RELIGIOUS TRADITIONS OF THE WORLD

RELIGIOUS TRADITIONS OF THE WORLD

James F. Lewis and William G. Travis

ZondervanPublishingHouse
Academic and Professional Books
Grand Rapids, Michigan

A Division of HarperCollinsPublishers

Requests for information should be addressed to:
Zondervan Publishing House
Academic and Professional Books
Grand Rapids, Michigan 49530

Library of Congress Cataloging-in-Publication Data

Lewis, James F.
   Religious traditions of the world : historical and evangelical
perspectives / by James F. Lewis and William G. Travis.
      p.   cm.
   Includes bibliographical references and index.
   ISBN 0-310-51900-4
   1. Religions. 2. Christianity and other religions. I. Travis,
William G. II. Title.
BL80.2.L40   1991
291—dc20   91-17929
                                            CIP

Edited by Tom Raabe and Leonard G. Goss
Interior designed by Vicki B. Heetderks
Cover designed by Lecy Design

Printed in the United States of America

      93 94 95 96 / DH / 10 9 8 7 6 5 4 3 2

This edition is printed on acid-free paper and meets the American National Standards Institute Z39.48 standard.

To Marylan, Dan, Amy and Tim—
Fellow-travelers in the adventure of learning

J.L.

———————————————

To Lucille—partner extraordinaire

W.T.

Contents

Preface

The authors and publishers have prepared this text to meet a need that exists in some institutions of higher learning and in the public generally. While a large number of well-written introductions to religious traditions of the world are available, few, if any, have approached the subject with sensitivity to the special interests of the orthodox Christian community. Like all others, they require accurate historical summaries to guide their understanding, but they are also seeking an approach that is cordial to their convictions about the truthfulness of the biblical faith. The authors share these convictions and hope the approach taken in the ensuing chapters will meet this need and serve both to inform and to stimulate.

William Travis, drawing upon his many years of research, writing, and teaching as a historian, contributed chapters three, five, and six on religions of the ancient Mediterranean, Judaism, and Christianity.

The plan for the text was conceived by James Lewis, who has written all other chapters. Travels in China and long-term residence in India and Southeast Asia have enriched his formal studies in religion by providing living contact with Hindus, Muslims, Buddhists, Marxists, ancestor worshippers, and others. It is hoped that nothing in this text will offend any member of the religious communities herein treated. Certainly every attempt has been made to be accurate and even sympathetic.

Chapters eleven through fourteen review recent approaches to the theology of religion and undoubtedly shall stir debate. Any deficiencies in the treatment of these theologies lie with its author, in spite of the kind efforts of a number of readers who offered suggestions including John Borelli of the Catholic Secretariat for Ecumenical and Interreligious Affairs and Bruce Reichenbach, professor of theology at Augsburg College.

We would also like to thank the many friends who contributed photo material and several colleagues and students at our respective institutions who have helped in ways too numerous to record.

Part One

Introduction

1 Studying World Religions—Purpose and Value

The Purpose

This book attempts to do two things, though perhaps not with equal emphasis. It sets out primarily to describe important features of major religious traditions as they have developed through the centuries, and it concludes with an analysis of contemporary theologies of religion. No reasons need be cited for treating most of the religions contained herein, since they already qualify as world religions. However, some rationale might be offered for including the religions of traditional societies and of the ancient world.

Little is known of the historical development of religions in traditional societies. But the large population of such societies in the world, perhaps around 250 million, warrants some representation in a book on world religions. The classical religions of the Mediterranean are now defunct except for those features that may survive in living religions today. Because of this, and because of their importance for Western world culture, these religions deserve discussion as well.

All but the final section depend on historical methods, while the concluding chapters evaluate world religions from the perspective of the biblical faith. Readers will judge for themselves whether the evangelical commitments of the authors have prejudiced the descriptive chapters.

A careful and thoughtful study of religions shows the error in thinking, as so many do, that the religious world, including one's own religion, is simple, uncomplicated, and uniform. Because of this diversity no one can claim success in comprehensively and exhaustively describing any of these religions. All we claim here is that we have been true to the facts about the religions presented and true to the believers who hold those facts.

World religions are complex in the extreme. While the Christian religion, in its hundreds of particular denominations, certainly has some beliefs in common, there are assuredly very significant differences among those groups calling themselves "Christian." The same can be said of every other major religious tradition. Even evangelical belief and practice, to which the authors adhere, lacks uniformity, and evangelical evaluations of the truth claims of other religions vary considerably as well. Nevertheless, the normative position expressed in the concluding chapter is offered as a sincere attempt to come to terms with the issues. Other evangelicals may see things differently.

One of our concerns is to provide the Christian student with both accurate and helpful information about the religions of the world as they respond to Jesus' mandate to 'be my witnesses' (Acts 1:8) in a religiously pluralistic world. While there is an abundance of material regarding evangelism and cross-cultural ministry, studies in religion that are cordial to the Christian's global responsibility are not in great abundance. To be sure missiologists and Christian anthropologists have made excellent contributions to understanding world religions. But there is clearly a need for religious studies alongside these other disciplines so that the religious life of mankind may be better understood and their needs addressed.

Those concerned for global mission cannot do without the descriptive work of history of religions and other disciplines which have the goal of accurate and value-free reporting about religious persons and communities. Some scholars will deny the possibility of a nonnormative or purely descriptive study of religion. We believe this is possible, and we cite all chapters but the last as examples of it. We do not argue for it philosophically since it has been adequately dealt with elsewhere.[1]

Those engaged in the task of world evangelism need an accurate description of the religions for several reasons. First, in a general way, it should be obvious that getting people to consider Christ requires us to speak of the Christian faith in categories with which they are familiar. To do this Christian witnesses need to understand the religious language and ideas held by those to whom they witness. The apostle Paul sought bridges of understanding when communicating the Gospel to the non-Christian world as seen in Acts 17. This he was able to do because his educational background familiarized him with Greco-Roman religion. Unfortunately, there seems to be little commitment to understanding other religions except for apologetic purposes. But it is doubtful that one can understand a religion if one studies it only to attack it. One may be critical only after one understands, and this requires the descriptive approach.

Christian colleges have not kept pace with their secular counterparts in offering courses in non–Judeo-Christian traditions. The importance of such studies is, in general, inadequately recognized in evangelical institutions in North America. Few offer the study of religions beyond an introductory level. By contrast, most public institutions in America offer majors in the study of world religion or religious studies. Christian institutions in Asia, such as Union Biblical Seminary, Pune, India, regularly offer courses in Islam, Hindu and Buddhist religious texts, and religions of traditional societies because they know effective Christian witness requires such understanding.

Many practical questions which the world Christian inevitably confronts in cross-cultural witness could be addressed in the classroom first. What concept of ultimate reality is held by the people? What words express this reality, and how do these words relate to biblical ideas of ultimate reality? What daily problems are encountered by non-Christians, and how or to what degree do indigenous ideas of the spirit world answer these concerns?

Some evangelical leaders and educators have, in the past, acted as if all one needs to know in order to effect religious change in others is the Bible and the living God. To be sure, without such knowledge no Christian work can succeed. But cross- cultural witness demands penetration into the religious worldview of those one wishes to reach. It might be pointed out that in this century anthropology has made continued advances in understanding the cultures and religions of others. Some missionaries have been at the vanguard of this effort. James Legge of China and William Carey of India translated several religious classics into English. The case studies and ethnographic field notes of R. H. Codrington in Australia and the Wisers in India advanced scholarly understanding about the religious world of the people they served. Others such as Wilhelm Schmidt, Eugene Nida, William Smalley, and Paul Hiebert have joined the ranks of professional anthropologists and scholars of religions and offered helpful insights for those in world evangelism.

Anthropology has gained a secure place in the academic preparation of persons for cross-cultural ministry. However, while religion is important to anthropological investigations, it seems that religious studies as a separate discipline has failed to get the attention it deserves. Cultural awareness is important, but understanding indigenous religions is essential to achieving religious change. The time

has come to devote attention to religious studies in proportion to the significance which religion has for the people who have yet to accept the biblical faith.

Perhaps one reason religious studies have been so ignored is because specialists in the study of religion have sometimes adopted unhelpful methods and proposed unfriendly normative positions. An example of an unhelpful method is that of phenomenologist Mircea Eliade who, through collating a wealth of ethnographic material on many interesting topics, aims to show how all religions seek the experience of the sacred. However, the connection between the "sacred" and the actual religious concerns of people is by no means very clear. Others, under the label of "science of religion," interweave normative positions that reject any claim to uniqueness for biblical faith, while still others prefer the truth claims of competing religions to that of biblical faith. Freudians regard religion as illusion; Durkheim and Malinowski see only its social function.

Ignorance of indigenous religions may not hinder evangelism as seriously in cultural areas which have a long history of Christian influence due to colonial presence. While animists and Muslims are found in large numbers in the Philippine Islands, vast sectors of that island nation are nominally Christian and continue to hold to many Christian assumptions. Animists and non-Christian religious minorities abound in South America. But, on balance, wherever you go on that continent the masses understand certain basic Christian concepts. Theological education to prepare individuals to aggressively evangelize in these places requires little preparation outside of what is available at any quality evangelical seminary.

But things are vastly different elsewhere. In Asia, where one-third of the global population exists, one finds religious ideas and practices which are quite foreign to Christian understanding and experience. If the Gospel is to be communicated effectively in this context, the religious traditions of these people must be studied seriously, not superficially. Furthermore, discipleship, Scripture translation, and contextualization of theology must be undertaken with a full knowledge of indigenous religions.

A second reason why the religions may not have been carefully studied is the nervousness mission leaders have about syncretism and theological accommodation. Their concerns are amply demonstrated in the documents on missions and evangelism that came out of the 1966 Wheaton and Berlin congresses on evangelism.[2] Fears about the pitfalls of universalism are not unwarranted, but the conclusions arrived at gave no encouragement to serious study of non-Christian traditions. Only in the Lausanne Covenant (1974) did a more moderate attitude surface signaling an improvement in the climate for the study of world religions.

The Value

At the heart of the Christian faith is the responsibility to witness to all people. It could be argued that whatever facilitates better witness should be prized. If so, we should highly prize the study of religions from an evangelical perspective. We cannot witness effectively to people of other religions without knowing the broad outlines of their religious goals and their means of achieving them.

Regretfully, even missionaries can spend a lifetime in physical contact with non-Christians without taking many steps to understand them religiously. To understand Buddhists, Hindus, or Chinese ancestor worshipers one must listen to them and learn. Eugene Nida wisely says: "It is not enough to avoid contemptuous attitudes toward another person's ideas. One should be vitally and sympathetically concerned with what other people think. This, of course, does not necessitate compromising one's own ideas; it is simply the basis for effective communication."[3] Jesus called us light and salt, which assumes we will find ourselves where darkness and decay need to be dispelled. Our ignorance of the true beliefs of others only hinders effective witness. It is interesting that it was Paul rather than Peter who was called to communicate the Gospel to the Gentile world due, no doubt, to the fact that he knew that world so well.

New social and technological developments have changed the world. Since the midtwentieth century, people of various religions and cultures have immigrated in great numbers to new homes on other continents. The emergence of travel and communications technology has made the world a global village. The nations and cultures of the world are in closer contact through increased international business and political contact, United Nations activities, satellite audio and video reception, and cultural and educational exchange programs at educational and national levels. Direct-dial telephone service is now available to the Baliem Valley of Irian Jaya among people only a few years out of the Stone Age. People from many religions and cultures of the world are now next-door neighbors in what used to be solidly Christian communities in Europe and North America. India and Southeast Asia have been religiously pluralistic societies for centuries, and now North America itself is experiencing a similar pluralism. Within a short distance of most Christians in America's larger cities live immigrants from Hindu and Buddhist lands. Islam is the third-largest religious group in the United States, and Buddhists in Canada in the 1980s had the fastest decadal growth rate of any religious group. It is said that there are now more Muslims than Protestants in France and more Muslims than Methodists in Britain.

The new reality to which Christians must adjust in today's world is that we live in a multireligious context with followers of non-Christian religions pervading our heretofore exclusive Christian enclaves. The physical nearness of these non-Christian neighbors naturally calls us to learn about them and share the Gospel with them. Emilio Castro has said: "What is new today is that nearly all Christians are exposed to personal relations with people of other faiths. Mission as witness to people of other convictions is no longer something carried on in faraway regions and to unknown people; it is also the practical problem of

relationships with neighbors. The population movements over the last few years have created in almost every nation a religiously plural situation."[4]

Asian Christians know the importance of understanding the religions of others. Students of Union Biblical Seminary visit a mosque in Yavatmal, India. J. Lewis

A second reason to study world religions is so that we can become better citizens in a world to which religious factors fuel fires of political and community unrest. In most of the world few persons distinguish between the religious realm and the nonreligious. The division of life into two distinct realms—the sacred and the secular, a concept popular in the Christian West since the Middle Ages—has no significance whatsoever for vast numbers of people committed to other religious traditions. There is no such thing as "religion" that is confined to a distinct and limited segment of their lives. All of life interfaces and is unified around certain beliefs and values which they share in common with members of their religious community.

Accordingly, there can be no understanding of Arab economic and political policies without understanding Islam. The American failure to understand Iranian Shi'ite longing for a return to the ways of the Quran precipitated an international crisis involving the United States and Iran in 1979. The largely secularized foreign embassy and diplomatic corps in Tehran and Washington had forgotten the importance of religion in general and the power of martyr-oriented Shi'a faith in particular. While religion may have lost its force in the lives of western diplomats, it certainly had not in Iran, nor has it diminished in the lives of most world citizens. The Buddhist majority and the Tamil Hindu minority in Sri Lanka have long been at odds over issues such as political representation and quotas for education and employment. These concerns are closely related to religious commitments and identity, and no solutions are likely without understanding them. Community peace and harmony require community leaders to understand community religions.

Third, Christians must seek to understand the religions around them to dispel the misunderstandings they have long held about others. The Christian church and evangelicals in particular have not seen it as in their interest to improve relationships with those of other religions. In part, this is because it seems difficult to be simultaneously aggressive in witness and tolerant toward others in the religious marketplace. Undeserved and unfair

criticism has been a part of our interreligious relations. A Muslim lawyer gave a guided tour of his mosque to Indian students from a Christian seminary in Maharashtra. After an introductory explanation about the physical layout of the mosque and the practice of *namaz*, he invited questions. One student asked, "Is it true that Islam in its first century was spread by the sword?" The gracious host responded, "That is probably not any more true than that Christianity was spread in Muslim lands by the sword of the Crusaders." It is probably undeniable that both used the sword to force religious conversion, but old animosities and fears live long in the history books and die hard in the memory. It is no doubt true that Christians of this century are more informed about world religions than those of previous generations. But Christians are still woefully misinformed, underinformed, and apathetic about the people in those religions. This will not do.

Fourth, the study of other religions sharpens the uniqueness of each religion. Some have held that the essentials of all religions are the same. This position, taken by the notable philosopher S. Radhakrishnan and some radical Christian theologians, often results from failing to take the emphases and doctrines of the different religions seriously. Radhakrishnan sees the center of the New Testament in the ethics of Jesus and his consciousness of God, but he gives little play to the doctrines of sin and atonement. To gloss over these matters, however, is to fail to see the central emphases of historic Christianity.

The Christian Richard Drummond in his book *Gautama the Buddha* similarly fails to take seriously enough the distinctive Buddhist doctrines of *anatta* and *anicca*, which teach the doctrines of nonsoul and nonpermanence, respectively.[5] Taken together, these exclude the possibility of a biblical God. But in an attempt to find an "essential" congruity with the Christian faith, Drummond represents Buddhists who follow the *Tipitaka* as believers of personal immortality and theism, both of which they vehemently deny. In view of the need for extreme care in these matters, descriptive studies are most helpful, for they sharpen differences between the religions and thus promote understanding.

The study of other religions can demonstrably broaden and deepen our understanding and appreciation of the biblical faith simply by clarifying its uniqueness. The world religions operate within the limits of natural theology, but at the same time they remind us of how sublime unredeemed human thoughts about God can be. When we read the Sikh Japji hymnal or the *Abhangas* of the Hindu bhaktist Tukaram, we learn of a God who is sometimes transcendent, glorious, and even redemptively gracious. Yet human religious traditions often have their darker side as well. Seen from an evangelical perspective, scriptures and rituals have perceptions of the nature of humanity and reality that are a mixture of truth and error. In some cases the error of a particular religious text is not in what is said but in what is left unsaid. In the *Narada Bhakti Sutras* love to God is described as the highest goal one can pursue. But the love of God for humanity is nowhere acknowledged. The deity grants grace, to be sure, but this is because of the purity of the seeker's heart in pursuit of God. The deity does not freely offer his grace equally to all. The *Analects of Confucius* teach: "Do not do to others what you would not want others to do to you." This is truly a sublime social ethic. But there is a quantum leap between this and the Golden Rule of the Lord Jesus Christ: "Do unto others what you would have them do unto you." We may never see the beauty of Jesus' words quite so clearly as when they are viewed in the larger context of world religions.

Discussion

1. What factors in the modern world call upon educated persons to be informed about the world's religions?
2. What reasons can you cite, preferably from your own experience, for Christians to study world religions?
3. Discuss reasons why some individuals might be hesitant to undertake the study of other religions.

Notes

[1]Robert D. Baird, *Category Formation and the History of Religions*, Religion and Reason Series, no. 1 (The Hague: Mouton, 1971), 28–53.

²Efiong S. Utuk, "From Wheaton to Lausanne: The Road to Modification of Contemporary Evangelical Mission Theology," in *Missiology* 14, no. 2 (April 1986): 205–20.

³Eugene A. Nida, *Customs and Cultures* (New York: Harper & Row, 1954), 71–72.

⁴Emilio Castro, "Mission in a Pluralistic Society," in *International Review of Missions* 75, no. 299 (July 1986): 198.

⁵Richard Drummond, *Gautama the Buddha* (Grand Rapids: Eerdmans, 1974), 138–52.

2 Approaches to the Study of Religion

A Preliminary Concern: The Definition of Religion

The study of the religions of humanity must begin with an understanding of the word *religion*.[1] World religions have usually been understood to be those major systems of beliefs and practices accepted by identifiable communities of persons.[2] Examples would be Christians, Jews, Muslims, Buddhists, and Hindus. When examined closely, however, each of these religions shows such diversity of beliefs and concerns that names must be found to distinguish different groups within them. Thus, Buddhists have sometimes been divided into Hinayana and Mahayana schools, each of which must be subdivided further if understanding is to proceed to a higher level.

But what makes a particular set of beliefs and practices a "religion"? Human beings have a wide range of shared and transmitted beliefs and practices which together make up the characteristic way they as a group or society act. The word *culture* might be used to embrace that totality. But within the totality called culture, what are the marks of "religion" which distinguish it from things political, economic, and social? The need to identify clearly what is meant by "reli-gion," and to arrive at a practical definition of the word, is a problem that has bedeviled scholars since the rise of the modern study of religion in the nineteenth century. Only recently have solutions been proposed which remove much of the prevailing confusion.

Robert D. Baird has proposed that the study of religion needs to follow some clearly understood method.[3] Central to his argument is the need for definitions of key words and the importance of recognizing several distinct levels of understanding. Most of what follows here reflects Baird's approach.

There have been many answers to the question, What is religion? Fundamental to arriving at a practical answer is to see the difference between viewing religion as a "thing" and viewing it as a "word."

It may seem strange to refer to religion as a thing. But consciously or not, some writers and speakers of religion have treated it as though it has some bona fide or quasi-real existence somewhat independent of persons or groups. In fact, a careful reading of the second paragraph of this section shows how easy it is to unintentionally give that impression. Reread it and see if you can find anything there that suggests that religion exists as a "thing."

Nineteenth-and early twentieth-century anthropologists and others who first launched the modern study of religion often viewed religion as something which virtually had a life of its own. The focus for them was not on the religious person or religious groups but on the "religion" which belonged to the person or group. This difference of perspective is significant. Some of these scholars were often unaware that "religion" was a mental construct. Rather, they reified religion and treated it as though it had some *sui generis* existence in the real world. For example, anthropologist E. B. Tylor and sociologist Emile Durkheim were influenced in their studies by the ideas of Comte and Spencer, who applied Darwinian developmentalism to the social sciences. What that meant was that religion was like an organism with an origin, a special unique existence, and a history with stages moving from early and simple to late and maturely complex. Important questions for them included: "What was religion's origin?" (Tylor) and "What will be the future of religion?" (Durkheim). Both questions are based on an assumption that religion has some reality of its own.

Such questions are of little or no interest to many today because, for the most part, religion is no longer looked at in this way. However, the conception of religion as existing independently in the world continues to befog scholarly studies. Jonathan Z. Smith succinctly summarizes his position against the view of religion as a thing:

[W]hile there is a staggering amount of data, of phenomena of human experiences and expressions that might be characterized in one culture or another, by one criterion or another, as religious—there is no data for religion. Religion is solely the creation of the scholar's study. It is created for the scholar's analytic purposes by his imaginative acts of comparison and generalization. Religion has no independent existence apart from the academy.[4]

In contrast to the view of religion as a thing having in some sense an existence of its own, this study regards it as a word. It is a word which has reference to something in this world, but this "something" is not freestanding nor independent of objective human experience. It is not that the word *religion* refers to nothing in the real world. *Religion*, like any word, may refer to something, but we communicate clearly only as we identify what that something is through a definition. Through definition, which is the use of many words to specify the meaning of a given word, we link a word to something in our experience. A word may refer to something tangible or intangible, imaginary or real, abstract or concrete. The word *religion*, as defined here, will refer to something which all persons can investigate if they take the time and pains to do so. The definition accepted here will limit our study of religion to certain kinds of human beliefs and behaviors. But which of all the multitudes of beliefs and behaviors should we identify as referring to "religion"?

A review of the literature shows no lack of definitions of religion offered by scholars over the years. Short definitions were given by G. Bleeker (the divine, a superhuman power), van der Leeuw (mana; power), and R. Otto (the Holy). Others proposed longer definitions, such as J. H. Leuba with his forty-eight articles.[5] Each of these proposals has failed to gain wide acceptance and has been rejected by those who felt it was either too broad or too narrow. Such conclusions are based on the assumption that religion is a thing to which the word should conform. If, for example, belief in a supreme god was accepted by a scholar as central to religion, it could be pointed out that Tipitaka Buddhists either did not believe in God, did not depend on God, or were indifferent to God or gods. If the definition was broadened to refer to the placation of spiritual beings, it might include more groups but exclude people like India's Shankara, who is regarded by many as that country's most famous religious thinker. Imbedded in most of these competing proposals was the view that religion had, nonetheless, some discernible essence or core, no matter how ineffectual and problematic the definitions were.

Other scholars solved the problem differently. Some concluded that, since there was no consensus, definitional attempts should be ignored or abandoned. Harvey Conn seems to be one who prefers to ignore the issue of the definition of religion. He indicates that the discussion of the nature of religion was an important issue in the nineteenth and early twentieth centuries. But his book, which describes attempted answers in that earlier period, leaves out the question almost entirely in his own contemporary reflections.[6]

In *The Meaning and End of Religion*, Wilfred Cantwell Smith went so far as to maintain that it was best to abandon the use of the word *religion* altogether and substitute for it some other word such as *faith*. In contrast to Smith, others judged it best to retain the word *religion* but leave it undefined since it seemed impossible to find a definition general enough to apply to all that they understood to be genuinely religious.

Throughout these scholarly discussions an assumption was often made that religion had some central core or essence of which all particular religions partook. That essence was understood differently by different persons, but it was accepted widely that some such essence did exist and that the best hope for achieving agreement was to concentrate on this issue.

All things considered, one definition did seem to have the most support. The essential or central features of religion were commonly thought to be beliefs and practices associated with the supernatural. One missionary scholar holding to this idea is Eugene Nida, who said religion "constitutes a componential feature of all the basic motivations thus providing meaning with supernatural sanctions."[7]

Baird discusses the full range of these problems and proposes that scholars give up the fruitless search for a definition of the "thing" religion. He argues that definitions should be of words and proposes the following functional definition of religion: "Religion is that which is of ultimate or supreme concern to individuals or groups."[8] The following considerations show the advance of this over previous proposals.

First, such a definition removes many of the ambiguities which have plagued religious studies by locating religion on the historical level of the observable and the empirical. This is important since studies in the history of religion have often involved a non-historical intuitional approach. That is, religion has too frequently been defined as having to do with what the researcher felt was religious rather than being founded on more objective bases. The missionary theologian J. H. Bavinck is an example of an intuitionist who defined religion as the observable responses to the "religious consciousness" inherent in the inner constitution of all human beings.[9] Those behaviors which Bavinck and others like him, call "religious" are, to a great extent, intuitively identified because they are connected to an inner awareness of something transcendent. This approach to defining religion is not grounded in that which is public and depends upon subjective convictions.

Baird wants to begin the study of religion by proposing a definition that focuses on that which can be studied and recognized without having to "sense" a person's religiousness. Baird would thus study what historically observable individuals and groups hold to be supremely important, as found in their writings, scriptures, testimonies, rituals or ceremonies, and daily living. Of related interest is how such ultimate concerns affect other areas of their lives. The study of religion thus centers on subject matter which can be historically described: individuals and groups and the complex of activities and beliefs associated with their supreme concerns.

Second, such a definition is practical and flexible. It is practical when studying theists, such as Muslims or Hindu bhaktists, as well as those who do not recognize any god, such as Tipitaka Buddhists. Any definition of religion which makes belief in a god a criterion of religion automatically excludes atheists and dialectical materialists. Yet many such persons have matters which are, by their own testimony, of supreme concern to them. Mundane concerns, if valued supremely, may properly be called religious concerns. The definition is flexible in that it facilitates the study of both the ideal and the real. The ideal may be seen to apply primarily to religious leaders, priests, and functionaries. The expectations for the common believers may be considerably reduced in terms of ethical achievement or religious goal. It has often been charged that religious studies focus exclusively on formal matters such as scriptures, organization, religious systems, or priests and fail to notice how or to what extent the ideals found there are embraced, modified, or even ignored in the everyday lives of ordinary believers. Further, it is important to trace out how supreme concerns change over stretches of time. According to some, the study of Chinese religion has too often been dominated by a fascination with the Confucian *Analects*, Daoist literature, and Buddhist texts but has failed to study the practiced folk-religion of the masses. But Baird's definition can apply equally to the textual or priestly ideal as well as the actual lay implementation which may closely or only distantly approximate that ideal. For example, the ethics of Jesus, centering on the Sermon on the Mount, are nearly universally regarded by Christians as their ethical ideal. But the interpretation and practical application of the sermon in the lives of individuals and groups varies considerably and even conflictingly. Religious persons are commonly found consenting intellectually to a textual or community ideal from which they nonetheless frequently and possibly unconsciously depart. This fact provides opportunity to study the interesting interplay between the community's ideals and the individual's behavior. Both may hold to a similar supreme concern, but the actual outliving of it may be considerably different.

Finally, this definition makes objectivity in the study of religion more possible. It does not, however, guarantee objectivity. It is a complex question whether the values of a researcher can be suspended while in pursuit of an accurate account of another's religion. There may be no entirely value-free researcher; but research may be more or less free of distortion. Some have argued one must be an insider to accurately understand a religion, while an opposite view says one must be an outsider or even former insider. However, there are good arguments that, in principle, historical objectivity is possible for the sensitive and thoughtful person. There are rigid requirements to achieve this, such as a sympathetic attitude toward a religious group, rigorous honesty with one's sources, careful observation, and a knowledge of the language or languages involved. If these and other requirements are followed, and if objective knowledge of the religions is achievable, what then are the implications for the evangelical student of religions?

First, it is helpful to know one can objectively understand the religions of others. It is not necessary to compromise or modify one's truth commitment to get at another's religious position. There may be emotional strain where conflicting views are acute. One may even find considerable agreement with others in their search for reality and truth. One might have a sense of frustration or bewilderment with their assumptions or truth claims. But the process of gaining religious understanding with this approach does not involve relativism.

Second, if objectivity is possible, one may be confident that a thorough and accurate study of the religions will teach helpful lessons enabling more effective witness. William D. Reyburn has argued that missionaries have a primary responsibility to study the religious ideas of the people they seek to win. In his view this is the first step in building cross-cultural understanding and relationships. In a study of the ideas of god in two tribal groups, the Quechua of Ecuador and the Kaka of the Cameroon in Africa, he posited that, "the missionary who will know his people will have to first know their god."[10] Put another way, it is not enough for the missionary to know his or her own God and the Bible that declares this God. It is imperative to know the religious traditions of the people as well since these are at the

25

center of their existence as a distinct people.

In this connection, one begins to understand a religion by answering two broad questions: What problem or problems about the human condition are implied in the ultimate concerns of persons and groups? and, By what means and methods are the problems resolved? For example, in the Christian faith the central problem may be described as how humanity can cope with the basic fact of sin and separation from God. This problem is addressed through the redemptive activity of God culminating in Jesus Christ, and the appropriation of that redemption through personal faith. On the other hand, for a Buddhist monk following the Tipitaka, the religious problem is how to cease from grasping and the suffering attending it, escape *samsara*, or the rounds of birth and death, and experience *nirvana*. The means is to join the *sangha*, or monastic community, learn the disciplines of meditation, ethics, and wisdom, and make progress toward, perhaps not fully achievable in this life, the religious goal of nirvana.

Third, since personal values neither prevent nor guarantee objectivity, religious understanding may be had by any individual so long as there is a commitment to objectivity. Evangelical students need to understand that they can learn from informed and careful scholars whether these persons are Christians or not. There is an immense amount of help for evangelicals in the fields of anthropology, sociology, psychology, philosophy, and history of religions provided they understand the limits of the methodology. Some non-Christians can teach Christians a great deal about the religious traditions of humanity. Conversely, simply because a scholar has evangelical commitment does not validate his or her conclusions or insights into the religions of others.

Other Important Terms: Explanation, Description, and Theory

Having accepted a definition of religion which avoids problematic intuitionalism, we need now to turn to three other words used consistently in the study of religion: *explanation*, *description*, and *theory*. Is there a difference between explaining religion, describing religion, and offering a theory of religion?

Explanation

Explanation is a word widely used by scholars and, like the word *religion*, is not used in any uniform or consistent way. Wilfred Cantwell Smith uses it interchangeably with *interpretation* in some of his writings.[11] Baird and some others prefer to define "explanation" as that which demonstrates a cause-effect relationship in a lawfully controlled situation. Thus, explanation provides answers to the question why. Why does the busy Japanese executive stop at a *kami* shrine daily to make offerings before the Shinto deity? An "explanation" for Baird would be to provide a causal answer indicating some necessity for the believer to stop there, perhaps of a financial, psychological, or sociological nature.

But we intend to broaden the word to

include answers to questions such as who, what, when, where, why, and how.[12] Answers to these questions call for information which can be provided by appealing to two very different sources: the descriptive and the theoretical.

Description and Theory

Answers derived from empirical or historical sources should be called descriptive explanations or explanations based on material that is limited to the observable and the public. However, either by circumstance or choice, answers may not be either available or satisfying if one is limited to historical data alone. What happens in the experience of *satori* calls for an answer that may be supplied by either description or theory. If one seeks answers in testimonials, written material, physiological data collected from telemetry attached to the body of a Zen Roshi, *koans*, or reflections of scholars, then the question is being approached from the standpoint of description since these sources are primarily historical in nature.

But if the person asking the question, What happens in the experience of *satori*? is seeking to know what, if anything, is truly encountered in the transrational experience of *satori*, it should be readily admitted that historical evidences are of very limited help. One can only turn to nonhistorical and theory-based answers derived from other disciplines such as psychology, philosophy, or even theology. Such answers may be based, at least in part, on ideas as diverse as theories of consciousness or the existence of demons.

Putting the two levels of explanation side by side, we can call the former descriptive explanations and the latter theoretical explanations. Thus, explanation may involve either description or theory or a combination of the two—theory which is based on description but which goes beyond it.

Why did the Reformation happen? may be answered with reference to descriptive data found in the rise of German nationalism, the impact of biblical studies, the corruption of the institution of the papacy, and other historical factors. But the why question may also be answered by taking these matters into account and going beyond them. Erik Erikson's *Young Man Luther* turns to psychoanalytical theory to find basic reasons for the actions and attitudes of Martin Luther in the experiences of childhood, youth, and family. Apart from these realities and their interrelationships in Luther's life, history might have been different according to Erickson. In short, explanatory studies of the Reformation can be of two kinds. The explanations may be descriptive and historic, or they may go beyond the strictly historical and involve conclusions based on the theoretical.

Thus the word *explanation* seems best not used exclusively to refer only to theoretical answers as Baird suggests, but with reference to all answers of all kinds ranging from the historical to the extrahistorical as it seeks to understand humankind and its religions.

Approaches to the Study of Religion

The study of religion has been a major academic field in Western universities and schools since the early part of the twentieth century. But scholars have taken contrasting approaches and continue to research new ways for the understanding of *homo religiosis*. The following are some of the current methods employed in the effort to understand religion.

The Personalist Approach: What Do the Followers of This Religion or Religious Community Believe to Be True?—W. C. Smith

Wilfred Cantwell Smith, noted scholar of religions, is known for taking this approach to religious studies. Basically, this may be called a descriptive approach not based on any theory or appeal to a transhistorical level. It is the approach which asks, What does this belief or ceremony mean to the person or persons who accept it? It seeks to understand what the believer accepts as true and important. Smith says:

> It is our glory that we study not things but qualities of personal living. Ideas, ideals, loyalties, passions, aspirations, cannot be directly observed but their role in human history is not the less consequential, nor their study less significant or valid. The externals of religion— symbols, institutions, doctrines, practices—can be examined separately. . . . But these things are not in themselves religion which lies rather in the area of what these mean to those that are involved. The student is making effective progress when he recognizes what he has to do not with religious systems basically but with religious persons; or at least, with something interior to persons.[13]

Smith has been a leading critic of categories used by scholars which

Wilfred Cantwell Smith's approach asks the question: "What do believers say is true?" Rural setting Gujarat State, India. J. Lewis

implied that "religion" was an object with an existence of its own. A growing chorus of scholars have joined him in this, including R. D. Baird, Hans Penner, and Jonathan Z. Smith. W. C. Smith hammered away at the need to base studies in religion on that which was recognized by the believers themselves. At one point he even opposed the use of the word *religion* itself since it seemed to connote, erroneously in his opinion, that there was something corresponding to it in the real world. His view was that this distracted attention from the proper locus of religion, which was persons. Smith preferred the word faith as it seemed more person-centered and verifiable.[14] He also opposed categories such as

"Hinduism" and "Buddhism" since they falsely suggested unified wholes which his experience in the field as a researcher contradicted. The term *Hinduism* is not useful since diversity among those who call themselves Hindus calls for more precision than the word implies. Language that suggests a unity that does not exist should be rejected.

Smith's focus on the religion of persons caused him to see the great diversity within the world religions as well as between them. He says:

> It is not the case that all religions are the same. The historian notes that not even one religion is the same, century after century, or from one country to another, or from village to city. So much is this so, that I have found myself pushed to dropping the word religion as a concrete noun altogether, and also terms such as "Hinduism" and "Christianity", since I find nothing on earth, or in Heaven, that will consistently answer to those names; and have argued at length that modern awareness requires—and rewards—dropping them.[15]

The value of the word *faith* is that it is more useful in describing beliefs and rituals since it points to what can be demonstrated, described, and analyzed in a person's life, in written texts, and in testimonies—all of which are public and hence of the nature of historical data. Furthermore, *faith* has the advantage of calling attention to the dynamic relation between the beliefs and practices of the past and the contributions to that past tradition by those of the present. Hence *faith* can also refer to that collection of ideas and ceremonies which are handed down from generation to generation

and from the group to the individual. The individual is a receptor of a tradition which has accumulated in prior generations like the strata of rock sediment or the bricks of a wall. Every generation assists in the construction or reconstruction of the faith of the community, by either preserving it or adding another brick to the received tradition and thereby modifying it.

The premises of the personalist approach would include the following:

1. An understanding of the beliefs, practices, and ideals of persons, whether separately or in groups, that are central to their understanding of religion.

2. The study of the categories of sacrifice, worship, prayer, God, sin, or any tangible external without reference to its meaning within the framework of the religion leads to misunderstanding rather than understanding.

3. Any understanding of the faith of persons by outsiders of that faith is to be tested for accuracy and depth by inviting the evaluation of the persons being studied. There is no meaning or understanding unless the believer's meaning and understanding is made the object of the scholar's analytical work. A scholar's study is not valid if the person of faith "does not recognize the substance of that in which he is involved."[16]

In order to see how Smith's approach is applied, we will examine the Hindu *upanayana* ceremony and suggest the way Smith might describe it. (To our knowledge, Smith does not focus specifically on this rite in his writings.) First, let us give a description of the ceremony.

The *upanayana* rite is an initiation rite and one of many *samskaras* (Skt., purification) practiced today in India and which originated in Vedic times. Other *samskaras* performed are at birth, naming of the child, taking of first solid food, marriage, pregnancy, and death. There were once as many as forty or more *samskaras* (now greatly reduced) that had as a major purpose the removal of impurities. The *upanayana* is a so-called rite of passage with a purificatory purpose. In short, it purifies boys so that they can have the standing of Hindu adult men.

The ceremony is for boys only, and only for those in the upper three castes. For the Brahman caste it is ideally performed in the eighth year, for the Kshatriyas the eleventh, and the Vaishyas the twelfth. In modern times the timing is usually flexible.

Boy undergoing upanayana ritual in the presence of Brahman priest and sacred fire. J. Lewis

One or more priests officiate at the ceremony, themselves bare to the waist and wearing the sacred thread—a mark of having undergone the investiture ceremony—looped over the left shoulder and under the right arm. The household preparations are weeks in the making as the ceremony is held in the home and witnessed by family and friends. Special foods are purchased or prepared to be consumed before and after the ceremony. It is a happy time for all concerned.

The night before the ceremony the boy is to remain silent. In the morning he has breakfast with his mother in a symbolic final meal in the child-mother dependent relationship. After this he will eat with the men. A barber is called, possibly a *shudra*, whose caste is not permitted this ceremony, who shaves the boy's head leaving, in many instances, a hank of hair at the crown. If the barber is a *shudra*, he is not permitted in the home proper but does his work in an outer courtyard or in front of the house. To admit him would be to pollute the home. Following this the candidate ritually bathes, dons the traditional one-piece cloth pantaloons for men called the *dhoti*, and at the appropriate moment takes his place to the right of the priest-teacher, the *acharya*.

A partial description of the ceremony would include the following. It begins when the *acharya* pours clarified butter on the fire in the ritual fire urn—the hub of all movements during the ceremony—situated in the center of the room. The *acharya* recites some *slokas* (verses) from Vedic texts addressing the deities Agni and Prajapati. The priest-teacher fills the boy's hands with water while invoking Savitri's protection. The boy is then asked his name. After the name is given, the water is released and the *acharya* holds one hand of the boy while touching the boy's right shoulder, navel, heart, and left shoulder. He then addresses him as *brahmacarin*, meaning one who remains celibate while a student under instruction in the Vedas.

At this point the youth is invested with the sacred thread in token of his new status. It is placed over the left shoulder and looped around his body and under his right arm, hanging at waist level. The *acharya* then instructs in the sacred Gayatri Mantra: "OM. Let us meditate on the desirable splendor of the Sun God, Savitri. May he stimulate our thoughts." The student may be given a staff, which must reach to head-height, and begins the first task as a *brahmacarin*; he asks alms of his mother, who gives a gift. Others who have come to celebrate this rite of the "twice born" present gifts of money or other gifts. The ceremony over, everyone relaxes to enjoy the sumptuous meal the family has prepared to serve in honor of the newly encasted son.

While Smith does not comment extensively on the *upanayana* rite, he does study the *shyn byu* ceremony, a Burmese Buddhist boy's initiation rite, which can give us a general understanding of his approach.[17] For Smith, a place to begin would be to realize that the boy and all concerned understand this generally as a rite of transformation. The boy knows that prior to the ceremony he is casteless and the rite will be a step of great importance for him personally and for the family. Equally significant is that with

this ceremony he will qualify to receive instruction in the Vedic scriptures which have been withheld from him to this point in life. Having been invested with the sacred thread, he is said to be "twice born"—once physically and now into the life of an adult Hindu male. Accordingly, he becomes a fully accepted member of his caste and eligible for instruction in the ancient texts.

This is the general understanding which the boy and all observers and participants share. But when we consider the meaning in more specific terms for the boy, his parents or observers, and the *acharya*, we may add important points. First, the *acharya*. The *acharya* who officiates was once in the same situation as the boy. He will have experienced the same, or nearly the same, ceremony he now presides over. It calls to his mind his own initiation long years ago and, depending on his sensitivity and earnestness, the ritual he now performs will cause him to recall his own excitement, family pride, fears, anxiety, or concern. In short, the ceremony is an occasion for him to relive existentially, along with all other initiated males present, the feelings and perhaps questions which came to him years ago. This is not to claim that reliving it will be entirely positive. He could be rather indifferent to the whole affair, since he undoubtedly officiates at many *upanayana* rites and all of this may be too familiar and too routine. What is the meaning of the ceremony to him? There is no sure way of knowing what the ceremony means to him or to others without asking questions of them. This makes a significant point for Smith. The "faith" of other people is something that is not directly observable since it has to do with ideals, values, feelings, hopes, loyalties, aspirations, and possibly transcendent experiences. Yet it is possible to study these matters indirectly through interviews, written records, and scholarly observations. Such efforts may be sufficiently accurate and insightful to provide an adequate description of the meaning of the rite to some involved.

From the standpoint of the parents, a variety of emotions may coalesce in their experience. They are proud their son is experiencing the rite which confers the status of their caste and transforms him into a Hindu. He is no longer the son of Hindus but a Hindu. While there is pride in this, there may also be a tinge of sadness. They know he is beginning to open that chapter in his life when he will be less dependent on them. A brahmacarin traditionally left home to live with the acharya. His independence troubles them less than it would were he to move outside the familiar bounds of Hindu beliefs and practices. They know he is tethered to that tradition to which they themselves are tethered. In the past, the boy would be initiated for a shorter or longer time in Vedic and general education. In modern times, however, he may only symbolically attach himself to the acharya, since the Indian government and private schools provide the education that only religious teachers gave in the past.

And what about the meaning of the rite to the boy himself? It is on him that the attention of the family, including brothers and sisters, the acharya, and well-wishers is focused. How does he view it all? Certainly with some excitement and yet with some solemnity. Nirad Chaudhuri says: "The ceremony is very arduous, and in my young days my Brahmin playfellows looked forward to it with terror as well as pride."[18] The boy has known for some time that boys his age become Hindus in this way and are given special secrets then. But that excitement is tempered by his knowledge that the ceremony is expected of him and impossible to reject. This leaves him somewhere between anticipation, passivity, and resignation.

Much depends on the sensitivity of the boy and his interest and alertness to the mantras and references to Vedic deities. Will he sincerely believe prayers to Savitri, Agni, or other deities are effective? Does he personally seek the help of the deities to stimulate his thoughts and grant him knowledge, even as the Gayatri Mantra indicates? This depends on the boy, his inner nature, and many hidden factors. We could find answers only by talking with him either immediately after the ceremony or at some subsequent time.

One thing is certain. The social and religious consequences are such that he is transformed into a Hindu who has caste where before he was casteless. In these two facts are bound up many of the most important factors that will influence his life from this time forward. To some extent the boy will inevitably feel this because this is a once-in-a-lifetime experience. While less significant initially, the ceremony's profundity may take on greater meaning in time. The fact that one is not born a Hindu but becomes one in this way makes the experience unforgettable.

While the personalist approach is primarily concerned with the *upanayana* rite as understood and experienced by individuals, it also takes an interest in how persons participate in and modify the traditions handed down from generation to generation. The rite has been modified slightly since ancient times as to length, complexity, and requirements. Caste ranking, region, and family financial and economic status impinge on the details of its performance as well, since more than one priest may be engaged if the family is wealthy. Future modifications are also likely. What is significant is the extent to which the rite follows the main outline as suggested in the *Shatapatha Brahmana* of Vedic literature, where it is first mentioned. The longevity of the rite may tell us that it is of such significance that no change of any great importance is ever likely to occur.

The Structuralism of Hans Penner: What Hidden Structure Is Understood by the Structuralist?

Hans Penner of Dartmouth College takes a structural approach to the *upanayana* rite based on research in linguistic analysis.[19] The questions he seeks to answer with his approach are, What does the behavior mean? and What does the language mean? His approach does not seek primarily to discover the meaning of the ritual to the participants, as does the personalism of Smith. It seeks answers to the above questions by collecting a full

description of the ritual. What are the premises of this approach?

1. Penner disavows that his structuralism seeks to study or understand religion or any part of it as an essence which can be intuited. What he seeks to explain is the multifaceted beliefs and practices of Hindus, Buddhists, and others. He wishes to study the concrete historical facts as they are observable primarily in the language, documents, and texts of the given religion.

2. Structuralism is a rational search for formal rules for the explanation of religious beliefs and practices. These rules, when discovered, constitute a "system."

3. The structure, or system, is not consciously known by the participants of the ritual, nor can it be discovered in the surface events; that is, the observable movements, expressed ideas, or opinions of the *acharya*, the boy, the parents, or friends. In this respect Penner departs sharply from Smith. Even the instructions and meaning of the rite as given in the Vedic texts do not circumscribe the structure of the rite. This would be "mere description"' to Penner and amounts only to the "general structure." He seeks the "deep structure."

The texts themselves indicate that the rite transforms the boy from casteless to caste, from the once-born to the twice-born, from unfit to study the Vedas to fully qualified. Penner seeks the "deep structure." This cannot be learned by any one or even a combination of the following: the exegesis of the Sanskrit text; observation of the

Hans Penner's approach is that believers are not conscious of the deep structure of their religion. Muslim prayers after Ramazan, India. J. Lewis

ritual; interviews; and observation of external behavior. These he calls the "empirically observable traits or units." The structure is there, but the participants are not themselves conscious of this. No one knows the deep structure except those who take the approach of structuralism.

4. The deep structure of religion is the unconscious possession of the social group which is imposed upon individuals from without. It is encased in their language and is "independent of the decisions" of the participating individuals.[20]

5. Though the structure operates through the group's communications, both verbal and nonverbal, the "deep structure" is the scholar's mental construct of the operative rules existing in the religion or the ritual. These rules

are extrapolated by the scholar but are unconscious operatives among the believers.

The above explanation of the premises of structuralism may leave many gaps in our understanding of its methodology. But so far as it can be applied, how does it provide understanding to the *upanayana* rite?

First, the ritual mediates between two contrasting stages in the boy's life by utilizing similarly paired opposites of directions and deities which enable him to pass successfully from the one stage to the other. Structuralism attempts to explain precisely how the ritual accomplishes the transformation from once-born to twice-born; from casteless to encasted; from non-Hindu to Hindu; from boy to man; from polluted to purified.

How does the ritual accomplish this? Penner emphasizes the movements and directional orientations of the participants during the ritual and the way these correlate with the symbolic meaning of the four directions and deities invoked. From a variety of relevant Sanskrit texts Penner draws the following pairings for the directions:

NORTH	•		man	dawn	life
EAST	•		gods	daytime	creation
	•	stands for			
SOUTH	•		ancestors	twilight	death
WEST	•		demons	night	destruction

In the course of the ritual there are two significant directional changes or reorientations which have meaning when the above pairings are considered. These changes provide an explanation of how the ritual transforms the boy's status. Early in the ritual the boy looks west and the *acharya* looks east, thus the two are facing each other. Both stand north of the centrally located fire. These positions reflect the deep structure of the ritual: north stands between the two directions and their meanings. North/man/life mediates between east/gods/creation and west/demons/destruction. At the beginning of the ritual the following constitutes the deep structure: the *acharya* is to gods as the boy is to demons. Being not yet "born-again," the uninitiated boy belongs to the demons while the *acharya*, being initiated, belongs to the gods. At a subsequent stage in the ritual a significant reorientation takes place. The boy is transferred to his new status when, after donning the sacred thread and circumambulating the fire, he hears the *acharya* pronounce the sacred word OM and then is made to reverse

himself so that he faces not west but east. This change now identifies him with the gods. He receives the Gayatri Mantra and concludes the ritual by pouring out ritual vessels which at the first was done only by the *acharya*. The boy, having gone from west/demons to east/gods, has undergone a transformation of directions which symbolizes the transformation of status.

Some comments comparing Smith and Penner are called for. That Penner's structural approach is primarily concerned with the structure he sees in the texts, ritual orientations, and language of the participants is obvious. Smith's interest is primarily in that which the individuals consciously experience and express or at least would understand and acknowledge. It is their understanding that is important and to seek elsewhere for the "meaning" of the ritual is, in his opinion, to miss the point and make the "faith" of persons a point of noninterest. Here are two approaches which are different without being contradictory. One could learn something from both. Neither appeal to transhistorical matters and both might be called descriptive in nature.

The Functionalism of Emile Durkheim: What Role Does Religion Play in the Life of Society as a Whole?

The most widely accepted approach to religion by sociologists and anthropologists is functionalism. There are many variations, but basically the question being asked is, How does religion function in the life of society and individuals?

The first to call attention to this question in modern times was Emile Durkheim in his work *The Elementary Forms of the Religious Life*.[21] Bronislaw Malinowski adapted and expanded Durkheim's ideas in a major work entitled *Magic, Science and Religion*.[22] Robert K. Merton has shown how functionalism, as held subsequently by some scholars, took on certain nonempirical postulates that, if recognized, could be removed without destroying the basic usefulness of functionalism as an approach to religion.[23]

Durkheim's functionalism had its own nonhistorical concepts; he referred to society as an entity not reducible to its constituent parts. For him society was a complex concept that included a notion that something emerged from the aggregate of individuals coming together in social gatherings. This transhistorical emergent entity acted back on those individuals to coerce their behavior. But this apart, Durkheim and his successors presented a new approach to the study of religion.

Durkheim and other functionalists were concerned to ask, What are the social consequences of religious rites and beliefs upon the individuals and their groups? Durkheim's answer was as follows:

1. Religious rituals often require ascetic and self-denying practices. These serve social ends because they require individuals to accept restraints and limits to their independence. Such self-denial is essential to social harmony, cohesion, and existence.

2. Religious ceremonies function as a cohesive factor binding individuals into a group. Social solidarity and bonding occur when individuals meet together for religious ceremonies. "Rites are, above all, means by which the social group reaffirms itself periodically."[24]

Functionalists believe social solidarity and bonding occur when individuals meet for religious ceremonies. Devotees of Minakshi pulling her cart through the streets of Madurai, India. J. Lewis

3. Ceremonies transmit social values and traditions through myths, stories, and religious texts, thereby bringing

past traditions into present life and introducing the newer generation to its heritage. Perpetuation of the group is guaranteed only as its common heritage is understood and internalized by the newest uninformed member. While not all rites serve this end, those that do function "to attach the present to the past or the individual to the group."[25] In short, the ceremony serves to transmit the social heritage without which there can be no ongoing existence for society.

4. Some ceremonies assist at crisis moments of death by drawing individuals together to give mutual comfort in their loss. Durkheim showed how mourning ceremonies provided channels for the expression of grief while requiring the participation of all. This reinforced society. Malinowski's study of the Trobriand Islanders made much more of this by graphically describing how the funeral ceremonies drew people together at a time when they may have felt like fleeing the presence of death, which would have been socially destabilizing.[26]

How does functionalism approach the *upanayana* rite? Durkheim never studied this, but if he had the following would be a reasonable application of his approach. Durkheim would have found Smith's personalism interesting but, on the whole, too individualistic, since Durkheim was interested in the consequences of religion for society more than for its individual participants. Smith's concern was to show how the received traditions of a group, so determinative of their behavior, may nonetheless be modified by individuals. He thus explores the changes the fixed tradition undergoes

in the process of its transmission.[27] Similarly, Durkheim would have had little interest in Penner's structuralism, as it too ignores questions about society.

What would Durkheim have proposed about this ceremony? First, Durkheim would have taken full note of the preparatory restrictions placed on the boy prior to the ceremony: the fast of silence, the exchange of ordinary clothes for ritual ones, the segregation from family and friends the night before, and the breakfast meal taken with his mother. These disciplines heighten the importance of the occasion and prepare him for participation in the duties of his caste. He can eat, dress, speak, and live only in a way that his society dictates to him. Second, the rite serves to bind the participants together. Those in attendance will be caste members: the immediate family, extended family, and friends of that caste. It is an occasion for social communion and serves to make for unity and identity. Third, the rite passes on the past traditions, thus assuring the life of that society. The boy becomes a Brahman through a Vedic thread-investiture ceremony that permits him to study the Vedas. The sacred knowledge of the Vedas is now, in a preliminary way, preserved for the next generation. This knowledge, though never fully mastered due to its vastness, forms the convictional glue binding him to his social group. By withholding Vedic knowledge from him until now, society has made it all the more probable that the boy will value it and, at the proper time, make certain of its transmission to others in his caste.

In conclusion, functionalism explains religion by reference to its value for society: how it serves to discipline individualism, bind individuals together into social units, and preserve and transmit the traditions which give individuals identity and cohesion.

The Normative Approach of Hendrik Kraemer: Are the Beliefs of This Religion True?

The normative approach to religion asks the question, Is it true? of religious beliefs and practices. This is the approach of most theologians and some philosophers. The normative approach evaluates the truthfulness of a claim according to some accepted standard. It is not infrequently the case that descriptive studies are laced with the normative. To the extent that any study makes pronouncements as to the truthfulness of a belief, the reality or other qualities of deities and spiritual beings, or the effectiveness of purification rites, it is a normative study. It is not merely a question of whether the followers of a particular religion believe such and such a thing is true. This would be a matter of primary concern to Smith's personalism. Of concern for the normative approach is whether deities exist, scriptural statements are true, Krishna lives, spirits haunt. Can a ceremony exorcise evil spirits? Will the prayer of the Gayatri Mantra fall on the ears of a god existing somewhere whose name is Savitri? Is there a spiritual reality inhabiting the *lingam* of Shiva? The normative approach intends to give true answers to these and other questions. For the other approaches, the truthfulness or reality of putative enti-

ties play no central part in answering their questions. For the normative approach it is central.

It should be apparent that the normative approach is the one Christian theologians would typically take in studying their own faith or the faith of others. Theologians may take an interest in other approaches, since they often do provide helpful insights, but they are primarily concerned with truth questions. They want to know what it is in their own tradition, as well as that of others, that is true and worthy of allegiance.

Hendrik Kraemer's approach asks the question: "Are the beliefs of a religion true?" Billy Graham preaches the Gospel at one of his Crusades. The Billy Graham Evangelistic Association

The normative approach does not decide truth questions on empirical grounds alone, or even primarily on empirical bases. Hence its explanations are not fundamentally descriptive but theoretical. It may be problematic for some theologians to accept the point that such an approach is a theoretical one. We do not intend to suggest that a theologian's conclusions are only as good as, equal to, or no different in value from other theoretical statements. We make no attempt to relativize theological conclusions. For example, the theoretical approaches of psychoanalysis and theology are not regarded as having, in principle, equal validity. We only claim that every approach appealing to the transhistorical for its answers is a theoretical one.

The theologian appeals to an authority which is not, ultimately, founded on history or historical factors alone. The biblical theologian works from the Bible, which is, to be sure, a book we can handle as a historical document. But the claim of its truthfulness, for the conservative theologian, rests on a belief in a transcendent God who authoritatively speaks in and through the book. At that point we leave the historical arena and enter the transhistorical. Whether the Bible is or is not a book of divine revelation is not a matter for historical documentation alone. This is not to say the Bible is not historically accurate. It may be. But at crucial points the evidence for its claims does not derive exclusively from the historical arena. When the theologian preaches Jesus Christ to the world, he or she intends more than to show that Jesus is a historical person. To argue for the historicity of Jesus one may bring forward historical evidences which are convincing to some though perhaps less convincing to others. But orthodox Christians claim something more than historicity for Jesus; they claim he was God of very God. The support for this, though within a historical framework,

has its basis in something more than the merely historical and descriptive. As Jesus said to Peter after his confession at Caesarea Philippi: "Simon son of Jonah, you are favored indeed! You did not learn that from mortal man; it was revealed to you by my heavenly Father" (Matt. 16:17 NEB).

When Judeo-Christian theologians examine the ancient Greek pantheon, they are likely to view it as a superstitious belief in nonexistent deities. Indeed, the apostle Paul makes this point in 1 Corinthians 8:4–5. In short, these gods do not exist and claims for them are regarded as either false or misinformed. Paul passes judgment on the truth of their existence and meaning according to some authority that is regarded as dependable.

Hendrik Kraemer takes a normative approach to the world's religions in his book *The Christian Message in a Non-Christian World*.[28] What are the premises he accepts?

1. There is no such thing as "religion." This is merely an idea or "essence" which corresponds to nothing found in the real world.

2. While there is no such thing as "religion," there are religions in the plural. But what is more important is the religious consciousness of individuals, of which the concrete religions are concrete expressions. This religious consciousness is, Kraemer claims, an empirical reality which is a given constitutional fact of human nature and points beyond to the transcendent, however it is defined.

3. Religions, including the Christian

religion, are a combination of the sublime and the foolish, truth and error, life and death. It is not that the Gospel itself combines truth and error, but that the followers of the Gospel, being fallible, do not inerrantly interpret the Gospel. The social and historical expression of the Gospel in the Christian church through the centuries has never perfectly reproduced the perfect Gospel; hence, it is flawed and corrupted.

4. Jesus Christ is a real revelation of the transcendent God whose message and redemptive mission are timelessly true. Because of his unique character he rightly judges all religions in all their dimensions, and this includes the Christian religion. Liberal theologies which reject or subvert the revelation of God in Christ misunderstand and mistreat the Bible. A fair-handed interpretation results in what Kraemer calls "biblical realism": a straightforward acceptance that the Bible's message is of the one true God acting in history and in Jesus the Messiah of God for the world's redemption.

How should one undertake the study of religion according to Kraemer? How can the religions be studied, compared, and evaluated? According to Kraemer, the discipline of the science of religion (*Religionswissenschaft*) has erroneously claimed for itself an objective, scientific approach while regarding theology to be unscientific and biased. Kraemer states that every approach to religion, including the so-called scientific one, begins with presuppositions and is therefore interpretive and subjective, whether self-aware of this fact or not. Objectivity is a fiction. The way of wisdom is for each scholar to explicitly acknowledge and articulate the starting points of his or her approach because scientific objectivity is "eternally unattainable."[29]

Kraemer begins his own study by laying forth his assumptions and starting points. He acknowledges that his is a theological approach, that he is a believer in Jesus Christ, and that the judgments of Jesus apply to all religions, including the Christian religion. Christ is the measure and standard of true religion. This is an act of faith, but it places him at no disadvantage since the approaches of the so-called scientific historians have faith positions which are often unacknowledged. Put theologically, Kraemer's starting point is revelation which is not to be confused with intuition and is not derived from religious consciousness. Revelation is in the person of Christ and is not identical with the propositional, verbal statements of the Bible, which merely testify to and about the revelation of God in God's mighty acts and in the person of Jesus Christ.

Kraemer wants to ask two very important questions: Are the religions places of encounter between God and man? and Are the religions responses to a divine activity? The answers to these questions, in his view, are always dialectical. By that he means that to some extent the answer is yes, while at the same time one must say no.

The natural knowledge of God found in the religions rests on two poles, the first of which is a sense of a transcendent, superhuman reality whose consciousness is divinely implanted in humankind. This, however, has been corrupted or distorted in such a way that humankind cannot take advantage of the second pole of the natural knowledge of God, which is the manifestation of God in and through nature. Since God has a covenant with all humankind, even the religions lie within the compass of God's concern. "God is not absent from them."[30] But the religions, nonetheless, belong to the realm of unredeemed humanity, having their ideas and values determined by the old or Adamic man. All of the highest achievements of the religions, as well as their Satanic deviancies, are under judgment. The religions reflect all that is true about those who create them and those who adhere to them. The adherents of the religions and the religious systems that they embrace are alike marked by paradox showing that they are related to God but also separated from him. They grope toward him yet rebel against him. In the world religions the individual dimly responds to the God who registers in his or her consciousness. But these same religions are expressions of human needs which blend things both sublime and base. What might be called the highest aspirations and achievements of the religions are mere gropings marked by ignorant or futile speculations. The religions are human responses to God which fall short of God's glory while being, at the same time, genuine longings for him. The only hope for finding what one longs for is through God's sovereign act of reconciling God and humankind through Christ.

How would Kraemer's normative approach view religious rites generally and the *upanayana* in particular? He is of the opinion that in the religions, their beliefs, and rituals there are intuitions of truth in such topics as sin, guilt, surrender to the divine will, expectations of a savior, grace, and the idea of divine sacrifice. For example, in the Indonesian myth of Ceram there is a teaching that the life of the world is established in the death and sacrifice of a god, and when this is ceremonially reenacted the tribal life is itself perpetuated. Such a myth comes close to the truth, according to Kraemer, since the cosmic order is the pivot for the social order. Though this rite is certainly a magical human act, it senses some truth about God. But many central truths remain unknown to the adherents, chief of which is God's holiness and saving acts in Christ.

Specifically, Kraemer might well point out how in the *upanayana* the *acharya* takes a mediating position in attempting to lead the boy from ignorance to knowledge. Jesus Christ mediates between God and humanity. Yet Kraemer might point out how frequently human pride permits human beings to take the place of God in mediating divine things. On the other hand, the boy, whose condition is that of spiritual ignorance, is identified with demons, which is a remarkably true intuition. Thus there are both negative and positive points in the ritual. The change of the boy from the once-born to the twice-born state shows positively the need for a new spiritual standing. Yet it grossly errs in providing a false substitute for Christ who alone can give humans a new status.

History of Religions Approach of Robert Baird: Does the Object and Method of Religious Study Rest on Historical Grounds?

The history of religions approach, as the name indicates, studies religion from a historical perspective. This means that both in its object of study and in the methods used to understand religion it is governed by historical considerations.

The historical approach differs from each of the foregoing in a number of ways, though it has more in common with the personalist approach, as both have an interest in describing the concerns of individuals, than with the others.

The study of religion has been undertaken historically in a variety of ways.[31] In the work of some scholars of the past, the historical approach meant the attempt to trace either religion itself or some belief, practice, or tradition to its starting point. While this approach may have achieved some limited success, it often faced the problem of the scarcity or even absence of data to provide historical answers to the question of origins. Without written or even artifactual sources, mountains of meaning or interpretation were built on molehills of data and evolutionary theories. This difficulty has led most modern scholars to give up the search for historical origins.

But what is history, anyway? This is a fundamental consideration. Many historians have written on this subject, and there are conflicting opinions on the limits and objectives of historical writing. Robert Baird begins his history of religions approach by stating what he understands the discipline of history to be. He defines the word *history* to mean "the descriptive study of the human past."[32] The past includes the present as well, since the present is nothing more than the "soon past." Thus Baird is interested in anything in the past that deals with humans and their religion.

This leads naturally to a consideration of the word *religion*. As we have seen earlier in this chapter Baird defines religion in such a way that it is subject to historical methods of investigation. Religion is given a functional or stipulative definition as "that which is of ultimate concern to individuals or groups." Functional definitions differ from what might be called "real" definitions. A real definition may be said to be true or false and carries with it the idea that there is one fixed and unchangeable meaning for a word. Baird holds that, rather than attempting such a definition, it is better to define religion in a way that more easily facilitates historical study. Religion defined as that which people believe to be of supreme importance serves in a useful way to learn about individuals and communities on historical grounds. It has heuristic value by getting at one of the most important of human issues: what counts most to people. Further, this study of primary concerns makes possible an examination of related matters and secondary concerns in the complex interrelationship of the hierarchy of interests. Thus history of religion undertakes a dimension of religious life that is very helpful.

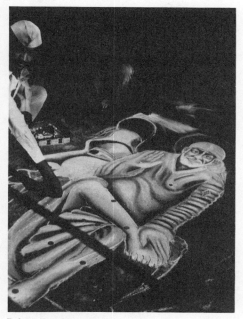

Robert Baird's approach is that religion is that which is of supreme or ultimate concerns to individuals or groups. Street puja *in Bombay.* J. Lewis

Since so many people think of religion as dealing with "Ultimate Reality," it is important to distinguish this from Baird's definition. The study of "ultimate concerns" is something different from studying Ultimate Reality, as Baird so clearly explains.

It is perfectly legitimate to make the object of one's study God, Ultimate Reality, the Ground of Being or Dharmakaya. But the object of historical study is the study of man and not the study of any of these. The historian is certainly interested in Shankara's or Gaudapada's view of non-dual Reality. . . . But, historically speaking, these are all man's views of Ultimate Reality. While it is undoubtedly true that all views of

Ultimate Reality are human in the sense that it is men who hold them, to ask "What is the nature of Ultimate Reality?" is a different level question from "What is Shankara's view of Ultimate Reality?"[33]

It is the claim of the historian of religion that in principle it is possible to have a valid understanding of the religion of others without entering into the personal experience of that religion. Some have questioned if this is possible. H. Presler says:

Primitive religion, or any religion for that matter, is not fully understood when observed from the outside; it must be observed from the subjective side. The field worker must acquire at least a vicarious experience of that primitive religion by prolonged participation within the group and sharing its subjective aspects with devotees.[34]

However, as has been argued by W. Cantwell Smith, if the believer can acknowledge the accuracy of a study, then this is a strong indication of its validity and objectivity. Numbers of studies have been done by those who have not personally participated in the religion but whose work has been confirmed by believers as substantially accurate.

This is not to say that the historian of religions claims he or she describes the entirety of another's religion. In fact, Baird's definition restricts the scope of the study by asking the extremely important question about ultimate concerns. There are some levels it does not claim to explore. An example is the inner religious experience of a person. There is a sense in which this is not open to the historian because it is not public, observable, and subject to examination like other historical phenomena such as texts, testimonials, rites, and rituals. This inner core of religious experience, since it is so private and unique, cannot by its very nature be confirmed since it cannot be truly compared. Hence, we may speak of the inner experience as being largely outside the scope of this method. It is unobservable, unexaminable, existential, personal, and sometimes even indescribable by the person having the experience, though it may be studied in a secondary way by the oral or written testimonies of those who have had the experience. Interestingly, the moment the experience is committed to oral or verbal testimony it is subject to historical investigation. One might say that experience may be studied, but only in this secondary way.

History of religions indeed recognizes that there are religious topics which its methodology cannot address. It would seem that this approach cannot verify the existence of deep structures such as those claimed in Hans Penner's structuralism. Neither can it deal with the topic of the origin of religion. Such topics hold no promise for the historian because there are no data which can supply probable answers to the questions of the existence of structures or the beginnings of religion. If these questions are to be answered, they will not be answered by responsible religious historians. Again, questions about the existence of a "religious nature" in humans or the existence of the "essence" of religion are subjects which necessarily fall outside the methodology of the historian. The existence of structures, the origin of religion, the innate religiousness of

humankind, and the essence of religion are not topics which the historian of religion needs to answer in order to deal with the question: What is of ultimate importance to this individual or group?

Notwithstanding these limits, history of religion does make its contribution. Baird's version seems to call for stricter limits to be placed on historical methodology than some others. Specifically, he seeks carefully to limit historical conclusions to those which can be empirically supported or inferred by empirical data. Because of this, Baird has been categorized as an empiricist historian. Conclusions based on the intuitive, the theoretical, and personal experience are not historical in the stricter sense.[35] In his view, what others have called "history" has often been a mixture of history, philosophy, and even theology. Baird wishes to restrict history of religions to a historical methodology and thus render distinctions between history and other disciplines more explicit.

The history of religions approach is not reductionistic. That is, it does not claim that religion in all its aspects is reducible to the historical level. There are no doubt mysteries of religious experience which historians cannot, by the limits of their methodology, examine. That does not make these mysteries less important. Theology, structuralism, psychology of religion, depth psychology, and other disciplinary approaches may each have its own questions about and approaches to these mysteries. The historian of religions only hopes that each discipline be as explicit as possible about its method and outcomes so that these outcomes can supplement each other for the broadest possible understanding of religion. Methodologies will differ. History of religion has its own methodology but does not, thereby, negate the usefulness of other approaches, provided they are internally consistent. Thus the historical approach makes no claim to exhaust the material or alone offer complete knowledge of *homo religiosis*. Rather, it sees itself as one of many approaches to religion in culture. History of religions is happy to incorporate the analysis of other disciplines, including the behavioral sciences such as anthropology, sociology, and psychology where the outcomes of these disciplines meet two criteria. First, where these outcomes are contingent on the search for understanding the pattern of ultimate concerns. Second, where the research is descriptive in nature and not merely theoretical. For example, historians who seek to understand Buddhist concerns in India in the period around 250 B.C.E. are interested in the conclusions of art historians about the Great Stupa of Sanchi constructed in approximately the same period. A historian would pay careful attention to the *Mahaparinibbana Sutra*, which comes from the period, but also to the bas-relief on the gateway pillars which depict a thriving *stupa* cult. The text describes activities of piety with crowds circumambulating the *stupa* which served as a reliquary of the Buddha's remains. But the art shows a commingling of additional interests which do not totally square with the description of the text itself. S. N. Dutt says, "the sculptured renderings [on the *stupa*] show fine shades of difference from their

textual originals. . . . Between the scriptural legends and their sculptural counterparts, the disagreements suggest in subtle ways fresh approaches to the religion, new angles in regarding the Lord's life and personality and the pressure of a new Buddha-concept."[36]

History of Religions approach may draw on the knowledge of art historians to help arrive at conclusions about the ultimate concerns of early Buddhists. Gateway pillars of the Great Stupa of Sanchi. J. Lewis

How does the historian of religion's approach to the *upanayana* rite compare to the approaches taken by phenomenologists, functionalists, or structuralists? First, there is a concern to put the rite into some kind of a social and temporal context against which one can attempt to learn of its place in the value system of the individual, family, or community. The ritual is not to be isolated from that context nor grouped by similarity with other rites of passage from other traditions, as though these collectively have some meaning in and of themselves due to some common universal form. This would be more the approach of some phenomenologists. Nor would the approach taken be identical to that of functionalists, who find social meaning for the *upanayana* rite as it serves to keep the youth within the Hindu religion, preserve Hindu traditions, and bind the community to its heritage. The structuralist's emphasis on deep structures, while depending on certain historical realities for the context of its work, is not founded on strictly historical descriptive methods.

The historian of religions will want to know, if possible, how and in what way the rite relates to some broader pattern of ultimacy in the life of its participants. The functionalist's observations are of special interest in this search, since they demonstrate rather conclusively that rites of passage function to conserve ideals, traditions, and values. The historian wants to go beyond this, however, to explore more precisely what matters are of highest importance to the participants and how the rite relates to that.

Thus the *upanayana* will be understood in the context of other experiences and possibly examined more longitudinally, that is, over time, rather than being limited to the particular moment of the rite. The longitudinal approach might be especially important if the focus is on the initiate himself, since it

is possible that his own sense of ultimacy is only in its earliest stages of development. At the time of the ritual it may be mostly a social event for the boy and only later take on more significance. If, however, the study extends to the family and the community, then the rite might provide some important clues as to what things count most in their lives.

Still, it would probably be recognized that little can be known about the ultimate concerns of individuals by reference to the *upanayana* rite alone without reference to other matters. It is nonetheless preliminary and, taken together with other matters, at least the following is recognized by the historian of religions.

First, the ritual makes the boy a Hindu and identifies him as a member of one of the upper three levels of caste. Second, he is permitted to study the Vedas; this gives him access to its secrets and truths. Third, all the diverse options found in the Vedas are opened for him, from theism to atheism to nondualism, and from *bhakti* commitment to a personal god to indifference to an impersonal force. The ritual opens many doors but by itself determines no narrow road for him within the Hindu community.

In the end, it could probably be said that the history of religions approach does not contribute much that is new to understanding the *upanayana* rite. Rather, its value is in seeing how the rite is a part of the broader picture and serves to give further direction to emerging concerns of the individual and his family and the community surrounding them. And since history is the story of change, Baird's approach might prove especially helpful in documenting how initiates over the generations have differing views of the rite's significance and meaning. Whether meaningful generalizations can be made relative to such changes is another matter.

In conclusion we can say that the approach of history of religions begins with a definition of religion that limits the object of study to the historical realm. Proceeding on these grounds it describes and explains what persons and groups consider of supreme or ultimate importance. Humanity's religious experience is so varied and rich that the application of these methods by sensitive and skilled observers leads to informative results.

Discussion

1. What are some ways religion has been defined? Which definition does the text subscribe to?
2. What does it mean to say that religion has no existence except in the mind of the scholar (Jonathan Z. Smith)?
3. What practical value does Baird's definition of religion have for us as we take up the study of the religious world?
4. What kinds of "explanations" are there for religious phenomena?
5. Can one learn something about religion from each of the approaches discussed in this chapter? Which of these approaches appeals to you and why?
6. Take a rite of passage with which you are familiar, say baptism or confirmation, and discuss it from the standpoint of one or more of these approaches.

Notes

[1]For a full discussion of the history and logic of defining the word *religion* consult Robert D. Baird's *Category Formation and the History of Religions* (The Hague: Moulton, 1971).

[2]There is no universal agreement as to what constitutes a "world religion." It might be said, however, that a world religion is one that is widespread geographically or found among a large number of persons, has a more or less systematic organization of beliefs to which a majority of the community give assent, is rooted in written scriptures and/or enduring oral traditions, and finds a focus for its community in a definable commitment to some supremely important goal or ultimate concern. See also Eugene Nida, *Customs and Cultures: Anthology for Christian Missions* (New York: Harper & Row, 1954), 170.

[3]Baird, *Category Formation*, 17–27.

[4]Jonathan Z. Smith, *Imagining Religion: From Babylon to Jonestown* (Chicago: Univ. of Chicago Press, 1982), xi.

[5]Referred to in Claas Jouco Bleeker, *The Sacred Bridge: Researches into the Nature and Structure of Religion* (Leiden: Brill, 1963), 39.

[6]Harvie M. Conn, *Eternal Word and Changing Worlds* (Grand Rapids: Zondervan, 1984), 60f, 90f, 106f.

[7]Eugene A. Nida, "New Religions For Old: A Study of Culture Change," in William A. Smalley, ed., *Readings in Missionary Anthropology II* (South Pasadena, Calif.: William Carey Library, 1978), 22.

[8]Baird, *Category Formation*, chap. 2.

[9]J. H. Bavinck, *The Church Between the Temple and the Mosque* (Grand Rapids: Eerdmans, 1966), 15.

[10]William D. Reyburn, "The Transformation of God and the Conversion of Man," in William A. Smalley, ed., *Readings in Missionary Anthropology* (Tarrytown, N.Y.: Practical Anthropology, 1967) 26.

[11]Wilfred Cantwell Smith, "Methodology and the Study of Religion: Some Misgivings," in Robert D. Baird, ed., *Methodological Issues in Religious Studies* (Chico, Calif.: New Horizons Press, 1975), 1-25.

[12]David Hackett Fischer argues that why questions are inappropriate for historical inquiry. However, it is not the word itself that leads to a nonhistorical approach. Rather it is the level at which one seeks the answer to the why question. *Historians' Fallacies* (New York: Harper & Row, 1970), 14–15.

[13]Wilfred Cantwell Smith, "Comparative Religion: Whither and Why?," in *The History of Religions: Essays in Methodology* (Chicago: Univ. of Chicago Press, 1959), 35.

[14]Wilfred Cantwell Smith, *The Meaning and End of Religion* (New York: Mentor Books, 1964), chap. 7.

[15]Wilfred Cantwell Smith, *Toward A World Theology: Faith and the Comparative History of Religion* (Philadelphia: Westminster, 1981), 4.

[16]Wilfred Cantwell Smith, *Meaning and End*, 9.

[17]Wilfred Cantwell Smith, *The Faith of Other Men* (New York: Mentor Books, 1961), 37–49.

[18]Nirad C. Chaudhuri, *Hinduism: A Religion to Live By* (New Delhi: B.I. Publications, 1979), 211.

[19]Hans H. Penner, "Creating A Brahman: A Structural Approach to Religion," in *Methodological Issues in Religious Studies* (Chico, Calif.: New Horizons Press, 1975), 49–64.

[20]Ibid., 61.

[21]Emile Durkheim, *The Elementary Forms of the Religious Life* (New York: Free Press, 1965).

[22]Bronislaw Malinowski, *Magic, Science and Religion* (New York: Doubleday Anchor, 1954).

[23]Robert K. Merton, *Social Theory and Social Structure* (New York: Free Press, 1957).

[24]Durkheim, *Elementary Forms*, 432.

[25]Ibid., 423.

[26]Malinowski, *Magic, Science and Religion*, 47–53.

[27]Wilfred Cantwell Smith, *Meaning and End*, 142–53.

[28]Hendrik Kraemer, *The Christian Message in a Non-Christian World* (Grand Rapids: Eerdmans, 1963).

[29]Ibid., 140.

[30]Ibid., 257.

[31]Descriptions of types of history of religions can be found in *Abingdon Encyclopedia of Religion*, S.V. "religion, the study of," and *The Encyclopedia of Religion*, S.V. "history of religions."

[32]Baird, *Category Formation*, 32.

[33]Ibid., 19.

[34]Henry H. Presler, *Primitive Religions in India* (Madras: Christian Literature Society Press, 1971), 32.

[35]See Eric J. Lott, *Vision, Tradition, Interpretation: Theology, Religion, and the Study of Religion* (New York: Mouton de Gruyter, 1988), 155ff.

[36]Sukumar Dutt, *The Buddha and Five After Centuries* (London: Luzac, 1957), 180.

Part Two

Religions of Ancient and Select Contemporary Societies

3 Ancient Religions

The polytheisms of ancient times (prior to the beginnings of Christianity) are more than simply religions from the past. Some of them, through their stories, have exercised influence on ideas in Western civilization. Their use as allusions in literature is extensive and they need to be studied as part of the heritage of that literature. Further, study of the religions in the Mediterranean basin provides background for Judaism, Christianity, and Islam. Beyond that, polytheism, whether ancient or modern, is indicative of one more way that human beings have of grappling with spiritual reality.

Polytheism literally means "many gods." Most ancient peoples and many modern ones have constructed a spirit world with multiple good and evil beings, often as personifications of the forces of nature. But polytheism is more than nature religion; it is also an attempt to explain human experience, the longings of the human soul, and encounters with the divine.

Religions of the Ancient Middle East

The ancient city of Jericho in Palestine is the oldest known human settlement, dating to about 9000 B.C.E.* Evidence of walls around the site, a settled agricultural system, and the religious rite of burial of the dead date to the eighth millennium B.C.E. Jericho was intermittently occupied between 7000 and 3500, and urban culture reappeared by the late fourth millennium. About that same time, civilization—often defined as the building of cities and the use of writing—began in Mesopotamia. And from the beginning, temples were built and the literature abounds with references to the gods.

Contrary to earlier views about religious "development," based on the belief that religious thought moved from the simple to the complex (or some other development model), it now seems unfair to speak about the development of religions like those in ancient times. That changes occurred cannot be questioned. That influences from other religious systems impinged on a given religion cannot be doubted. Also, social and political factors influenced religion (and vice versa). But the neat schemes of the historians of religion of two or more generations ago have been put aside. In the following descriptions we shall look at

*The terms "Before the Common Era" (B.C.E.) and "Common Era" (C.E.) are now commonly used to replace the older B.C. and A.D. terminology.

Excavations at Jericho reveal what may be the oldest city on earth. Israel Tourism Bureau

the various religions as whole systems that experienced change and underwent influence.

Sumer and Akkad

Sumerian civilization goes back to about 3500 B.C.E. Located in Mesopotamia (the land "between the rivers"— the Tigris and Euphrates—roughly equivalent to present-day Iraq), Sumerian civilization developed the potter's wheel, ox-drawn plows, and cuneiform writing, which was done with a stylus on a wet clay tablet that, when fired, became a lasting record. Hundreds of thousands of clay tablet fragments have been found, giving us valuable insights into the Sumerian and later cultures of Mesopotamia. The Sumerians were active traders in the region of the Persian Gulf and Asia Minor. The stone, ores, and timber they brought back, all in short

supply in their homeland, enabled them to build ziggurats, tall, pyramid-shaped towers with temple shrines at the top. The temples were important in the social and religious life of the Sumerians.

Cuneiform writing was made in wet clay using a utensil called stylus. Roy Cuny

For a thousand years the Sumerians held sway in southern Mesopotamia, then about 2340 B.C.E. an Akkadian army led by Sargon the Great subjugated the Sumerian city-states to his own kingdom. The two cultures intermingled in the following centuries, their religious systems becoming virtually one. Around 2060 B.C.E., after a period of political stagnation in the region, a Neo-Sumerian Empire was established, restoring prosperity to Sumer and Akkad for about a century. The first king of Neo-Sumeria, Ur Nammu, issued the first known law code in history.

While there were hundreds of Sumerian deities, six emerged as prominent ones; each was the deity of a large city. An (Anu) was the sky god and presumed ruler of the gods, but the air god Enlil (Bel) was the god of the lands beneath the sky; he conferred power on kings and was a great warrior. Nanna (Sin) was the moon god, Utu (Shamash) the sun god, and Enki (Ea) the water god (and also the god of wisdom). Ninhursag, the mother goddess, was unmarried, so she did not fit with the typical arrangement of male god and female consort. An's daughter, Inanna, was the virgin love goddess and mistress of the sky.

Each city had its chief deity, but the gods were not exclusive of one another; temples to gods other than the reigning deity were found in all the Sumerian cities, though the temple of the chief god was usually the largest.

Over the course of time the gods were placed into groups or families of natural grouping like the seasons of the year, the physical universe, etc. There was a netherworld also, the land of no return, ruled over by the gods of pestilence, death, and sterility.

The deity who came closest to being universally worshiped was the goddess of fertility, Ishtar (the Akkadian equivalent to the Sumerian Inanna, the Phoenician Astarte, the Greek Aphrodite, and the Roman Venus). Ishtar gave conception to women and life to the ground. She was also the queen of heaven, and a warrior goddess to some. Worship of Ishtar continued beyond the life of Sumer and Akkad, moving to Palestine and Egypt.

Knowledge about the Sumerian and Akkadian god system comes from inscriptions in cuneiform script on clay tablets, walls, and rock surfaces. Many of the clay tablets, most in fragmentary condition, come from the Sumerian library at Nippur; others are from the library assembled by the Assyrian king Assurbanipal in the seventh century B.C.E. The Sumerian language died out as a spoken tongue about 1800 B.C.E., but it remained the classical language of the Middle East until the beginning of the Christian era. Akkadian succeeded it as the spoken language and, known successively as Babylonian and Assyrian, was the main cuneiform language of biblical times.

The temple was at the center of Sumerian and Akkadian life. The statues of the deities, usually wood plated with gold, were an important feature of temple rites. Consecrated in secret rituals called the "opening of the mouth" that signified their transition to god status, they could "see," and even "eat" the twice-a-day meals served to them. Probably most often kept in the shrines and away from public inspection, the god statues were treated as if they had life.

Life even in urban Sumer was heavily agricultural, and the temples owned large segments of the land surrounding the cities. This gave the temples and the priests a good deal of social and political power. When the Akkadians became dominant, however, the power shifted to the royal palace because the king, as the servant of the temple god, became the locus of sacred power.

For the ordinary worshiper, prayer was the center of experience, and prayers for assistance, as gratitude for dangers averted and favors granted, and as invocation of the gods are the common features in the textual materials. Prayer was often accompanied by sacrifice ceremonies, including animals and vegetables and gifts of jewels, perfume, and clothing. Since fertility was so important, prayer for good harvests and for human conception was necessary, and temple prostitutes performed fertility rites aimed at securing these blessings. In all, the men and women of Sumer served the gods as best they could.

Babylon

The Neo-Sumerian Empire ended about 1950 B.C.E. After a period of unrest the city-state of Babylon rose to power under Hammurabi (ruled c. 1790–50). An energetic ruler with a large professional army and a government bureaucracy, Hammurabi issued a law code which became the most famous of antiquity outside the Mosaic legislation. The code was based on the principle of "an eye for an eye" and included religious elements as well as political and legal ones. While similar in content to earlier law codes, Hammurabi's is noteworthy for its completeness and for the relation some of it bears to the Mosaic code.

Hammurabi's Babylon did not last long, but the city came to represent a succession of empires that prevailed in the region for almost two thousand years. After periods of rule under the Hittites and Kassites, the Assyrians came to power in the ninth century B.C.E. From their capital at Nineveh they dominated the Fertile Crescent, an area running in an arc from Mesopotamia to Palestine, and ruled in Egypt for more than a century, creating thereby the first "world" empire. A very warlike people, the Assyrians often uprooted the populations which they conquered.

In 612 B.C.E. the Assyrians were overthrown by two of their subject peoples, the Medes and the Chaldeans. The Chaldean king Nebuchadnezzar (ruled 605–562 B.C.E.) rebuilt Babylon and established the Chaldean or Neo-Babylonian Empire. He continued the Assyrian custom of removing conquered peoples, among them many of the inhabitants of Jerusalem in 587/6 B.C.E. Babylon at this time became a city of great splendor, with walls and terrace gardens (the famous "hanging gardens") and a ziggurat 300 feet high.

As the successors to Sumer, the Babylonians continued some of the same god system but added other concepts, including several stories that in some ways parallel accounts in the Bible. These stories continue to hold interest many centuries after their time, for they demonstrate the common belief in the supernatural origin of the world and at the same time show the great differences among accounts of the origins.

The Epic of Creation

Called *Enuma elish* ("when on high") from its opening words, the Epic of Creation begins with the watery realm that existed before the world was created. Ruled by Apsu and Ti'amat, god and goddess of the deep, this primeval realm was disrupted by their unruly family of gods. Apsu wished to kill them, but he was killed by the water god Enki, and this roused Ti'amat to the angry creation of monsters, snakes, and demons. She gave the tablets of destiny to her second husband, Kingu, and started war on the gods. Only Marduk, great god of the Babylonians, was able to subdue Ti'amat, which he did in exchange for absolute rule over the assembly of gods. The battle was fierce:

Ti'amat and the champion of the gods,
    Marduk,
engaged, were tangled in single combat,
    joined in battle.
The lord spread out his net encompassing
    her;
the tempest, following after, he loosed in
    her face.
Ti'amat opened her mouth as far as she
    could;
he drove in the tempest lest she close her
    lips.
The fierce winds filled her belly,
Her insides congested and she opened wide
    her mouth;
he let fly an arrow, it split her belly,
cut through her inward parts, and gashed
    the heart.
He held her fast, extinguishing her life.[1]

Marduk cut her in two and used her carcass to create the universe, one half the sky, the other half the earth. From her eyes flowed the Tigris and Euphrates rivers. Turning next to Kingu, Marduk took from him the tablets of destiny and mixed clay with the blood from Kingu's cut veins to create humanity.

Begun in the conflict among the gods, chaos remained always a threat to the order that Marduk had imposed. Since the blood from the defeated demons was in them, human beings were seen ambiguously; they had life but not immortality, and the breaking of order was always a possibility. Annually at the New Year's festival in Babylon the king and the high priest went through a ceremony that reestablished Marduk's superiority among the gods and reinstituted the king's rule: humanity and the cosmos in harmony once again.

The Epic of Gilgamesh

A morality tale in the Akkadian language, the story recounts the adventures of Gilgamesh, harsh ruler of Uruk (the Erech of Gen. 10:10). In response to appeals from his subjects, the gods create Enkidu, a wild man who at first lived among animals but eventually fought Gilgamesh at Uruk. Defeated, Enkidu becomes a companion of Gilgamesh and the two men later kill Huwawa, guardian of a forest of the god Enlil. Enlil condemns Enkidu to death, and after seven days of lamenting the loss of his friend, Gilgamesh journeys to look for immortality. Along the way he encounters a woman who runs a tavern, and she seeks to dissuade him from his quest:

Gilgamesh, whither hurriest thou?
The life that thou seekest thou wilt not
    find.
When the gods created man,
They fixed death for mankind.
Life they took in their own hand.
Thou, O Gilgamesh, let thy belly be filled!
Day and night be merry,
Daily celebrate a feast,
Day and night dance and make merry!
Clean be thy clothes,
Thy head be washed, bathe in water!
Look joyfully on the child that grasps thy
    hand,
Be happy with the wife in thine arms![2]

Traveling beyond the western waters, Gilgamesh encounters one of his ancestors, Utnapishtim, who recounts the story of the flood. Warned that the gods were sending a flood to destroy life on earth, Utnapishtim built a large boat and took refuge in it with his wife and two each of all the animals. Safe in the boat that comes to rest after the flood waters recede, Utnapishtim and his wife are rewarded by the gods with the gift of immortality, which they explain to Gilgamesh can be obtained by eating a plant that grew at the bottom of the sea. Gilgamesh finds the plant, but before he eats from it a snake robs him of the plant and gains immortality for itself. A much-chastened Gilgamesh returns to Uruk, bereft of his friend Enkidu and aware that he does not have immortality.

The story is unresolved at the end, thereby demonstrating that life too is unresolved, that human beings face a futile struggle against evil and death, and that human beings are at the mercy of fate. The Babylonians had no hope of good in the world beyond death; much like the lament sections of the book of Ecclesiastes with its depiction of life "under the sun," the most that Gilgamesh can hope for is joy in earthly life.

Zoroastrianism

The successor state to the Chaldean Empire was the Persian Empire. Shortly after the death of Nebuchadnezzar, Cyrus of Persia moved into the region, and he and his successor, Darius (522–486), created an empire that lasted until defeated by Alexander the Great in 331 B.C.E. That defeat signaled the shift of power from the

Middle East to Greece and inaugurated the Hellenization of the Mediterranean world.

King Darius was a convert to Zoroastrianism, a religion founded by Zoroaster (the Greek form of Zarathustra), born sometime around 600 B.C.E. This religion became ultimately the state religion of Persia (Iran), and some adherents are still found in India and Iran. A corrupted form of Zoroastrianism called Mithraism (after the ancient Persian god of the sun) flourished in the second and third centuries C.E. in the Roman Empire, especially in the Roman army, and for a while offered strong competition to Christianity. It is virtually impossible to separate the teachings of Zoroaster from those of his later followers, but the chief source of the teachings, the *Avesta*, contains hymns called *gathas*, which likely were written by Zoroaster.

Zoroaster apparently was unhappy with the older Persian pagan polytheism and substituted a mixed monotheism and dualism in its place. The chief of the gods, and the only one deserving of homage, was Ahura Mazda ("wise lord"; at times improperly translated as "lord of light"). Ahura Mazda is in an agelong struggle with Ahriman, the spirit of evil, who came into existence with Ahura Mazda at some distant past point. Human beings are enlisted in the battle on the side of Ahura Mazda, who will be triumphant ultimately through the work of the Saoshyant, a messiahlike figure.

Later forms of Zoroastrianism made the dualism very pronounced. Each person, and each spirit, has the responsibility of choosing between the Wise Lord and Ahriman, the Lie. From this it follows that humans are responsible for their own fate. Through good deeds the righteous person earns an everlasting reward, and through choosing the lie the unrighteous faces an eternal misery which more or less corresponds to the Christian understanding of hell. In addition to the sharp dualism, some sacrificial practices and other forms of the older Persian polytheism also crept into Zoroastrianism.

The relation between Zoroastrianism and the chief monotheistic religions, Judaism, Christianity, and Islam, is debated. Part of the problem is due to the fact that the collection of Zoroastrian teachings was not completed until the fourth century C.E., leaving in some doubt who may have influenced whom in such matters as angels, resurrection, and eschatology.

Religion in Egypt

Egypt's religion came to an official end in the fourth century C.E. when the nation converted to Christianity. For three millennia before that the native religion held sway.

Political Life

Egypt and the Nile were intertwined. The annual flooding of the Nile, usually in September or October, left a rich deposit of silt in the area immediately adjacent to the river. Hence the name Kemet ("black land") applied to the agriculturally rich Nile valley, while the desert nearby was known as the red land. Two and sometimes three crops could be harvested in the rich soil. A failure of the Nile to flood could cause immediate famine conditions because Lower Egypt (north of the city of Memphis and including the delta region) received only ten inches of rain per year and Upper Egypt (south of Memphis), less than an inch. The sharp division between black and red land provided a barrier between the Egyptians and other peoples, allowing the creation of a self-contained culture governed by *ma'at*, the concept of an order in society, religion, and government.

The newly united kingdom of Egypt with its capital at Memphis was established about 3100 B.C.E. by Menes, who founded the first of Egypt's dynasties (royal lines that succeeded one another). The system of writing known as hieroglyphics (pictures and other symbols representing the sounds of syllables and consonants) was devised in this the Archaic Period of Egyptian history. The kings were believed to be incarnations of one of the gods, at first Horus, the falcon god, and later Re, the sun god. The god-kings divided Egypt into districts called *nomes*, each with its own deity worshiped in a temple complex in the main city.

In the era of the Old Kingdom (c. 2700–2200 B.C.E.) Egypt became a major civilization. The rulers, the pharaohs, claimed divine origin and therefore ruled as gods, not as representatives of the gods as in Mesopotamia. Large structures were built during this "Pyramid Age" as stairways to heaven for the king's spirit to ascend into the afterlife, during which he would accompany the sun god Re in his daily boat journey across the

False door from a tomb at Giza, C. 2400 B.C.E. *The inscriptions ask for offerings to aid the dead man's journey to the afterlife.* Minneapolis Institute of Art

sky. The Great Pyramid at Giza was the outstanding achievement, built by Khufu (Gk., Cheops; d. 2494 B.C.E.). Covering thirteen acres and nearly 500 feet high, the pyramid was built with over two million limestone blocks, most of them several tons in weight, which were cut, floated along the Nile, and put in place. It was an impressive work of engineering. Toward the end of the Old Kingdom, nobles from Thebes mounted a rebellion against the pharaohs and the priests of the sun god, creating a period of civil war and anarchy.

Order was restored in the Middle Kingdom (c. 2050–1800 B.C.E.), centered in Thebes. Viewing themselves as the "shepherds" of the people, the kings undertook large-scale irrigation and other public works projects aimed at improving conditions for the peas-

ants. The pyramid building that had died out late in the Old Kingdom was not renewed during this time. Shortly after 1800 B.C.E. a people known as the Hyksos crossed the Sinai peninsula, invaded the delta and, with the aid of the horses and chariots they brought with them, ruled Egypt for more than a century.

After the expulsion of the Hyksos, the New Kingdom (c. 1500–1150 B.C.E.) was put in place by a series of aggressive kings who brought peace at home and engaged in foreign conquest. The empire they created extended from Nubia in the south to the Euphrates in the northeast. The priests gained power and wealth because much of the spoils of war went into the temple complexes. The chief god of Thebes, Amun, was combined with Re to form Amun-Re, the supreme god of the state. The New Kingdom was the golden age of Egyptian painting and architecture, especially in temples and tombs, and the Egyptians became famous for their religiosity.

After the reign of Ramses II (d. c. 1090 B.C.E.) Egypt went into a long period of decline. Its empire was gradually lost, and a succession of invaders came in: the Assyrians in 673 B.C.E., the Persians in 525, and the Greeks in 332, followed by the Romans in the first century B.C.E. Egypt remained a part of the Roman Empire and following that the Byzantine Empire until its conquest by the Muslims in the seventh century C.E.

Texts

Like most ancient peoples the Egyptians never composed a systematic account of their religious beliefs, and since they were syncretists (those who combine practices or principles that are contrary to each other), such an account would have been well-nigh impossible in any case. The texts fall into three categories.

1. The *Pyramid Texts* consist of the inscriptions on the walls of the pyramids and are concerned with the ruler's life in the hereafter and with funerary (burial) rites.

2. The *Coffin Texts* are inscriptions on the inner and outer lids of coffins of persons who died during the Middle Kingdom period. These texts contain religious myths, temple rites, and items related to the cult of the dead.

3. The *Book of the Dead*, probably the most famous of the Egyptian religious texts, consists of prayers on papyrus rolls dating from the New Kingdom and the later decline. Not really a single book, the papyrus rolls vary in length from many prayers to just a prayer or two, but together they constitute an important understanding of the Egyptian concepts of earthly life and the afterlife.

Cosmologies

The creation myths of the Egyptians emerged from their polytheism. Though the stories about the gods and goddesses differ in detail, several common points stand out. The goddess of the sky was Nut; her body stretched out to form the heavens, beneath which lay the sun, moon, and stars. Shu was the god of winds or air, the support of Nut. The circular ocean was Nun, and Geb the earth. A part of

Geb was red, to represent the hostile desert, and a part was black, the Nile valley and delta. To these gods were added several others, making most often a list of eight or nine (an *annead*) of the "high gods." The various creation myths retained the basic relationship between sky and earth, the role of the pharaohs, and the funerary rites. Added to these was the idea of a primal hillock, probably a reminder of the hillocks of good soil that remained when the Nile receded each year after its flood.

Scholars distinguish four creation myths, each connected with a different city.[3] The priests at Heliopolis, as is true of many other accounts of origins, assumed that a watery chaos existed before time began. Atum, the high god, emerged from the waters of Nun in the form of a hillock at the moment of creation. Bringing light to the dark world, Atum appeared each day at dawn and each month in the new moon. He was also present in the rebirth of a soul after death and in the rites accompanying the installation of a new pharaoh.

Atop the hillock, Atum created the universe. Bisexual, he produced both the male principle, Shu, and the female principle, Tefnut. Somehow separated from the two principles, Atum was later reunited with them, and from his tears of joy human beings were formed. Shu was made into the air god and became the principle of life. Tefnut, though not distinctive at first, became in the Coffin Texts the goddess Ma'at (justice or order).

Shu and Tefnut produced Geb and Nut, who in turn produced Osiris and

Isis. The latter's son Horus was the symbol of the pharaohs.

The Hermopolis priests saw eight deities, four couples, at the beginning. The watery chaos, Nun, was stirred by Amon, the wind god, and the city of Hermopolis appeared as the hillock. The universe was formed from an egg laid by a heavenly goose or, alternatively, came from the opening of a lotus flower which revealed a divine son, Re. A third version has the opening lotus produce a scarab beetle, the symbol of the sun god. The scarab is transformed into a weeping boy from whose tears came human beings.

The Memphis account centered on Ptah, the chief god at that city, whose various forms produced the eight major gods. For example, Horus, the god associated with the pharaohs, was the heart of Ptah, and Thoth was the tongue; each was regarded as an agent of Ptah. Ptah established the world order (ma'at) and was identified with Tatenen, the god of the primeval mound (and therefore by implication the creator of the physical universe).

Amun, the successor of Re, was the chief deity at Thebes, capital of Egypt during the New Kingdom. Accompanied by his wife, Mut, the vulture goddess, and his son Khonsu, the warrior god, Amun assumed control over the other gods and was attached to the pharaohs like Re had been, blending all together as Amun-Re.

These accounts supported the Egyptian political and social order, particularly the crucial role played by the pharaohs. The accounts also relate the universe to the local Egyptian way of life, thereby sanctioning both the people and their place in the cosmos.

Osiris and Isis

The Osiris myth first appeared in the Pyramid Texts, but was told in its entirety only by Plutarch, a Greek writer of the second century C.E. Osiris appeared as both a god of fertility and the personification of the dead king. The Egyptians believed that when the king died he became Osiris and the new king was Horus, the falcon god.

Osiris and Seth, the sons of Geb and Nut, were married to their sisters, Isis and Nephthys, respectively. Osiris's rule over Egypt was a golden age, but his brother Seth, out of envy, persuaded him into a coffinlike box and either killed him outright or drowned him by throwing the box into the Nile. The coffin floated out into the Mediterranean and finally ended up near the Syrian port of Byblos. Isis recovered the body and brought it back to Egypt, but Seth again appeared and cut the body into many parts, which he scattered over various parts of the country. With the help of Nephthys, Isis found the parts and together they constructed the body into the first mummy. Osiris did not come back to life, but Isis was able to conceive a son by him, Horus, who led in a war against his uncle Seth. Eventually victorious, Horus reigned as the new king over Egypt, and Osiris became the god of the underworld. Osiris was honored as the giver of immortality and fertility, and Isis as a model of dignity and fidelity.

Devotion to Osiris increased over time, and during the long period after the New Kingdom he came to supersede the sun god as the chief of the Egyptian deities. Some felt that devotion to Osiris would guarantee to them a good afterlife, now conceived as an underworld parallel to the Nile valley, entered through the use of passwords. Once in the underworld, each person's heart was judged on the balance scales by Anubis, the god of death. If the heart on the one balance did not outweigh the feather on the other, the person was pronounced "justified." Guilty spirits were torn to pieces by a fierce monster. The justified dead were led into the kingdom of the afterlife and united with family and friends in a pleasant existence, though inferior to life in the world.

Isis played a double role. She was chiefly seen as an enchantress, whose power was greater than that of other deities. She was invoked in all forms of illness because her power was said to be greater even than that of Anubis. She was also seen as a mother goddess, because of her association with Horus. Isis was represented in statuary as a woman with the sign of the throne on her head, sitting on a throne, alone or with the child Horus, or kneeling before a coffin. The most popular goddess among Egyptians, she was received as such by the Greeks and was acclaimed throughout the Mediterranean world for centuries.

The Book of the Dead

The myth of Osiris and Isis demonstrates not only the Egyptian understanding of the role of the king, it also shows the popular Egyptian concern about death and the afterlife. Graves

of family members were regularly visited with offerings of food and

First century C.E. statuette of Isis, who wears the double crown of Upper and Lower Egypt and holds two of her attributes—a serpent and a libation jug. Minneapolis Institute of Art

drink, and funerary rites were performed to aid the deceased in attaining immortality.

The Book of the Dead is a compilation of such rites, made up of spells and magic formulas. Reedited perhaps in the sixteenth century B.C.E., the collection includes material from both the Pyramid Texts and the Coffin Texts.

Later materials were also added. Scribes made copies of the texts on papyrus rolls, often with illustrations, then sold them for burial use. Copies of some of the texts have been found in many Egyptian tombs, but none has all the approximately two hundred known chapters. The Book of the Dead also signifies an extending to all the privilege of an afterlife, which in the age of the pyramids was reserved exclusively for the pharaoh.

The soul consisted of three elements. The *ka* was a kind of double of the person which, at death, united with the body, remaining in the tomb and needing food offerings to survive. The *ba* was the spiritual aspect of a person. Depicted as a bird, it flew off into heaven at the person's death. Some contended that, since the *ba* returned to the dead person each night, mummification was necessary. Whether believed this way or not, mummification included an elaborate system of religious ceremony in the embalming process. The *akh* was the dead person's spirit, which inhabited the underworld and reflected in a hazy way the person's deeds on earth. Since each of these components needed care, the Book of the Dead filled an important function.

Akhenaton

A pharaoh of Egypt in the midfourteenth century B.C.E. and a religious reformer, Akhenaton has often been linked to monotheism. He assumed the throne as Amenhotep IV, for a while worshiped the old gods, and then in a few years built a temple to a rather obscure god, Aton, the sun disc. In the sixth year of his reign he changed his name to Akhenaton ("glory to the Aton"), indicating his loyalty to Aton as Egypt's sole god. He transferred the capital from Thebes to a site on the Nile where he built a new city. With his wife Nefertiti and their six daughters he devoted himself to exclusive worship of Aton.

His excessive interest in religious matters led to military and administrative failures, and his reforms were doomed. After his death, the priests of Amon-Re quickly recovered their former authority and the changes of Akhenaton were soon gone.

Whether or not Akhenaton's reforms were a move to genuine monotheism is widely disputed. He struck a blow at Egypt's polytheism and syncretism, but the latter had such staying power that even the pharaoh could not alter its hold on the culture. Through thirty centuries Egyptian religion was a strong force among the people.

Greek Religion

It is hard to overestimate the influence of Greek civilization on Western culture. Although our thinking is probably more than a series of "footnotes to Plato," and our scientific advances far outstrip the ancients', and Greek religion has long since lost its strength, we keep coming back to the Greeks again and again. We do so probably because they raised the basic issues of life in ways not often done outside the context of Scripture. The Greeks are endlessly fascinating both for their artistic and literary achievements and for their desire to understand the nature of things. In philosophy and literature they seem acutely modern, and in religion, too, there are matters worthy of study.

Greece in History

Aegean Civilization

In the third millennium B.C.E. a new civilization, called Minoan after a legendary king, appeared on the island of Crete. The ruins of a very rich, advanced civilization at Knossos reveal a seagoing commerce, artistic expression, and the worship of a fertility goddess, the Great Mother, which was similar to the worship of the Babylonian Ishtar.

By 1600 B.C.E. a similar way of life was flourishing along the Greek mainland coast and in the islands of the Aegean Sea. Called Mycenean after the site discovered in modern times on the mainland, these people also were traders. Evidence shows that the Myceneans were warlike, with massive walls around their cities and citadels. They engaged the Minoans for control of trade in the eastern Mediterranean, and around 1400 B.C.E. the Minoan civilization fell (apparently from a natural disaster rather than from military action).

Greek-speaking peoples called Achaeans had already begun to move from central Europe into the Aegean area as early as 2000 B.C.E. After 1200 B.C.E. more warlike Greeks, called Dorians, came into the region and sacked Mycenae around 1150. Tradition says that shortly after this victory Greek forces captured the city of Troy on the northwestern coast of Asia Minor.

For the next four centuries Greek civilization entered a "dark ages," during which time the Greeks forged

The Lion Gate at Mycenae, site of a major city in the development of Greek civiliation. William Travis

their own distinctive culture. By the eighth century B.C.E. that culture included the mainland, many of the islands in the Aegean, and the western coast of Asia Minor. The famous Greek poet Homer may have lived at this time, so it is often referred to as the Homeric Age.

The Greeks called themselves Hellenes, and their domain Hellas, after their mythical founding father, Hellen. Located in an agriculturally poor region and surrounded by the sea, the Greeks became a different kind of people from the river-bound civilizations in Mesopotamia and Egypt. Sea trade was their commercial strength, and Greek colonies dotted the shores from the Black Sea in the east to the Spanish coast in the west.

The Archaic Period (750–500 B.C.E.)

The chief development of the archaic period was the city-state (Gk., *polis*), similar to the temple-states or city-states of Mesopotamia and Egypt before they were merged into larger political units. In Greece, however, the city-state remained the characteristic unit while Greek civilization was at its height, so the city-state was integral to Greece's most creative phase.

Most city states were located near a commanding hill with a fortress on the summit, the *acropolis*. At a lower level was the marketplace, the *agora*, the center of political and social life. Religious activity was carried out at both the acropolis and the agora. The population lived in the city proper or in the surrounding countryside. Most city-states had relatively small populations, numbering only a few thousand; the philosopher Plato envisioned a population of five thousand citizens in his ideal state. By contrast, Athens, in several ways untypical of the city-state, may have numbered three hundred thousand at its peak.

The citizens (adult males) and their families conceived of themselves as belonging to a single kinship group. This concept made for good solidarity among the citizenry, especially in war situations, and meant that the conflict between the state and the individual common in modern times was not present. But it also meant that the city-states fought among themselves over disputed territory and commercial enterprise, and had difficulty uniting to face a common enemy.

The city-state functioned as the people's church. Though most Greeks believed in a pantheon (a group of gods), each city-state had its special deity to whom particular homage was given. Usually the deity was connected with the founding of the state (such as Athena in Athens), giving to the state a divine or semidivine quality and uniting the people further. The priests were not a separate class, but performed their duties as civic officials.

Classical Greece (500–338 B.C.E.)

The Greek city-states emerged as important military powers, and among them Athens sttod out as the most important. The Athenians, Spartans, and their allies engaged the Persians in a long war in the first half of the fifth century B.C.E., with decisive victories at Marathon (490) and Thermopylae (480). This war, concluded in 445, was followed by the Peloponnesian War (431–04) between Athens and Sparta, the two chief claimants for Greek supremacy.

The city-state system, although fragile, created elements of civilization that endured. For even in the midst of the wars, the Greek culture was flowering. Political developments at Athens led to the creation of the quintessential democracy. Sparta meanwhile came to symbolize the state as a military ideal. Architecture reached new attainment when the Athenians rebuilt their acropolis buildings after the Persians had burned them down. Poets, philosophers, and sculptors exercised their talents in ways that affected other civilizations for centuries to come. These developments continued into the fourth century B.C.E.

The Hellenistic Period (338–146 B.C.E.)

The failure of the city-states to unite was dramatized in the rise of Macedon, a power to the north of Greece proper. Philip became king in 359 B.C.E. and within twenty years had defeated

One of the most famous buildings of antiquity, the Parthenon atop the Athenian acropolis was a temple for the worship of Athena. Built in fifth century B.C.E. William Travis

the Greek alliance mounted against him. His treatment of the vanquished was evenhanded and he wished to see the Greeks avenged of their bad treatment by the Persians a century previous. But he was assassinated in 338, before his plans could be realized.

Philip was succeeded by his twenty-year-old son, Alexander, who went on to world conquest. By the time of his death in 323, Alexander had conquered Persia and Egypt, had established himself in Babylon, and had pushed to the frontier of India. His dream of one world in which Greek culture would dominate, and east and west would overcome their hostilities, was not realized. Three states emerged from his empire, and they

survived until the Romans conquered the eastern Mediterranean.

Greek culture did spread throughout the region, however, in a form now called Hellenistic (to distinguish it from the Hellenic culture of earlier Greece). Since the Greek city-states in their weakened condition would be overrun repeatedly in the centuries ahead, the broadcasting of their culture saved their valuable works and ideas for posterity, and allowed for the considerable Greek influence on Western civilization.

Texts

Well developed in the classical era, Greek religion permeated Greek society, but it had no authoritative works of dogma. The works of two poets of the eighth century, Homer and Hesiod, and the works of several lesser writers, plus incidental references in other writings constitute the major sources for our understanding of Greek religion.

Homer

Whether the *Iliad* and the *Odyssey* were written by the blind poet of Ionia (now Turkey's western coast) as tradition dictates is a matter of great dispute. Some now see the works as the creation of wandering bards who told and retold the stories; others assign Homer at least some role in the resulting works. For the sake of convenience, they are still called the Homeric epics.

The *Iliad* is the story of the Greek military expedition against the city of Troy (Gk., Ilion). The war begins when Paris, a son of the king of Troy, abducts Helen, the wife of Menelaus, king of Sparta. Agamemnon of Mycenae is the leader of the Greek forces sent to recapture Helen, and Achilles is the warrior hero. In the midst of the siege these two quarrel over a captive woman, and Achilles retires in anger to his tent. Achilles' mother, Thetis the sea goddess, persuades Zeus, king of the gods, to send losses to the Greeks and thereby convince the Greeks they need Achilles for battle. Zeus does so, and Achilles is approached by the Greek leaders, but he remains in his tent.

The fighting continues without Achilles, who allows his close friend Patroclus to enter battle wearing Achilles' armor. Patroclus is killed by Hector,

the chief Trojan warrior. Thetis brings new armor to Achilles, who reenters the battle, slaughters many Trojans and kills Hector. Funeral games are held in honor of Patroclus, and Achilles is restored to a revered position in the warrior society.

The tragedy is the story of two men, Achilles and Hector, facing each other and the vicissitudes of life; Achilles as the protagonist of the tale is filled with the ambiguity characteristic of Greek and later tragedy. The gods play a role, but a muted one. Achilles seeks "honor from Zeus"; and references to the will of Zeus remind the reader that human beings face a destiny in life beyond their control. The gods frequently intervene, but human motivation plays a large role. The levity assigned by Homer to the immortal gods serves as a counterpoint to the serious and short life of the human mortals.

The *Odyssey* interweaves the ten-year return trip of Odysseus from the Trojan War with events taking place at his palace in his home city of Ithaca. Long delayed in coming back from Troy, suitors have taken up with his wife, Penelope, and threaten Odysseus with the loss of both kingship and family. His son Telemachus plays an important part in the return of Odysseus, who eventually slays the suitors; righteous judgment wins out.

The goddess Athena, the protectoress of Odysseus, is given a free hand by Zeus to do what is necessary to bring Odysseus home. She appears to Telemachus, persuades him to seek out his father and helps him procure a ship to do so. Athena complains that

Odysseus is held against his will by the nymph Calypso, and Hermes is dispatched to get his release. Put on a raft wrecked by Poseidon, Odysseus is rescued by an emissary of the sea goddess. Athena influences Penelope through a dream, and is influential in bringing Odysseus safely home.

In each of these epics the presence and influence of the gods is a foregone conclusion. These are the gods of Mount Olympus, and their power and relationships are drawn out through the Homeric works. What strikes one immediately about the Olympians is their human quality; indeed, they have human forms, and they engage in very human conduct. In order to placate the gods a variety of rites were used: libations of wine; slaughter of cattle, goats, and sheep; sacrificial burning of animal parts; and festivals.

Chief of the Olympians was Zeus (Jupiter),* father of the gods and ruler of the universe. Connected with the sky, Zeus brought lightning bolts and storms, as well as rain. He fathered many semidivine creatures through his mating with mortal women, and was the progenitor of animal species as well. His symbol was the eagle, and he received the sacrifice of bulls.

Hera (Juno), Zeus's jealous wife, was the goddess of women, marriage, and childbirth. Apollo, son of Zeus and a mortal woman, was associated with the sun and was the prototype of youthful male beauty. Hermes (Mercury) was the messenger of his father Zeus and the god of the highways and the marketplace. By extension he was also the god of travelers and highwaymen.

Aphrodite (Rome: Venus), the goddess of sexual love and beauty, important as a promoter of fertility, sometimes worshipped as a goddess of the sea and of war. Minneapolis Institute of Art

The god of the sea was Poseidon (Neptune), whose emblem was the trident. Artemis (Diana), Apollo's twin sister, was the goddess of the moon and of hunting. Respected for her virginity, she punished any of her attendant nymphs who were unchaste. Athena (Minerva), goddess of wisdom, came from Zeus's brain fully grown. Worshiped primarily at the Athenian acropolis, she held sacred the owl, snake, and olive tree.

Other members of the Olympian family were Ares (Mars), the god of war;

*Latin names, if different, are shown in parentheses.

Aphrodite (Venus), goddess of love and beauty; Hephaestus (Vulcan), god of fire and husband of Aphrodite; Demeter (Ceres), god of vegetation and grain; and Hestia (Vesta), goddess of the hearth.

Beyond the humanized gods was the concept of fate or destiny (*moira*). *Moira* was not quite a full-blown determinism, but even the gods respected the destiny given to a person. And while human beings had some choice, avoiding disasters and death was out of their hands.

Hesiod

Much more is known about Hesiod than Homer, and he emerges as a clear historical figure compared to the shadowy Homer. The son of a farmer, Hesiod lived in the region in mainland Greece called Boeotia, probably in the late eighth century B.C.E. In addition to his epic poem called *Theogeny* (*Birth of the Gods*), he also authored *Works and Days*, a poem describing the life and work of a Greek farmer.

The *Theogeny* is Hesiod's attempt to give order to the mass of conflicting myths that had developed by his era, and to provide an understanding of the beginning of the universe. The world, he wrote, had been created by four primary spirits: Chaos (Space), Gaea (Earth), Tartarus (Abyss), and Eros (Love). Gaea creates Uranus (Heaven), then she takes him as her husband and gives birth to Titans, monsters, and hundred-headed giants. At Gaea's urging the powerful Titans, under the leadership of Cronos, revolt against Heaven, mutilating him and severing him from Earth. Cronos and Rhea, his wife and sister,

become rulers of the universe. Knowing he is going to be supplanted by one of his children (just as he had supplanted his father), Cronos swallows each of them as they are born. But Rhea saves Zeus from such a fate and compels Cronos to disgorge all the children.

The Titan Prometheus deceives Zeus and steals fire from Heaven. Zeus then sends Pandora, the primal woman, to plague men, and Prometheus is bound. Then Zeus and the children of Cronos defeat the Titans in a great battle, the Titans are thrown into Tartarus, and the gods make Zeus their king over the sky. His brothers Poseidon and Hades are made rulers over the sea and the realm of the dead. After this, Zeus's marriages and progeny are enumerated, as are those of the other Olympians. Finally, the sons born of goddesses in union with mortals are named.

What Hesiod attempted was to make some order out of the complexity of Greek polytheism, and he did that to some extent. In his other major work, *Works and Days*, he pictured the succession of ages: from a golden time when Cronos ruled; to the silver and bronze ages put in place by the Olympian gods and during which the human beings of that time came to an end because of rebellion and wars; and finally the present iron age in which Zeus created a world of burdens and cares. Still, the gods watched over humanity, and at the end Hesiod argued for a moral order:

For Zeus has appointed this law unto men: that fishes and beasts and fowls of the air should devour one another, since there is no justice

Roman amphitheater at Bet She'arim, Israel, built in the second century C.E. *Plays in antiquity were often performed under religious auspices.* Israel Tourism Bureau

among them; but to man he gave justice, which is far better. For if a man will speak just sentences, Zeus will give him prosperity.[4]

Religious Observances

Religious observance began in the household with its host of everyday gods and spirits: gods of the hearth, the field, and fertility; spirits like the daimons and furies who might punish individuals for their lapses; the "heroes" or noble dead who were half-human and half-divine and still powerful; the chthonic deities of the earth who were important in death and fertility; and the powers that brought on old age or destructive passions like jealousy and pride.

In addition to household religion, public festivals were held in all the city-states, though most is known about the ones held in Athens. The year began in summer with a festival to Apollo in which a hundred head of cattle were sacrificed. In late summer and early fall three more festivals celebrated his power.

The Panathenaea in honor of Athena was held annually in midsummer, and every fourth year with special pageantry. A statue of the goddess was carried from her temple on the acropolis, bathed in a special rite, given a newly woven mantle by the women of the city, and returned by torchlight to the temple. Feasting, sacrifices, and athletic games accompanied the event, which renewed the city's alliance with its patron.

Dionysus, the god of wine, was the recipient of many festivals. The Anthesteria festival, held at the god's sanctuary in the marshes, combined both the joy of the new wine and the seriousness of death. The spring festival in Athens ran for six days, during which plays were performed at the theater named in his honor. An image of the god presided at the theater, thus linking religion and drama.

Other festivals were held in honor of Zeus, Demeter, and Artemis. All told, perhaps thirty festivals were held each year at Athens, indicating the strong tie between civic life and religion.

Mystery Religions

At the opposite end from the public religion openly celebrated at the civic festivals were the secretive and personal mystery religions. By the fifth century B.C.E. philosophical criticism had cast doubts on the virtues and existences of gods and goddesses like Zeus. The Greek *polis* linked to them ceased to be the chief political basis after the late fourth century. As people looked for new religious experiences the mystery religions flourished.

The origin of many ancient mystery religions is unknown, though some seem to have developed from agrarian festivals celebrating the fertility of nature. The Asian Adonis who died and was reborn, the Anatolian Attis, and the Egyptian Osiris were all gods who died and were linked to the life cycle of nature—the rebirth of fertility in nature—and the human cycle of life and death. The concept of a divine mother nourishing and protecting earth was tied to worship in early agricultural festivals and is seen in figures such as Demeter, the grain mother, and her daughter Persephone of the Eleusinian mystery religion. Followers of the Magna Mater (great mother; Cybele) sometimes castrated themselves as the great mother's dying lover, Attis, was said to have done.

Led by a *hierophant*, the one who revealed the secrets of the god, each candidate went through a purification rite, received instruction in the special knowledge of the cult, observed a pageant or play or objects telling a story about the god, and was given a task to perform. Initiates received a symbol of their membership in the religious group. Singing and dancing in public processions preceded the private ceremonies with much colorful display.

The Eleusinian mysteries worshiped Demeter, the goddess of grain. Demeter once loved Zeus and by him had a daughter, Persephone (Prosperine), the spirit of spring. While gathering flowers in a meadow Persephone was carried off to the underworld by Hades. Overwhelmed with grief, Demeter refused to give life to the earth, and the land became flowerless and cold.

Disguised as an old woman, Demeter reached Eleusis, where the ruler of the city made her a servant in his home. Later, Demeter revealed her true identity and ordered the ruler to build a temple to her. Once done, Demeter lived in the temple at Eleusis, but still withheld her favors from the land. To break the deadlock Zeus sent Hermes to Hades to order the restoration of Persephone to her mother. Hades complied but cunningly made her eat a pomegranate seed, which put her in his debt, for which she had to spend four months each year in the underworld. Each year Persephone returned to her mother on earth, and nature was reborn. The myth provided an explanation for winter death and spring rebirth and gave comfort to humans as they faced sorrow and death.

The Eleusinian mysteries were decorous compared to those that surrounded the cult of Dionysus. Born of Zeus and a woman from Thebes named Semele, Dionysus' mother was tricked by Hera into making a request of Zeus that led to her death just before the baby was born. Zeus rescued the infant Dionysus and kept him from the jealous Hera.

When fully grown, Dionysus wandered from place to place teaching people how to grow grapes and encouraging them to worship him in secret rites. The king at Thebes, Dionysus' home city, refused to allow the worship, and in anger Zeus blinded the king. Later, Dionysus descended to the underworld, from where he took his mother to Olympus, and the gods agreed to let her live because, even though she was a mortal, her son was divine.

The cult of Dionysus demonstrated both the joy and the danger associated with drinking wine. Identified with vitality, it was easy for the rites to become excessive. The orgiastic dances and wild ecstasies of the initiation ceremonies pushed the devotees to excess. At times, they tore apart and ate the flesh of a kid or bull,

thinking that in so doing they could attain union with the god and rise above their mortality.

A third important mystery religion centered on the tale of Orpheus and Eurydice. The child of a Thracian prince and Calliope, the muse of music (the nine muses were the patrons of the arts), Orpheus could play the lyre so beautifully that both trees and animals followed him in delight. He married Eurydice, a beautiful maiden, but she was bitten by a snake and died. Like Inanna of the Sumerian myth, Orpheus went to the underworld to get Eurydice released. Affected by the music of Orpheus, Hades allowed Eurydice to return to earth on the one condition that Orpheus precede her and not look back until they were outside Hades' domain. Overcome by curiosity, Orpheus did look back, only to see Eurydice fade from his sight. Overcome with grief, he left the company of human beings and roamed through the forests of Thrace.

Here, a variation of the Dionysus myth enters. Dionysus Zagreus, the son of Zeus and Persephone (not the Dionysus of Zeus and Semele), was so favored by Zeus that the Titans seized the boy, killed him, and ate the pieces of his body. Incensed, Zeus killed the Titans with his thunderbolts. In the meantime, Athena had saved the heart of Dionysus Zagreus, gave it to Zeus, and he ate it. Dionysus Zagreus was later born again, to symbolize rebirth and immortality, and half-divine human beings were born from the ashes of the Titans, symbolizing the mixed quality of humanity.

Orpheus now lined himself up with

the Dionysus cult, which he spread throughout Greece. Encountering a group of devotees of the cult one day, Orpheus was torn to pieces by them, himself a victim of the Dionysian mysteries.

Followers of the Orphic cult did not engage in the orgiastic rites associated with Dionysus. They lived a mildly ascetic life in the hope that they could free themselves from the Titanic influences in humanity and be admitted to the Elysian Fields, the part of the underworld reserved for the blessed. The way to self-realization was through knowledge, not rapture.

The mysteries were ways of coping with the major issues in life—evil, mortality, injustice, death, and hope—and holding the possibility for understanding, but only to the initiated, who "claimed to have tasted death and life and to have been touched by the divine. United with one another of the deities of the mystery religions . . . they beheld the light, and their lives were renewed."[5] The idea that only some have knowledge (GK., gnosis) is present in many religious systems, the mystery religions being a primary example of the concept.

In addition to the claims of initiates to be changed people, and the attractiveness of the public celebrations preceding the secret meetings, Plato points out in Phaedo 696 that there were also social attractions for the alienated, bored, or lonely, and for some an egalitarian appeal where slave, free, rich, and poor mingled.

Greek Philosophy and the Gods

Not all the Greeks explained the nature of the universe through the gods.[6] Beginning in the sixth century B.C.E. a whole series of Greek thinkers offered other explanations. The earliest philosophers sought to discover the one (or few) elements that gave permanence and stability to the universe. The idea was to find something other than the coming into being and passing out of existence that seemed to be the lot of human beings and the way of the natural order. Earth, air, fire, and water, either singly or in combination, were offered by different thinkers as the basic elements. One philosopher, Heraclitus, believed that everything was in flux; the essence of the universe was change. With but few exceptions, these thinkers believed in the gods, but the myths about the gods were inadequate to explain the nature of things.

Greek philosophy reached its greatest achievement in three Athenians who lived in successive generations. Socrates (c. 470–399 B.C.E.) did not deny the existence of the gods, but the Athenian elders accused him of atheism and of undermining the youth of the city with his teachings, and forced him to drink hemlock poison as his death. He tried to teach critical thinking, and in so doing at times seemed to mock the gods. He also began at the human level; "know thyself" (a phrase from the temple to Apollo at Delphi) was his motto. If we can just use clear thinking to find out what is the "good"—the chief virtues—then we will do the good. Not against the gods, Socrates wished to discover truth through the power of reasoning. He used a dialogue method of teaching to get his points across.

Plato (427–347 B.C.E.) was the most famous of Socrates' pupils. The author of the Socratic dialogues and other works, Plato has left a complete philosophical system. It begins with the world of ideas or forms, which constitute reality. The world in which we live is but a shadow of the real world of ideas. The contact between the two worlds is the *nous,* the thinking faculty in human beings. The human soul has observed the realities (all souls were once in the world of forms), but has also gotten tied to the human body (a distinctly lesser category than soul), thus human beings are caught in the duality of soul and body. The soul longs for the real world; the body plunges the person toward the shadow world. The way out is to turn from the illusions created by the bodily senses and live according to the correct understanding of the good.

In his famous book, *The Republic,* Plato gives an example of this way of thinking as he addresses one component of the good, the issue of justice. *The Republic* creates a state and society built on the real-world idea of justice. Presumably, similar explanations could be made for all the major elements in life: the good, the true, and the beautiful. The myths about the gods are present in Plato's writing, but he uses them as symbols to communicate philosophical concepts, not as pictures of reality in themselves.

Plato's pupil Aristotle (384–322) established his own system of thought. He rejected Plato's dualism of soul and body, and the world of forms, working instead to explain nature as it was observed on earth. For Aristotle, ideas existed in their embodiment; there was no abstract idea of justice, there were operating systems of justice. His concept of God was as the Unmoved Mover or the Prime Mover, the one beyond which we cannot go as we look at the sequence of cause and effect. God is not so much person as he is the logical consequence of thinking about the nature of things.

All three of these philosophers had enormous impact on the monotheistic religions. Judaism, Islam, and Christianity all had to come to grips with the thought of these influential Greek thinkers.

Roman Religion

The Roman State

According to legend, Rome was founded by Romulus and Remus, twin boys born to Mars, the god of war, and Rhea Silvia, a princess from the Trojan city of Alba Longa. Indirectly, then, Rome could be traced to the city of Troy that Homer described in the *Iliad* and the *Odyssey.* Indeed, the Roman poet Virgil (70–19 B.C.E.) made that specific connection in his *Aeneid,* which he ended with the marriage of Aeneas the Trojan hero to Lavinia, an Italic princess. The legend says that Romulus and Remus were abandoned in infancy and suckled by a she-wolf. After coming of age they decided to found a city, but could not agree on which of the two would give his name to the city. Romulus killed Remus and settled the issue, establishing the city of Rome in 753 B.C.E.

Later in heaven, as the god Quirinus, he continued his watch over the city and its people.

Indo-Europeans moved into the Italian peninsula sometime around 2000 B.C.E., and over the next several centuries made their way south, some of them settling in the plain and hills around the Tiber River. They called their territory Latium and they were called Latins. By the ninth century another people, the Etruscans, had come by sea to the region and for a long time were the foes of the Latins. By the eighth century the Greeks had established colonies along the Adriatic coast, from which they exerted some cultural influence.

The city of Rome may have been founded as early as 850 B.C.E.; it became a market center around 575. By 500 the Romans had overthrown the last of their kings and established a republic form of government, with power in the hands of the noble class. By 270 B.C.E. the Romans controlled all of the Italian peninsula south of the Po River. This was followed by the Punic Wars with Carthage, the result of which put Rome in power in the western Mediterranean. From there she moved east, gradually extending her power through the whole Mediterranean basin.

By the first century B.C.E. the Roman Republic had been eclipsed by its far-flung domain, and the result after a long period of internal strife was the Roman Empire, begun under Octavian (Caesar Augustus) in 27 B.C.E. His rule initiated what has been called the *pax Romana*, two centuries of relative peace in the Mediterranean world that ended with the death of Marcus Aurelius in C.E. 180. The third century C.E. was an era of turmoil for Rome brought on by internal factions and external pressures, with Diocletian (ruled 284–305) restoring order through his administrative division of the empire. The fourth century saw the official introduction of Christianity into Roman life and the permanent division of the empire. Rome "fell" late in the fifth century, the capital already well reestablished in the east at Constantinople and the successor empire, Byzantium, in place.

The Forum was both the administrative and religious center of ancient Rome, temples and other public buildings intermingled in imperial times. William Travis

Texts

Roman religion is often seen through the later influence of Greek religion and sometimes as a kind of outpost of Greek polytheism. But Roman religion had forms of its own quite different from the Greeks, and these need to be noted. The Romans created a system of divine law (*jus divinum*), a body of rules by which the gods could be placated and the unknown forces in life controlled. To follow the rules was to live successfully. Early in Roman history, the rules emphasized the performance of the rites, their ceremonial quality, but as the Roman state grew the public rites became a part of patriotic tradition. Later, moral elements played a larger role in the rites, especially for individuals.

The difficulty in reconstructing original Roman religion is the sparsity of texts available. Since Roman religion lacked the human forms and the myths of other peoples, no cosmology similar to Hesiod's theogony exists. The few literary sources come from the antiquarians and poets of the first century B.C.E. and first century C.E., hundreds of years after Rome's founding. And these sources are already under some influence from the Greeks. Other sources are archaeological in nature: inscriptions, calendars, coins, buildings, and works of art. For later Roman religion the number of sources, both literary and archaeological, is more numerous.

The Development of Roman Religion

All sorts of human activities (from bearing a child to opening a door) and natural phenomena (like the seasons of the years) were invested by the Romans with some sense of divinity. Divinity was involved not only in such repeated actions but also in one-time occasions such as being saved from an accident. This led to multiple deities, what some call "religious atomism," the assignment of specific dieties to specific acts. The veneration of acts was carried over to objects, fields and hearth for example, which were seen as more than natural. Even if the name of the divinity was not known,

it was best to presume a divinity in all these actions and objects.

The power behind the actions and objects was described as horror, or sacred thrill, and since the power was both mysterious and alarming, it needed both to be propitiated and made into an ally. The system of sacrifice aimed to do both. Central in the sacrifice, usually of an animal, was the belief that the power (and the divinity behind it) needed nourishment in order to be revitalized and therefore able to carry out the request of the one performing the sacrifice. Accompanying the sacrifice was prayer, the words used to flatter or cajole the divinities into acting (or not acting destructively). Some elements of magic crept into the sacrifice system also, though the state at times forbade such practices.

The Romans were influenced by the Etruscans in two important ways. One was the use of statuary, introduced perhaps as early as the sixth century B.C.E. (Images were apparently not used earlier by the Romans.) This in turn allowed for the introduction of the Greek myths, for the human forms of the statues led to thinking of the gods as humanized and the stories of the humanlike gods naturally followed. The second influence was the use of a religious calendar. The calendar fixed the annual feast days (eventually numbering over fifty) and gradually moved many of the rituals connected with home and farm into the public domain. State religion gave a sense of stability to life and ensured that relations with the gods were being carried out correctly.

The formal nature of public religion meant that not all religious aspirations were met, and so other religious forms came to Rome. Mystery religions made their appearance around 200 B.C.E. with the cult of the Great Mother (Cybele), imported from Asia Minor, and the cult of Dionysus (Bacchus) from Greece. Though not officially welcomed at first, these and other cults later became a permanent part of Roman life. Astrology also became very popular in the two centuries prior to the common era. Oddly enough, Stoic philosophy, introduced into Rome in the second century B.C.E., aided the growth of these foreign religious expressions. The Stoic concept of determinism aided belief in fate, a common ingregient in religion, and its notion that the human soul was part of the whole universal *logos* tied individuals to the gods and to belief in an afterlife.

The Roman Pantheon

The high gods in the Roman state cult were presided over by Jupiter, the sky god. Temples to Jupiter were common in all the cities where Rome prevailed. A triad of gods—Jupiter and his wife, Juno, and daughter Minerva—was also common, some temples having three chambers to house them. Juno's chief function was to supervise women, especially their sexual life, and Minerva was the goddess of craftsmen. Mars, the god of war, and Quirinus, the god of the city of Rome, also held special places in the system. These last two, along with Jupiter, were the only ones who had a special priest (*flamen*) attached to them. Ceremony connected to the other public gods was run by the various priestly orders.

Janus and Vesta were important state deities. Originally in the home as the powers of the door and the hearth, their move into the state cult is another indication of the general switch from private to public religion. The gates at the temple to Janus were open when the state was at war, and closed during times of peace, thus imbuing Janus with the role of doorkeeper for the whole society. Vesta's temple contained an eternal flame, indicating her protection of Rome; she was attended by six virgins, young women drawn from patrician families.

A series of deities showed how powers or spirits around the home might get transformed into gods of state. The *manes*, *penates*, and *indigentes* were various categories of the spirits of the dead, who helped control the destiny of families and of Rome. The *lares*, originally connected with the boundaries of adjoining properties, became the gods of the crossroads, where shrines might be erected to them. The *penates* were national protectors who had begun as the powers that ensured sufficient food to eat. Two of the *penates*, Castor and Pollux, had helped Rome in one of its ancient battles, and annually a festival was held in their honor.

Other deities personified abstractions. Thus, gods like those of health, peace, fortune, and plenty had their temples. Our conception of justice, pictured as a blindfolded woman holding a balance-scale, is a contemporary expression of this ancient practice.

Ritual

The Lares were domestic deities guarding family prosperity and well-being who were worshipped by Romans at the door and hearth. Minneapolis Institute of Arts

Four boards of priests had charge of the state religion. The pontifices, headed by the *pontifex maximus* (a term later used by the Roman Catholic Church), had general oversight of public religious practice. The *augurs* were those charged with discovering if a contemplated state action was indeed suggested by the gods—often done by observing the flight of birds. The other two boards had charge of foreign rites—Rome earlier had forbade the presence of non-Roman deities, but later allowed their pres-

ence—and supervision of religious festivals.

The Latin word *templum* apparently referred at first to that portion of the sky from which a priest collected and interpreted omens. Later it meant a piece of ground, probably projected from the sky portion, set aside to the god(s). In the sixth century B.C.E., buildings—temples in our usual sense—were erected for the shrine to the deity, and temple building became a common activity of Roman civilization.

Like other peoples, the Romans engaged in animal sacrifice, the pig the most common animal, though sheep and oxen were also used. The heart, liver, and kidneys were considered the best parts for sacrifice. Prayer or a vow invariably accompanied sacrifice. Except for those who belonged to the mystery religions, most Romans had only a vague sense of the afterlife, so the use of sacrifices was basically for temporal matters.

Once the Roman Empire was established, a cult around the emperors developed. Typically this entailed a deification of the emperor after his death, and involved the emperor's genius (originally defined as the procreative power of a person, it later came to mean something akin to one's spirit). The emperors were in a category below the high gods and worthy of veneration and gratitude, but apparently were not the object of prayer. By the third century C.E. the ruling emperors were treated more and more as divine, but the cult of divinity apparently was stronger in the eastern sections of the Roman domain.

In all the civilizational centers discussed in this chapter belief and unbelief existed side by side. Some, like the Roman playwright Plautus and the Greek writer Aristophanes, ridiculed the gods. No doubt others lived a basically material existence. But the pervasiveness of religion in these cultures cannot be denied, whatever the level of belief and doubt.

Outside the Mediterranean basin other god systems held sway. The Celtic in Ireland, Gaul, and other parts of western Europe; Germans and Scandinavians in northern Europe had their own pantheons. Little is known of Celtic religion, except what can be reconstructed out of Irish legend and some comments by Romans like Julius Caesar and Tacitus. Teutonic and Viking gods appear in a number of sagas and poems whose compilation or creation dates from the Middle Ages. Concerned mostly with fertility, death, and the end of the world, these writings are noteworthy for their influence on later literature.

What is one to make of the myths of these polytheisms? Some of the myths seem so crude and material and immoral that it is difficult for us to classify them as "religious." Yet, from the myths about the dying and rising god who gives new life to humans, C. S. Lewis draws the principle that these are "real though unfocused gleam[s] of divine truth falling on human imagination." Lewis says the myths are more than stories, they are the "dim dreams of premonitions" that conscience-endowed humanity created in its attempt to discover the full revelation of God that only came in Christ.[7]

Discussion

1. Each of the religions in this chapter seemed to have "high gods." What was their function? What do you think prompted this division among the gods?
2. How do you relate to Christianity some of the elements that appear in the polytheisms, like eating the god's flesh or the dying and rising of a god?
3. Draw parallels, where applicable, among the god systems of Mesopotamia, Egypt, Greece, and Rome.

Notes

[1]Thorkild Jacobsen, *The Treasure of Darkness: A History of Mesopotamian Religion* (New Haven: Yale Univ. Press, 1976), 178.

[2]Morris Jastrow, *Aspects of Religious Belief and Practice in Babylonia and Assyria* (New York: Putnam, 1911), 374.

[3]Detailed in Nielsen, Niels C. Jr., et al., *Religions of the World* (New York: St. Martin's Press, 1983), 37–38.

[4]F. M. Cornford, *Greek Religious Thought from Homer to the Age of Alexander* (Boston: Beacon, 1950), 18.

[5]Marvin W. Meyer, *The Ancient Mysteries, A Sourcebook: Sacred Texts of the Mystery Religions of the Ancient Mediterranean World* (San Francisco: Harper & Row, 1987), 13.

6 While the definition used in the text could easily include "philosophy" in religion, this section follows the common usage that refers to Socrates, Plato, Aristotle and others as philosophers, i.e., persons who engage in "the rational, methodical and systematic consideration of those topics that are of greatest concern to man." [Quotation is from *New EB: Macropedia*, (1977) vol. 14, 248.]

7The Lewis quotes are found in William Luther White, *The Image of Man in C. S. Lewis* (Nashville: Abingdon, 1969), 37–38.

4 Religions of Select Contemporary Societies

Chil tribals on the trail near Dalat, Vietnam. Montagnards maintain good relations with the spirit world by periodic animal sacrifices. J. Lewis

The Search for Useful Categories

Robert Moffat, father-in-law of David Livingstone, stated after twenty-five years in southern Africa that the aboriginal peoples to whom he ministered had no "religion" at all. By that he certainly meant "true" religion, such as the monotheistic ones of the Jewish and Christian traditions. When Moffat discovered that the African worldview was dominated by spirits and ances-

tors and that the creator-deity occupied a position of lesser importance in daily affairs, he could only conclude that they were not monotheists and therefore had no religion at all. But religion in the life of a people, if we accept the definition of religion used in this text as that which is of supreme importance to individuals and groups, cannot be denied to exist simply because it does not tally with another's point of view.

The religious beliefs and practices of any two tribal societies seldom are similar, even though some may share general features such as a concept of *mana*, spirit beings, ancestor worship, and the existence of sacred places and taboos. Even the combination of these general characteristics is usually sufficiently diverse to prevent generalizations, easy classifications, or neat groupings.

In fact, no uniform language has been accepted by scholars in reference to the religions of select peoples like those we will examine in the following chapters: the Zulus, the Quechuas, and the Santals. Most anthropologists would agree that these are tribal peoples, and on that basis one might be tempted to use the category "tribal religions" or the "religion of traditional peoples." Other categories include "primal religion," "animism," or "primitive religion."[1]

Many of Vietnam's tribals were driven from their mountain homes by war in the 1960's. Social displacement has led to conversion to Christianity for some and modification of traditional ways for others. J. Lewis

"Primal religion" has the disadvantage of suggesting the existence of an archaic system brought into modern times in some slightly altered or evolved form. The evolutionary implications of this term do not seem to promote historical understanding and hence should be rejected. Also used in some studies is the word *animism*, but it is questionable whether animism can be satisfactorily defined in such a way as to include the beliefs and practices of all tribal people. Nida and Smalley define animism as "belief in spirits including the spirits of dead people as well as those that have no human origin." But in their study of specific societies they themselves find this too narrow and are forced to include other religious elements "not precisely animistic."[2]

"Primitive religion" as a term seems pejorative and condescending. It is also open to the implication that such a religion is crude, undeveloped, and uncivilized. This would be inconsistent with our commitment to the historical approach to describe ultimate concerns of individuals and communities and not pass them under the review of some cultural bias. Moreover, it implies the existence of its opposite—that there may be some religion that is nonprimitive, more developed, or possibly even sophisticated. But by what elitist standard would we judge one religion primitive and another developed? Like "primal religions," "primitive religions" as a category is inadequate since it too suggests a view of religion as having some characteristics which can be traced from earlier through later developmental stages. Should the religion of a tribal society be called primitive religion? Probably not. A religion may be true or false in a theological or normative sense, but it cannot be judged as primitive or sophisticated if our approach is to be basically a descriptive one.

One is tempted to use the term "religions of primitives." That there are genuinely primitive people yet in today's world is undeniable, though their numbers are shrinking rapidly due to acculturation and encroachment by neighboring peoples.[3] However, the religion of a primitive people can be found among their nonprimitive tribal cousins who are acculturating in urban settings. They are no longer "primitives," yet they continue to follow the ways of their ancestors. Naturally there are other tribals who have significantly departed from traditional beliefs, not a few of whom may have become thoroughly secularized or changed religion. In sum, while "religions of primitives" may serve to describe the religion of a truly primitive people, nonprimitives may hold the same traditional beliefs. The category seems inadequate for that reason.

"Religions of selected societies" seems the best term in view of the historian's commitment to description. The religions of the Zulus, Quechuas, and Santals are particular to their societies and have little to say about other tribal societies. There is a great deal of religious diversity not only between societies but also within societies over a period of time. This makes it extremely difficult to fashion categories that are truly descriptive and constitute a "fit" in describing religion. The Shoshoni Indians of the American plains performed a sun dance whose ritual forms remained relatively constant while the purpose and function changed considerably over the years.[4]

But when speaking of the religion of these societies in terms of our definition as that which is of supreme concern, it is possible to maintain that there is a surprising common thread running through them. The need to provide daily the essentials for life causes tribals often to make subsistence their main concern. It has been said of African religious traditions that they are "oriented toward and con-cerned with the continued vitality of living human beings and their environment."[5] There are or may be other concerns unique to each society at that moment and in that setting. But in many settings the ultimate concern as a society is a rather practical one. Hence, their dealings with one another, with outsiders, and with the spiritual world often have to do with survival through success in hunting, farming, fishing, mastery of human and natural enemies, and coping with sickness and death. In their dealings with the spirit world, the spirits are seen as a means more than an end. The spirit world is useful for practical purposes.

Complexity in religious beliefs and practices often comes about because of the difficulty of dealing with the spirit world. It is unknowable, vague, shadowy, amorphous, unsystematic, unpredictable, flexible, inscrutable, and even irrational. It is this fact, and the nearly infinitely variable way in which particular societies cope with the interface of daily needs and the spirit world, that gives each religion its unique pattern.

The Zulus and Their Religious Traditions

Background

About four million Zulus live in and around the Republic of South Africa. Originally arriving from the north, they belong to the Bantu-speaking peoples, whose migrations were complete by the seventeenth century. These several ethnolinguistically related tribes have similar social and religious traditions. While other tribal groups have much larger percentages living in rural or semirural areas, about forty percent of the Zulu people

Zulu's continue to maintain many traditional beliefs and practices though urbanization has brought significant changes. South African Tourism Board

are rural and continue to perpetuate tribal beliefs relatively undisturbed by modern ideas and education. What follows here is more descriptive of the rural Zulus though many ideas are still found among their urban cousins.

The rural Zulus live in a unified world in which their lives as cattle farmers are regularly affected by the spirit world. Indeed, it might be best to think of their view of the world as consisting of both scientific cause and effect as well as spirit realities governed by the irrational and unpredictable. There is both the known and the unknown; the objective world of things and the subjective world of real but unpredictable spirit realities. In general it could be said that Zulus, like other traditional peoples, live in a

world of beings as much or more than in one of things.

In this chapter we will identify several sources of power in the life and experience of the Zulu people. In order to provide some context we need first to look at their general understanding of the world.

The Cosmology of the Zulu

There are a large number of spiritual beings in the consciousness of the Zulus.[6] It may be best to begin with God of the Sky (*Inkosi Yezulu*), not because he is the most important figure in their religious concerns but because of the logical priority of his associations with creation and origins. It is said that the Zulu people gave little thought to God of the Sky prior to the arrival of Christian missionaries in the nineteenth century. This was because he was both near and yet far, knowable and yet for the most part unknown. Christian emphasis on the creator God and his direct activity in human affairs through creation, incarnation, and redemption prompted Zulu elders to reflect on their own tradition of a distant but creator god which, in general outline, they share in common with other sub-Saharan Africans.

God of the Sky created the Zulus' early ancestors, called "that which appeared first" or *umvelingqangi*, and is the object of special praise names on ceremonial occasions. God of the Sky is apparently a twin, and in contrast to Earth is called "first of twins." He is male and father compared to Earth, who is female and mother. At death a person goes to be with Earth and only in rare cases returns to God of the Sky.

The Zulus depend for their livelihood on cattle, which are kept in an enclosure (*kraal*), which in turn is surrounded by their huts arranged in a semicircular way. Sufficient grazing depends on sufficient rains. God of the Sky is important in this connection since he has control of weather, rain, and wind. He is primarily a being of power who controls storms, lightning, and thunder. The Zulus believe they came from some interrelationship between God of the Sky and Earth. A sexual union between the two is not made explicit. However, because one legend posits that the first Zulu came down from the sky still sporting his umbilical cord, we may assume such a relationship. Some early records of Zulu traditions merge God of the Sky with First Man, so this cosmology is not consistent.

The Zulu kraal *is the scene of much of the religious life of the Zulus.* South African Tourism Board

This god has special human assistants called "heaven-herds" (*izinyanga zezulu*), who, through some natural event such as lightning or a thunderstorm, believe they are chosen for a special relationship to the god. Cuts on the face during a period of initiation mark

the chosen. Ordinary Zulus do not speak with God of the Sky but depend on these or other specialists (diviners, sorcerers, herbalists) to intercede for special needs. However, it is possible that in extreme circumstances an individual might seek help directly if all specialists are ineffective. Certain unpopulated hills away from the *kraals* are known to be favored places for such contacts.

In summary, God of the Sky has power, but this power is limited to controlling the weather and to capricious acts which the Zulus can neither predict nor anticipate. This uncertainty does not seem to increase God of the Sky's importance in their lives. Rather, in practice he is of little importance or consequence for personal affairs. Ordinary persons do not deal with him. He is approachable by certain specialists, but then only under dire circumstances. Power over storms is his main, if not exclusive, attribute that affects the daily life of the Zulu. He also has creative powers, but these are not absolute, as seen in the fact that he colabored with Earth to form man, who issues from his sexuality. He is worthy of praise poems directed to him on special occasions, but he is not a companion of the Zulu in life or in death since few deceased go to be with him. He is capricious and unpredictable, able to bestow either good or evil.

The Headman and the Ancestors

The Zulus believe the ancestors and spirits strongly and regularly affect their lives. A recent survey among both Christian and non-Christian Zulus indicates a high percentage of persons who believe an ancestral spirit accompanies a person to bring good fortune.[7] Perhaps equally important is the belief that the spirits assist the Zulu in coping with those crises moments common to all humans: birth, puberty, marriage, and death. Ceremonies performed on these occasions, known as "rites of passage," ensure that the dangers associated with the occasion are avoided and that the transition from one status to another occurs safely.

The headman (*umnumzane*) serves as the village representative to the ancestors and thus acts not just as headman but as headman-priest. His hut in the Zulu village (also called a *kraal*) is on the west side of the nearly closed semicircle of huts, directly opposite the gate to the east. The inner *kraal*, maintained for the cattle, stands in the middle and provides a secure place for the animals, but it has another important function. Rituals are most often performed there. Lawson says "some scholars call the cattle enclosure the 'temple' of the Zulu people," in part because it is here that the ancestors linger and special protective rituals are performed.[8]

Each hut will have an *umsamo* positioned on a wall directly behind the centrally located cooking hearth. The *umsamo* is a place for objects of ritual significance and it is here that spirits dwell if they are not in the cattle *kraal*. The headman's *umsamo* has special significance since he has primary responsibility for gaining the blessing of ancestors or coping with their displeasure. The ancestors are departed family members who are thought to abide with Earth in their after-death life. Though buried in the earth upon death, they are very much present on earth in village life and affairs, and thus death does not separate them from the survivors. They are alive to benefit or punish the living. The approval of ancestors is guaranteed so long as the headman continues to inform them of major village events such as births, marriages, and deaths.

Since Zulu society is patrilineal, male ancestors are of special importance and receive special attention in rituals. Famous chiefs and past headmen become especially important, as can be seen in the treatment their funeral ceremonies receive. The headman is buried near the main hut in the *kraal*. It is a time for mourning and a solemn attitude prevails for a month. A period of yearlong mourning will follow for the widow of the headman. Others will observe certain taboos and take certain medicines to ward off danger in case the death was unexpected. For them the one month of mourning will end with the *Ilambo* ritual called "washing of spears," a combination of animal sacrifice and praise poems in memory of the departed.

The final event occurs on the one-year anniversary of the headman's death. This is the *Ukubuyisa Idlozi*, "the bringing home of the ancestor." At this time the deceased, considered in the interim to be in a sort of undefined state, is invited to join the other ancestors who live in, below, and around the *kraal*. Sometimes the departed ancestor is symbolically "guided" to the *umsamo* by twig markings and verbal invitations. Henceforth he will be addressed and praised together with other departed ancestors by the new headman, typically the oldest son. The ceremony closes in a festive occasion for the entire village with the slaughter of an ox and feasting for all.

The headman is, therefore, the single most significant person in the life of the Zulu *kraal*, since the lives of all the community depend upon his priestly duties, as their representative, to gain and sustain the favor of the ancestors.

Diviners and Other Power Brokers

While the headman's mediatory functions affect the entire community, other functionaries powerfully serve individual needs: physical, psychological, spiritual, and social. These persons may be called power brokers in that they have power to affect the lives of individuals in a variety of ways and are regularly called on to do so.

The Zulu, like most other African peoples, have a strong sense of unity with family and community. Individual existence is understood only within this broader social setting. Harmonious relations with family and community are essential, and sickness may occur when that breaks down. When sickness occurs the individual may resort to medicines of either a folk or a scientific nature, without any thought of a malevolent cause. But there are also nondescript diseases, it is believed, which result from mysterious forces or activities of one's enemies which disturb the person's internal balance of health or the normal relationships within the family or community. It is at this point that those with special power are sought out in order to return the situation to normal. "The main aim is to restore the disposition, the balance of the affected person in the context of his or her family and community. The person has been put into a disarranged, disturbed, disordered situation and this has to be rectified. The main aim of such a person's adversary is to either destroy him or to influence negatively his social equilibrium which results in all types of misfortune, ill-health, or even death."[9]

The power brokers who act at several different levels include diviners, sorcerers, herbalists, and witches. One scholar arranges these practitioners and the services they provide along a continuum with wisdom at one end and spirit possession at the other. The nature of the powers held by these specialists ranges from knowledge of what causes the problem (the diviner) to counteracting the agent with powerful offsetting means (sorcerers) to spirit possession and the use of power for evil ends (witches).

1. Diviners, as is indicated by the name, function primarily to provide information about the cause of the problem. Usually women, diviners are believed to be appointed by ancestors or experience a special vision or dream calling them to their work. They are specialists with a "calling," which only a few who have the sanction and approval of society can perform. Their work is essential to Zulu well-being, since it is widely believed that much misfortune, illness, and even death is the result of malevolent forces directed against the victim. The diviner is viewed as morally neutral or positive; her powers, through which she provides a needed service to the community, are not due to any evil source.

2. Sorcerers, however, may use black or evil magic to gain their information. Anyone can become a sorcerer by paying a fee to another sorcerer. An ordinary person who has reason to feel offended by another may learn from an herbalist or sorcerer some techniques to use against his or her enemy. The sorcerer's task is essentially to dislodge the enemy or destroy that force or power which is causing a problem. It is an appropriate action in the face of a justifiable grievance.

3. Herbal healers may deal in herbal medicine or combine it with Western medicine and function either to heal or provide medicinal substances to counter evil influences directed against one who intends harm. If the physical problem can be treated with medicine, an herbal healer with knowledge of medicine may be consulted. Both the diviner and the sorcerer may have medicinal skills to supplement their mystical powers and serve their respective ends.

4. Witches, usually women, gain their status through spirit possession and have the superhuman ability to fly, become invisible, and act from a distance. Witches differ from both diviners and sorcerers. Diviners provide information concerning the cause of a problem and hence engage in a morally good, or at least morally neutral, enterprise. Sorcerers use occult means, to be sure, but they seek a remedy to a perceived evil. They may even use evil to combat evil. But witches use evil against good, work clandestinely, and are considered a threat to society. "Witchcraft is a threat to public order, an unbearable strain on traditional social organiza-tion, a challenge to revered tradition. Witches derive their power from, and base their operations in, a shadowy world that is neither that of the ancestors nor that of the God of the Sky. And their purpose is the destruction of what is good, especially those processes that create and enhance life."[10]

Religious Change

While belief in God of the Sky is foundational to other Zulu beliefs, its impact on personal daily living is rather insignificant. Changes have been noted in Zulu life and practice through the impact of Christian movements, however. As noted above, the average person would not usually seek to communicate with God of the Sky. But just as Christians commune directly with God in their worship services, there has been an increase in hilltop worship of God of the Sky among non-Christian Zulus. The theistic beliefs of Christian neighbors have led to greater recognition and a more important place for God of the Sky in the thinking of traditional Zulus.

But change has worked the other way, too. Traditional Zulu religion has brought changes in the ideas and acts of Christian Zulus, as seen in Isaiah Shem be (d.C.E. 1935), the Zulu founder and leader of the Amanazaretha Church, who incorporated into church life certain ideas and practices common to non-Christian Zulus.

Religion of the Quechuas

Background

Six to seven million Quechuas live in Peru, Bolivia, and Ecuador. In Ecuador these mountain agriculturalists, the cultural and religious heirs to the Inca civilization, make up forty-one percent of the population. The present Quechua beliefs and rituals have been so influenced by Catholic Christianity that some scholars refer to the faith as simply a specialized form of Catholicism. Distinct non-Christian beliefs and practices persist even today among many Quechuas, however, and it will be these that we will study.

While it is no doubt true that the different Quechua groups dispersed throughout South America differ in some respects, in the main their religious traditions are similar enough to be treated as one.

The Supreme Being

The pre-Colombian Inca heritage of the Quechuas is not entirely lost, as is evidenced in the survival of the idea of a supreme being whom the Incas called Viracocha. The exact nature of the deity is disputed. Some suggest Viracocha was a sun god, others think he was god of thunder and lightning, and others still believe he had the form of a white sheep. Whatever his form, Viracocha was a creator god, as is seen in a poem preserved among Quechuas in Peru. The following is an excerpt.

> The world awakes
> And is filled with light
> To worship thee,
> O Creator of man.
>   The lofty sky
> Sweeps away her clouds
> In homage to thee,
> The Maker of the world.
>   The king of the stars,
> Our father, the sun,
> Submits to thee

> His power and might.
>   The wind lifts up
> The tops of the trees
> And waves each branch
> In tribute to thee.
> . . . .
> At the dawn of the day
> My heart sings praise
> To thee my Father
> And Creator of man.[11]

While a supreme god may have been extremely important to their ancestors, the Quechuas of today are less concerned and no pagan rituals of importance deal with him. The following is a description of their present understanding of a supreme being.[12]

The Ecuadorian Quechua give the name Taita Dios, "Father God," to the supreme being; the word *Dios* being derived from the Latin *deus*, "God." The presence of ancient Quechua concepts persists despite the Christian vocabulary, as can be seen in the following considerations:

1. The idea of a father "out there" exists, but he can be personal or impersonal, as he chooses. He may be coaxed into being personal, but he shares the impersonality of nearby volcanic peaks, which are also divine fathers.

2. He may do either good or bad acts. He is considered good if he does what the Quechua consider to be good and bad if his acts are bad. His nature contains no sense of moral perfection and thus perfection is not ascribed to him. He is capricious and subject to whim in things both moral and material. The implications for the Quechua are that there is no cosmic purpose that derives from him, nor is there purpose for individuals directed by a

caring and interested being. Impersonal fate controls human affairs not Taita Dios.

3. Though things owe their existence to Taita Dios, in our analysis it might be best to think of him as "source" rather than creator, since he himself is a part of the cosmos and neither infinite nor transcending it. He is part of the cosmic world and not "other than" it. Volcanic peak deities are also said to have given origin to humankind through marriage union.

4. Taita Dios is an ethical judge of the world but not a lawgiver. His judgments are not according to any established standard and hence his fairness is open to question.

5. Humans are dependent on him for things material but not things moral. He gives and requires no moral perfections since moral perfection is not his nature.

6. Taita Dios is neither source nor symbol of universal moral values, which the Quechua find only in the sanctions of the group. There is no concept of universal truth stemming from him.

7. He is neither eternal nor omniscient. Taita Dios is durable but not eternal; he is static and passive. For Quechuas who are nominally Christian he may learn information from the saints or the Virgin Mary, whose good will is gained through special religious festivals.

The Spirit World

Supernatural beings are much more central to the real concerns of the people and may be classified in a binary way: higher and lower, good and bad, heavenly and earthly, traditional and Catholic. They are much like people in that they have moods, humanlike desires, and the full range of personality traits. But they also have superhuman powers and can be influenced through food, drink, and impressive ritual.

As the Quechua are dependent on the land, the weather, and the productivity of crops and animals, the motivation for seeking and maintaining a relationship with the spirit world is to gain help in controlling natural factors. Health, family, and financial problems are occasions for spirit intervention as well.

The Quechua use rituals and public festivals to seek spirit help in daily-life needs. Examples of supplications for practical needs are the following prayers:

At the Beginning of Planting

This is your due which I serve you in August at the beginning of the year. You, the one who nurtures me, receive this offering. You, the one who feeds me as a mother giving the breast, as a bird that feeds its young, receive this kindly and from all things defend me; from illness, cause it to be removed far from me; may I be free of all trouble; may I live happily for another year.

To Mountain-Peak Deity

Father, . . . bless—breathe on my animals. In the month of August I am offering what is your due. Receive this my offering as I serve it to you with all my heart.

The *Shaman*

Found among the Quechua and other Amerindians of South America are *shamans*. This word, borrowed from the Tungus of Central Asia, describes a variety of different practices. The *shaman*, in whatever tribal setting, is typically a kind of spiritual medic who cures sickness, but he or she can also contact the dead and mediate with them through ecstatic experiences. Ventriloquism and manipulation, alcohol, drug consumption, and spirit possession may play a part in the *shaman's* work.

The *shaman* typically works alone or with assistants in the homes of those seeking help. Illness is believed to be caused by the intrusion of something supernatural into the body, which must be purged. Alternately, some attribute illness to the departure of the soul.[14] The technique of the *shaman* may be mechanistic with various ceremonies in evidence, or it may call for direct spirit contact. By "cupping," which is the application of a heated bowl or cup to the body, the *shaman* may hope to remove the malevolent force or spirit causing the disorder. If that fails, efforts to recapture the soul may require bargaining, arguing, or contesting in the spirit realm.

In summary, it can be said that the Quechua have largely merged the beliefs and practices of their Inca forebears with quasi-Christian ones and cope with life less through the remote supreme being Taita Dios than with the spirits by the help of a *shaman*.

The Santals of India

The Santals in Their Context

The Santals number a little less than ten percent of India's officially recognized tribal population of nearly four million. Spread through the states of Orissa, Bihar, and West Bengal, they speak Santali—a language of the Munda family—and are the largest tribe to retain their language in the face of competing national and regional languages. The Santals of this study live in the village of Pangro in the northern part of Bihar in the district called Santal Parganas.[15]

There are 12 exogamous (males marry outside the clan) clans of Santals in India, each having numerous subclans, for a total of 405 clans and subclans. In the village of Pangro the Santals comprise 8 clans and 25 subclans for a total of 283 people. A few non-Santals live in Pangro as well. Since each clan has its own clan spirits, and each subclan its own spirits, the total number of spirits are several score in number.

The Santals engage in paddy farming from April through December-January, during which time they fertilize, plow, sow, transplant, weed, harvest, and thresh. Domestic animals serve as a secondary source of food and income and include fowl, goats, cattle, water buffalo, and pigs. The Santals are agriculturalists who know the rhythm of the seasons and weather, the properties of plants, soils, and pests, and most factors on which their agrarian economy rests.

Religion and the Growing Season

The entire village is involved in farming and concerned with all factors that affect production. The Santals believe in a large number of spirits who directly affect the success or failure of their all-important farming. Dealing with the spirits, which exist at several levels and whose character is of differing kinds, is the concern of the entire tribe.

The Santal religion enables them to cope with factors beyond their technology, factors that lie in the realm of spirit influence. Both nature and the spirits are understood to some extent and are seen by the Santals as being both dependable and uncertain. Though there are a large and uncounted number of spirits and a great

In addition to these there are three other festivals, but many Santals observe only the above four plus Baha, which is a New Year's festival. The Sohrae festival is considered the most important and more time and attention is given to this than any other. These festivals, with accompanying rituals, are geared to further guarantee success in farming by enlisting the help of the many spirits recognized in the Santal world.

The Santals and Their Spirit World

All of life for all of the villagers revolves around agriculture. Around it centers the whole of family and village life. Rituals and ceremonies involving *bongas* (spirits) are integrated with and tied to the agricultural cycle. Rituals performed at annual ceremonies are as indispensable as manual labor. Manual labor is necessary to deal with the things Santals can see; spirit ritual is equally necessary to attend to factors one cannot

MONTH	TASK	RITUAL
April-May	manuring	
May-June	plowing	
June-July	sowing rice seedling	Erok Sim
July-August	transplanting	Hariar Sim
August-September	weeding the paddy	
November-December	harvesting	Janthar, Sohrae
December-January	threshing	

diversity of rituals connected with them, those which affect tribal and village life most correlate with the agricultural calendar. The following shows the calendar of events for rice production and those festivals which correspond to it.

directly control. The spirits serve village economic and social needs, not primarily individual needs.

Though the Santals know many kinds and categories of spirits, they do not know all of them, since many have not yet been encountered. It might be fair to say that the Santals regard themselves not as living in two worlds, spirit and material, but in one world. Santals live in a spirit world rather than spirits inhabiting a Santal world. This is not to say that Santals are overly attentive to or preoccupied with the spirit world. They accept the spirit world as readily as they do other aspects of their existence. The visible and invisible, categories Santals recognize but make little of, interpenetrate. Though different in obvious ways, they are in continuity in most other ways.

Santals have names for many but not all spirits and vocabulary differences exist between clans. The spirits are the real lords of the fields, houses, crops, and nature, and it is to them that Santals pay tribute through sacrifice, offering, and libation. In many ways there are few differences between spirits and humans, since both are motivated by complex factors, subject to whim and caprice, and if offended can express malice, spite, mischief, and anger. As with humans, Santals do their best to influence spirits, but in the end they simply hope for the best. Spirits, like humans, are sensitive to neglect, fussy about rights, and express displeasure at being wronged.

Ten classes of Santal spirits are dealt with today. The Santals do not generally think of them in any hierarchy of authority or importance.[16]

1. Thakur. A supreme deity also called Cando, he is a benevolent source of the Santals. Since he is generally good and satisfied with them, there is little reason to show much concern, although he is mentioned at every im-portant festival and specifically in ceremonies of marriage and death.

2. Tribal (clan and interclan) spirits. Maran Buru, Moreko-Turuiko, and Jaher Era are the major ones.

3. Subclan spirits. These *bongas* are numerous, as at least 405 subclans have been counted. Their names are known only to the headmen of the subclans, who keep them secret from women and others.

4. Household spirits. Considered to be the most personal, they have power to protect individual household members, who may pray directly to them in distress or sickness. These spirits are inherited patrilineally. Married women take on their husbands' household spirits and leave the spirit of their fathers behind.

5. Ancestral spirits. These are deceased members of the family who continue influence as senior kinfolk, assisting at times of births, weddings, and household crises. On appropriate occasions offerings are given to at least the most recent generation of ancestors.

6. Spirits belonging to *ojhas*. These are *bongas* retained by *ojhas* (*shamans*) whose work is to heal sickness and deal with trouble-causing spirits.

7. Spirits exorcised by *shamans*. These are disease- and mischief-causing *bongas*, including spirit-husbands of *bongas*.

8. Spirits belonging to non-Santals. Because they live in a Hindu society, Santals also regularly worship three

female Hindu deities: Kali, Durga, and Ganga Mai.

9. Spirits whose territory is beyond the village. A variety of spirits control affairs on the edge of the village, in the mountains, hills, and water. They are malevolent and must be kept inactive.

10. Ghosts and others. These stray and occasional *bongas* are dealt with by amulets, incantations, exorcisms, and rituals.

Dani Tribesman from the Baliem Valley of Iran Jaya. Alliance Life

The Sohrae Festival (November-December)

A complete description of all rituals performed during the yearly farming cycle might be interesting but tedious.

The Santals believe each of them makes an important contribution to production. The rituals effect success in their own way and without them a serious loss of confidence would ensue. Unless replaced with an equally convincing worldview, such as that held by Christian Santals, life would be intolerable.

The first day of Sohrae involves water purification rites for all. Each home should also be tidy in order to receive guests that are sure to come. The *naeke*, "headman-priest," takes some male members to a rice field to perform *puja* (worship). On a low, makeshift altar an egg is placed and marked with vermilion powder. The fowl to be sacrificed is made to eat of rice from the altar. The *naeke* addresses the *bongas*, asking for their presence at the sacrifice and their blessing in return for the items to be presented. The fowl is beheaded, blood drips on the egg and rice, and *handi* (rice beer) is poured over the altar, to which has been added the head of the fowl. All present seal the ceremony by drinking from a ready supply of *handi*. A second altar is attended by the *naeke's* assistant. In conclusion the *naeke* reminds all present of the taboo against sexual contact within one's clan. Apart from this restriction persons are free to make merry.

Cattle are then driven over the altar. The cow that breaks the egg is honored and its owner is believed to have a year's good luck. Other cattle ceremonies of the day seek the spirits' protection from disease or misfortune and blessing to make them fruitful.

The second day is called Daka Hilok

(food day), during which heads of households lead their families in offerings of fowls and rice beer and consumption of a family meal of fowl and rice. Early in the day bands of men tour the village from house to house dancing and drinking in mock gestures of begging. After returning, these men offer sacrifices to Maran Buru and other spirits, including spirits of the ancestors.

Maran Buru is the head of Santal spirits. According to Santal mythology he taught the primal Santal couple how to brew rice beer and copulate. He left instructions for them to offer rice beer when calling on his name. Though he is acknowledged as the most powerful spirit, he is described as a genial and kind grandfather and thus a distant and highest ranking ancestor.

As this festival is accompanied by dancing and prodigious drinking bouts, drunkenness and sexual license are widespread. A carnival spirit prevails through the village and hence Sohrae is easily the festive peak of the year. Its contravention of the usual norms of behavior has earned for it a bad reputation among Christians.

The third day centers around the bull buffalo. Poles are erected in front of their enclosures, and gifts are placed atop each pole and in a circle around it on the ground. The bulls are washed and curried and then tied to the pole as guardians of the gifts. Villagers sport with the bulls, who drive back any who attempt to take the gifts. This diversion lasts into the evening and is accompanied by singing, dancing, and drinking.

The fourth day sees the removal of the poles by youths who ask owners for rice and vegetables in exchange for their services. These foods are taken to the house of the official government representative where a common meal is consumed followed by singing, dancing, and merrymaking into the night.

The fifth day is designated for fishing. It is believed that the life of anyone who eats fish or crab on this day is prolonged. Irrigation ditches connected to the nearby Ganges River make it a relaxing and sporting day.

The last day is called Sakrat. After an early meal men go for a hunt, singing as they go. Upon return they ceremonially bathe and offer rice beer offerings to Maran Buru and the ancestors. The *naeke* offers libations to Manji Haram, the chief village deity, who is believed to represent either the original headman of the village or the patron spirit of all village headmen. He resides in the *manjithan*, a special shrine opposite the headman's house consisting of a wooden post surrounded by a low, flat stone upon which offerings are placed. Manji Haram is believed to be a spiritual adviser to the headman, who communes with him by presenting and consuming rice and rice beer. He is to be propitiated without fail, and those headmen who are lax may be fined by villagers. He is a benevolent *bonga* who exercises some control over other *bongas*. Thus he should never be neglected, insulted, nor polluted.

Myths Among the Santals

There is no agreement about what constitutes mythical literature nor how to understand it. Theories of the interpretation of myths are often complicated and contradictory, and while none seems fully satisfactory some have been given greater reception than others in the scholarly world. It is useful to categorize these theories as psychological and psychoanalytical, sociological and transcendentist.

Psychological theories differ according to whether their proponents regard the thought processes of primitives as irrational, speculative, and emotional, or whether their reasoning processes are reasonable and rational. Persuaded that the latter was the case, Levi Stauss, in his structuralist view, believed myth demonstrates there is a logic imbedded in the thought processes of primitive people of which they are not fully aware. Myth has meaning on two levels: the obvious meaning understood by the primitive individual and the latent meaning understood only by the scholar. According to structuralists, myth served primitives well by enabling them to deal with the conflicts found in their experiences. Psychoanalytical explanations see in myth a manifestation of inner personal drives calling for satisfaction (Freud) or an expression of the collective unconscious (Jung). The evidence Jung and his followers cite is that myths contain archetypes found universally among people of all cultures and eras.

Sociological theories rooted in the ideas of Durkheim and Malinowski say that myths encapsulated in story are not merely humanity's response to its hopes and fears but function to reinforce social realities upon which life depends. Further, myth contains a model or paradigm to which a people must conform. It is by reciting tribal myths that social institutions are safeguarded and society's stability is ensured. Malinowski's basic position is this: "The function of myth, briefly, is to strengthen tradition and endow it with a greater value and prestige by tracing it back to a higher, better, more supernatural reality of initial events."[17] The transcendentist approach, by contrast, may combine some ideas from any of the previous theories. However, it centers its explanation of myth around references to an irrepressible consciousness of a transcendent entity such as God (H. Kraemer, Andrew Lang) or, as in the case of Mircea Eliade, involves references to some quasi-transcendent reality, "the sacred," manifested in "hierophanies" found in most mythical literature.

A Santal Myth of Origins[18]

Toward the rising of the sun was the birth of man. At first there was only water, and under the water there was earth. Then Thakur-Jiu (lit., the Lord) created the beings that live in water: the crab, the crocodile, the alligator, the boar fish, the prawn, the earthworm, the tortoise, and others.

Thereupon Thakur said: "Whom shall I now make? I will make man." He decided to make two of earth. He had just finished making the two; then when he was going to give them souls the Day-horse (sun) came down from above, trampled them to pieces, and left. Thakur became awfully grieved by this.

Then Thakur said: "I will not make

them of earth; I shall make birds."
Then he made the two Has Hasil birds
(swans) pulling the material off from
his breast. He placed them on his
hand; they were looking very beautiful. Thereupon he breathed on them,
and they at once became alive and
flew upward. They moved about
flying, but as they could not find a
place to alight anywhere, they therefore always alighted on Thakur's
hand. Then the Day-horse came down
along a gossamer thread to drink
water. When he was drinking water
he spilt some froth of his mouth and
left. It floated on the water; thereby
foam was formed on the water.

Thakur then said to the two birds:
"Do alight on the froth." They did so.
When they had alighted they moved
about over the whole sea, the froth
carrying them along like a boat. Then
they implored Thakur: "We are moving about, that is so, but we do not
find any food."

Then Thakur-Jiu called the alligator.
He came and said to Thakur: "Why
did you call me, Thakur?" Thakur said
to him: "Would you be willing to
bring up earth?" The alligator answered him: "If you tell me to do so, I
might bring it up." Having gone
down in the water, he worked to
bring up earth but all was dissolved.
Thereupon Thakur called the prawn,
the fish, and the crab. All attempted
to bring up earth but all the earth was
dissolved.

Thereupon Thakur called the earthworm. He came and said to Thakur:
"Why did you call me, Thakur?"
Thakur said to him: "Would you be
willing to bring up earth?" The earth-

worm answered Thakur: "If you tell
me to do so, I might bring it up,
provided the tortoise stands on the
water."

Thereupon Thakur called the tortoise.
He came and said to Thakur: "Why
have you called me, Thakur?" Thakur
said to him: "No one is able to bring
the earth up. The earthworm has
promised to bring it up, provided you
will stand on the water." The tortoise
answered Thakur: "If you tell me to
do so, I might stand." Then he stood
on the water. When he had taken his
stand there Thakur chained his four
legs in the four directions. The tortoise
became immovably quiet on the water. Then the earthworm went down
to bring up the earth. He put his tail
on the back of the tortoise and with
his mouth down below he began to
eat earth, and this he brought out on
the back of the tortoise. Then it was
spread out and fixed like a hard film.
He continued to bring up earth; he
brought up enough for the whole
earth. Then he stopped.

Thereupon Thakur caused the earth to
be harrowed level. By continual har-
rowing some was heaped up on the
implements; this became mountains.
Then when the earth had been
brought up and leveled, the foam that
was floating on the surface of the
water stuck to the earth, and as Thakur sowed *sirom* seed on this foam the
sirom plant sprang up first (before all
other plants). After this he let the
dhubi grass be sown and come up;
after this the *karam* tree, thereupon the
tope sarjom, the *labar atnak*, the *ladea
matkom*, and after this all kinds of
vegetation. The earth became firm. In
all places where there was water,

there he let sods be put, and in all places where water was bubbling up, there he let it be closed up by pressing pieces of rock down on it.

Thereupon, having made a nest in a clump of the *sirom* plants, the two birds laid two eggs. The female bird would sit on the eggs, and the male bird would find and bring back food. Keeping on in this way they hatched the eggs. O mother! Two human beings were born, one boy and one girl. . . . The names of these two human beings were Haram and Ayo. Some people call them Pilcu Haram and Pilcu Budhi (male and female first parents). . .

So they implored Thakur saying: "How shall we two support these two human beings?" Thakur gave them some cotton and said to them: "Whatever you two eat, press the juice out of these things and make a place on the cotton wet therewith, and put this into their mouths to suck." By sucking and getting food in this way they grew and commenced to walk. But as they were growing the anxiety of the two birds increased, viz., where they should put the two when they grew up.

So they besought Thakur, and he said to them: "Do fly round and find for us a place for them to stay." Then they flew toward the setting of the sun; they discovered Hihiri Pipiri and once they returned they told Thakur of this. He said to them: "Do take them there." Then they took them along carrying them on their backs. They put them down and left them there. What became of Has Hasil, this the

ancestors of old have not told us; therefore we do not know. . . .

One day Maran Buru (lit., Lita) came to the humans and said to them: "Where are you, grandchildren? How are you? I am your grandfather; I have come to pay you a visit. I see you are well; but there is one great joy that you have not tasted. Do brew beer, it has a very sweet taste." Then he taught them to prepare the fermenting stuff. All three went to the forest. Maran Buru showed them the roots. The two dug up and brought these. When they had brought them Maran Buru said to Pilcu Budhi: "Now you make the rice wet for us." She did so. Having made it wet she pounded it into flour. She and Pilcu Budhi jabbed the "medicine" (fermenting stuff); they squeezed it and kneaded it to flour with the "medicine" juice. Having kneaded it into a dough they made balls of it; having made the balls they put these into a basket together with straw and put this aside. . . . In five days the fermentation was complete. In the afternoon they poured water on it. Then Maran Buru said to them: "Now both of you drink this after first pouring on the ground some to Maran Buru. Tomorrow I shall come again and visit you."

Thereupon they made three leaf-cups and filled these; having done this they poured on the ground the contents of one in the name of Maran Buru; then they drank themselves. When they were drinking, they commenced to toy amorously; continuing this they both drank much and became very drunk. It became night, they lay down together.

When it became dawn Maran Buru suddenly came. He called out to them: "How is it, grandchildren? Have you got up or not? Do come out." When they had regained consciousness they recognized that they were both naked and felt very ashamed; therefore they answered him: "O grandfather, how can we possibly go out; we are awfully ashamed; we are both of us naked; last night when we had become drunk from beer, we did something bad."

Maran Buru then said to them: "It does not matter." And smiling to himself he went away. To cover their shame Pilcu Haram and Pilcu Budhi made a skirt and a loincloth for them-selves of ficus leaves. Then they begat children, seven boys and seven girls.

The Santals and Their Religion

No attempt has been made here to review all the relevant facets of Santal religious life. The major concern in Santal life appears to be the manipulation of material and spiritual realities for success in farming. Whether Santals could stand to gain from the modern science of farming we are not qualified to say. We have, however, shown how important control of the spirits is to that enterprise.

Discussion

1. Evaluate how useful the terms "religions of primitives," "primitive religions," and "animism" are to discussing the religions of selected societies presented in this chapter.
2. In what ways are the religious concerns of Zulus, Quechuas, and Santals different? In what ways are they similar?
3. How does the following, said of the Konds of India, relate to the peoples studied in this chapter?
   The great concern of the Kond is with this world, and only with the next in so far as it affects himself and his family or village in their this-worldly experience. His world-view, therefore, is his conception of man, society, the natural and the supernatural in relation to his daily life and behavior.[19]
4. How does the conception of a supreme being among these peoples compare or contrast with that of the Judeo-Christian tradition?
5. On myth:
   A. Who are the principal figures in the Santal myth of origins and what relation do they bear to one another?
   B. What do you see as the purpose of this story? For what reason might it be told?
   C. It has been said that mythical stories reflect the social structure of the people more than they explain origins. Is there any evidence of this in this origin story?
   D. What does the story teach about origins? about society? about the spirit world? about the relation between the human and spiritual planes?

E.   Are there parallels between this story and the Genesis account? Are there differences? What might account for this?

F.   Which (if any) of the approaches to religion described earlier in the book would be useful in giving an "explanation" of the story?

Notes

[1]Eugene A. Nida and William A. Smalley, *Introducing Animism* (New York: Friendship Press, 1959), 5; Edwin Arthur Burtt, *Types of Religious Philosophy* (New York: Harper & Brothers, 1957), 33–73; and Robert S. Ellwood, Jr., *Many Peoples, Many Faiths*, 2d ed. (Englewood Cliffs, N.J.: Prentice-Hall, 1982), 29f. Ellwood points out problems in using the phrase "primitive religion" but accepts it nonetheless since he believes the religion of primitives is foundational to later religious developments.

[2]Nida and Smalley, *Introducing Animism*, 3–5.

[3]For a good survey of primitives in the Asian context read under the words "tribes" and "adivasis" in *Encyclopedia of Asian History*, ed. Ainslie T. Embree (New York: Scribner 1988).

[4]Ake Hultkranz, "The Peril of Visions: Changes of Vision Patterns Among the Wind River Shoshoni," *History of Religions* 26, no. 1 (August 1986): 34–46.

[5]Niels C. Nielsen, Jr. et al., *Religions of the World* (New York: St. Martin's Press, 1983), 29.

[6]E. Thomas Lawson, *Religions of Africa: Traditions in Transformation* (San Francisco: Harper & Row, 1984). Most of the information in this section about the Zulu religion comes from Lawson.

[7]G. Dal Congdon, "An Investigation into the Current Zulu Worldview," *Evangelical Missions Quarterly* 21, no. 3 (July 1985): 296–99.

[8]Lawson, *Religions of Africa*, 19.

[9]George C. Oosthuizen, "Interpretation of Demonic Powers in Southern African Independent Churches," *Missiology* 16, no. 1 (January 1988): 4.

[10] Lawson, *Religions of Africa*, 23.

[11]Eugene A. Nida, *Customs and Cultures: Anthropology for Christian Missions* (New York: Harper & Row, 1954), 189–90.

[12]William D. Reyburn, "The Transformation of God and the Conversion of Man," *Readings in Missionary Anthropology*, ed. William A. Smalley (Tarrytown, N.Y.: Practical Anthropology, 1967), 26–30.

[13]Norman Anderson, ed., *The World's Religions*, 4th ed. (London: InterVarsity Press, 1975), 30.

[14]Quentin Nordyke, *Animistic Aymaras and Church Growth* (Newberg, Ore.: Barclay Press, 1972), 27–34.

[15]J. Troisi, *Tribal Religion* (New Delhi: South Asia Books, 1979). I am indebted to this book for its description of the Santals.

[16]Ibid., 79.

[17]Bronislaw Malinowski, *Magic, Science and Religion* (Garden City, N.Y.: Doubleday Anchor, 1954), 146.

[18]*Traditions and Institutions of the Santals*, P. O. Bodding, Translator, Oslo Etnografiske Museum, Bulletin 6 (Oslo: A.W. Broggers, 1942): 3–6.

[19]Barbara M. Boal, *The Church in the Kond Hills* (Lucknow, India: National Christian Council of India, 1963), 27.

Part Three

Monotheistic Religions of the Near East and the World

5 Judaism

Hear, O Israel: The LORD our God, the LORD is one. Love the LORD your God with all your heart and with all your soul and with all your strength. These commandments that I give you today are to be upon your hearts. Impress them on your children. Talk about them when you sit at home and walk along the road, when you lie down and when you get up. Tie them as symbols on your hands and bind them on your foreheads. Write them on the doorframes of your houses and on your gates. (Deut. 6:4–9)

This call to worship is known as the *Shema*, from the first word of verse four, *sh'ma*, "hear." The first sentence of these verses is the Shema proper, but the whole six verses refer to the foundational truth conveyed by verse four. Sabbath worship in the synagogue begins with the Shema proclaimed, and religious Jews recite it three times a day. The heart of the Shema is the teaching that God is one, that Israel's God, Yahweh, is supreme God of the universe—hence the command elsewhere, "You shall have no other gods before me." Since God is the sole God, then the obligations that follow the proclamation are inevitable: love God with your whole being; remind yourself in every facet of life just who God is.

The "Israel" of the Shema refers to the descendants of the twelve sons of Israel, (the name God gave to Jacob, Gen. 32:28), to the descendants collectively—the people of Israel—and to the land in Palestine where the Israelites lived.

The word *Jew* comes from Judah, one of the original twelve tribes of Israel. Later the name Judah was given to the southern region of Palestine where the people of Israel settled. First used in 2 Kings 16:6 to mean the citizens of Judah, the word *Jew* had come to mean all members of the nation of Israel by the time of the prophet Jeremiah in the sixth century B.C.E. Once in exile, a religious meaning was added to the term: Jews were different from other peoples in that they kept alive their tradition of the one true God.

By the first century C.E., *Jew* and *Israel* had become roughly synonymous terms, and in the pages of the New Testament the words are used interchangeably. Further, *Jew* contrasts with *Gentile*—any people that does not have the same national/religious quality that Jews have. *Hebrew* at times in antiquity referred to the Jewish people but nowadays almost exclusively denotes the language of the Jews.

Palestine is the name (probably as a corruption of Philistia) given by the

Romans to the territory running from Gaza on the south to Syria on the north, the land described in the early books of the Bible as Canaan, the location of the modern state of Israel.

The simple definition—Judaism is that religion practiced by Jews—does not work well because the term *Jew* has both an ethnic and a religious meaning. Certainly, Judaism in its several forms is the religion of the Jews, but not all ethnic Jews follow the tenets of Judaism. In fact, the Knesset, the parliament of the state of Israel, defines Jew in such a way that atheists may be included in the category. The question of whether the term *Jewish* has primarily an ethnic or a religious meaning has for centuries plagued Jews, their friends, and their enemies. We shall use the term in both ways, though the religious meaning will naturally predominate.

Since Judaism is intricately bound with the historical experiences of the Jewish people, the history of the Jews recounted in the following pages is necessary for a fuller understanding of that religion. As Nicholas de Lange states it:

> [T]he character of Judaism is to be sought not in ideas or beliefs but in history. This is not to say that Judaism has no ideas or beliefs, which would be patently untrue, but rather that it is the historical experience which is primary, and the ideas and beliefs in some sense flow from that experience.[1]

The basic texts of Judaism are the *Torah*, the written Law (the books of the Bible; what Christians call the Old Testament); and the *Talmud*, originally an oral law but later written down.

Each has been the subject of myriad commentaries, so in an extended sense the commentaries are also the texts of Judaism. Exposition of the primary texts will be given in the context of their historical appearance.

Beginnings in Ancient Israel

The Patriarchs

The story begins in the book of Genesis, chapter twelve, which recounts the call of Abraham, a native of the city of Ur in Mesopotamia. Abraham was told by God to leave his homeland and travel hundreds of miles to the land of Canaan, where God would make from him a great nation. Abraham heeded the call, went at age seventy-five to Canaan, and by the time of his death had fathered the son of promise, Isaac.

Although Abraham used his wife Sarah to carry out deceptions in Egypt, and while he had family difficulties with his nephew Lot, he is remembered for two things: he was the father of the Jews—the children of Abraham—and he was a person of great faith. He had so much faith, in fact, that it was counted as righteousness for him (Gen. 15:6; Rom. 4:9) and became an important symbol in Christianity as well as in Judaism. The supreme test of Abraham's faith came when God ordered him to sacrifice Isaac: at the last moment, when Abraham showed his willingness to obey God even in this act, an animal was provided as the sacrifice.

Isaac is briefly described in the Bible as a transition to the longer story of Jacob (renamed Israel), the immediate progenitor of the Jewish people. The twelve tribes of Israel were named after the sons of Jacob. The lengthy story of one son, Joseph, provides background for the removal of the Israelites from Canaan to Egypt and the subsequent four hundred years of servitude in that country. Joseph's trust in God when sold into slavery by his jealous brothers, and when victimized in Egypt, is a tribute to the righteousness the patriarchs exhibited.

Moses: Law and Covenant

At the end of the four hundred years in Egypt God raised up a deliverer in the person of Moses. Saved by his mother's subterfuge when Jewish male infants were ordered killed, Moses grew up in Pharaoh's household, became an important figure in the government, later turned against the Egyptians, spent forty years in exile after killing a man, and then returned to demand release of the people from Egyptian bondage.

After the dramatic series of plagues recounted in the book of Exodus, the last being the death of firstborn males, Moses led the people out of Egypt and into the desert regions south of Palestine, where they wandered for forty years because of their unbelief.

Early in the wanderings God revealed to Moses at Mount Sinai the code of laws that was to govern the nation. The law code, which the rabbis said contains 613 commandments (365 negative ones and 248 positive ones), marked the special relationship the Jews had with God. To this day, strictly observant Jews see the need

for following these commands, each of which is called a *mitzvot* (pl., *mitzvah*); rabbinic history is marked by controversy over the understanding and interpretation of the *mitzvah*.

Giving the law code indicated that God was in a special covenant relationship with the Jews, his chosen people. Initially described in Genesis 15 where God covenants to make a great nation from Abraham, the covenant relationship is repeated many times over in the Hebrew Bible. Each important event in Israel's history was one more mark of the covenant established with the people.

Since a covenant by definition describes a particular set of relationships that embody mutual obligations, the parties to a covenant need to act faithfully. Faithfulness (or the lack of it on the part of the covenant people) is a recurring theme in Israel's history. God, for his part, undertook to provide for the people and to establish an enduring relationship with them. For their part, the people were to carry out consistently the beliefs and practices given at Sinai, from motives of faithfulness and love. At Sinai this relationship was formally established. The people of Israel were to be "a kingdom of priests and a holy nation."

In addition to the Ten Commandments, the summation of the Law found in Exodus 20, there are three codes in the Mosaic legislation. The Book of the Covenant (Ex. 20:22–23:33) contains the stipulations that Israel agreed to observe in upholding its part of the covenant. The Priestly Code (Ex. 25–Num. 10) describes the

duties of the priests in carrying out temple worship, and was instituted right after completion of the tabernacle. The priestly line was in the family of Aaron, Moses' brother, and was aided by the Levites. Forty years later, just prior to Moses' death and the entrance into Canaan, came the Deuteronomic Code (Deut. 1–30), a series of speeches by Moses calling the people to faithfulness to God in the new land and listing the blessings and curses that come with obedience or disobedience.

The Hebrew word most often used for the Law is *Torah* (teaching), which has several referents. Specifically, Torah is the first five books of the Bible, the Pentateuch; in these books most of the specifically legal material is found. By extension Torah might also apply to the whole of the Hebrew Bible (though more often the Hebrew Bible is called *Tanakh*, an acronym formed from the Hebrew words for the Bible's three sections: law, writings, prophets). By further extension Torah might include the commentaries made on the Mosaic Law, thus embracing a very large body of material. In this chapter, Torah is most often used in its specific sense.

Periodically the covenant was renewed to remind the nation that obedience was the human necessity in covenant-keeping and to reiterate God's choice of his people for special blessing. Lack of obedience, which occurs often in the biblical texts, could lead to the loss of the land and a return to the kind of bondage experienced in Egypt. The covenant always had a blessings-cursings component in it.

Kings, Priests, Prophets

Kings

After Moses' death, the new leader, Joshua, led the people out of the wilderness and into the Promised Land (Canaan). The books of Joshua and Judges describe the various campaigns against the groups in Canaan which, though not totally successful, were sufficient to make the land into a Jewish domain. The people both kept the Law and transgressed it, producing an uneven quality in the life of the nation. During the time of the judges, a sharply contrasting period of victories and defeats, spiritual height and disobedient depth occurred. The book ends on a discouraging note of moral and political decay: Everyone did what was right in his own eyes. The Jews were in the land God had given them, but not happily so.

The way out of this, so the majority thought, was to have a king as their ruler; he could bring stability and, with it, prosperity to the land. Though this desire marked a shift away from

God as the king, God granted the request and Saul was chosen. After a good beginning, Saul turned away from God in the by-then frequent pattern of life in Israel and had the kingdom taken from him (though he did not give it up right away) and given to his successor, David.

After years of struggle, David succeeded Saul and became the king whose kingdom has since been perceived as the height of Israel's political and spiritual power. Though harassed by family turmoil and political infighting, he extended the borders of the nation to the largest they would become, was a spiritual force in the land, and through his psalms exerted an influence on the later generations of the people. In succeeding generations, David's kingship took on spiritual and eschatological overtones, often tied in with the hope of a Messiah who would come, set things right in Israel, and usher in a new age.

David's son Solomon, noted for his wisdom and wealth, initially maintained the kingdom, but during his reign the first breaks began to appear. Internal problems and Solomon's disobedience led to a divided kingdom after his death, the northern half (usually called Israel) in the hands of other than Solomon's heirs, the southern half (called Judah) in the Davidic line.

The northern kingdom lasted from the division in 931 B.C.E. to the Assyrian conquest in 722. Starting with the first king, Jeroboam, all the kings of Israel followed idolatrous ways, and were frequently at war with their neighbors. The south, Judah, had the tem- ple worship, periodic religious revivals, and some kings who were godly monarchs. But Judah also went into idolatry and was conquered by the Babylonians in 587/6 B.C.E. Both conquests meant exile for large numbers of the Jewish population.

Restoration came in the fifth century B.C.E. under Ezra and Nehemiah. The returning Jews met opposition from those whose families had not been taken into exile, had intermarried with surrounding peoples (producing the mixed people known as Samaritans, who built their own temple on Mount Gerizim, probably in the fourth century B.C.E.), and therefore did not welcome the Babylonian Jews. But the restoration was completed in Jerusalem and temple worship continued, keeping the Law and the covenant alive.

Priests

The initial place of worship for the Jews was the tabernacle, a portable house of worship used in the wilderness wanderings. Once settled in Canaan, they went ahead with plans to build a permanent temple. Denied to David, the temple was built in the reign of Solomon, and was the center of Jewish worship until the Exile and then reemerged under the restoration. The tabernacle and the temple was where God "dwelt."

Associated with the places of worship was the main function of the priesthood, animal sacrifice. Pivotal in the life of Israel, sacrifice provided the ritualistic demonstration of atonement, the means by which the sinful person could approach a holy God. The whole procedure of sacrifice, from the choosing of a spotless animal to the fellowship meal at the end, suggested the atoning nature of the system.

Entrance into the system was by means of circumcision, done by a priest on the male infant's eighth day of life, symbolizing entrance into the covenant with God, the removal of sin, and the assurance of continuation of the family line in the household of God.

Holy seasons with their appointed feasts occurred throughout the year. In addition to the Sabbath (*shabot*), the weekly day of special worship, there were seven special times. Five were associated with feasts—Passover, Pentecost, the blowing of trumpets, tabernacles (booths), and the Day of Atonement. The other two celebrated the sabbatical (seventh) year release from debts, and the Year of Jubilee (the fiftieth year) when all land was returned to its original owner. (Whether a Year of Jubilee was ever held in ancient Israel is a matter of debate.)

Three of the celebrations—Passover, Pentecost, and the Feast of Tabernacles—were pilgrimage feasts, when adult males were expected to appear before God at the temple. The Feast of Trumpets introduced the fall harvest season. The Day of Atonement, most solemn of all, was when the high priest made his annual entrance into the Holy of Holies of the temple, there to get forgiveness and restoration for the whole nation.

The ritual elements in the Law, such as sacrifices and holy days, were the means of worship by which the people sought to make up for failure to keep the moral law. But forgiveness was not automatically achieved through following the ritual; faith was necessary. Ritual without faith was ineffective, and "to obey [was] better than sacrifice" (1 Sam. 15:22). Thus, moral and ceremonial matters were mixed together in the various codes.

In addition, what modern legal systems would consider the criminal and civil codes were also a part of the moral and ceremonial, all presided over by the priests. Clearly, the Mosaic legislation saw life as a single piece, with "love your neighbor as yourself" (Lev. 19:18) and "love the LORD your God with all your heart" (Deut. 6:5) serving as the anchor posts for life.

Prophets

Along with the kings and priests were the prophets, a group of individuals through whom God made known his teaching and himself to the people. The line of prophets began with Moses and continued through ancient Israel's history.

Typically the prophet received a divine call from God to take some special message or messages to the people. All the prophets claimed inspiration from God, and therefore had authority for the messages they delivered. But there were false prophets as well as true prophets, and the people had to exercise judgment to know one from the other: the true prophet taught correct doctrine (i.e., in keeping with the Law), had his prophecy confirmed by the turn of events, and led a holy life. The false prophet failed in one or more of these categories.

The prophets brought God's message. But why was a message needed if the Law was already revealed? One reason was the prediction of future events; often these were tied to the sinfulness or faithfulness of the Jewish people, but some applied to other nations as well. Another reason was to bring about moral change in the people; the prophets frequently reminded their hearers (often in very strong language) of personal and social failings and their need to turn to God in repentance; thus, the prophets were preachers of righteousness. Too, the Law was revelation from God, but not the whole of the revelation; the prophets gave further explication of the nature of God and his ways with human beings. The message was most often delivered in preached form, occasionally aided by some symbolic action.

Exile-Diaspora-Return

As noted above, the northern kingdom fell in 722 B.C.E. and the southern kingdom in 587/6. In both instances thousands of persons were deported out of Palestine, resettled, and lived as aliens in a foreign land. Little is known about life in Assyria, the place of exile for persons from the northern kingdom, but both the biblical and Babylonian records give a fairly full account of Judah's exile. After initially serving as a forced labor supply, the Jews in Babylon were allowed to live quite normal lives, though never as full citizens. They could marry, engage in business, achieve some political role, and even correspond with those who remained in Judah. When the opportunity to return was granted by Cyrus, the Persian king who had conquered Babylon, some chose not to leave Babylon because they felt well established there.

In Babylon, the Jews adopted the Babylonian calendar, still the basis for the Jewish year, and adopted Aramaic, at that time the language of international diplomacy, as their second language. Hebrew continued in use, but most of the people in Babylon and Palestine used Aramaic as their everyday language from this time through the New Testament era and until the Arab conquest in the seventh century C.E.

Since those in exile had no access to temple worship, they were forced to think more of the Law as their source of religious guidance, though the documents mention functioning priests as well. It is possible that synagogue worship developed out of the exile experience as a subsitute for lack of access to the temple's sacrificial system. Synagogue worship precluded ritual sacrifice, forcing the worship toward the written word of the Law. The altar, which had been at the center of the temple, was replaced in the synagogue by the ark with its scrolls of scripture.

Exile hastened the absorption into Gentile life for some, while others had their faith strengthened in exile, setting the tone for the many centuries of adversity that lay ahead for the Jewish people. Perhaps no other people in history has had to face as much anti-ethnic feeling as have the Jews.

The Exile came to be known as *diaspora*, a Greek word meaning a "sowing" or "scattering," and the term applied

The triumphal arch erected by Titus, Roman general (later emperor), to commemorate his victory over the Jews in 70 C.E. William Travis

both to the exiled people and the place of exile. Most Jews over most of their history have been in diaspora. Most dispersion was forced, like that imposed by the Assyrians and Babylonians and later by the Romans, but some was voluntary, such as might be experienced through trade or commerce. By the time of Christ the Diaspora population far outnumbered that in Palestine. Diaspora and Palestinian Jews were held together by attendance at the great feasts like Pentecost (note the list of homelands in the second chapter of the New Testament book of Acts), payment of the temple tax assessed on all males worldwide, and recognition of the authority of the Jewish council in Palestine, the Sanhedrin.

The return to Judah was carried out by a small band of exiles allowed by King Cyrus to rebuild Jerusalem. Though faced with a number of difficulties, including opposition from some of the nonexiled inhabitants in Judah, the city wall and the temple were rebuilt, the Law reinstated as the normative

code, and a strong Jewish community established.

Hellenistic Period to Late Antiquity

The Maccabean Revolt

About the time of Ezra and the restoration of the temple, the Greeks were beginning their rise to prominence. In the fourth and fifth centuries B.C.E. the Greeks achieved political, intellectual, and artistic ideas and ideals that had enormous influence on Western civilization.

At the end of this period of creativity came the world conqueror Alexander (d. 323 B.C.E.). His early death caused the dissolution of his fragile empire, which was divided among his generals. Out of that milieu came the Ptolemaic power in Egypt and the Seleucid power in Syria. Among the effects of Alexander's sweep was the establishment of Greek culture in the Middle East in what has become known as the Hellenistic era.

The small Jewish communities in Palestine still had the temple as a worship center, but parallel to that was the developing synagogue worship, held both in Palestine and in the diaspora. The synagogue (Gk., assembly) was a center for prayer and learning. At the heart of the learning was the study of Torah (specifically the Pentateuch, the first five books of the Bible). Over the course of time Torah experts emerged who could interpret and apply the laws to everyday life; eventually this group created the Pharisee party.

One of the results of Hellenistic culture was the need for a translation of the Hebrew Scriptures into Greek. The translation was made in the city of Alexandria, Egypt, with its very large Jewish population, and done, according to tradition, by a group of seventy, hence the name Septuagint given to the translation. Completed about the middle of the third century B.C.E., the Septuagint was the common version of the Bible among the diaspora in Hellenistic times.

Palestine was caught between the Ptolemys and the Seleucids, subject to the control of one or the other. After a century and a half of rule, the Jews revolted. The immediate cause was the desecration of the temple by Seleucid ruler Antiochus IV, who in the year 167 B.C.E. set up an altar of Zeus in the temple and forbade Jewish rituals. The Maccabean family led the revolt against the overlords, cleansed the temple in 165, an event noted to this day in the celebration called Hanukkah, and created an independent state that lasted for more than a century. The Maccabean dynasty had control over this small state and, contrary to earlier Jewish practice, for some time combined the offices of king and high priest in the ruler. (The family name was actually Hasmon, but one of the brothers, Judah, was nicknamed "the hammer" and from this the name Maccabee was derived. In historical literature both Hasmonean and Maccabean are used to denote the family.)

The Jewish state could not long survive in face of a rising Rome, and in 63 B.C.E. the Roman control of Palestine began. No Jewish state would reappear there for two thousand years.

The Romans ruled Palestine with a fairly light touch, and during the reign

Since at least the second century B.C.E. the synagogue has played a crucial role in Jewish life. Jewish Historical Society of the Upper Midwest. St. Paul, MN

of Herod, a puppet king, extensive building was carried out in Jerusalem, the most noteworthy being a new temple, commonly called the second temple.

But many Jews chafed under Roman rule, and a revolt begun in 66 C.E. led to the destruction of the temple in the year 70; no temple ritual has since been carried out. In the wake of the destruction of the temple, rabbinic Judaism, already born before this time, came to the fore and Judaism since that era has been a religion of synagogue, Torah, and Talmud.

Varieties of Judaism to C.E. 70

With the work of Ezra and Nehemiah in rebuilding the city of Jerusalem in the last half of the fifth century B.C.E., the Jews in Palestine were encouraged to live by the rediscovered Law of Moses. Not much is known about the Judaism of the next two centuries, but by the second century B.C.E. several parties had emerged.

Perhaps the earliest were the Hasids (pious ones) who supported the work of the Maccabees in the revolt against Antiochus. From this group may have come either or both the Essenes and the Pharisees. The former group, most noted from the discovery of the Dead Sea Scrolls in the 1940s, was a sect that lived separate from the general population in tight communities led by authoritarian leaders.

The Pharisees are much better known, through the pages of the New Testament and in rabbinic Judaism. They held to a strong belief in rigorous observance of the Law and avoided contact with those who were contaminated by not keeping certain Law observances. Interpretations of the Law were carried down from one generation to the next in what were called "the traditions of the elders."

The Sadducees were a religious and social elite, associated with the temple hierarchy and priests. They did not believe in angels, resurrection, or punishment and rewards after death. The origin of the Sadducees is not clear, but they emerged sometime in the second century B.C.E.

A smaller group, the Zealots, were perhaps founded around the time of the death of Herod the Great (6 B.C.E.) as a militantly anti-Roman and pro-Torah organization whose ideology can be traced to the Maccabean Revolt. Zealots saw themselves as defenders of a pure Judaism and opponents of idolatry and collaboration. They were influential in the Jewish

revolt begun in C.E. 66, and a group of more than 900 of them committed suicide at Masada in C.E. 73 rather than surrender to the Roman siege.

The Talmud and Rabbinic Judaism

The word *rabbi* (and its variations, *rebbe*, *reb*, *rav*) is a title of respect meaning "(my) master," applied by the first century C.E. to those who were skilled in knowledge and understanding of the Law. It is likely that the rabbis as a group came out of the Pharisee party, so while not every Pharisee was a rabbi, virtually all rabbis were Pharisees.

With the fall of the temple in C.E. 70, the Sadducees as the temple party simply faded out of existence, and the Zealots, who helped bring on the revolt that led to the destruction of Jerusalem, were of little continuing influence. This left the Pharisees alone among the Jewish parties to carry on the Jewish faith in the years that followed. Through a series of circumstances they were allowed by the Romans to set up an organization (initially at Jabneh, between Jerusalem and the Mediterranean coast; later, elsewhere in Palestine), part of which reduplicated the Sanhedrin, the council that had for generations been the chief Jewish governing body.

The result was the creation of the Patriarchate, a quasigovernment that included the Sanhedrin and was recognized by Rome as speaking for the Jews in Palestine. The Patriarchate was held by the family of Gamaliel II (grandson of the Gamaliel mentioned in Acts 5 and Acts 22), the successive

Students studying the Talmud in the centuries-long tradition, at a yeshiva in the Jewish Quarter of Jerusalem's Old City. Israel Tourism Bureau

sons holding the post of *nasi* (patriarch). The line continued until C.E. 425 when Gamaliel IV died without a male successor and the Romans closed off the system. By that time the center of Jewish life had moved away from Palestine.

The posttemple Sanhedrin created the system by which the templeless Jews were to live. Emphasis was on the Law and its interpretation for various facets of life. The Sanhedrin decided on the canon of the Bible (omitting the *Apocrypha*, some books written after the time of the prophet Malachi); and set dates for the cycle of festival and fast days (the present Jewish calendar was fixed in the fourth century C.E.), transferring their observance to the synagogue and the home. They consolidated the teachings of the two schools of law interpretation, those of Shammai and Hillel, with Hillel prevailing. More precise form was given to the daily prayers. And the term *rabbi* was brought into general use, referring to a sage so recognized by

his fellows, thereby introducing rabbinic Judaism.

One of the beliefs that had long been held by the Pharisees was that in addition to the written Law, the Torah, there was also an oral law, passed down from Moses to Joshua to the prophets and thence to the sages. Much of this oral law explained and elaborated on the written Law. The Palestinian rabbis were the continuators of this oral tradition, both as receivers of the tradition and as those who gave answers to questions of interpretation of the Law for their contemporaries.

The materials were of three kinds: *halakah* (by far the largest body of material), interpretations of the Law, especially as questions were raised about the meaning of this or that commandment; *aggadah*, the non-halakhic materials such as proverbs, parables, and sermons aimed at inspiring a person to live correctly; and *midrashim*, brief commentaries on passages in the Bible.

113

With the destruction of the temple and the loss of the sacrificial system and the consequent emphasis on synagogue worship and Torah learning, pressure mounted to have the rabbinic material written down (the tradition had said it should remain in oral form). In the second century C.E. this process began in Palestine, and was completed under the supervision of Rabbi Judah (132–217). Called the *Mishnah*, this collection of precepts, decisions, and other comments, a kind of New Testament in Judaism, became the basis for rabbinic Judaism.

Parallel to these events in Palestine were developments in Babylon (Mesopotamia). Babylonian Jews, already there for centuries, had made trips to Palestine for study, but beginning in the third century C.E. they founded schools of their own at several locations in Babylon. These schools dominated Jewish religious and intellectual life for the next several centuries as the influence from Palestine faded. The *Mishnah* as compiled by the *tannaim* (teachers) in Palestine was terse and raised questions about its own interpretation. From the third to the fifth centuries C.E., the *amoraim* (speakers, explainers) in Babylon added their commentaries to the *Mishnah*; their additions are called, collectively, the *Gemara*. Together, the *Mishnah* and the *Gemara* make up the Talmud, the major source for rabbinic training from that era to the present. (A *Gemara* was created in Palestine in the same centuries as the one in Babylon, but the Palestinian Talmud is significantly shorter; the Babylonian Talmud has been the more authoritative one.)

Three-fourths of the Talmud is taken up with jurisprudence (*halakah*), and it is often difficult reading because of the disputations in the text and the labyrinthine reasoning used. So great was the respect for the tradition that very little attempt was made to achieve unity of style, and this further complicates understanding. The Talmud is divided into six orders (*seders*), each of which covers a major area of law concern and is subdivided into units called *tractates*.

To illustrate the complexity, the *tractate* which deals with the Sabbath has a section on work forbidden on the Sabbath. Thirty-nine categories of work are defined, and discussion centers on whether particular acts related to one or another of the categories is work or not: if not, the person is exempt and the act may be performed; if it is work, the person is liable and some penalty must be paid. One of the discussions on the category of sorting says this:

> Our rabbis taught: "If food of different kinds is lying in front of a man, he may sort and eat, or sort and put to one side; but he must not sort. If he does so he is liable for a sin-offering." What does this mean? Ulla said, "This is what it means: he may sort and eat on the same day, and he may sort and put to one side for consumption for the same day, but he may not sort and put to one side for consumption on the morrow. If he does so, he is liable for a sin-offering."[2]

With the creation of the Talmud, and its use as the center of study in the synagogue under the tutelage of the rabbi, the rabbinic system was put in place and remains so to the present. In place of the temple and its system of ritual was talmudic study in the hands of the rabbis. For the generations to come young Jewish boys entered the life of talmudic study and became the next generation of rabbis. The rabbi was at the center of control of the Jewish community and was looked up to as an able scholar, a sage who could provide answers to legal perplexities—the man who interpreted God to the people.

The Middle Ages

Under Islam

After the center of cultural and religious gravity shifted away from Palestine and toward Mesopotamia, the influence of the latter region continued to grow. Schools founded there were headed by leaders known as *geonim* (sing., *gaon*, excellency), who as spiritual authorities received the law questions posed by Jews in various parts of the world. Their answers were called *responsa* (responses), and these became another body of literature to study. The era from the fifth to the tenth centuries C.E. is sometimes called the gaonic era.

Perhaps the Mesopotamian center would have stayed influential even longer, but in the seventh century a new force appeared in the Middle East, Islam. Muhammad (c. 570–632) founded the new religion, and within a short time after his death it had spread around the eastern Mediterranean, across North Africa, and into Europe—to Spain, at least.

Not long after the Muslim conquest an important schism appeared in Judaism with the rise of Karaism. Probably

The Israel Museum's "Shrine of the Book" houses the original Dead Sea Scrolls, ancient manuscripts that authenticate texts of the Hebrew Bible. Israel Tourism Bureau

originating in opposition to the power of the Babylonian *geonim*, the Karaites rejected the jurisdiction of the Talmud and of rabbinic Judaism in general, extolling exclusive reliance on the Bible. Chief among the founders was the eighth-century figure Anan ben David, whose guiding principle, "search thoroughly in Scripture and do not rely on my opinion," pointed to the Bible as the sole source of law. His own opinions, however, were much like rabbinic opinions, and in some cases he took a stricter view of interpreting the commandments than the rabbis did.

New parties were founded after Anan's death, and ninth century Karaism became a conglomerate of antirabbinic groups. By the tenth century a more uniform movement had emerged with communities in Palestine, Iraq, and Iran (Persia). The academy in Jerusalem produced significant legal, biblical, and philosophical works.

Opposition came from a number of

quarters. The Karaites were opposed by the rabbis as a heretical movement, beginning with the attack by Saadiah Gaon early in the ninth century. Activities spawned by the First Crusade devastated the Jerusalem center. Karaism in Egypt languished. Moving into the Byzantine Empire in the eleventh century, Karaite communities were founded in several locations in eastern Europe. But in that same century the movement's influence diminished, and from that time to now has survived as only a tiny minority in Judaism.

Islam was relatively tolerant of other religions, but still it was difficult for the Jews to remain strong in Babylon. They had been in North Africa and Spain since Roman times, and in Spain they were destined to achieve a golden age. While under the influence of Islam, a number of Jews adopted the Arabic language and used it as the means of communication, though rabbinic studies remained tied to the Hebrew texts. Along with the general tolerance, Jews suffered some persecution under Muslim occupation.

In one place, the kingdom of the Khazars in southcentral Russia, the Jews apparently had the rule in their hands, the only Jewish state in history other than the ancient and modern states in Israel. Though at one time doubted, it is now generally agreed that in the middle of the eighth century the Khazar king, Bulan, along with many of his nobles, converted to Judaism. The kingdom remained a powerful one in its region until the eleventh century.

As for Spain, the Muslim Arabs had arrived there in the eighth century and in the ninth century had established the Cordova caliphate. Theoretically there was only one *caliph* ("successor [to Mohammad]") in the Islamic world, but rival *caliphs* occasionally appeared and such was the case in Spain. The authority of the Cordova caliphate was broken in 1034, and thereafter Muslim Spain was an agglomerate of small political units, fighting among themselves as well as against the Christian states of Castile and Aragon. The middle tier of these small states fell to Christian armies in the eleventh and twelfth centuries (Toledo in 1085, Lisbon in 1147). The fall of the southern cities (Cordova in 1236 and Granada in 1492) left only a small Muslim toehold in southernmost Spain.

During the centuries of the Muslim presence in Spain Judaism underwent further changes. The ties to the Babylonian schools were lost, as was the Aramaic language, and there was some mingling of Jews with Muslims, even in education. Rabbinic courts still settled most of the disputes among the Jewish population, but interaction with classical learning affected Jewish-educated persons. In Muslim Spain a burst of intellectual activity led to new ways of expressing Judaism.

Medieval Theology and Philosophy

Saadiah Gaon (882–942) marks both the end of the Babylonian era in Judaism and the beginning of Jewish medieval theology. His *Book of Beliefs and Opinions* set out the central doctrines of Judaism, used biblical and rabbinic citations to support his defense, argued against both Muslim and Christian beliefs, and used rational argument to state his case. Saadiah's work points to the writing soon to emerge from Spain.

The works of three important figures came out of the Spanish period. First was the *Book of the Laws*, a compendium of the Talmud done by Isaac Alfasi (1013–1103), a transitional person sometimes called a *gaon* by his disciples. Written partly in Arabic, the Alfasi text was for several generations used by Jewish students in their studies.

Judah Halevy (1075–1141) came from Muslim Spain, therefore he marks the transition of the Jewish intellectual tradition from the east to the west and, more important, the coping with the rise of Aristotelianism, a philosophy that had to be dealt with by Muslims and Christians as well as Jews.

Halevy's defense of the Jewish faith, in the *Book of the Khazars*, opposed Aristotle because Halevy believed the faith could not be defended rationally. The highest life was not the life of reason but the life of prophecy; the prophet (who alone can receive revelation) is more important than the philosopher. The genius of Judaism, he wrote, is not that it can be defended with reason, as Saadiah did, but that it is revelation from God. The Mosaic legislation has features in it that cannot be explained; since Judaism is suprarational, it cannot be explained by the intellect. Halevy was not against scientific knowledge and the use of reason, he simply denied that either science or philosophy

could adequately explain the universe, nor could they arrive at personal and social ethics.

The most influential of the medieval philosophers was Moses Maimonides (1135–1204). Though born in Cordova, Maimonides' family moved first to Fez in present-day Morocco and then in the 1160s to Cairo, where he remained for the rest of his life. By 1185 he had been appointed one of the court physicians to the Muslim ruler of Egypt, was a leader of the Cairo Jewish community, and had earned a high reputation among many in the diaspora for his handling of issues of *halakah*.

Quite in contrast to Halevy, Maimonides saw philosophy and religion pointing to the same truth, though philosophy by itself was insufficient; it needed revelation, such as at Sinai, to fully explicate matters. Thus, the Unmoved Mover of the philosophers was insufficient as a picture of God; only revelation could adequately describe God.

One of Maimonides' major works was the *Mishneh Torah*, a digest of Talmud and Torah and the accompanying literature, organized into fourteen books and resolving all conflicting interpretations (a point heavily criticized by some). The *Guide for the Perplexed* is his most famous work, an attempt to put together the findings of philosophy with the writings of the Torah. Intended for advance students of philosophy, the book sought to resolve the tensions between the moral values of Judaism and the intellectualism of philosophy. Maimonides deals with creation, providence, evil, and the biblical ceremonial law, affirming the primacy of reason even in the study of revelation.

In a third work, *Commentary on the Mishnah*, Maimonides lays out what he calls the thirteen fundamental principles of the Jewish faith, a document that probably comes closer than any other to being a Jewish creed. Along with principles on Torah, prophecy, human deeds, the messianic age, and resurrection are five principles on God, the fifth of which says:

> God is the one who should be worshipped and exalted, whose greatness should be proclaimed, and whom men should be called on to obey. We should not act thus towards anything beneath him in existence, whether angels, or stars, or spheres, or elements, or things compounded of them, for all these have been imprinted with their functions: they have no independent judgement or free-will, but only love for God. We should not adopt intermediaries through whom to approach God, but should direct our thoughts towards him and turn away from whatever is beneath him. This fifth fundamental principle is the prohibition against idolatry. The greater part of the Torah is taken up with forbidding idolatry.[3]

Though opposed by some later Jewish thinkers, he proved very influential, and some medieval Christian theologians like Albertus Magnus and Thomas Aquinas cite the *Guide*. Both Maimonides and Halevy sought to relate the traditions of Judaism with what for them was the new context in which to express their religious faith.

Kabbalah

The Jewish mystical tradition can be traced to Palestinian and Babylonian times. From the second century C.E. there was a steady development of the trend to find ways of contact with God other than the usual ways of religious practice and thought. The most important of the mystical movements is called the Kabbalah (literally translated, "reception," popularly used to refer to mystical teachings), which flourished from the end of the twelfth century. Rather than being given to visions, dreams, and other sources of revelation (there is that tendency in a form of Jewish mysticism called Hekhalot), the kabbalists saw themselves as transmitters of insights and secrets based on ancient texts, handed down to them or resulting from their own reflections on the texts.

Like most mysticisms, Kabbalah centers on a set of symbols that are used to support the claim that words cannot adequately convey truth. The words of the Bible are divinely inspired, but they symbolize truth that is beyond verbal expression. The symbols used by the earliest writers of the Kabbalah became the standard language to which later individuals and schools added their own meanings.

The chief work of the Kabbalah is the *Zohar* (Splendor), apparently compiled at the end of the thirteenth century by Moses de Leon of Spain, though attributed to the esteemed second-century C.E. rabbi, Simeon ben Yohai. The *Zohar* teaches the doctrine of the ten spheres, each called a *sefirot* (pl., *sefira*), through which God reveals himself. God in himself is *Ayn Sof*, beyond the reach of the human mind; human minds can only grasp the *sefira*. The material or lower world is the visible reflection of the spiritual world, with everything above having its counterpart below, and the two worlds influencing each other. Since humans live in both worlds they may through the mystical understanding of the Torah influence the upper world.

The *Zohar* posits a God from whom occur emanations, hence the ten spheres, with each succeeding emanation less spiritual than the preceding one. The last sphere, Kingdom, created the physical world. Through the spheres God rules the universe. Moreover, everything that exists is a part of deity, and humans can achieve union with God through moral conduct. The Jews in particular, the covenant people given the commandments, can influence the spheres and thus be involved in God's work. All souls were created at once in the creative act, and the soul which remains pure in spite of its contact with the body moves after death into the abode of the ten spheres. Impure souls must be reborn in other bodies until purity is attained. Evil is the negation of good and therefore does not exist by itself; it can be overcome by prayer, repentance, and observance of the Law.

Kabbalah influenced later Jewish history, both in a variety of messianic movements and in later expressions of mysticism, including some of those in the twentieth century.

Life in Christian Europe

The Jews in Iberia (Spain and Portugal) were known as Sephardim, a word taken from Obadiah 20 and mistakenly identified with Spain. The Sephardim developed a language of their own, Ladino, a Hebrew-Spanish combination written in Hebrew letters. They further developed differences from other Jews in some details of synagogue worship, the wearing of phylacteries, and several dietary matters. Today the Sephardim number about five hundred thousand, less than 5 percent of the world's 13 million Jews.

While the Sephardim were settling in Spain, other Jews were moving into northern Europe. They moved into France (eighth century), Germany (ninth century), and England (eleventh century), preparing the way for a shift of focus away from the Iberian peninsula after the twelfth century, when it became more difficult for Jews to live there, and for the development of another group in Jewish life, the Ashkenazim. The Ashkenazim took their name from a great-grandson of Noah (Gen. 10:3), created the Yiddish language, a Hebrew-German combination written in Hebrew characters, and came to predominate throughout non-Iberian Europe. Most Jews today, including most American Jews, are among the 11 million Ashkenazim.

As the Jews settled in northern European cities, they came to suffer persecution, isolation, and expulsion. Always an outsider group in Christian Europe, the Jews, after 1100, were treated quite harshly. This period included the two centuries of the Crusades, the attempts by Europeans to retake the holy lands then under Muslim control. One by-product of the original call for the Crusades, issued by Pope Urban II in 1095, was sporadic attacks on Jews in Europe, attacks that came to mark the whole Crusade era.

Sabbath at the Western ("Wailing") Wall of the Second Temple. Jewish tradition requires separation of the sexes during prayer.

Several accusations were made against the Jews. One was called "blood-libel," a contention that Jews engaged in ritual murder of Christian boys for eating or for use in some Passover rites. Another accusation was host desecration, the belief that Jews stole the bread consecrated for the Christian Eucharist. Jews were at times accused of bringing outbreaks of the plague, a sign, it was thought, of God's displeasure with them for their failure to accept the Christian faith. In some parts of Europe, Italy for example, the accusations and persecution were relatively mild.

Jews went through a changed economic position in the Middle Ages. Gradually divorced from the soil, earlier in Babylon and now in Europe, the Jews were virtually forced into the towns and cities. While they originally held a wide range of artisan occupations in urban areas, they gradually moved into trade, and the Jewish merchant became a common feature of European town life. In turn forced out of trade by the rise of the Italian trading republics, the Jews became bankers and moneylenders. Rabbinic teaching opposed the practice of taking usury, but Jews were involved in the system. By the fourteenth century Christian usurers were present and some Jews were driven down to the pawnbroker level. Technically, the Jews were royal serfs, much used by the rulers as sources of money. While many Jewish artisans continued to ply their crafts in the Jewish communities, contact outside the communities was mostly in finance.

With the increase in power of the Christian feudal monarchies, and the general hostility against the Jews, it was inevitable that they would be excluded from some areas. Exclusion was not new in Jewish history, of course, but now it was more extensive. England expelled its Jewish population in the year 1290; France, or at least parts thereof, expelled Jews in the fourteenth century. No general expulsion occurred in Germany due to the fragmented nature of the German state, but many German principalities expelled Jews in the fourteenth century.

The culmination came in Spain with the decree of expulsion issued in 1492 (Portugal issued its decree five years later). Jews had lived in Spain for centuries, but with the appearance of the Inquisition in the 1480s anti-Jewish sentiment intensified. The Inquisition could only deal with converted Jews (called *Conversos*, or New Christians, or *Marranos* [the Spanish word for swine]), many of whom were thought by the church to be insincere in their turn to the Christian faith. The *Marranos* were widely persecuted, some were put to death by the state, and the anti-Jewish feeling led to the expulsion decree.

Expulsion was never complete in any of the countries where it took place, and even after expulsion some Jews drifted back to the various countries in succeeding generations. But we dare not underestimate the disruptive effects of the expulsions, for many Jews fled to other areas: some back to the Middle East, others into southern Europe, and still others into central and eastern Europe. From the expulsions came ultimately yet another shift of the locus of Jewish population, this time from western Europe to eastern Europe, laying the groundwork for the large Jewish populations in Poland and Russia in the eighteenth and nineteenth centuries.

Early Modern Times

The Ghetto

Once the expulsions had taken place in Europe, a number of other developments occurred, among them the creation of the ghetto. Though the origin of the term is disputed, it probably dates from 1516 when Venice ordered all Jews into one sector of the city, the ghetto (It., *gheta*: foundry). The term spread throughout Italy, and in the sixteenth and seventeenth centuries became the common name for the segregated Jewish quarter so prevalent in the cities of Europe. Most segregated quarters had similar features: the area was walled off, often with only a single point of entrance; Jews were restricted in their movements outside the ghetto and were usually required to be in the quarter by sundown; since the ghettos typically remained fixed in size any population increase meant overcrowded conditions for the residents. Jews were not allowed to own real estate in other parts of the city. Often, Jews were required to wear either a badge or some distinctive form of clothing so that they were easily identified by non-Jews.

Repopulation began in Europe in the seventeenth century, as Jews both moved back to regions from which they had been expelled and out of ghetto areas. By the late eighteenth century many ghettos, in the strict legal sense, began to fall, though Jewish quarters remained a common feature well into the twentieth century, and anti-Jewish feelings persisted.

The ghetto was revived by the Nazis in the Second World War, but not with the aim of establishing permanent quarters for Jews. The ghettos in Polish and Lithuanian cities served as points from which the Jews were transported to the death camps. Despite the desperate situation, Jewish religious and cultural institutions were maintained. The rebellion in the Warsaw ghetto in 1943 marked a time of heroism in Jewish history. Virtually all the ghettos were closed by 1944. Since that time the term *ghetto* has come to refer to an area where any oppressed people reside.

The Levant

In the wake of restrictions on Jewish life contained in the Lateran decrees of the twelfth and thirteenth centuries, and the persecution and expulsions of the thirteenth and fourteenth centuries, a significant segment of the Jewish population in Europe shifted back to the eastern Mediterranean, a region sometimes called the Levant ("rising [of the sun]"). By this time several Turkish groups, already Muslims, had settled in the area, and beginning in 1300 the Ottoman Turks began to create an empire that would last into the twentieth century. While the Ottomans were not pro-Jewish, their treatment of Jews was better than what Jews were experiencing at the time in Christian Europe. When Constantino-ple fell to the Turks in 1453, the Ottoman Empire was in place and in it was a sizable Jewish population. Most of those who moved to the east were Sephardic Jews, whose numbers were increased in the sixteenth century by *Marranos* fleeing the Spanish and Portuguese inquisitions.

Some of the Jews in Ottoman Turkey held high government posts, others established flourishing communities, and a revival of rabbinic learning occurred in the sixteenth century. Chief among the rabbinic scholars was Joseph Caro (1488–1575), an émigré from Spain. His monumental work on Jewish law, *The House of Joseph*, was based on a number of previous codes. A shorter version, consisting of only those rulings that Caro felt were binding, was issued in 1564. This latter work, the *Shulhan Arukh* (*Prepared Table*), became the authoritative code of law in the Jewish world, and remains so at the present time.

While working on the *Shulhan Arukh* Caro moved to Safed, a city in the Galilee of Palestine. This small city had become a center for cloth manufacture, with ten thousand Jews residing there in the sixteenth century. More importantly, talmudic schools were established with an emphasis on kabbalistic studies in an atmosphere of mysticism and messianism. Collections, organization, and interpretations of the earlier mystical authors were produced.

The culmination of this interest in mysticism came in the work of Isaac Luria (1534–72), who arrived in Safed after a career in business and then seven years of study of the *Zohar*. For two years he taught a handful of disciples who circulated his teachings after his death.

At the heart of Luria's view is his belief that creation was in part a negative act; that is, God (the *Ayn Sof* of Kabbalah) withdrew within himself in order to create (the contraction is called *tzimtzum*). Divine light was sent into empty space and into vessels that shattered because they could not bear the light. The shattering divided the cosmos into two realms: the upper realm of divine light and the lower realm of the forces of evil. Even the lower realm has some sparks of light needed to maintain itself, since evil is not self-sustaining. The history of the universe, and of humanity in particular, is the process of releasing the divine sparks from the evil realm, sending them back to the divine light. When all the sparks are released the universe will be whole again. Human beings play a special role in the process (called *tikkun*: repair), for they are able by righteous acts to release the sparks. But they are also able by unrighteous acts to send more divine sparks into the evil realm; Adam did this when he fell, and the people of Israel did this when they made the golden calf. Thus, human acts have cosmic significance.

Israel and the Law hold special significance because, as God's chosen people, Israel uses God's chosen means of regulation, by which the divine sparks will be released. Luria and his followers felt that they were near the end of the process of *tikkun*, and therefore the messianic age was about to appear.

Messianism at its most intense was reached with Shabbatai Zevi (1626–76), a Sephardic Jew from Smyrna whose messiahship was proclaimed in 1665 by "prophet" Nathan of Gaza, his most important follower. Imprisoned by Turkish authorities in 1666, Zevi's quarters became a messianic court. Zevi was denounced by a Polish kabbalist and, given the choice of death or conversion to Islam by the Ottoman authorities, chose the latter. While this meant the loss of some followers, others explained it as a necessary act for the messiah in his fight against evil. His later life spent as both Muslim and Jew, Zevi handed on his teachings and some groups continued belief in his messiahship after he died.

A century later, messianism was given a bad name with the career of Jacob Frank (1726–91), who proclaimed himself the incarnation of Shabbatai Zevi and the second person of the Trinity. Frank and his followers were accused of indulging in licentious orgies. Traditional Jews disputed against the Frankists, Frank was imprisoned for thirteen years, he and his followers received Christian baptism, and he spent the last years of his life in Germany, still subscribing to the Shabbatean tradition.

Poland

Little is known about the Jews in eastern Europe in the Middle Ages, though there were some communities there. Poland, attacked by the Mongols in the thirteenth century, turned to Jews in German lands for help, and the result was an increase in Jewish emigration to Poland. In 1264, King Boleslav issued a charter of liberties for Jews who would come and settle in his lands; such charters became the norm for later Jewish settlements. By 1500, perhaps fifty thousand Jews lived in Poland (actually Poland-Lithuania, a confederation after 1569 and a major power in the sixteenth and seventeenth centuries) and by 1650 the number had increased to five hundred thousand. Virtually all these Jews were Ashkenazim. In fact, most Jews in the world today are descendants of these Jews in Poland.

Jews were often employed by the Polish and Lithuanian monarchs and nobles as fiscal agents and managers of estates. Some noblemen created private towns; often these were run by Jews and frequently had a majority of Jews in their populations. The means of administration of the Jews was through the community (*kehillah*) board, which collected taxes for the (Polish) government and provided educational and other facilities for Jewish life. Regional councils made decisions for the various Jewish communities, and twice a year the Council of the Four Lands met to allocate finances and discuss ordinances.

In this relatively prosperous environment, Jewish scholarship thrived. Reconciling conflicting rabbinic texts by the method known as *pilpul* ("pepper") was a common feature of talmudic study in this era, though its labyrinthine intricacies were sometimes branded as oversubtle. Collections of halakhic texts were made and commentaries on the *Shulhan Arukh* were written.

In the midseventeenth century a series of uprisings affected the Jews. In 1648 Cossacks led by Chmielnicki created widespread havoc as they fought against the nobles and attacked Jews as representatives of the nobles. Sweden and Russia, along with Ukrainians, were drawn into the fray in the 1650s and perhaps one-fourth of the Jewish population was destroyed. After this, life was more tenuous for the Jews of Poland, yet they increased in population in the eighteenth century.

Poland went through continuing decline in the eighteenth century, finally being divided up by Austria, Prussia, and Russia in the 1770s and 1790s. But Jews in Lithuania fared quite well, and a new center for Jewish life and scholarship developed at Vilna, where Elijah ben Solomon Salman (1720–97; known as the "Vilna Gaon") lectured on a wide range of subjects and wrote commentaries on both the Bible and the Talmud. Once again, just as Jewish fortunes in one area diminished, they picked up elsewhere.

As life in Poland deteriorated more and more, Jews felt confined to the small towns where most of them lived. From this experience life developed in the *shtetl*, a Yiddish word meaning "small town." *Shtetl* life was common not only in Poland but throughout eastern Europe after Poland was partitioned by the hostile powers. In isolated communities, cut off from the surrounding culture and led by their rabbis, the inhabitants lived in a degree of autonomy but always subject to threats from the outside.

Hasidism

This form of Jewish piety originated in the Ukraine, but achieved its greatest influence among the *shtetl* Jews in Poland. Founded by Israel ben Eleazer (1700–60), popularly known as the "Besht," Hasidism taught that devotion, zeal, and heartfelt prayers are more acceptable to God than great learning. Opposed to asceticism and self-denial, but not to humility or modesty, the hasidim (pious ones) made joy a central virtue: one should perform the *mitzvah* (commandments of the Torah) with fervor and enthusiasm.

An elderly Hasid makes his way down one of the streets in Safed, Israel, a city important in the Jewish mystical tradition.

One of the central features of Hasidism was belief that cleaving (*devekut*) to God was necessary in all areas of life, and available for all classes of persons, not just an intellectual or spiritual elite. Since divine sparks were in everything, even mundane physical actions like eating could be done with *devekut*. The highest form of *devekut*, though, was in the act of prayer; the greater the concentration in prayer, the greater the cleaving, and the higher up the rungs of spiritual attainment one could go. Some of the hasidic masters gave specific advice on how a person achieved *devekut* in the synagogue service:

> You have to go step by step in prayer, not using up all your strength right at the beginning. Begin slowly, and when you reach the midle of the service attach yourself to God in a more intense way. Then you should be able to say all the words of prayer, even at a quickened pace.[4]

A special feature of Hasidism was the *zaddik*, a holy man with greater access to God than average people. The *zaddik*, usually called *rebbe*, rose to prominence in the last half of the eighteenth century, and eventually the role became a dynastic one. About half of the Jews in Poland were affected by Hasidism, and it had some strength elsewhere in eastern Europe.

The movement lost some of its vitality in the nineteenth century, but hasidic communities are found presently in both the United States and Israel.

Modern Times

Emancipation and Its Consequences

The eighteenth century saw an important change in Jewish-Christian relations. The old view from the Jewish side was summed up in the word *exile*: Jews were living in the diaspora until God granted them redemption in a return to Zion. From the Christian side the view was summed up in the phrase "wandering Jew," that is, Jews were doomed to live in exile until the second coming of Christ. Each view acted as an effective rationalization of the situation where communities of Jews lived in Christian nations.

In the wake of the eighteenth-century Enlightenment, however, some began to question whether the Gentile nations should keep Jews in a permanent minority status. On September 28, 1791, the French National Assembly, the new legislature created in the French Revolution, removed the legal restrictions in France applying to Jews and Judaism. This removal is known as the Emancipation.

By about 1860 much of western and central Europe had followed France's lead and emancipated the Jews. Officially, this meant the end of religious hostility—though in reality this was not always the case. In some places the religious hostility was replaced by political anti-Semitism: since Jews are members of another "nation," they can be treated as foreigners within our domain. This question—Are Jews a people (ethnic group), or are they adherents of a religion?—has been a major issue wherever Jews have lived since the time of the Emancipation, and is still not resolved, not even in the state of Israel.

In the West, the breakup of Jewish religious solidarity found expression in the formation of sects or denominations, much like Protestantism in the Christian religion.

In eastern Europe—Tsarist Russia and the former Polish territories—the older repressive policies continued through the nineteenth century. In 1804 the tsar created a "Pale of Settlement," an area in western Russia designated as the only area where Jews could reside; travel or other movement out of the pale required government permission. In this situation the Jews living in the *shtetl* became the stereotype. From time to time, notably worsening toward the end of the century, unprovoked attacks (called *pogroms*) on Jews led many Jews to emigrate out of tsarist lands. Also in the east, radical political views surfaced among some of the Jews as they sought for ways to cope with their suppressed status.

Judaism in America

The first record of Jews in America noted the arrival of a group of Sephardic Jews in New Amsterdam (New York City) in 1654. Others came to Newport, Rhode Island, and Charleston, South Carolina. In all, there were fewer than a thousand Jews in America at the time of the American Revolution, and no rabbis on the North American mainland, though there were three in the New

World. The colonial Jews had a strong emphasis on community, a carryover from their European background. Further, they were heavily Americanized, with some loss of Jewish practices.

Reform Judaism

Changes in the composition and attitudes of American Jews came with the arrival of German Jewish immigrants. Most of the immigrants were Ashkenazi, and the increase of Jewish population from about three thousand in 1820 to two hundred fifty thousand in 1880 consisted mostly of German immigrants and their offspring. In contrast to the colonial Sephardic immigrants, who were mostly merchants and traders, the German immigrants were often shopkeepers and peddlers. Such trades meant a more mobile population, resulting in the spread of German Jews across the new nation into the heartland cities. By 1848 the approximately fifty congregations in the United States were mostly German, and usually led by reform-minded rabbis.

The rabbis who came with the immigrants brought with them the reform ideas derived in part from the situation created by Emancipation: Could one be both a Jew and a full member of some nation at the same time? Since the Jewish religious laws advocated separation, it was difficult to be both. Further, biblical criticism was making its beginnings early in the nineteenth century and some of the German rabbis were responsive to it.

The result was the creation of Reform Judaism, one of the "denominations" in the modern era. Reform Judaism changed the nature of synagogue ser-

vices to conform fairly closely to a Protestant model. Then, traditional Jewish education, the study of Torah and Talmud, was replaced with modern schools. *Bar mitzvah*, the entry into adult life, was changed into something resembling Christian confirmation. Finally, the very basis of Jewish life, the Bible, was attacked as many of the Reform rabbis dropped belief in the Bible as revelation.

A part of the reason for the change was the loss of the Jewish community as the center of Jewish life. Up to this time, the rabbi was most often seen as the community leader, and in fact a rabbi was not needed to conduct the traditional synagogue service. In America the community as a separate entity was no longer needed, and the rabbis became heads of the synagogues or, the common term among Reform Jews, the temples.

In their transition to what they felt was needed in the post-Emancipation world, Reform Jews faced two problems. One was the status of the Law. Reform typically said that Judaism was progressive, so the old Law need not be taken literally. It had much symbolic meaning, but science could also help in one's understanding of it. The other problem was the status of the Jew. If Jews were a people then they had to continue a separate existence because they were in exile. If Jews were followers of a religion then that religion was a denomination more or less like other denominations in the United States. Reform Judaism chose the latter view. Then what of the diaspora? Was it punishment for sins? No, the diaspora meant the

Jerusalem, the city of Peace. The Jaffa Gate is in the foreground, the Temple Mount in the center and the Mount of Olives can be clearly seen in the background.

dispersing of Jews for the spread of the true faith.

By the end of the century Reform Judaism had its own organization of synagogues, a theological seminary, and a conference of rabbis. And the German Jews who formed the backbone of Reform Judaism had moved up the socioeconomic scale. In both regards—economic success and religious change—they had adapted to the American scene.

Conservative and Orthodox Judaism

The Pittsburgh Platform, a summary of Reform teaching issued in 1885, marked Reform Judaism's break from the past as genuine; even God was called the "God idea." But three issues faced Reform Judaism, in spite of its overwhelming success. One, not all American Jews accepted the Reform changes; some thought they were too deep a break with the Jewish past. Two, among Reform Jews themselves items like the continued practice of circumcision and the ban on intermarriage meant they still had some attachment to the concept of the Jews as a people. Three, beginning in 1880 a large influx of Jewish immigrants came from eastern Europe, many of whom were orthodox in their beliefs and resistant to Reform ideas.

Into the situation stepped the Conservatives, who attempted to walk a middle road between traditional Judaism and what they felt was the too-modern approach of Reform. The Conservatives, who date from the 1880s, had several major thrusts to their thinking. While accepting the idea that the Bible was not revelation, they asserted that they would remain faithful to the Mosaic Law and ancestral traditions. They argued that rabbinical literature was worth studying, not merely as a historical matter but because it had relevance to the contemporary world. Such study meant that Hebrew education—in the language and in the rabbinic material—was a necessity for the continuation of Jewish life. Like the Reform movement, the Conservatives also formed an association of synagogues, a theological seminary, and a conference of rabbis.

One of the compelling motives for the Conservative approach was the large number of eastern European immigrants who arrived after 1880. Between 1880 and 1920 some two million Jewish immigrants came to the United States, the overwhelming number of them of Polish and Russian background. Most of these were Orthodox Jews. They accepted the written law, Torah, as revelation from God, and the oral law, Talmud, as providentially guided by

God and therefore the authoritative understanding of how the Torah should be practiced. They opposed the changes brought about in Reform Judaism and adhered to the practices of the *Shulhan Arukh* as the normative way of Jewish life. They felt modern Jewish approaches were deviations from the divinely ordered way.

The Conservatives, many of them German in background, were faced with the question of how to win over these coreligionists. To turn to Reform Judaism was too radical, given the traditional beliefs of many of the eastern Europeans. Some halfway measures, as outlined above, could save some of the Orthodox.

The Conservatives won many of the Orthodox to their side, at the expense of the influence of the Reform among American Jews. The effect of the eastern European immigration was to shift the influence in American life away from German control and toward an eastern European control, and to curtail the modernizing effects of Reform Judaism so that more of the traditions prevailed. Even the Reform movement was affected, because in the 1930s it issued a revision of the Pittsburgh Platform that moved more toward traditional language, and toward Hebrew education also.

Orthodoxy was also a loser in the battle for Jewish minds, because it became a smaller segment of American Jewry with each passing decade. Some Orthodox modified their orthodoxy between the two world wars, i.e., they were Americanized. Perhaps they would have continued to decline, or to modify in the Conservative direction, except that the Holocaust, the founding of the state of Israel, and a post–Second World War immigration led to an Orthodox revival.

Currently, Conservative Judaism claims the most adherents in the United States, Reform is the next-largest group, and the Orthodox are third. A large number of American Jews are unaffiliated.

Zionism and the State of Israel

Nineteenth Century

Nationalism burst onto the international scene in the wake of the American and French revolutions in the late eighteenth century. The revolutions throughout Latin America, the European revolts in 1830 and 1848, and the unification movement in Italy, Germany, and elsewhere were signs of the era. Coupled with Jewish emancipation, and the long-standing tradition about Return, the feelings of nationhood led some Jews into thinking about a homeland. Of course, the Jewish desire to be seen as a religion and not an ethnicity ran counter to this trend, and provided some fuel for anti-Zionism.

Nationalism and emancipation provided the atmosphere for the growth of anti-Semitism. The term dates from the 1870s, coined by a German journalist, Wilhelm Marr, who believed that German history in his time was a struggle between Semitic aliens and native Teutonic stock, with the aliens winning. In Germany in 1878 a Christian Social party was organized with a specifically anti-Semitic platform. The

1880s saw a number of anti-Semitic congresses held, and from the middle of that decade the "Jewish question" was a recognized political issue throughout western and central Europe. Politicians in both France and Germany achieved some success with political anti-Semitism. In Russia, which included large numbers of Jews in both Polish- and Russian-speaking areas, anti-Semitic feeling was manipulated to mount pogroms against Jewish settlements from the early 1880s on.

Jews had always lived in Palestine, from Roman times to the nineteenth century. In the midnineteenth century some increase in immigration into Palestine, from southeastern Europe, took place. Further, since the Western powers moved more and more into Ottoman affairs at the time, the natural concern on the part of European Jews for their compatriots in Palestine increased.

These concerns expressed themselves in a number of organizations whose aim was to support Jews wherever they were being oppressed. Some of these began to see a Palestinian homeland as a natural outlet for Jews. A network of Hovevei Zion (lovers of Zion) societies were in place by the last half of the century. Their advocates felt that emancipation was not working and that a homeland fit the long-standing belief in Return. The societies spread throughout Europe and the Middle East in the 1880s and 1890s.

Zionism

The concerted effort to settle Jews in Palestine and there create a homeland for them grew out of the forces noted above. Among the thinkers making Zionist proposals was Leon Pinsker (1821–91). Having studied law and medicine at the University of Odessa in Russia, for some years he promoted a movement known as Haskalah. This movement attempted to unite Jewish literature with the surrounding European culture by using European secular literary forms. Led by people known as *haskilim* (enlighteners), the movement had implications for education, for the use of science, and for social action.

Pinsker moved away from Haskalah in the 1870s and in 1882 published *Autoemancipation*, a Zionist tract. Anti-Semitism, he wrote, is "demonopathy," an irrational fear of the stranger, made worse by the fact that Jews were everywhere guests, not hosts. A "ghost people" without a home, the Jews attracted jealousy by their economic success, and their political powerlessness made them ideal victims. Religion is not the distinguishing feature of modern Jews; what anti-Semitism hurts is their esteem and dignity as a people. Drastic changes must be made. Since Jews could not depend on the goodwill of Europeans, they must emancipate themselves (hence the book title) by finding a homeland of their own.

Much more influential was *The Jewish State*, published in 1896 by Theodore Herzl (1860–1905), the father of Zionism. Like Pinsker, Herzl said that Jews must obtain a homeland, preferably Palestine. In contrast to Pinsker, Herzl argued for large-scale colonization since the current small efforts seemed ineffective. In the homeland, Jews must create a just economic system as an example to the world and for their own sake. Herzl also felt getting international backing for the move to Palestine was necessary. He believed the European powers would cooperate because it was in their interest to solve the Jewish problem, and he wanted to get a charter from the Ottoman ruler to legitimate the Jewish state.

Largely through Herzl's efforts, the first World Zionist Congress (WZC) met in Basel, Switzerland, in 1897. In 1901 the Jewish National Fund was created for the purpose of purchasing land and providing money for immigrants. Herzl worked hard at negotiations with the Ottoman sultan, but no charter was given. Internal splits plagued the WZC, and opponents of Zionism continued to voice their opinions. Still, progress was made. The Jewish community in Israel grew from twenty-four thousand in 1880 to eighty-five thousand in 1914, by which time forty-three agricultural settlements had been established in Palestine (some of them the communal kind known as *kibbutzim*, the first of which started in 1910), a new Jewish city, Tel Aviv, had been founded (1909), and schools, political parties, and the press were in operation.

While Herzl's hope of a fully recognized Jewish state was not realized in his lifetime, the British government issued the Balfour Declaration in 1917 and that became the basis for the Jewish state. Though widely disputed, it remains the international basis for the existence of Israel.

The Balfour Declaration was followed by the League of Nations Mandate in

1920. England was placed in control of Iraq, Transjordan, and Palestine, each of which was listed as a provisionally independent nation. Article Four of the mandate created the Jewish Agency, the means used to continue to provide for the presence of Jews in Palestine through the creation of the necessary infrastructure for a Jewish community.

The increasing presence of Jews in Palestine created increased tension with the Arab inhabitants. By 1933 the Jewish population numbered two hundred twenty thousand, and when Hitler came to power in that year further pressure was put on European Jews to seek asylum in the homeland. Jewish settlements and industries provoked clashes with Arabs. In 1936 the Arabs called a general strike and armed violence on both sides increased, despite the thousands of British soldiers in the region.

In May 1939 the British government issued a white paper, a blow to Jewish interests in Palestine. Jewish immigration for the following five years was to be limited to seventy-five thousand, bringing the number of Jewish residents to about one-third of the total population of Palestine. Further transfers of Arab land to Jews were restricted. Since the white paper came just at the beginning of the massive Jewish exodus from Europe, the Zionists saw it as a betrayal of the Balfour Declaration and the League of Nations Mandate, and the announcement became the starting point for struggle against the British.

The wartime and immediate postwar eras did not alleviate the difficulties faced in Palestine. Of the one hundred seventy-five thousand Jews who volunteered for service in the British army operating in the North African theater, only twenty-five thousand were accepted, the British apparently fearing to arm and train Jews who might engage in future hostilities in Palestine. After the war ended the British maintained their restrictive immigration regulations, and more conflict began, with Jewish paramilitary organizations fighting both Arabs and the British.

In the spring of 1947 the British turned the matter over to the fledgling United Nations, whose committee report in November recommended partition of Palestine into a Jewish state and an Arab state. Early in 1948 the British announced they were pulling out of Palestine on May 14. Shortly before midnight on that date David Ben-Gurion, chairman of the Jewish Agency, proclaimed the state of Israel. Within minutes the United States recognized the new state, and within a short time Israel was fighting a number of Arab nations.

Relations between Israel and the Arab nations have been difficult since the creation of the state of Israel. The hostilities of 1947 and 1948 ended in a truce, which is still the technical relationship between Israel and the Arab states, with the exception of Egypt, which in 1978 concluded a peace treaty with Israel known as the Camp David Accord. War broke out again in 1956, 1967, and 1973. Terrorist acts and preemptive strikes have been constants in the area. After the 1967 war, Jewish occupation of the Gaza Strip and the West Bank served to further

The Knesset, Israel's parliament building, symbolizing Israel's nationhood, stands on one of the many hills in Jerusalem. Israel Tourism Bureau

exacerbate relations with the Arabs. Very recently, the Palestinian *intifada* (uprising) has led to more bloodshed.

The importance of the state of Israel is hard to overestimate. Though some Orthodox Jews do not see it as the Return promised in the prophetic books of the Bible, most Jews understand the presence of a Jewish state as a major turn in the history of the Jewish people. Both Christians and Jews, though with differing interpretations, have welcomed the new nation. Jews around the world, especially those in the United States, have contributed much money, time, and energy into building up Israel, and they have provided enormous emotional support for Israel's existence. Surrounded as it is by hostile states, Israel is dependent on world Jewry for continued help.

The Holocaust

Adolf Hitler came to power on January 30, 1933. Within three months the German parliament began instituting a series of laws that by 1938 had the effect of severely restricting the lives of Jews. The culmination of the restrictions came in an event in November 1938 known as Crystal Night. A member of the German legation in Paris had been shot and killed by a Jew, and in retaliation the attack of Crystal Night was aimed at Jewish businesses and synagogues. Following the attack the government levied a one-billion-mark penalty on the Jews in Germany. By this time some two hundred thousand of the five hundred thousand Jews who had been in Germany as of 1930 had fled the country. Eventually, about half the prewar population got out of Germany.

Soon after World War II began with the invasion of Poland on September 1, 1939, instructions were given to move Jews around as the military authorities deemed necessary. Each Jewish community had appointed to it a council of Jewish elders whose job it was to carry out German orders. The wearing of armbands by Jews and the creation of ghettos also took place in Poland. Germany's invasion of Russia in June 1941 included plans for the killing of Jews in territory wrested from the Russians. Mass killings were carried out by units called *Einsatzgruppen*. These units incited anti-semitism wherever they went and used local people to help them as much as possible. Most of the killings took place in ravines, some of them dug by the victims. In all, aided by collaborators and the German armed forces,

Yad Vashem, Israel's memorial to the six million Jews murdered in the Nazi holocaust. Israel Tourism Bureau

about two million Jews were killed by the *Einsatzgruppen*.

At the Wannsee Conference in suburban Berlin in January 1942, plans were laid out for the "final solution." The chief means for extermination became the death camp, euphemistically called "resettlement." Between the end of 1941 and the summer of 1942 six death camps, all in Poland, came into operation. The largest camp, and the one that symbolizes the Holocaust, was Auschwitz. Resettlement occurred as quickly as possible without impairing essential war work; even the death camps had forced-labor camps connected with them where those who still had some strength were compelled to work. By October 1943 over five million Jews had been murdered. In all, about eight hundred thousand Jews escaped from Nazi-occupied Europe, approximately one in seven of the prewar population.

The Nazi invasions of Poland and Russia brought about five million Jews under their rule. The Judenrat (council of Jewish elders), successor to the traditional *kehillah*, was forced not only to carry out the German orders but also to care for the sick and needy and try to maintain some form of education. Most of the Jews were herded into urban ghettos, heavily crowded and made more so by the additional thousands sent in from the countryside. Rabbis relaxed the traditional halakhic rulings on food in order to spare as many as possible. Recreational and cultural activities continued as the various councils were able to provide them. In 1941 Oneg Shabbat came into being, a clandestine archival society that ended up creating many documents as a record of the Holocaust.

Anxiety and foreboding characterized the Jews as they thought about resettlement. The foreboding was confirmed when those who left for resettlement seemed to enter a void; that the transport was to mass murder was too bizarre to be believed. The Jewish underground made the first reports about mass extermination, but not everyone believed the reports. Some word was sent out to the Allied governments as early as May 1942. In December of that year the "Big Three" (the United States, Britain, and Russia) issued a document condemning the extermination of the Jews, but not mentioning death camps or gassing installations. The Europa Plan of 1943 and 1944 failed to get the Allies involved even in bombing Auschwitz or the rail lines leading to it.

The final tally of six million Jews killed by Nazi Germany led to the need to cope with such a horrific experience. How was this to be seen in the context of Judaism? Auschwitz was more than raising again the problem of theodicy—Why does God allow suffering in the world?—it seemed to stand out uniquely from the rest of Jewish experience, the "catastrophe" different from all other Jewish suffering.

A variety of views have been offered in explanation of the Holocaust. One contends that the Jews died for the sins of humankind as God's suffering servant and sacrificial lamb. To save what? Western civilization. Another view sees the issue as the 614th commandment: that God commands his people to survive. A third view maintains that the Jewish response to Auschwitz should be like Job's, i.e., although Job did not know where God was in his situation (at least not until the end), yet he believed in God. The hidden God was actually present as savior and redeemer, and so he was, inexplicably, in the Holocaust. Another solution is to see God as either unloving or impotent, which means giving up on the traditional view of a sovereign, immanent God. More radical is the belief that the sovereign, immanent God is "dead." In this case, Auschwitz is the ultimate refutation of belief in a providential God who acts in history.

Such despairing views are countered by that of Elie Wiesel, survivor of four concentration camps. Though God was silent, still he was there. Rather than asking, where was God? we should be asking, where was humanity? It should be asked not only of the death dealers at the camps, but also of those who in wartime turned a deaf ear, and of those who after the war mistreated the survivors. The suffering was caused by human beings for whom judgment awaits. As to those who suffered, God was there for them in the midst of the pain. And the carnage stopped. We wish it could have stopped sooner or better yet, never have started, but regardless, it did stop. The Jews were slaves in Egypt for four hundred years; God's intervention on their behalf was not immediate, but his intervention came.[5]

In recent years three issues have galvanized the Jews of the world, helping them maintain a strong sense of peoplehood and, for some, a strong sense of their role as a covenant people who espouse a particular religion. One of the issues is the Holocaust, whose study was stronger after the 1960s than in the years immediately following World War II. A second issue is the fragile and difficult situation for the state of Israel, surrounded by hostility but now into its fifth decade of existence. The third issue, probably now on its way to resolution (unlike the other two issues that will likely continue to provoke interest for many years to come) is the plight of Soviet Jews. Now that the eastern European regimes, including the Soviet Union, are going through massive changes and the Soviets are allowing more emigration, the situation has eased.

Jewish Beliefs and Practices

Beliefs

It is often argued that Judaism is not a religion of doctrines but of practices. While this argument has force, especially in light of the wide range of beliefs held not just by lay members of synagogues and temples but by rabbis also, it seems right to describe a few of the beliefs that have typified Jewish history, especially in rabbinic Judaism since that is the most common.

God

Monotheism is the anchor of Jewish faith. The God of the Bible hates idolatry and asserts the oneness of deity. God is at the same time the master of the universe, sovereign and omnipotent, and the tender Father who dwells with his people. God is a ruler with both justice and mercy: without mercy no human being could meet the stringency of God's commands; without justice rebellious humanity would never become responsible in its actions. God sometimes issues harsh decrees, but his love is constant to the righteous. Though God cannot be fully understood, yet he is to be trusted.

Humanity

Human beings form a family because God made them all from a single pair. And all are descendants from Noah, with whom he made a covenant. But even that relatively short document of seven laws was regularly broken. Therefore God brought into being a special covenant nation, the Jews, who are to serve God by keeping the 613 commandments of the Mosaic Law. Both Jews and Gentiles may achieve righteousness by following God's commands; those who do will enjoy God's blessing forever, those who do not will be annihilated.

Torah

The Law came at Sinai to Moses. It is God's direct revelation to his people, and by extension to all peoples. The Law existed before Creation as God's most treasured possession. Wisdom may be found among the nations (non-Jews), but the fullest truth for all humanity is the Torah, the arbiter among all contenders for truth. Added to the written Torah is the oral law, Talmud, handed down through generations of rabbis, explicating the meaning of Torah. Conflicting and abstruse as it is, the oral law created the Jewish emphasis on learning, for such learning was needed in order best to understand Torah.

God's People

The Jews are the special covenant community created by God. Though they bear great responsibility because they need to fulfill the commandments of Torah, still they are God's special people. For their sins they are punished, as in the Exile into Diaspora and in the destruction of the temple. But restoration awaits them in the fullness of time, with the temple restored and Messiah in leadership. Meanwhile, they must bear their situation and stay loyal to the commandments and devoted to God.

The Religious Year

The year is marked by a series of important days and by the recurring day, the Sabbath. The six workdays reach a climactic moment in the Sabbath, a time for rest, worship, study, and feasting. Beginning at sundown Friday and lasting until sundown Saturday, the Sabbath is the constant reminder of the goodness of God and of one's responsibility in carrying out his commandments. Each week in the worship service a portion of the Law is read, the whole completed in a single year. By beginning the Sabbath with the lighting of candles, saying of prayers, and feasting, and ending it

The Torah scrolls, here being carried in a formal service, are a central feature of Jewish liturgy. Jewish Historical Society of the Upper Midwest. St. Paul, MN

with wine and blessings, worshipers mark off the special quality of the day from the rest of the week, and carry out the command to keep the day holy, i.e., separate unto God.

Though the first month in the Jewish calendar, a lunar system tied to the solar calendar, is in the spring of the year, the religious year begins in autumn's ten-day penitence period from Rosh hashanah (head of the year) to Yom Kippur, the Day of Atonement, the most solemn day of the year. God's forgiveness is asked for the sins of the previous year, and blessing sought for the ensuing year as renewed commitment to God is made.

Three other major festivals highlight the year. They form a unit because in temple days they were pilgrim festivals when the people came from all over to worship and offer sacrifices.

Pesach (Passover) celebrates the Exodus from Egypt, Shavu'ot (also called Weeks or Pentecost) marks the giving of the Law at Sinai, and Sukkot (Tabernacles) celebrates God's care for the ancient Israelites in their wilderness wanderings.

Other festivals and fasts are also held. Purim remembers the salvation of Jews in Persia as recounted in the biblical book of Esther. Hannukah, or festival of lights, recalls the rededication of the temple under the Maccabees in the second century B.C.E. Tish'ah be-Av is a solemn reminder of the destruction of the temple.

The calendar year, fixed in its present mode in the fourth century C.E., is marked from the day of Creation, so in the very numbering of the year each Jew is reminded of God as the Creator of the universe.

Worship

The most frequent and regular worship occurs in the weekly Sabbath service, though there are prescribed prayers and other acts of worship for the festivals and fasts as well, and devout Jews pray publicly three times a day. The place of public worship is the synagogue, a "temple in miniature" where the service reflects as closely as possible the temple forms of worship, though now with words and not animal sacrifice.

Additions have been made through the centuries so that the original rabbinic ideal has layers of liturgy added to it, but the Torah remains central in the service, with set prayers, singing (both by the congregation and individually by the worship leader, the cantor), and the reading of portions of the Bible being the main components in worship. The people's words as offerings are given to God, and God's word, the Torah, is proclaimed to the people. Judaism remains a religion of the book.

Private worship is most often found at home, in the special events usually related to mealtimes. But spontaneous prayers are made also, on occasions of the miraculous or just in noting some of the normal events in life.

Rites and Observances

Several events mark initiation or transformation for Jews at the various stages of life. The origin of the observances goes back at least to the Middle Ages and in some cases to the Bible. They vary to some extent because of the division of Judaism into several streams of thinking. In general, the more liberal variations are found in non-Orthodox Judaism.

Circumcision of male infants takes place on the eighth day after birth (counting the birth day as the first day), even if the day falls on a Sabbath or a festival. It is the responsibility of the father, according to Jewish law, but it is most often done by a *mohel*, a trained circumciser. The child is welcomed into the covenant through the ritual that accompanies the surgery. The infant is also formally named at the circumcision ceremony.

Bar mitzvah (for boys) or *bat mitzvah* (for girls) marks the time of reaching religious maturity, in most congregations at age thirteen. At this time the youngster moves into adulthood as far as responsibility for the commandments is concerned, and the event is marked by participation in Sabbath worship. This usually means reading a portion of the Torah in Hebrew and saying the blessing of the Torah. The event is celebrated with a party or special meal.

Marriage in Judaism is both a sacred relationship and a legal contractual relationship, therefore it may be dissolved by divorce. The traditional elements in the wedding are sometimes omitted among the non-Orthodox, but commonly there is still the wedding canopy where words of greeting and blessing are given, the signing of the wedding contract that outlines the obligations of the husband to the wife, and the breaking of a glass at the end of the ceremony.

Mourning rites are clearly spelled out

and divided into three periods: from death to burial, the seven days after

Children celebrate Bar- and Bat-Mitzvahs as they assume adult roles in the Jewish community. Israel Tourism Bureau

burial, and from the seven days to thirty days after burial. In each period specific obligations and exemptions are detailed. On the yearly anniversary of a person's death a memorial light is kept burning for twenty-four hours, and contributions to charity are made in the deceased's memory. Four times a year, in connection with the festivals, a memorial service is held for all the deceased.

Domestic observances include the special meals connected with Passover, Yom Kippur, and other festivals, the partylike atmosphere connected with Purim and Hannukah, the maintaining of a *kosher* (ritually pure) kitchen, and some elements of conjugal relations. In Orthodox homes, prayers at mealtimes, ritual washing of the hands, and prayer services are added to the items listed above.

Discussion

1. Trace various ways in which the Diaspora has affected how Jews lived or thought.
2. Discuss Torah, both written and oral, and its central role in Jewish life.
3. To what would you attribute the ability of the Jews to maintain their communities in spite of all the years of persecution?
4. Does "Jewish" refer to a religious faith or to a people? Explain your answer.

Notes

[1]Nicholas de Lange, *Judaism* (Oxford: Oxford Univ. Press, 1987), 7.

[2]Philip S. Alexander, *Textual Sources for the Study of Judaism* (Totowa, N.J.: Barnes and Nobel, 1984), 86–87.

[3]Ibid., 112.

[4]Barry W. Holtz, ed., *Back to the Sources: Reading the Classic Jewish Texts* (New York: Summit Books, 1984), 390.

[5]The summation of Holocaust views is based on an unpublished paper by Patricia Halverson, "Views of the Holocaust," Bethel Theological Seminary, 1989.

6 Christianity

> I have been crucified with Christ and I no longer live, but Christ lives in me. The life I live in the body, I live by faith in the Son of God, who loved me and gave himself for me. I do not set aside the grace of God, for if righteousness could be gained through the law, Christ died for nothing! (Gal.2:20–21)

These words of the apostle Paul, the most important figure after Christ in the early church, reverberate with several themes in Christianity: the crucifixion of Christ; new life in Christ realized by faith and grace; the lack of righteousness in human beings and therefore the need for God's acts; and love as a major ingredient in Christian experience.

Christianity, the largest world religion in terms of members, has a two-thousand-year history and is multiform and pluralistic in its expressions. The following survey emphasizes the history and teachings of traditional Christianity in its main branches, noting variations along the way.

Beginnings

The Roman World

The Christian church began when the Roman Empire was in its first century of existence. Rome began as a republic (its form of the city-state) but outgrew the relatively small size needed for a well-functioning republic, and shortly after the defeat of Mark Antony by Octavian in 31 B.C.E., the empire was born. Octavian became Caesar Augustus, first of the emperors, and his reign (to C.E. 14) inaugurated the era that came to be known as the *pax Romana*, two centuries of relative peace in the Mediterranean basin, ending with the death of Marcus Aurelius in C.E. 180.

The relative political stability and ease of cultural movement in the Greco-Roman world made the spread of Christianity proceed more smoothly than might otherwise have been the case. The Roman Empire, stretching west to east from Britain to the borders of Parthia, was a marvel of efficiency. The central government allowed local legal and cultural institutions to remain in place as much as possible. Roman citizenship was a much-sought condition, and in only some cities of the empire were inhabitants born as Roman citizens. The ideal of justice, though not always realized, was foremost in Roman legal thinking. An excellent system of roads provided a communication network of great speed. The cosmopolitanism of Rome with its Greek culture meant a universal language side by side with the governmental and legal Latin. Within a relatively short time Christianity moved across the Roman world.

There were many religious rivals to Christianity. The Greek and Roman polytheisms were everywhere. In fact, the Greek god-system had influenced the Roman, so Greek Zeus was Roman Jupiter, Hera was Juno, and so on. The two systems were comparable, though the Romans were not so willing as the Greeks to embrace the scandalized gods as depicted in the Homeric epics. The polytheism really operated as a kind of civic religion in Rome with temples of Jupiter in every main city. Local deities were worshiped alongside the "national" ones, and no doubt in many places had more importance. Whether the populace believed in the gods is a moot point; educated persons often allegorized the god stories.

Alongside the polytheisms were the mystery religions, various religions (mostly from North Africa and the East) that provided insider knowledge for their adherents. Built on the principle of *gnosis*—special knowledge obtainable only to the devotees—the mystery religions were exclusive in nature, demanding the kind of loyalty among their followers simply not asked for in generalized polytheism. One of these religions, Mithraism, very strong in the Roman army, had several features comparable to the Christian faith, and in some regions posed a heavy competition to it.

Emperor worship developed in the first century C.E., and was strongest in the eastern part of the empire. Not all the emperors demanded it, and sometimes it was in place only for an emperor who had died. It posed a threat to Christians in that it became a kind of civic duty, often in the form of offering incense to a statue of the emperor, an act many Christians were loath to perform. The general accusation against Christians—that they were uncivic-minded—was supported by their lack of participation in emperor worship.

At the popular level belief in astrology, magic, the interpretation of dreams as oracles from the gods, and miracles—especially healing ones—caused conflict with Christian belief in what was an already hostile religious environment.

In the second and third centuries a group of Christian writers known as apologists disputed with classical thought, both religious and philosophical. The polytheisms presented not too large a problem, for some of the pagan thinkers were embarrassed by them. The apologists argued that the myths of the gods should either be admitted as false or, because of the scandalous nature of the myths, kept from the public's eye. Several of the apologists further contended that the origin of the gods was demonic, not angelic. On the more serious question of how to explain pagan virtues, the apologists took three tacks: the pagans had access to natural law (as all human beings did) and therefore could arrive at some of the virtues in life; or, they had access dimly to the *logos* who was now fully revealed in Christ; or, Plato and other thinkers knew of Moses and the Mosaic legislation and from this derived the virtues.

Several competing philosophies were

present in Rome. Epicureanism, founded in fourth-century B.C.E. Athens, had lost some of its earlier asceticism, and Epicurus's belief in the highest good as pleasure in the sense of freedom from cares and peace of mind had been transmuted into sensual pleasure.

More important than Epicureanism was Stoicism, also founded in fourth-century B.C.E. Athens. Central to Stoic belief was the *logos*, the reason that permeates and governs the universe (macrocosm) and ought to govern the life of human beings (microcosm); thus, humanity is integrated with nature, and all human beings belong to a single world community. Life ought to be lived in cooperation with the *logos* since it knows the universal design; thus, there was an emphasis on duty and fortitude. Stoicism even had an eschatology: time was punctuated with conflagrations, the destruction of eras, followed by a regeneration or restoration of all things, until the next conflagration. Here, then, was a philosophy that saw the universe as whole, emphasized moral values, and had a picture of human history. Stoicism was probably the most widely held of the philosophies in the second and third centuries C.E.

The Jewish Background

Christianity began within the confines of Judaism, with the claim that Jesus Christ was the Jewish Messiah fulfilling all the messianic prophecies of the Bible. Scholars still debate the Jewishness of Christianity—whether the Jewish influence on Christian practices was heavy or light—but no consensus has been reached. The central difference revolved around understanding who Jesus was. The Christians—and most of the earliest Christians were Jewish—contended that he was the Messiah (anointed one; the Greek equivalent is Christ) promised in the Hebrew Bible as the one to come at the end of time and restore all things, especially the Jewish kingdom. Hostile Jews saw Jesus as an imposter, while more irenic Jews lauded him as a teacher but not as the Messiah. This basic distinction lies at the heart of Jewish-Christian differences through the centuries.

As the differences between Jews and Christians became more apparent in the second century, a more elaborate relationship developed, chiefly around understanding the Hebrew Bible, what Christians call the Old Testament. Basically, this became a Christian document with several elements in it: the prediction of the coming Messiah was gathered together in Jesus of Nazareth as the fulfillment of the prediction; the Mosaic Law was seen as preparatory for the coming of the Gospel of grace, and the Law was stratified so that the ritual and ceremonial aspects were fulfilled in Christ and the moral components continued as binding on Christians; and the prophetic portions of the Hebrew Bible were emphasized more than the legal portions. Through the process of correction-and-fulfillment (correcting the Jewish understanding of the Bible so that it was fulfilled in Christianity), the Hebrew scriptures became the old covenant of the Christian Scriptures, followed by the new covenant centering on Jesus, described in the New Testament of the Christian Scriptures.

To highlight the contrast between Jewish and Christian understandings of the Bible and Jesus, the major Christian writers of the first five centuries wrote dialogues against the Jews. By the end of the second century these dialogues had become almost unnecessary, for by that time Jews and Christians had almost virtually lost contact with each other and the predominance of Jewish Christians in the first-century church had evaporated. None of the church fathers from the second century on were Jews, and the remnants of Jewish Christians died out by the seventh century.

Christians of many lands have often contextualized Jesus by presenting his ministry in the setting of their own culture. CARAVS, India. Artist: N.K. Mishra

Foundations

Jesus

Christianity begins with the belief that God the Son, the second person of the Trinity, came to live among humankind in the person of Jesus Christ. His life and teachings are an exemplar of how one is to live. His substitutionary atonement for sin by his death and resurrection ensure new life for all who trust in him by faith. He intercedes for believers as the ascended King and High Priest in heaven, and from there he shall return at the end of time to usher in the new heavens and the new earth.

Though it is virtually impossible to construct a strict chronology of Jesus' career, the Gospels suggest he began his ministry in Judea, spent a great deal of time in the Galilee and nearby parts of northern Palestine, with Capernaum as his base, and followed that with a lengthy final trip to Jerusalem with ministry in Perea and Judea along the way.

Jesus was born in Bethlehem before the death of Herod the Great (4 B.C.E.). The accounts of his birth in the books of Matthew and Luke describe Mary, his mother, as a virgin who conceived through the power of the Holy Spirit. He grew up in Nazareth in the Galilee, apparently learning the carpentry trade. One brief item from his childhood surfaces: he talked with the scholars in the temple precincts when he was twelve years of age.

Jesus' public ministry began when he was about thirty years of age. A prophetic figure named John the Baptist, who had been preaching repentance to the people of Judea, had announced the coming of the Messiah, and pointed to Jesus as that chosen one. Jesus' baptism by John signified his entry into public ministry, and shortly thereafter he endured temptation in the wilderness as a prelude to further ministry and as an indication he would do his Father's will and fulfill the commission given him. He announced his call at the synagogue at Nazareth when he quoted a passage from the prophet Isaiah that indicated the Spirit of the Lord was upon him.

There are a number of components in Jesus' ministry. He performed many miracles of healing, did much casting out of demons, and performed nature miracles (walking on the water, stilling the sea, etc.). Two aims were inherent in these miracles: to show compassion on those who were afflicted, and to demonstrate the power of God as a sign of his messiahship.

The teaching of Jesus centered on the kingdom of God. The kingdom was God's rule in the hearts of human beings. Jesus brought the kingdom, he was its king, and he laid out kingdom values (the way one was to live in the kingdom). The kingdom was not only present, it was also future, the new heaven and earth described by the Hebrew prophets that had broken into history in the person of Jesus—he was its inaugurator. In parables and discourses, especially the Sermon on the Mount, Jesus described the kingdom values, summed up as "love God" and "love your neighbor."

More than a teacher, Jesus made claims about himself that place him in a unique category. His death has meaning for all humankind. He clearly contends that he is the Messiah sent from God. The titles Son of Man and Son of God are peculiarly his. A series of "I am" statements in the gospel of John indicate his special nature. The fact that the high priest tore his own clothing when Jesus admitted to divinity shows that the ones who opposed him felt he had blasphemously claimed to be God.

Jesus' ministry was to the multitudes, often to those who were scorned by the religious leaders. He came, he said, not to call the righteous but sinners to repentance. The irony, as clearly disclosed in his stories and encounters, was that those who thought themselves righteous were usually as unrighteous as those who knew they were sinners. Both kinds of persons needed repentance from sin and faith in Jesus. In his teaching Jesus called for a righteousness far exceeding the legalistic concept of the day, demanding, for example, not only love for benefactors but also for one's enemies. By going to the sinners in society Jesus demonstrated one of the kingdom values: take the words of the Gospel (the term means *good news*) to everyone who needs them. In so doing he also extended the concept of who one's neighbor was, viz., anyone a person encountered, or better yet, all of humanity.

Jesus' work with the outcasts and fringe persons of society, coupled with his challenge to the religious establishment, garnered hostility from the religious leaders. One of the parties in leadership at the time, the Sadducees, was connected with the temple organization, the high priests, priests, and others who were part of the sacrificial and ritual system. The Pharisees, no friends of the Sadducees, were connected with the Law, the Mosaic legislation. As both interpreters and rigorous keepers of the Law, the Pharisees disdained the common people for their lack of scrupulosity. Members of both parties opposed Jesus because of his radical departure from their teachings.

Throughout his public ministry, Jesus gradually revealed himself as the Messiah, and on three occasions predicted his death and resurrection. The last week of Jesus' life, culminating in his death and resurrection, are treated extensively by the Gospel writers. Clearly they understood this as the central reason for Jesus' existence. The unfolding of the hostility leading to the Crucifixion, the betrayal by Judas, and the weak will of Pilate played a part in the story. But, the sadness of Good Friday is superseded by the joy of Resurrection Sunday. The denouement follows: appearances to the disciples, the restoration of Peter after his denials, and the commission to take the Gospel to the ends of the world.

Who is Jesus? Jewish and Roman officialdom saw him as a troubler of the religious and political orders. Up to the time of the Crucifixion his disciples knew him as Lord and Christ. Hearing (and recording) his acts and words led to further reflection about his ultimate nature. More than a prophet, more than the expected Messiah, he is viewed in the pages of the New Testament and in the early church as the divine Son of God, a view that has been the majority opinion in the church ever since.

Paul and the Earliest Church

Paul was born in the city of Tarsus located at the northeast corner of the Mediterranean Sea. A Jew trained in the Pharisaic tradition, he possessed Roman citizenship and was well aware of Greek culture. His two names, the Hebrew Saul and the Greek Paul, reflect the bicultural nature of diaspora Judaism which served him well on his missionary journeys. His rigorist approach to Jewish Law led him to condemn the church and try to destroy it. After his conversion he remained proud of his Jewish background, retaining an abiding interest in his people of origin.

In the midst of persecuting the church, Paul was dramatically converted, an event recounted three times in the book of Acts and referred to often by Paul in his letters. Paul saw the experience as coming from God, and came to believe that God had prepared him through his Jewish upbringing in a Gentile city to be an apostle like the original twelve apostles, though "born out of due time." Immediately after his conversion Paul was commissioned to take the Gospel to the Gentiles, though several years elapsed before the work began.

Paul and his associate, Barnabas, were commissioned by the church in Antioch (Acts 13), the first of the Gentile churches, and from this start Paul, with several different associates, made three missionary journeys in Asia Minor and Greece. On the journeys Paul

Ruins of the second century C.E. synagogue at Capernaum, built on the site where Jesus "entered into the synagogue and taught" (Mark 1.21). Israel Tourism Bureau

planted new churches (stressed in Acts 13–19) and visited ones already in operation. Several general features of his missionary activity appear in Acts: Paul's work brings him into contact with Jewish or government officials; opposition to his preaching frequently arises, and is usually overcome; Paul is bold and direct in his speech, and as a result of his preaching congregations of believers are established.

Paul ended up in Jerusalem with monies collected from various congregations to help the Jewish Christians in their time of poverty. While there Paul was arrested by Roman authorities for creating a disturbance, and the remaining chapters of Acts (22–28) detail his appearance, with speeches, before several authorities as he makes his way toward Rome, to which as a

citizen he had appealed. Of his life after arrival in Rome little is known; he may have been released, spent some time in traveling to visit churches, been rearrested, and sent back to Rome. Tradition says he was executed in Rome sometime in the 60s C.E. under the emperor Nero.

While he never wrote a systematic theology (sections of Romans and Galatians come closest to this), Paul expounded his theology as he wrote to meet the needs of the moment. He claimed the authority of apostleship equal to that of the other apostles, and therefore his words were from God. His work, accepted as normative by orthodox Christians, formulates and applies the essence of Christianity. Paul saw human beings as fallen creatures who could not through their own efforts please God, whether in keeping the Mosaic Law or in some other religious system. But God had provided a way of salvation through the death and resurrection of Christ, freely given out of grace and love to those who accept it in faith. The Gospel of grace, freely given, entailed ethical demands on the life and conduct of the believer, and significant portions of Paul's letters address these demands.

The union of the believer with Christ was an important point for Paul, as he often mentioned his own such union and encouraged others to think of the faith in that way. Dedicated to living for and with Christ, Paul admonished others to do the same. At the same time union with Christ was accompanied by union with other believers: being united with Christ brought persons into fellowship with the church, the body of believers, of whom Christ was the head. The church is the new Israel, put together by the new covenant in Christ, bringing Jews and Gentiles into the same domain and making obsolete the old community of God, the Israel of the Old Testament. Finally, there is an eschatological element in Paul's theology, for Jesus Christ is not only Lord of the church, he is also the coming King who will return and usher in the new age after the judgment.

Texts

The sources for the life of Jesus are the four gospels of Matthew, Mark, Luke, and John, and scattered references in other books of the New Testament. None of the Gospels are biographies in the modern sense, for they concentrate on the three years of Jesus'

public ministry, especially the events surrounding his death and resurrection. The first three gospels are called the "synoptics" (seeing together) because they relate similar events and seem to have similar sources; the gospel of John is quite different in form. Each of the Gospels consists of several kinds of literary materials: accounts of miracles, discourses by Jesus, parables, narratives of encounters with hostile persons, instructions to the disciples.

The fledgling church is chronicled in the New Testament book of Acts. Written by Luke as a companion volume to his gospel, the book begins with the account of the Ascension of Jesus accompanied by his admonition to his followers to carry the Gospel throughout the world. Acts describes the history of the church from its founding in Jerusalem to its arrival in Rome. The extension of the church is laid out in a threefold pattern (1:8): Jerusalem (1:1–7:60); Judea and Samaria (8:1–11:18); to the ends of the earth (11:19–28:31). In the course of the extension a shift is made from a Jewish-dominated church with its leaders—Philip, Stephen, James, Peter—to a church of the Gentiles, with Paul in leadership. Peter is the hinge person in the account, as he gradually accepts the notion of the church spreading to the Gentile world (chaps. 10 and 11); and the Council in Jerusalem (chap. 15) is the hinge event, as the Jerusalem leaders accepted the presence of Gentiles in the church without demanding of them extensive conformity to the Jewish law system.

Speeches make up nearly one-fifth of

Fourteenth century carved ivory diptych portrays scenes from the life of Christ. Minneapolis Institute of Art

the book of Acts, giving examples (and perhaps models) for the proclamation of the Gospel in the early church. Another feature of the book is the work of the Holy Spirit, from the initiatory moment on the day of Pentecost to his presence with believers in a variety of ways.

Some pieces of information about the founding of various church congregations, and much about the daily life of the church, are found in the letters of the New Testament.

From the end of the fourth century C.E. the canon (official list) of the New Testament books has been accepted by all branches of the church as revelation from God and therefore authoritative. Portions of manuscripts date from the second century, whole sections from the third, and complete manuscripts from the early fourth century. Seven of the books were debated in some regions of the church, but general agreement on the others was universal.

Early Church (to 600)

The Church Organizes

The church was called the catholic church by everyone through the first several centuries. Originally, catholic simply meant "universal"—the whole church—but by the end of the second century, due to the rise in heresies and schisms, it also came to mean orthodox (correct belief), so the catholic church became also the true church.

The kind of church government (polity) in which the bishops have authority is called episcopacy. From the second century to the Protestant Reformation in the sixteenth century episcopacy was the prevailing form, both West and East. Two other forms came out of the Reformation. Presbyterianism places authority in a group known as elders, sometimes elected by the church members, who make decisions for and in behalf of the congregation. A third form, congregationalism, places authority in the hands of the church membership, who make their own decisions as a voting body. The clergy in an episcopal system are ordained by the bishops, in a presbyterian system by the elders, and in a congregational system by the congregation.

In the first few centuries, bishops gradually assumed the chief role in various local churches, and among the bishops several (in Rome, Jerusalem, Antioch, Alexandria, and Constantinople) gained international influence and asserted their claim over other bishops. These were called patriarchs.

Further, by the fifth century the church divided along linguistic and geographical (and to some extent theological) lines, resulting in a Latin-speaking Western church and a Greek-speaking Eastern church. Each of the two bodies came to be known by terms originally applied to the whole church: the (Roman) Catholic Church in the West and the Orthodox Church in the East. Of course, each body claimed both catholicity and orthodoxy for itself.

As the church expanded in the cities of the empire, and as questions arose that seemed to require consistent solutions, inevitably attention had to be paid to the interrelations of communities. The apostles had already done this to some extent, and some of the second-century bishops like Ignatius of Antioch showed concern for the wider Christian community, though their functions were apparently not "official." Leaders of churches in large cities exercised some control over the Christians in the nearby areas. These factors prepared the way for the convening of synods (assemblies, meetings) in the latter half of the second century, occasioned by the Montanist schism (originating in Asia Minor, the Montanists were accused of overstressing the work of the Holy Spirit in the church), and the controversy over the correct date for observing Easter. A large number of local synods were held in the third century to discuss liturgy (church rites), doctrine, and discipline. The first general council was convened in the West at Arles in the year 314, and the first ecumenical council (all the bishops of all the churches) met at Nicea in 325.

Three motives were prominent in organizing the church. One was the desire to unite all Christians in a conscious fellowship. A second was to preserve, transmit, and spread the Gospel in its purity. The third was to bring all Christians together into a visible body of Christ. Three strategies were employed to achieve this. Apostolic succession placed the organizational and theological authority of the church in the hands of the bishops, who would choose their own successors—all candidates outside the approved line would not count as members of the true church. A second strategy was to work on the writings of the apostles to determine a fixed and authoritative collection, the canon. This endeavor began in the second century, prompted by the presence of competing canons. Third was the issuing of doctrinal statements as understandings of the basic teachings of the Bible; this was done at council meetings.

Church Life

Until the emperor Constantine (d. 337) made the Christian church legal in the empire in 313, Christians lived in a hazy legal condition. Technically the Christian religion was an *illicit religio*, an illegal religion, but whether or not Christians were hauled before the courts depended much on the whims of opponents and local conditions. Always subject to persecution because of their insecure legal status, Christians were largely persecuted on a local and regional basis until the middle of the third century. Then the emperor Decius (ruled 249–51) attempted an empire-wide persecution, which was abruptly halted by his

death. Under Diocletian (ruled 284–305), a longer-lasting and more devastating persecution broke out, which was continued by his successors. Political turmoil in Rome led to the rise of Constantine, thus putting an end to state-sponsored persecution. But in the process, both local and empire-wide, many Christians were killed for their faith (the number is impossible to know), and the concept of martyrdom as a sanctioned way of Christian death became a powerful force in the church.

The common form of entry into the church in the first three centuries was through a period of instruction (catechesis) of up to eighteen months in length, followed by baptism (often done on Easter Sunday). In the third century this began to change with the increase in infant baptism. The catechumenate had assumed adult converts, but now some argued for infant baptism. Over the next century and a half the issue was joined, though infant baptism became a common rite, and the doctrine was put together for the Western church by Augustine (354–430), who argued that infants were born with sin on their souls that could be washed away by the waters of baptism. From this it followed that infants were regenerated (born again) at baptism, and instruction in the faith would follow rather than precede baptism. This in turn led to the practice of penance (the "second plank" after shipwreck [original sin]; the first plank was baptism—one needed both planks for salvation) whose prescriptions took care of postbaptismal sins, and meant that the "body of Christ" was a mixed group of believers and unbelievers because one was never totally sure that the acts of penance would in fact wipe out the effects of postbaptismal sin.

Monasticism

The impulse that led to monasticism was the desire to banish sin and worldliness from church life and live up to what the monks felt were the superior virtues of poverty and chastity. The beginnings are not clearly known, but in the third century a group known as the desert fathers left the cities to live solitary lives fighting against sin and devoting their lives to God. Some lived extreme lives, more curiosities than spiritual examples, but others, the most noteworthy of whom was Saint Anthony, were an inspiration to the church.

The word *monk* is derived from a Greek word meaning "alone," but in the third century an Egyptian monk, Pachomius, designed a system that emphasized communal life, led by elder monks. Basil the Great (c. 330–79), whose rule—guide to monastic living—is still the basic one for Eastern monasticism, stressed communal monasticism and added the principle of social concern to monastic communities.

The chief founder of communal monasticism in the West was Benedict of Nursia (c. 480–c. 547), whose rule elaborated the role of each person in the community, forbade excesses of behavior, gave practical advice for every phase of monastic life, and bound the monks to a single monastery for life. Benedict's *Rule* became the standard in Western Christendom. Because the monks were strictly de-voted to the rule (L., *regula*), they came to be called the "regular" clergy as differentiated from the parish priests who served outside the monastic cloister in the world (L., *saeculum*) and were called the secular clergy.

> And in all things let all follow the Rule as their guide; and let no one diverge from it without good reason. Let no one in the monastery follow his own inclinations, and let no one boldly presume to dispute with his abbot, whether within or without the monastery. If anyone so presume, let him be subject to the discipline of the Rule. The abbot, for his part, should do everything in the fear of the Lord and in observance of the Rule.[1]

From the beginning, women were drawn into monastic life. Communities of nuns were founded in the vicinity of monks' houses as early as the fourth century. Under the aegis of Columbanus (d. 615) a number of "double" monasteries were founded in Gaul. These were basically communities of nuns, with monks attached to serve as priests and do some of the heavier manual labor; the head of the joint congregation was usually an abbess (the female equivalent of abbot, the head of a male house). The rule for the women's houses was usually Benedictine. With the founding of separate women's orders in the thirteenth century and following, other rules were drawn up. Like the monks, women's orders have varied from heavily cloistered groups to those that engage primarily in social action.

In addition to their works of devotion and help to those outside the community, the monks were instrumental in preserving some of the literature of antiquity and in providing education for some segments of European society at a time when education was piecemeal at best. Several monastic communities, especially in Britain and Ireland, were actively missionary, taking the Gospel to pagan peoples in western and northern Europe.

While monasticism in the East stayed fairly constant, monasticism in the West was in flux. The Benedictine form took hold by the ninth century and was the prevailing mode. One of its weaknesses, however, final authority in the abbot, held the potential for corruption. When the feudal system began to make its way in Europe in the early Middle Ages, the monasteries as holders of lands were drawn into the system, and the abbot in some regards was much like a feudal lord. This drew the monasteries into political and economic conflicts. Further, simony (the buying of church offices) and concubinage added scandal in some places. These resulted late in the eleventh century in the Cluniac reforms, which introduced more oversight into the system.

Further vitality appeared in the church in the thirteenth century. The Dominicans and Franciscans revitalized monastic life. These orders moved out of the cloisters to live in the world; did not have a financial base (so their monks were known as mendicants: beggars); and took special works under their aegis, the Dominicans becoming teachers, and opposers of heresy, and the Franciscans going to the poor. In contrast to these socially engaged mendicants, new orders like the Carthusians and Cistercians emphasized uncompromising wihhdrawal from the world. Lay movements like the Brethren of the Common Life added yet another dimension to the vitality of special orders in the church. Women's groups like the Sisters of Clare (founded c. 1215) enhanced the role of nuns in the church.

Church Councils

The church is always more than a school, but it can never be less than a school, and so one of the concerns of the early church was to lay out carefully the correct understanding of the faith. What came to be authoritative, besides the Scriptures themselves, were the findings of the ecumenical councils (councils at which all the bishops met). From Nicea I in 325 through and including Nicea II in 787, the bishops of the church met seven times to deal with important doctrinal issues. The first two councils debated the question of the Trinity, the next four dealt with the nature and person of Christ, and the seventh approved the use of icons in church worship and liturgy. For the Orthodox Church these seven are the only ecumenical councils, and only their findings are demanded of the faithful. Roman Catholicism argues for twenty one councils, the most recent being Vatican II in the 1960s. Most traditional Protestants would agree with the declarations of the first six councils.

What the councils did was to answer the question, What does the Bible teach about . . . ? The Trinitarian issue in the fourth century revolved around the issue of the nature of the persons in the Godhead, concluding that both the Son and the Holy Spirit were separate persons from each other and the Father, but that all three were *homoousios* (Gk., of the same substance) with one another. The next four councils, in the fifth through the seventh centuries, concluded that Jesus was one person with two natures:

> Therefore, following the holy Fathers, we all with one accord teach men to acknowledge one and the same Son, our Lord Jesus Christ, at once complete in Godhood and complete in manhood, truly God and truly man, consisting also of a reasonable soul and body; of one substance with the Father as regards his Godhead, and at the same time of one substance with us as regards his manhood; like us in all respects, apart from sin.[2]

The Middle Ages

The Orthodox Tradition

The division in the church, East and West, was promoted in part by the divided Roman Empire. The emperor Constantine ordered the building of Constantinople for good reasons. Imperial trade routes were enhanced, the new city could serve as a bulwark against the eastern tribes that threatened the empire, and the division of empire begun under Diocletian in the late third century was solidified. Over the next one hundred fifty years a shift in importance from Rome to Constantinople (the "second Rome") occurred, so that when the German Odoacer took the Roman throne in 476, the traditional date for the "fall" of Rome, there was little concern in the East. Also by this time there were already several kingdoms in the West.

The height of the eastern empire (also called the Byzantine Empire or Byzantium; from the ancient city of Byzantium, the site of Constantinople) was reached in the reign of Justinian (ruled 527–65). Under his rule Byzantium became a Mediterranean power and conquered some of the western areas that had been lost. He ordered the building of Hagia Sophia, the most famous church in Byzantium, and oversaw a codification of law called the Justinian Code, extremely influential in both church and state. The form of the Byzantine state was called *symphonia*, a harmony between the spiritual and the temporal (sometimes more negatively called caesaropapism, rule in both church and state by the emperor).

The Byzantine Empire lasted officially until the fall of Constantinople in 1453, but its history was a series of risings and fallings, due to pressure from Islam beginning in the seventh century and from the Turks from the eleventh century on, and a gradual diminishing of political and military strength over the centuries.

The eastern church, Orthodoxy, grew in this political context. Some of the difficulties it faced included the "mono" heresies: monophysitism, an emphasis on the divine nature of Jesus at the expense of his genuine human nature; and monothelitism, the belief that Jesus had but one will. These heresies, augmented by nationalism, led to the creation and perpetuation of several separate church bodies in the East, like the Syrian Orthodox Church and the Coptic Church.

In the eighth century the church was

An Orthodox service conducted before the congregation, with the bishop (center) chanting the liturgy.
St. Mary's Orthodox Cathedral, Minneapolis, MN

riven by the iconoclastic controversy, a debate over the use of images (Gk., *icon*): whether paintings, mosaics, or statuary of Jesus, Mary, and the saints should be used in church worship. The iconoclasts wished to see all icons removed from the churches, but they were defeated at the second council of Nicea in 787. Iconoclasm reemerged in the following century, only to be subdued again. The long-term effect of the controversy was far less use of statuary in the eastern church than in the West.

A more celebrated controversy centered on the *filioque* (L., "and from the Son"), a phrase added to the Nicene Creed in the West sometime in the sixth century. Condemned in the East in the ninth century, it gradually achieved currency in the West. When East and West split in 1054, the main doctrinal issue was the *filioque*, the

East arguing that only an ecumenical council could alter the creed and that this alteration in fact demeaned the Spirit because it read, "the Spirit proceeds from the Father and from the Son," whereas the creed said that the Son proceeded only from the Father.

The immediate cause of the breach in 1054 (not officially resolved until 1965) was the role of the papacy in the church. Orthodoxy sees the church as all those believers who remain in fellowship with the historic patriarchates—the five mentioned above and, later, Moscow. Rome's claim that its bishop was the unique successor to Peter, with power to define dogma, was an innovation. The Orthodox argued that all right-teaching bishops are equally successors of Peter, therefore only ecumenical councils attended by the bishops can arrive at teaching the faithful must believe.

Cathedrals like this one expressed the hopes and aspirations of people in the Latin-speaking medieval West. William Travis

The eastern church has several other characteristics that make it different from the West. For one thing, monasticism in the East has been highly contemplative, i.e., it has tended to stay in the cloisters, quite in contrast to the western mendicant tradition for some monks, who lived out their service in the world. Further, the eastern churches are heavily liturgical, the central activity of many congregants being the attendance at the weekly service. In part, this derives from the Orthodox emphasis on the community of believers as the abode of the Spirit.

In early centuries the eastern church was quite missionary in its work, particularly to Slavic peoples. Most of the time, however, the Orthodox have been content with a "presence" kind of evangelism, rather than an active missionary one.

Since the doctrinal statements of the seven ecumenical councils are the only required creedal beliefs, the Orthodox Church has been patristic and traditionalistic, but the belief that the Holy Spirit dwells in the ongoing church preserving his people in all truth gives a measure of theological freedom. Two creedal formulations in the seventeenth century, the more important one adopted at Jerusalem in 1672, are the standard definitions of Orthodoxy in the modern era.

The eastern church views the West as far too rational in its explanations of the faith, the East being content with the mysteries (their term for sacraments), and content not to carry every idea out to its logical conclusion. For example, there are saints in the eastern system but no formal purgatory, no formal doctrines about the Virgin Mary, no formal development of canonization and beatification for the saints. Their theology is apophatic, stressing what is not known, rather than kataphatic, emphasizing what is known.

Church and Empire in the West

After the breakup of the Roman Empire in the fifth century a series of smaller kingdoms succeeded in its place, until the time of Charlemagne (c. 742–814), who was crowned emperor at Rome in the year 800, the only medieval ruler to control most of western Europe. His short-lived empire was divided among his sons, but the empire idea refused to die, and in 962, Otto I was crowned as head of what came to be called the Holy Roman Empire. Voltaire, the eighteenth-century French critic, quipped that it was neither holy, nor Roman, nor an empire, but it lasted at least on paper until Napoleon abolished it in 1806. Always a haphazard arrangement of territories, primarily in German-speaking lands, the empire lived side by the side with the western European feudal monarchies, and provided together with the church the medieval ideal of Christendom: church, state, and society forming a single whole.

The question of who should be in charge in Christendom embodied a long-standing issue for the Christian church: how to relate to the political order. The medieval maneuverings were just one episode of such relationships. Pope and emperor gave mutual support to each other, at least in theory, but they also fought against each other. In 1077 Pope Gregory VII, first in a line of strong popes, disputed with Emperor Henry IV and forced him to wait in the cold three days at Canossa until Gregory allowed Henry back in the church. Papal strength was more pronounced in the era from Innocent III (ruled 1198–1216) to Boniface VIII (ruled 1294–1303), the lawyer popes who marked the zenith of the medieval papacy. As a summary statement of the Roman church's power, Boniface issued in 1302 the papal bull (decree) *Unam Sanctam*, which declared "no salvation outside the church"—which meant no salvation for members of church bodies like the Orthodox Church which did not recognize papal supremacy.

Symbolically enough, the following year Boniface was humiliated at Anagni by Philip the Fair of France, a counterpart to the Canossa incident and an indication of the beginning of at least a temporary papal decline. The so-called Babylonian Captivity of the church, when the popes resided not at Rome but at the French city of Avignon, lasted from 1304 to 1374. This was followed by the Great Schism (1375–1415) when two and occasionally three different claimants to the papal chair were vying for authority. The papacy emerged from these two events with a greater strength, only to see in the fifteenth century the rise of national monarchies, first in Portugal and Spain, as rivals to papal power.

Completed in the sixteenth century, St. Peter's Cathedral in Rome is the symbol for papal authority in the Roman Catholic Church. William Travis

Intellectual Life

The original meaning of the word *university* was corporation, and it was applied to organizations other than educational ones. But by the year 1200, with the reemergence of urban centers in parts of Europe, the growth of trade, and the introduction of previously unknown Greek and Roman works, the educational universities were growing. Bologna was famous for law studies, Montpellier and Salerno for medicine, and Paris and Oxford for theology and philosophy.

Out of the university came the philosophy-theology known as Scholasti-

cism. Its proponents were called Scho-
lastics or Schoolmen because virtually
all of them were university teachers
(and also members of monastic orders). Where the theologians in the
early church were usually bishops,
now the monks were the theologians.

One of the questions faced by the
Schoolmen was the relation between
faith and reason, to some extent an
issue joined by the presence of philosophical works outside the Christian
tradition. The question was not new,
having been faced by the church
fathers in their encounter with classical thought, but it was now newly
posed. Three answers were given to
the issue. First was the idea that faith
and reason did not fit with each other,
that they were opposing forces. After
all, the Bible with its revelation had
been given because the human mind
could not figure out who God was nor
what was needed for salvation. This
meant that when faith and reason
apparently opposed one another, one
should choose faith. Indeed, men like
Saint Francis were somewhat fearful
of education because to them it had
the potential to damage one's faith.
This compartmentalizing approach,
summed up in Tertullian's famous
dictum "What has Athens to do with
Jerusalem?," has been a constant feature in Christian life and thought.

A second approach, held by only a
very few thinkers, accepted the idea
that faith and reason opposed one
another, but also said that one must
hold to both. When faith and reason
have conflicting principles or results,
both should be subscribed to. This
idea (sometimes called the "double-
truth theory," i.e., something true in

theology might be false in philosophy,
and vice versa) could lead to the
restriction of the faith to areas where
reason did not flourish, and further
had the potential for diminishing the
realm of faith as reason moved into
more and more disciplines.

A third approach, typified in the
greatest of the medieval thinkers,
Thomas Aquinas (c. 1225–74), suggested that faith and reason were
separate realms, but that faith was the
natural next step after reason. In other
words, reason (God-given in any case)
could help human beings unravel a lot
about the nature of humanity and the
universe and some qualities of God,
but only revelation (apprehended by
faith) provided the fuller picture of the
character of God and of the means of
salvation. This view allowed for the
full expression of reason without fear
on the one hand and contradiction on
the other, but still left a vital place for
faith as a natural outgrowth of the use
of reason. Reason had limits that only
faith could exceed.

Aquinas's system, here only touched
on, was the high point of the medieval
intellect and has influenced Roman
Catholic thought in the centuries since
his time. But in the fourteenth and
fifteenth centuries Scholasticism became overelaborated and lost the dynamic of the thirteenth century.

Christian mysticism, the belief that a
personal religious experience can give
one an immediate knowledge of God,
can conceivably fit with each of the
foregoing positions, but has probably
been most compatible with the first
one. Most often achieved in prayer,
Christian mysticism opposes the idea

of absorption present in other mysticisms in that it maintains the distinction between Creator and creature; the mystical experience is one of love and will. Visions, dreams, and ecstasies are reported by Christian mystics, but such phenomena are not inherent in Christian mysticism and frequently are seen as only a small part of mystical experience. Forms of mysticism vary considerably, but it is present in virtually all branches of the church.

The Protestant Reformation

> Unless I am convicted by the Scriptures and by plain reason—I do not accept the authority of popes and councils, for they have contradicted each other—my conscience is captive to the Word of God. I cannot and will not recant anything, for to go against conscience is neither right nor safe.[3]

With these dramatic words Martin Luther (1483–1546), the German monk and doctor of theology turned reformer, closed his statement before the imperial Diet (parliament) of the Holy Roman Empire gathered at the German city of Worms in April 1521. In the four years since posting his ninety-five theses on the church door in Wittenberg, he had moved away from the mother church in which he had grown up and which he served.

From 1512 a professor of theology at the new university at Wittenberg, he was aware of some of the abuses in the church, especially in the matter of indulgences—the church's practice of granting reduced time in purgatory in exchange for pious works. His investigation of the abuses led him back to

Reformation Monument, Geneva, Switzerland, commemorating the founders of the Protestant Reformation, including Luther, Calvin and Zwingli. William Travis

the theology that had spawned the abuses, and this in turn led him back to the Bible to check on the validity of that theology. By 1520 he was publishing antipapal material and in that year the pope condemned his writings. His recalcitrance to give up his criticisms and his demand for reform had brought him before the imperial diet to stand for his alleged heresies.

Luther's reforms were notably successful, but he was not the first reformer in the late medieval church. John Wycliffe (c. 1330-84) led a reform movement in England in which he attacked the wealth and power of the church, criticized its view of the priesthood and the Mass, and initiated a translation of the Bible into English. Rome condemned Wycliffe and had his body disinterred and burned years after his death. His teachings caught on among the Czech students at Oxford, leading to the Prague reformer John Hus (1374–1415, condemned by the Council of Constance in 1415 and put to death at the stake in that year by the city of Constance. At the end of the fifteenth century another reform appeared, led by Girolamo Savonarola (1452–98) of Florence, who for several years in the 1490s changed church and other practices in that Italian city.

Principles of the Reformation

Several issues divided Luther and the other sixteenth-century reformers from the Catholic Church. One of the initial ones was the issue of authority. In the summer of 1519 Martin Luther debated Cardinal Johann Eck, in the course of which Eck asked Luther if the Council of Constance had been right to condemn the ideas of John Hus. Since Luther answered that the council had been wrong in part, he was implying that a major belief in the church, that councils had final authority, was itself wrong. Eck did not raise the issue of the pope as final authority, but had he done so Luther would no doubt have denied that, too. What appeared here in embryonic form became a rallying cry of the Reformation: Scripture alone (*sola scriptura*) is the authority for the church.

Luther believed the Holy Spirit was the proper interpreter of the Bible, not the church, and he translated the Bible into German to show his desire for laypersons to read the Bible in the vernacular. He also changed the liturgy, translating it into German, encouraged congregational singing, and offered both bread and wine in Communion (not Catholic practice at the time).

On the issue of salvation the Reformers also differed from Rome. Luther, Calvin, and the others argued for justification by faith alone, in contrast to their perception that the church asked its members to engage in a works-righteousness to achieve salvation. Luther had been through a long personal struggle on this matter while still a monk, finding no relief for the guilt he carried. While preparing for lectures he gave at Wittenberg, he discovered the Pauline dictum of grace alone (*sola gratia*) by faith alone (*sola fide*). One could do nothing to deserve the merit of salvation, but God had provided it through grace to be received by faith. Such a doctrine, based on the inability of the human will to carry out obedience to God, undercut the whole penitential system (including indulgences) that the medieval church had developed. If human beings could merit salvation or cooperate with God, then Christ's death on the cross was not needed. And the faith Luther described was not simply assent to a list of doctrines, the common understanding of faith in his time, but an act of accepting God's grace in providing salvation in Christ. Thus, Luther rediscovered a dynamic to Christianity that had been lost for many in preceding generations.

A third matter was summed up in the phrase, "priesthood of believers." At its heart this idea meant there was no need to go through an intermediary like a priest to get to God. The only mediator was Christ himself, immediately available to all believers. This had a major effect on the concept of calling, as elaborated by Luther and Calvin. In the medieval understanding calling belonged to those who entered a religious profession—priests, monks, nuns, certain lay religious. The Reformers contended that all were called, those in secular professions as well as those in religious ones. This had a transforming effect on the laity in the Reformation congregations and, combined with the emphasis on lay reading of the Bible, created a common characteristic of Protestantism: the informed laity.

For the Reformers the priesthood of believers did not imply democracy; except for a small minority, the Protestants retained belief in hierarchy in church and state with the implication that most people would remain in the stations in life into which they were born. Political democracy was a creation of the seventeenth century. Also, priesthood of believers did not mean abandonment of a learned clergy. Gifted persons in the church called into clergy positions needed special training to perform those gifts. Though the Bible was perspicuous enough for all to read to understand salvation, further exploration into biblical truth and the need for congregational leadership demanded education.

Evangelical, a term derived from the Greek *euangelion* ("good news"), has been used since New Testament times but came into frequent use only with the Protestant Reformation. Thus, in its more restricted usage, evangelicalism describes the inheritors of the Reformation tradition. Specifically, evangelicalism has three components. First, salvation for all through the death and resurrection of Christ. Second, belief in the Bible as the only rule of faith and practice, a belief that results in several central doctrines. Third, the missionary desire to share the Gospel, producing the evangelism and missions emphases so characteristic of the last several centuries.

A variation within evangelicalism was the rise of fundamentalism in the United States late in the nineteenth century. Adding to historic evangelicalism a stress on premillennialism and a principle of separation from strictly defined worldliness, fundamentalism won over a great many theologically conservative Protestants by the 1920s, and battled with the modernist movement in the Protestant denominations and schools. Fundamentalism suffered a public defeat at the Scopes Trial in 1925, but continued to flourish in the 1930s and 1940s in missionary activity, education, and the use of media to propagate the Gospel. After World War II, fundamentalism divided, an evangelical center emerged, and both became politically involved in the 1970s and 1980s. Evangelicalism also spawned a left-wing group while fundamentalism remains on the right.

The Spread of the Reformation

After Luther's hearing before the Diet of Worms he was condemned, declared an outlaw, and his books were banned. Rescued by a German prince, he spent several months in the safety of a castle and then returned to Wittenberg, and the Lutheran Reformation was begun in earnest. The sacraments were reduced from seven to two: baptism and the Eucharist (the Lord's Supper), the latter was given a new understanding and the Mass was eventually proscribed; bishops were retained but not archbishops, cardinals, and popes; and clergy celibacy was abolished, and Luther married a former nun. Attempts at reconciliation with the Catholic Church were made.

At the Diet of Speyer in 1529 the Lutherans brought a "protest" against some of the Catholic princes, and from this event the name Protestant derived. In 1530 at Augsburg a last attempt at reconciliation was unsuccessful and Catholic and Protestant views hardened into hostility.

By 1530 other places in Europe also felt reform. Huldreich Zwingli (1484–1531), a Catholic priest, in the 1520s reformed the church in Zurich in German-speaking Switzerland. Initially influenced by Luther, he later split with him over the meaning of the Eucharist and developed a more rationalistic and biblicistic theology. His view of the Lord's Supper as virtually a memorial influenced a number of later Protestants.

Anabaptists, on the so-called left wing of the Reformation, also developed in Switzerland. They strongly affirmed baptism of believers (and therefore a believers-only church), and though they were called Anabaptists (rebaptizers), they saw infant baptism as an invalid form. Some of them advocated communal living. They were persecuted by Catholics and Protestants alike, including the Protestants in Zwingli's Zurich, for the following reasons: some persons and groups at the fringe of the movement engaged in what was seen as bizarre behavior; the Anabaptists held a low view of the state; and Anabaptists were willing to publicly denounce those with whom they disagreed. Further, many Anabaptists were pacifists in an era when pacifism was incompatible with much Christian thinking.

Consisting of a number of small groups like the Mennonites, Hutterites, and various Brethren sects, the Anabaptist movement never achieved unity, but its voice was heard. The Anabaptists advocated a "free" church—free from state intervention—in contrast to Luther, Zwingli, and Calvin, the "magisterial" reformers who turned to the state for help in reforming the church. The free-church tradition gathered force in the following centuries and predominates today in many parts of Christendom.

John Calvin (1509–64) was the reformer of Geneva and the creator of Reformed theology, the theology influential in several bodies of Protestants, especially Presbyterians and Baptists. Born in France a generation later than Luther and Zwingli, Calvin left the Catholic Church in 1533, well after the Reformation had begun. The first edition of his *Institutes of the Christian Religion* was published in Basel in 1536. Though it went through several revisions and editions in the following years, the central teachings remained the same. Like Luther, Calvin believed in justification by faith, but he began his theology with the knowledge of God and emphasized the sovereignty of God. Contrary to popular opinion, Calvin did not make predestination the centerpiece of the *Institutes,* but his view of it was more sharply drawn than the views of Luther and Zwingli (and for that matter Aquinas and Ignatius Loyola, Catholic theologians who also held to predestination of the elect).

Accompanying his belief in sovereignty and predestination was the assurance of the elect. This led to the whole

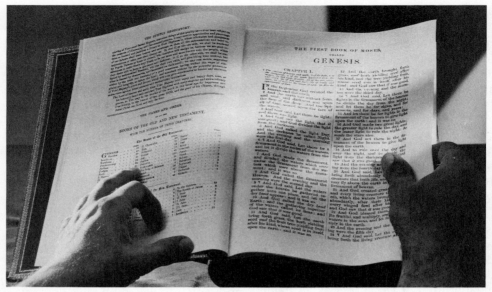

Christians believe the Bible, written over a period of 15 centuries, is inspired by God and contains the truth about God, man and salvation.

question of what were the marks of the true Christian. Catholic theology seemed to cast into some doubt whether a person could be assured of his or her salvation, but the Protestants, other than Luther, suggested some tests. Calvin noted three marks of the Christian; to the Zwinglian profession of faith and the Anabaptists holy living, he added faithful attendance at the sacraments. Later Calvinists like the Puritans added a fourth test: a known conversion experience, what in the United States came to be called the born-again experience. This array of marks of the Christian became the standard understanding for most Protestants outside the Lutheran tradition.

Since the elect were recognized by their beliefs and practice, it became possible to create a holy commonwealth in which God would bring to bear the principles of the kingdom on

all facets of life—political, economic, and social as well as religious. Calvin and his cohorts in Geneva attempted to do just this, and it became a model for all such Calvinist attempts in later generations.

In Geneva the program for the holy commonwealth led to an understanding of the relation between church and state differing from that of Luther and Zwingli. The church ought to be free to determine its own liturgy and exercise discipline of its own members. Luther and Zwingli saw these as state matters, but Calvin persuaded the Geneva magistrates to relinquish these powers to the church. Even the community became a group of the elect, in part because the disaffected left Geneva. But Calvinism as an international movement, which it quickly became in the middle decades of the century as it spread to Scotland, France, Hungary, and elsewhere, was most often unable, because of its minority status, to transfer to other places the total Genevan pattern of church, state, and community.

Much debated is the relation between Calvinism and capitalism. The older view of a direct causal relation has now diminished, and the idea that the rise of capitalism stemmed as much from the waning of religious faith as from the rising of religious faith is now established.

Education was important in Geneva, an academy being established there in 1559. Calvin appreciated the arts more than Zwingli did, and that too has shown in later Calvinist emphases. H. Richard Niebuhr's idea that Reformed theology has a transformist dimension seems correct.

The Reformation in England stands as a unique one. Lutheran ideas were felt as early as the 1520s, but they were rebuffed by the monarch Henry VIII, whose tract against Luther earned him from the pope the title "defender of the faith." But Henry soon ran into his own difficulties with Rome, centering on his marriage and succession problems. He disbanded the monasteries and asserted his headship of the church in England, but did not fully break with the Roman Catholic Church.

After Henry's death in 1547 the religious situation oscillated. His successor, the young Edward VI (ruled 1547–53) was influenced by Protestant advisers, and the next monarch, Queen Mary (ruled 1553–58), was under Catholic tutelage. All the while, the English church was disputing over creeds, liturgy, and its relationship to the state. Finally under Elizabeth I (ruled 1558–1603) a settlement of the religious issue was made. The thirty-nine Articles, quite Reformed in their theology, was issued as the church's creed, and the Book of Common Prayer was revised. The church in England accepted royal supremacy, episcopacy, and the liturgy as defined therein; the break with Rome was realized.

The Anglican Church, as the church in England is known, often sees itself as a fourth force in Christendom, the one organization that can be the means of bringing the three major branches together. Especially in the twentieth century, Anglicans have worked hard in the ecumenical movement to bring about church unity.

The Reformation created the issue of what was the nature of the church. The prevalent idea was that it was a "school for sinners": all the persons in the immediate area, the parish, were baptized into the church community and then schooled in the faith. First was belonging and then (it was hoped) believing. Some Reformers contended for a believers-only church, in which one first believed the faith and then was allowed to belong; for them the church was a "society of saints." Even some who baptized infants, like the Presbyterians, saw such baptism not as creating belonging in the full sense, but as anticipation of belief yet to come. Luther took a middle position with his *ecclesiola in ecclesia*: the "little church" of truly devout believers, the saints, was embedded in the larger group of more nominal members of the congregation.

The Counter-Reformation

It was evident by the 1530s that Protestantism and Roman Catholicism were moving away from each other, in the process creating a tripartite division in Christianity: Orthodox, Roman Catholic, and Protestant.

One expression of the growing religious hostility in the West was the religious wars, military conflicts in which Catholic or Protestant loyalty was a chief component, in France, Germany, and other parts of the Continent in the sixteenth and early seventeenth centuries. England escaped at the time, only to have its religious wars in the midseventeenth century— after the signing of the Peace of Westphalia in 1648, usually seen as the end of the era of religious wars.

Ultimately more important than the wars was the Counter-Reformation in Catholicism. The Council of Trent, probably the most important council meeting in Catholic history until Vatican II in the 1960s, met periodically from the 1540s through the 1560s. What Trent did was to gather up a whole series of doctrinal developments from previous centuries and make them into a single theology, which in turn became accepted Catholic teaching into the twentieth century.

At Trent, reaffirmation was made about many beliefs: Scripture and tradition had equal authority; justification was accomplished by God and man working together; sanc-tification was also the work of God and man; the Mass was a propitiatory sacrifice achieved through the changing of the bread and wine into the very body and blood of Jesus; and purgatory, prayer to the saints, and the veneration of images and relics were affirmed. In most cases, the positions taken were opposed to Protestant teaching.

Concomitant to the Tridentine faith were continuation of the Inquisition (founded in the thirteenth century as a means to uncover and eliminate heresy) that had achieved notoriety in late-fifteenth-century Spain and Portugal, and the Index of Prohibited Books (first issued in 1557; abolished in 1966), a list of works deemed not suitable for reading by the faithful.

In the latter part of the sixteenth century, a new vitality flowed through the Catholic Church in the founding by Ignatius Loyola (1491–1556) in 1540 of the Society of Jesus (Jesuits), whose special obedience to the pope created a kind of papal militia, and in the work of the Spanish mystic Teresa of Avila (1515–82), who revitalized the Carmelite order in Spain and was influential in other parts of Europe through her writings.

Both education and missionary activity surged in the Counter-Reformation. Jesuits in East Asia and Franciscans, Dominicans, and Jesuits in the New World were part of the renewed interest in spreading the Catholic faith. High standards for scholarship and learning, especially among the Jesuits, indicated an educational dynamic in the church also.

The Orthodox in Russia

The Protestant Reformation touched only briefly in the domains in eastern Europe where the Orthodox Church prevailed. Two brief flirtations with the Reformation ended with a denouncing of Protestantism, and the reassertion of Orthodox tradition.

Probably the most important development was the move of the Orthodox into Russia. Legend has it that Prince Vladimir of Kiev (now capital of the Ukraine) listened to Jewish, Muslim, Roman Catholic, and Greek Orthodox advocates present their respective faiths and was convinced of Orthodoxy by the beauty of its liturgy and the splendor of its icons. Vladimir was baptized in 988 and thus began the thousand years of Orthodoxy in Russia just recently celebrated.

Not noted for theological innovation, the Russian Church did produce a vital monasticism, beginning with the eleventh-century monastic leader Theodosius. Influenced by the Greek monks, Theodosius added a social dimension—special regard for the poor—that became characteristic of Russian monks. The Mongol invasion of 1237 led to two centuries of Mongol overlordship, during which time the liturgy of worship and the activity of the monks (who eventually spread all the way across the Asian landmass, crossing the Bering Strait into Alaska in the eighteenth century) kept the church alive.

The Mongol power weakened in the fifteenth century and the duchy of Moscow moved into the political vacuum, uniting the Russians by 1449.

The Byzantine Empire was about to expire and the Orthodox Church in Russia, rather than continuing its deference to Constantinople, became independent (autocephalous, a term used in Orthodoxy to describe the various semi-independent communes in worldwide Orthodoxy). Over the next one hundred years, with Constantinople's approval, the church leaders in Moscow assumed the title of patriarch. About the same time the princes of Moscow began calling themselves tsar (emperor), and Moscow began to be called the Third Rome, the center of Orthodoxy as well as of tsardom.

Few sectarian movements surfaced in Russia, though the Nonpossessors-Possessors controversy of the fifteenth and sixteenth centuries (over whether monasteries should have extensive landholdings) created tension for some time. In 1667 the Old Believers were excommunicated for refusing to accept the liturgical reforms of the patriarch Nikon. Persecuted in both the eighteenth and nineteenth centuries, they had no bishop until 1846. Before that time they had split into two sections, the one section fragmented into many sects.

In the Russian system the church was simply a department of the state, with little room for church leaders to admonish the rulers. The westernizing reforms of Peter the Great and Catherine the Great in the eighteenth century did little to affect the church's role vis à vis the state, so that down to the Revolution of 1917 the church supported the absolutism of the tsars. During most of the seventy years of

Communist rule, the church was in an even more repressed condition.

Today, over eighty percent of the world's Orthodox population is Russian, and now with the new openness in the Soviet Union a resurgent Orthodoxy no doubt will be evident in that nation, as a companion to the recent Orthodox presence in the ecumenical movement and increasing strength in North America.

Early Modern Times

With the religious lines in Europe relatively fixed by 1600—Catholics in southern and western Europe, Protestants in the north and west, and the Orthodox in the southeast and east—the way was prepared for entry into the modern era. Each of the branches of Christendom exported its own variation of Christianity as the European powers spread through the rest of the world economically and politically, reproducing the ecclesiastical systems of the sending nations. One new place, North America, in turn became a missionary-sending center, adding further variety to the European mix.

Beyond the globalization of the church, movements internal to church life and challenges external to the church further added to the mosaic that Christianity became in modern times.

Puritanism

After the Elizabethan Settlement in the Church of England, opposition arose both from pro-Catholics on the right and from those on the left who wished to take the reforms further.

The reformers, called Precisians or Puritans, wanted to reform the church in England in polity (church government), worship, and teachings. Their norm for such reform was the Bible. In their view the English church simply retained too many features from the medieval church; the Bible, the Puritans felt, called for expulsion of those features.

Beyond the general call for reform, several other features characterized Puritanism. One was the demand for a known conversion experience, the recounting of which (the recounting was called a "relation") became for the Puritans in America their requirement for full entry into the congregation. Another was a strong sense of stewardship: time, talent, and money were all to be husbanded to bring glory to their author, God. For some this led to an overly rigorous discipline that created among outsiders the view that Puritans were repressive and inhibited. But the discipline was not extreme for everyone, and while the Puritans were a serious group they were not without mirth and joy.

The Puritan theology was in the Reformed (Calvinist) tradition, in the form called covenant theology, begun by a contemporary of Calvin named Heinrich Bullinger and brought to refinement under the English Puritans. The two covenants, one of works, the other of grace, included all of life in them. All humanity was under the covenant of works, to live according to God's principles. But since sinful human nature precluded that, God graciously gave to the elect the covenant of grace, salvation in Christ. This latter covenant provided the justification unattainable in the covenant of works. Even for the elect the covenant of works still applied, but now there was aid given through grace.

When some of the English Puritans went to New England in America, they saw the opportunity for creating a holy commonwealth in the Geneva tradition. The church consisted of visible saints—those who acceptably related their conversion experience to the congregation—plus their baptized children. But infant baptism was not regenerative, it was a sign of the new covenant the way circumcision was a sign of the old. Most of the adults assumed their children would later experience conversion and become full members of the church, the sign of which was participation in the Lord's Supper. The state in its fullest expression—those adult males who could vote and run for office—was limited to full church members; theoretically, then, the state was run by the visible saints.

This holy commonwealth put in place in the Massachusetts Bay Colony in the l630s was quite short-lived, but the idea of being God's special people passed into the American consciousness and in both religious and secular versions gave later generations of Americans the sense that they had a special role to play in history. As John Winthrop put it in his famous shipboard sermon in l630:

Now the only way to avoyde this shipwracke and to provide for our posterity is to followe the Counsell of Micah, to doe Justly, to love mercy, to walke humbly with our God, for this end, wee must be knitt together in this worke. . . for wee must consider that wee shall be as a Citty upon a Hill, the eies of all people are uppon us.[4]

By the beginnning of the eighteenth century Puritanism was starting to fade as a vital movement, but it had by then produced an enormous literature that carried over into succeeding eras, inspiring later generations of Protestants. To the present time it is the era of American church history most studied, a clear indication of its continuing influence.

Pietism

Seventeenth-century Protestantism, apart from Puritanism, is sometimes branded as "scholastic," a rather pejorative term meaning that Protestants had fallen into dead orthodoxy; the intensity and dynamism of the Reformation had been lost. Into that situation, first in Lutheran Germany, entered a movement known as Pietism. The term, like Puritanism, has suffered from its critics, often being viewed as stuffiness or pretension in religion. But Pietism originally fused a warmhearted faith, holy living, and lay Bible study with missionary work and social philanthropy. Such qualities characterized the university town of Halle, where Philip Spener (1635–1705) and August Francke (1663–1727) created a Pietist center that inspired others.

Furthered by Count Zinzendorf (1700–60), who resuscitated the Moravian Brethren into the Moravian Church, Pietism continued its effect into the eighteenth century. The Moravians were especially missionary, establishing churches in America and elsewhere, and they influenced John Wesley and Wesleyanism. By the end of the century some forms of Pietism had become inward-looking, leading to its poor reputation, but it revitalized Scandinavian Christianity in the nineteenth century and continued to affect British and American Protestantism into the twentieth.

Revivalism

Revivalism is the movement that promotes periodic spiritual intensity in church life, during which the unconverted come to faith and the converted are shaken out of spiritual lethargy. Although it is thought of as a particularly American Protestant form, the Catholic Church's parish missions were of a similar nature, and the long history of renewal movements in the church are at least related forms of spiritual awakening. American Protestants have been its most common practitioners, however, and some historians see it as the distinguishing characteristic of American church life. Since American Protestants have been extensively missionary, revivalism has been exported to other parts of the world as well.

The general sources of revivalism are the Protestant emphasis on preaching (the Word as the center of the worship experience, in contrast to the Catholic emphasis on the Sacrament as the center), the Puritan emphasis on a known conversion experience, and the pietistic emphasis on warmhearted faith. Add to this the notion that the Spirit works in "seasons of harvest" and by the early eighteenth century the concept of periodic awak-

enings had emerged in both Britain and America.

Revivalism in America began with the Great Awakening of the 1730s and 1740s, and was furthered with the rise of camp meetings around 1800 and the Second Great Awakening of the first third of the nineteenth century. The great apologist of revivalism was Jonathan Edwards (1703–55), an American Congregational minister noted for his erudite Calvinism as well as his interest in revival. Edwards published four works on the Great Awakening and they were extremely influential in justifying the movement. He asserted that the whole person (intellect, will, emotion) was affected by conversion, that the true marks of conversion were in the holy life that follows the experience, and that changed hearts produced a changed society.

By the time of evangelist Charles Finney (1792–1875), the general outlines of modern revivalism were set (including some important distinctions from Edwards's thought): protracted meetings held once or twice yearly; preaching for decision; professional itinerant revivalists; and techniques for preparation and conducting of meetings. Later revivalists like D. L. Moody, Billy Sunday, and Billy Graham have followed these general practices.

Revivalism was always more than emotional appeals in frontier conditions. Both urban and rural, rational and emotional, revivalism has cut across all class lines. It has also been tied to social reform movements, most notably in the antebellum United States, but since that time and in other

Famed revivalist Dwight L. Moody preaching to a large crowd at Islington in London, England.
Moody Bible Institute

places as well. Education has been a feature of revivalism's social impact, from the founding of several pre-Revolution colleges to scores of schools founded in the nineteenth and twentieth centuries under the auspices of revivalism.

Parallel to the rise of revivalism in eighteenth-century America was the Evangelical Revival in England, spearheaded by George Whitefield (1715–70) and John Wesley (l703–91). Whitefield preached to large crowds, often outdoors, in England, Scotland, and North America (where he died and to which he made seven trips). Ordained in the Anglican Church, Whitefield was a friend of Wesley, but they disagreed on free will and predestination (Whitefield remained a Calvinist) and thus had separate careers.

John Wesley was also an outdoors itinerant preacher, continuing his work until a few weeks before his death at age eighty-eight. Wesley's genius was the creation of societies which gathered and sustained the awakened and converted. These groups became the center of the Wesleyan revival, emphasizing as they did the need to disciple young converts in the faith; in fact, many conversions took place in the small society meetings. Agreeing with the Reformation doctrine of justification, Wesley made a departure on sanctification in advocating that the Holy Spirit imparted righteousness to believers, thus making it possible for them to be delivered from sin, not just from future judgment.

Wesleyan thought had great influence in Britain and especially America where the Methodist Church was the most rapidly growing church in the nineteenth century. The movement broke over varying emphases, some on sanctification, others on doctrinal purity, still others on social action.

Science, Reason, and Revelation

The seventeenth and eighteenth centuries saw the rise of modern science and the Enlightenment (the use of reason in understanding life), and with them the beginning of long-standing debates about how science and reason should relate to religion.

The Age of Reason (roughly 1650–1800) posed a specific challenge to Christianity when its advocates became thoroughgoing rationalists. Rationalists argued that humanity could understand its experience by thinking logically and objectively. While such an approach can make compromises with Christian belief, the push is away from Christianity because rationalism says the reasonable is the natural and therefore there is little need for invoking the supernatural. At most, we have the unknown, which it is hoped will someday be known. This leaves little room for a personal God or faith.

The cluster of dominant ideas in the Age of Reason were nature, reason, and progress. Nature, quite in contrast to previous thinking in Christendom, was a benign concept, not something suspect because of the presence of sin. Nature was orderly and untroubled, the simple working of the universe as properly understood. To properly understand nature one needed reason. Reason was clearest in mathematics, but it would also enable human beings to found human institutions and human relations that are "natural." Society needs to clear away its superstition and other relics of the past, and then think its way to the clear understanding of human relations.

Reason properly understanding nature leads to progress, a relatively new concept for Western thinking, pagan or Christian. Progress implied a new picture of history: no longer was it a repeatable cycle or a relatively flat line going from point to point, but now it was a line on an upward slant. As humanity gets more and more enlightened (uses reason more), both technological and moral progress are possible.

The chief rational religious form was called deism. The deists, perhaps the majority of intellectuals in western Europe in the eighteenth century, believed in a God who was apprehended through the created order (i.e., with reason) rather than through revelation. The Bible simply confirmed what God had built into the universe: both the natural laws discoverable by science and the moral principles discoverable by philosophy. There was an implied continuity between God, the natural order (God's creation), and humanity. The picture of a fallen natural order and humanity was not subscribed to. At its best, deism was a gentle humanitarianism, but it could be scathing in its denunciation of traditional religion.

The flaw in deist thinking was pointed out by David Hume, the Scottish skeptic, who argued that the deists assumed that God was benevolent when such an argument could not be inferred logically from human experience. At times, like the Lisbon earthquake of 1755 that killed twenty thousand, it looked as though nature (and therefore nature's God) was malevolent. It all depended on how one "read" nature; the deist reading was only one possibility, but their system was built on the assumption that it was the only right reading. Skeptical, Hume disagreed.

Where science fit in the reason-revelation debates is ambiguous. Science as such had no necessary connection with rationalism, but some scientists were rationalists, and some scientific discoveries seemed to place God farther away from the natural world. A related issue is whether Christianity (in Catholic or Protestant forms) spawned modern Western science or science had risen in spite of Christianity. While these ambiguities persist, and while the relation between science and religion remains as an issue, two things seem clear: science as science need not oppose religious faith; and the older picture of a "warfare" between Christianity and science was overstated—recent studies show a closer partnership between the two than the warfare metaphor allowed.

Church and State

From the fourth to the seventeenth centuries the normal arrangement for church-state relations where the church was in the majority was the state church. Any historical argument on the issue would have to conclude that such was the norm.

In the sixteenth and seventeenth centuries two questions began to be asked. Does the state have the right to suppress heresy? The centuries-long response had been a resounding yes, but some were beginning to say the

opposite. Does an individual have the right to express publicly a dissenting religious opinion? The centuries-long answer here had been no, but some were beginning to suggest the opposite.

This ferment over state involvement in internal church affairs and individual dissent reached a point in the seventeenth century where toleration was advocated. Several arguments called into question the validity of nontoleration. For one, coercion did not work well; the wars of religion demonstrated that, with the result being a kind of regional toleration that was still dependent on what the state saw as the majority religious opinion (or what the prince said it ought to be).

In England, John Milton's famous tract on liberty, *Areopagitica* (1644), contended that in religion people ought to be convinced by argument, not coerced by the state.

John Locke (1632–1704) laid out a detailed argument in his *Letter Concerning Toleration* (1689). The state and the church have to be seen as separate entities, he wrote, with the church being concerned about people's souls, the state about their bodies. Their differing concerns mean different approaches: the church uses persuasion, the state uses coercion. Since the two concerns and the two means ought not to cross, and since finality in religion is hard to arrive at, there should be some toleration of dissent. Locke restricted the toleration, however, excluding atheists (they could not be trusted to speak the truth), Roman Catholics (their ultimate loyalty was to the papacy, a power foreign to the English crown), and disruptive sects (a catchall category referring to all who might create social turmoil).

In the same year as Locke's essay, the English government issued its Act of Toleration, the first such in the modern world. And despite some restrictions (a few of which were not removed until the nineteenth century), toleration gradually assumed a role in European and American states. Roman Catholic countries were less ready to move to toleration than Protestant ones, some of them waiting until the twentieth century to do so.

Toleration of dissent did not necessarily lead to the next step: separation of church and state. Two sets of arguments were offered in the United States when that nation was founded. The religious argument stated that God founded the church and that human beings under God's aegis founded the state. The authority in the two was radically different, therefore the state should not, indeed could not, intrude in church matters.

The moral argument, in the hands of Jefferson and Madison in Virginia, stated that morality derived from human nature, not from religion. Therefore, the presence of religion per se made no difference to morality nor, by extension, to society. In light of that, it followed that a person could believe what he or she wished, so long as no harm was done to others. Religion, then, was not a state matter but an individual matter, and the church as such should not be involved in state affairs.

The two sets of arguments laid the basis for two approaches. On the one hand, the separation of church and state means the state should not interfere in internal church matters: it does not mean that religion should be without influence on the state. On the other hand, separation of church and state means there should be a wall of prohibition between the two, the state not interfering in the church, and the church having no influence in the state. These differing opinions have been held in tension in the United States, one side or the other being emphasized by different people at different times.

Other nations have moved toward the separation of church and state, though not always on American terms, and the idea is quite strong in the twentieth century.

The Modern Era

The last two hundred years have seen remarkable changes in the church. Globalization, pluralism, and ecumenism stand out as three of the major features in this time span.

Globalization

Overseas missions in the seventeenth and eighteenth centuries flourished among Roman Catholics, but was relatively weak among Protestants. The Jesuits, Franciscans, and Dominicans all carried out extensive missionary work in the western hemisphere, India, and East Asia. Protestants did some work in North America, the East Indies, and elsewhere.

The modern missions movement

The Kowloon Tong Alliance Church in the British territory of Hong Kong, a symbol of the globalization of Christianity. J. Lewis

among Protestants began with William Carey, who went to India in 1793 under the sponsorship of the Baptist Missionary Society. Carey's struggle to be appointed, followed by his triumph over family difficulties and internal mission problems in India, served as an inspiration for others to go overseas from Europe and America. The formation of missionary-sending agencies continued unabated through the nineteenth century, sometimes called the "great century" of missionary activity.

By the end of the century thousands had gone from their homelands to circle the globe with the Gospel message. Contrary to common belief, Protestant missions were not always closely tied to commerce. Recent studies show that missionaries and traders were as likely to oppose each other as to engage in mutual reinforcement for their enterprises. Thus, while it is true that both Protestant and Catholic missionaries went to areas newly opened to European enterprise, it did not mean that the missionaries were dependent on commerce for carrying out

their work. Nor were Western missionaries sympathetic to the race theory that prevailed in the late nineteenth century. Common to many academics at the time was the belief that each race had certain characteristics, built in genetically. In European and American hands race theory usually favored whites as the leadership race. The determinism of the theory was what bothered missionaries, who argued that what made the charcteristics of civilization was religion, not genetics, and while European groups clearly seemed to be ahead of other peoples in a number of ways, the source for the lead was the presence of Christianity in the culture.

At the end of the century a great burst of missions activity was fostered by the student movement, particularly strong in Britain and North America. Propelled by the slogan "the evangelization of the world in this generation," thousands of university students offered themselves for missionary service. Though the original movement lost direction in the 1920s and 1930s, another student movement began after World War II and still continues.

Not all missionary activity was direct evangelism. Medicine and education from the beginning played important parts, and they still do. Translation was integral to missions, and its positive effect was to sanction the language (and by implication at least some of the culture) of the peoples among whom it was done. Recently, missions organizations have included economic development as another part of their global outreach.

Women played an important role in missions. Most of the women who went overseas in the early nineteenth century were missionary wives. But about the middle of the century single women were accepted by mission boards, and by World War I women missionaries (both single and married) outnumbered men by two to one. Most boards did not accept single men for missionary appointment.

Missions growth continued through the first half of the twentieth century at a steady pace, but then another major burst of activity followed World War II, and that thrust has not abated yet among more conservative agencies (liberal Protestant denominations have all suffered personnel losses in the last three decades). If anything, the approach of the millennial year has only spurred missions more.

The more liberal Protestants have moved away from missions to mission. The dropping of the final *s* is an important ideological matter. "Mission" means social engagement, dialogue with other religions, and decline in evangelism; "missions" smacks of triumphalism. Mission is a more humble approach to others, say these folk.

Another development since World War II has been the rise of mission-sending agencies in missionary lands. Asian nations like Korea and Japan are sending missionaries to other parts of the world. Some African nations are doing the same. The prediction that Africa may become the most Christianized of all the continents is an indication of the possible shift away from Europe and North America, though financial considerations will probably mean continued North American presence. The decline of church attendance in Europe (Catholic Poland is the exception) has meant a dramatic shift there, so that conservative organizations in North America are sending missionaries to "Christian" Europe. Some changes are evident in Roman Catholic nations: for example, Chile has more Protestant Pentecostals than Roman Catholics in attendance at Sunday services. Other South American countries may be moving in the same direction as they feel the effects of the strong Pentecostal tide in Latin America.

Pluralism

Pluralism can be defined as simply the fact that more than one expression of Christianity exists. It can also be an argument that all theologies are equal; no one Christian theology is normative. Some further argue that, in regard to Christianity and other religions, no one religion has truth (i.e., there are no false religions). This last point has gained currency in the contemporary world. Such a view is counter to the belief that Christianity is exclusive, i.e., it is true and therefore some aspects of other religions are false.

In regard to the first matter, it can hardly be argued that there is no pluralism in Christianity. There are literally scores of variants within groups who claim allegiance to traditional Christian belief, to say nothing of the hundreds of additional groups who claim the name Christian while not espousing traditional beliefs.

Are there theological norms in Christianity? For two centuries a whole array of theologies has bewildered and confused the church. Classic liberalism, neo-orthodoxy, religionless Christianity, "death of God" theology, process theology, and the various liberation theologies (feminist theology, Latin American liberation theology, black theology, et al.) vie for the allegiance of the person in the pew and the marketplace. The presence of this array leads some to conclude that no theology is normative. Others, more inclined to accept some limits to theological speculation, rule out these theologies. The basic question is, What are the parameters outside of which a theology can be branded as not Christian?

One reason for theological diversity stems from the variety of ways in which Christianity has related to culture, whether preliterate or modern. Another is biblical criticism (which began in the nineteenth century) with its historical approach to the Bible and reformulation of some of the long-held understandings about the Bible. Biblical criticism has both aided in interpreting the text and has had the effect of keeping the Bible from the layman, an undermining of the Protestant belief in the perspicacity of the Scripture. Roman Catholic biblical scholarship, perhaps two generations behind Protestant movements, has since the 1950s displayed the same variety of views of the text as Protestants have.

Are there false religions in the world? Recent thinkers like Paul Knitter (Roman Catholic) and John Hick (Anglican) say that Christianity cannot claim exclusiveness among the world's religions. Their arguments have been advanced, defended, and criticized—and have captured the more liberal-minded in the churches. Christian traditionalists argue the other side, contending that without exclusivity Christianity (and for that matter virtually every other world religion) is vitiated: its canonical texts misunderstood, and its core meaning lost.

Ecumenism

Hopes for unity among the churches are based on the principle of oneness laid down by Christ in John 17. The oneness is to be achieved throughout "the inhabited world" (Gk., *oikoumene*; hence, ecumenical and its variations). But diversity, if not outright hostility, has characterized much of church history. At times, appeals for unity were made from within the diversity. The exclusive idea contained in "no salvation outside the church" meant that the Roman Catholic and Orthodox communities each claimed they alone were the true church—here, unity is located in a person (the bishop of Rome) or in a tradition (Orthodoxy). With the breakup of unity in the western church that came with the Reformation (to say nothing about internal battling among Protestants), new understandings of diversity and unity had to be considered.

One approach among Protestants was to begin with the concept of the invisible church (all believers in all times in all locations) as the ultimate unity and to suggest that due to human limitations (including sinfulness) and the inability for anyone to know all the truth, the creation of separate church factions was inevitable. These factions hardened into separate church groups (called denominations in Protestantism) by the later eighteenth century, and the modern diversity was born. This view was a positive picture of denominationalism; the question was not, what is the true church? but, which are the true churches? This still drew lines between church bodies, some of which were branded as not true and therefore did not qualify as "churches." And at the time neither Catholics nor the Orthodox accepted this Protestant approach.

Others took a dimmer view of diversity, suggesting it derived from the loss of an established (state approved and supported) church, or that it came from geographical sources, or worse yet that it resulted from social differences among adherents, some denominations appealing to the disinherited in society while others appealed to the social elites. Each of these views was a picture of diversity that, according to these writers, should be overcome.

Whether diversity was seen positively or negatively, attempts at unity were made. The visible church could never achieve the unity of the invisible church, but perhaps it could achieve unity on some grounds. So, in the nineteenth century a number of transdenominational enterprises were begun—Bible societies, missionary organizations, and the like—culminating in the English-speaking world in the Evangelical Alliance of the middle and late decades. The unity in the alliance was around the core doctrines of the faith; polity, ritual, and other diversities could remain. The alliance broke up at the end of the century

over doctrinal issues—the core could not be agreed on. Still, ecumenism was a matter for discussion.

The contemporary ecumenical movement dates from the World Missionary Conference, Edinburgh, 1910, attended by representatives of more than 150 Protestant organizations. From this meeting came the International Missionary Council, which, with the conferences on Life and Work (1925) and Faith and Order (1927), became the sources for the creation of the World Council of Churches in 1948. The Orthodox communions and the so-called younger churches of Asia and Africa were part of the movement. The Roman Catholic Church made a major concession toward ecumenism with the publication in 1964 of the Second Vatican Council's Decree on Ecumenism. Calling those in Orthodoxy and Protestantism "separated brethren" (rather than seeing them as outside the church), the document paved the way for wider Catholic participation; the Roman Catholic Church, however, is not an official member of the World Council.

Begun in hope and optimism, the World Council achieved both organic union among some denominations and unity of purpose among many of its members. National and local branches appeared; some of them, like the National Council of Churches in the United States, very formidable organizations. However, the ecumenical movement has lost vitality in recent years. Funding for the various levels has declined; the union movement, especially in the United States, has stalled; and the reputation of the movement has suffered because of its emphasis on social and political issues and its generally liberal theology.

The ecumenical movement—whose advocates are called ecumenists or conciliarists—has never included significant portions of the Protestant churches, nor has it always enjoyed full grass-roots support in its member churches (most of them the mainline denominations). The recent upsurge of evangelicalism, for centuries the dominant view in Protestantism, has served to demonstrate this division. Counter organizations of ecumenism like the World Evangelical Fellowship, umbrella missionary organizations, and, on the right wing, fundamentalist organizations, compete with the World Council and its various regional expressions. While the term *ecumenical* often refers to the World Council and its religious ideology, these other groupings are ecumenical as well.

Church Practices

Sacraments

Sacraments are the signs of Christian initiation and ritual. Since the time of Augustine of Hippo, the term *sacrament* has often carried the meaning of an outward and visible sign of an inward conferring of grace. This definition depends on what one sees as the nature of the church. The Augustinian view, strong in Roman Catholicism, is that the church is the means of grace from God to the communicants, and the various sacraments are the vehicles that carry the grace. Roman Catholicism numbers seven sacraments in the system; the Orthodox Church numbers seven mysteries, but takes a less rigid approach to the significance of the number seven. Most Protestants have a different view of the church, one that sees grace coming directly from God to the individual member, and therefore typically do not have a sacramental system. Many Protestants prefer the word *ordinance* to *sacrament*, because the latter is freighted with the Augustinian meaning. Typically in Protestant groups there are two sacraments, Communion and baptism.

Communion

A major ingredient in Christian worship is the Eucharist (Gk., thanksgiving) service—also called Communion or the Lord's Supper. Based on the Last Supper recorded in the Gospels and on passages from Paul's letters, bread and wine (or grape juice) are taken by the participants. The Eucharist has been variously understood by different branches of the church, usually revolving around the issue of the real presence—whether Jesus is present in the meal.

The Roman Catholic position, official since the Fourth Lateran Council in 1215, is that in the Eucharist (the Mass) the bread and wine are changed into the body and blood of Jesus (the body born of Mary and which died on the cross) by a process called transubstantiation. The external "accidents" like taste and appearance remain the same, it is the internal "substance" that changes. Further, the Mass is a bloodless sacrifice, in which Jesus is immolated and provides propitiation for sins to those who take the Eucharist in faith. The Orthodox Church accepts the belief in transubstantiation, but its emphasis is not on the sacrificial nature of the Eucharist meal, but on how it achieves unity between the believer and Christ. Also, the change in the elements does not occur at the words of institution— "this is my body"—but at the invocation of the Holy Spirit: "Send thy Holy Spirit . . stronger emphasis on the Holy Spirit in the church than do Roman Catholics.

The Protestants disagree with the Catholics and Orthodox. Luther rejected both the accident-substance theory and the Mass as a propitiatory sacrifice, replacing them with what is called consubstantiation. Jesus is bodily present in the Eucharist, in, with, and under the elements of bread and wine, and the body is received by all who partake in faith. Calvin accepted neither transubstantiation nor consubstantiation, saying that the body and blood of Christ are received in Communion, but in a spiritual manner; the real body of Christ is in heaven. Zwingli held to a memorialist position, that neither "the essence nor the reality" of Christ was present; Christ was seen through "the contemplation of faith."

Baptism

The universal rite of initiation into the church, baptism (to wash, to purify with water) has, like the Eucharist, received various interpretations. The subjects of baptism are either the children of professing Christians or adult confessors of the faith. In the earliest church adult baptism was the commonest, and is still the demand among groups like the Baptists who require a personal confession of faith prior to the rite, but since about the

third century the baptism of infants has been prevalent.

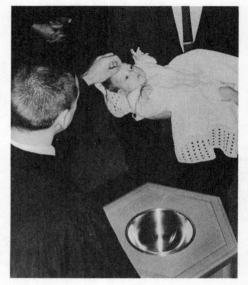

Baptism is an initiatory rite common to all Christian groups, though its mode and meaning vary.

A further issue concerns what happens in the baptismal act. According to Roman Catholic, Orthodox, and Lutheran doctrine, when infants are baptized they are regenerated. Other infant baptizers, like Presbyterians and Congregationalists, say the act is a sign of presence in the covenant but is not regenerating; each person must come to conscious personal faith as an indication of regeneration. Virtually all who baptize adults believe that it is believer's baptism, viz., the person has experienced conversion prior to the baptism event; some sections of the Churches of Christ denomination believe that believer's baptism is a regenerating act.

As to mode, three methods are used: sprinkling (aspersion), pouring (affusion), and immersion. While virtually everyone agrees that in classical Greece the word *baptizein* meant "to immerse," some argue that in its theological use the word means "to wash" or "to purify with water," without reference to the means of washing. Immersion advocates also contend that union with the death and resurrection of Christ, the picture baptism is meant to portray, is best seen in that mode. Nonimmersionists say that the mode is not relevant to meaning. Most groups that practice infant baptism do so by sprinkling, though the Orthodox Church practices trine immersion, and most groups that practice believer's baptism use pouring or immersion.

Role of Women

Beginning with their presence in Jesus' ministry, women have played important roles in the life of the church. References to women are scattered throughout the book of Acts and the Epistles. Women monastics appeared almost simultaneously with the founding of monastic orders. Active membership in the churches has at times been preponderantly women, and women have often been in the majority in membership.

The chief issue of the last two centuries has been the role of leadership for women, specifically, ordination to priestly and ministerial positions. Neither the Roman Catholic nor the Orthodox churches ordain women to the priesthood. A few Protestant groups began ordaining women to the pastorate in the midnineteenth century, but most Protestants did not allow women's ordination. In recent years, many more Protestant groups have ordained women into the ministry, though the question of ordination remains a much-debated matter.

Discussion

1. How did Christianity relate to its Roman and Jewish background?
2. What issues separated the western (Roman Catholic) church from the eastern (Orthodox) church?
3. What were the causes and results of the sixteenth-century Protestant Reformation?
4. What kinds of diversity were present among Protestants in the seventeenth and eighteenth centuries?
5. Discuss the issues of the modern era: What are the components of controversy in the issues?

Notes

[1]From *The Rule of St. Benedict* quoted in Henry Bettenson, ed., *Documents of the Christian Church*, 2d ed. (London: Oxford Univ. Press, 1963), 117.

[2]From *The Definition of the Council of Chalcedon* (451), ibid., 51.

[3]Quoted in Roland Bainton, *Christendom*, (N.Y.: Harper and Row, 1966), vol. 2, 21.

[4]Quoted in Robert R. Mathisen, *The Role of Religion in American Life* (Washington: University Press of America, 1982), 18.

7 Islam–Unity and Diversity

Taj Mahal. Agra, India. 1643 C.E. This most well known (to Westerners) of all Islamic structures is not a mosque but the tomb of Mumtaz, the beloved wife of the Mughal ruler Shah Jahan.

Background

The word *Islam* is an Arabic noun meaning "submission" or "surrender" and is used to refer to the faith of at least 700 million persons in the world today. This religion calls them to surrender their lives to the will of God as it affects every area of their lives personally and collectively. The word *Muslim* (variant: *Moslem*) means "one who submits" or "one who commits himself to surrender." The faithful hold to many beliefs and practices that are quite uniform throughout the world. Yet there are also sectarian differences that sometimes lead to quarrels and even fratricide.

Muslims begin their calendar with the year A.H. 1 (*anno Hegira*), or C.E. 622, when Muhammad was forced to flee Mecca because his doctrines and claims were unpopular. Islam is thus more than fourteen centuries old, though it remains the youngest of the major world religions. Because of their common spiritual heroes such as Abraham, Moses, David, and Jesus and because of a mutual belief in monotheism, Christians and Jews are respectfully called *Kithabia*, or "people of the book."

Apart from the Dome of the Rock in Jerusalem, all the places of greatest importance to Islam are found in the modern state of Saudi Arabia.

The Land and the People Before Islam

The Arabian peninsula forms a vast rectangle of some 1.4 million square miles. It is bordered on the north by the biblical Fertile Crescent, on the east and south by the Persian Gulf and Indian Ocean, and on the west by the Red Sea. The most significant religious sector is the narrow western corridor from Yemen on the south to the Gulf of Aqaba on the north, in which are found the cities of Taif, Mecca, Medina, and Petra, which were linked by caravan traders since pre-Islamic times. The southwest districts of Yemen consist of a well-watered mountain country which from an early date permitted the rise of an agricultural and sedentary civilization. Most of the rest of the peninsula consists of waterless deserts broken by the occasional oasis.

The deserts of Arabia are of various kinds. The most important is the Nefud, a sea of enormous shifting sand dunes forming a landscape of constantly changing topography that separates Damascus in the north from Medina in the south. There is steppe country near Syria and Iraq, and between these zones communication and travel is limited and difficult. The center and northern part of the peninsula is traditionally divided by the Arabs into three zones: the Red Sea coast, the *Hijaz* or (barrier), and the Najd coast.[1]

From very early times Arabia had formed part of the trading network between Mediterranean countries and countries farther east. This east-west traffic has had much to do with the growth of ports of trade and routes of commerce on the peninsula. One route ran from the coast of Palestine, along the Red Sea coastal range, through places like Medina, Mecca, Jeddah, and Taif, and then southward to present day Yemen. This was at various times a route for caravan traffic between the empire of Alexander and countries in more distant Asia.

There has been no archaeological investigation in Saudi Arabia like that in modern Israel, and therefore very little about pre-Islamic history is known. One is left only with theories about the past. One, called the Winkler-Caetani theory, is that Arabia was originally a land of great fertility and the first home of the Semitic peoples who dispersed from there. Through the millennia it has been undergoing a process of steady desiccation with the drying up of water sources and a steady spread of desert across cultivatable land.

The national tradition of the Arabs divides the Arabian people into two main groups: the northern and the southern. This distinction is echoed in Genesis 10 where two distinct lines of descent from Shem are given for the peoples of southwest, central, and northern Arabia. The southern Arabian dialect is different from that of the north, which ultimately developed into what is now known as classical Arabic.

The chronology of early southern Arabian history is obscure. One of the earliest kingdoms named in early records is Saba, which is perhaps identical with the biblical Sheba. It may have been in existence as early as the tenth century B.C.E. About the year 750 B.C.E. one of the Sabean kings built the famous Marib dam, which for a very long time regulated the agricultural life of the kingdom. Commercial links were maintained between this kingdom and the African coastline to the west.

From the time of the conquests of Alexander the Great there has been increased contact and information about southern Arabia. The basis of society in southern Arabia was agriculture, and the inscriptions, with frequent references to dams, canals,

boundary problems, and landed property, suggest a high degree of development. The political organization of southern Arabia was monarchic and appears to have been solidly founded with regular dynastic successors. The kings were not divine and their authority was limited by councils of nobles and later by a kind of feudalistic system.

Of the history of central and northern Arabia there is much less information. There were apparently some semicivilized border states in Syria and across the northern Arabian desert. They were strongly influenced by Hellenized Aramaic culture and used the Aramaic language for their inscriptions. One kingdom was Nabatea which built its capital at Petra.

At some time in the fourth century C.E. the trade routes seem to have been diverted from western Arabia to other channels, probably via Egypt and the Red Sea, or the Euphrates valley and the Persian Gulf. The period between the fourth and sixth centuries was one of decline and deterioration of trade and economic viability. Historians note a movement away from trade and cultivation and toward nomadism.

The dominant Arab social feature on the eve of Islam was tribalism. In Bedouin society the social unit is the group, not the individual. The latter has rights and duties only as a member of the group. It is held together externally by the need for self-defense against hardships and dangers of desert life and internally by the basic social bond of bloodties of descent within the male line. The livelihood of

A Some trade routes at the time of Muhammad ➝

B Islamic expansion to 750 CE

1 Mecca (Muhammad born 570CE)
2 Medina (Muhammad died 632CE)
3 Damascus
4 San'a
5 Muscat

Conquests before the death of Prophet Muhammad in 632CE

Muslim conquests under the rightly guided Caliphs 632–661CE

Islamic expansion under the Umayyads 661–750CE

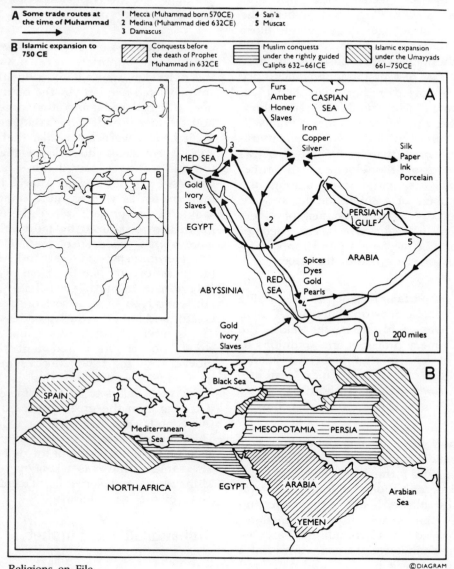

Religions on File

©DIAGRAM

the tribe depended on the flocks and herds, and on raiding neighboring countries and the caravans that passed through them. It was by a kind of chain of mutual raiding that things from the outlying areas made their way into the interior. The tribe did not permit private holding of property but exercised mutual rights over pastures, oases, and water sources. Only movable objects were subject to personal ownership.

The tribe was organized politically

around an elected leader who was called a *sheikh* (Ar., one who bears the marks of old age; a title given to those who are respected or venerated). His authority was never absolute but more like that of a first among equals since he followed rather than led tribal opinion. He could neither impose duties nor inflict penalties by himself. The function of the *sheikh* was arbitration rather than command. He was elected by the elders of the tribe, usually selected from among the members of a single family, and advised by a larger council of elders called a *majli*, which consisted of heads of the families and representatives of clans within the tribe.

An important fact of pre-Islamic life for Islamic developments is that tribal life was regulated by the *sunna*, the customary practices and traditions of tribal leaders that had accumulated through the years to guide tribal life. The *sunna* was the authoritative guide for all aspects of appropriate behavior.

While most of the population was nomadic, some of the people lived at oases and formed a rudimentary political organization. Typically, one family established a sort of petty kingship over the inhabitants and sometimes extended it to surrounding tribes. One ruling family might gain control of a nearby oasis as well and thus put together a sort of desert empire. The petty empire of Kinda, in the fifth to sixth century C.E. was one such example. This empire succeeded in binding together competing tribes in a confederation that was celebrated by Arabic poetry. Though their languages differed, they shared a common poetic technique which was valued for its beauty of expression.

One of these oases, Mecca, grew to considerable importance and power. Part of its significance had to do with a shrine visited regularly by the population, who believed it and other shrines housed many gods and goddesses. Their beliefs were not unlike that of ancient Semites who acknowledged the spirits of trees, sacred stones, and shrines. Some tribes were attached to local deities as well as more universally accepted ones. Three of the major deities recognized by most tribes were Manat (goddess of fate), Uzza (the morning star goddess), and Allat (goddess of the sun). These were subordinate to the highest deity, Allah, conceived of as a sort of far-off creator and father of these goddesses. The symbol of Allah was usually a stone, housed in a red tent that moved with the tribe. Mecca's most important pre-Islamic shrine is believed by scholars to be the same one that stands in the great courtyard of the Grand Mosque in Mecca today. This meteorite was made the center of a shrine for the worship of the deities. The same shrine was taken over by Muhammad and serves as a centerpiece of the *hajj* pilgrimage.

Muhammad the Prophet

Sources on the Life of Muhammad

It is difficult to speak of a history of the life of the prophet Muhammad. Though helpful inferences can be made, the *Quran* does not chronicle his life in any way similar to the treatment Jesus receives in the Gospels. What is believed about the prophet's life comes from a body of oral tradition called a *hadith*, which authorities wrote down in the first and succeeding generations. It is difficult to evaluate the historical accuracy of *hadiths*. There were also biographies written in the early centuries such as that of Ibn-Ishaq (d. c.e. 767), which survives only in fragment form, while that of Ibn Hisham (d. c.e. 833) is more complete. What follows is what Muslims generally believe about Muhammad and his times.

Muhammad and the Early Mecca Years

Muhammad was of the Hashim clan of the tribe of Quraish and lived in Mecca, where he was born about c.e. 570. He was left an orphan at age six and lived with either his maternal or paternal grandfather and his uncle. He is believed to have engaged in the caravan economy, traveling with entrepreneurs who bought and sold. Like his peers he believed in *jinn* (Ar., spirits), Satan, goddesses such as al-Uzza, and the remote creator Allah (a general term meaning the "deity" and cognate to the Hebrew *El*). At the age of twenty-five he married the widow Khadijah, who was fifteen years older. She was wealthy from commercial ventures which Muhammad subsequently managed. They had several children but only their daughter Fatimah survived.

Almost everything indicates Muhammad was dissatisfied with society in his day. He opposed the fratricidal strife between tribes and clans and had some doubts about the existing polytheistic beliefs and practices. At the heart of this opposition may have been excesses of his day, or what he felt were corruptions from the past. Most of all he was critical of moral degeneration and the belief in many deities. It is widely believed he was subject to visions and trances and was given to meditation and prayer. This led to the revelations Muslims believe he received. His contact with Jewish and Christian communities or their beliefs concerning one god and eternal judgment for those rejecting him probably conditioned the development of his ideas considerably.

Dome of the Rock in Jerusalem. Next to those in Mecca and Medina, it is the most sacred shrine since it is believed to cover the rock from which Muhammad ascended to heaven with the angel Gabriel to talk with God. Mike Saunier

Tradition has it that during a moment of solitary meditation and prayer in a cave outside Mecca he received the first of many revelations. The first word the angelic messenger said was "recite" (translated "read" in the following *sura* [Ar., chapter]). This word, from which the word *Quran* is derived, marks the beginning of both Muhammad's prophetic call and the final revelations of God to man through him. Sura 96:1–5 is believed to contain the exact words from God on this occasion. The following is the complete chapter with title.

96. The Clot
In the name of Allah, the Beneficent, the Merciful.

1. Read: In the name of thy Lord who createth,
2. Createth man from a clot.
3. Read: And thy Lord is the Most Bounteous,
4. Who teacheth by the pen,
5. Teacheth man that which he knew not.
6. Nay, but verily man is rebellious
7. That he thinketh himself independent!
8. Lo! unto thy Lord is the return.
9. Hast thou seen him who dissuadeth
10. A slave when he prayeth?
11. Hast thou seen if he (relieth) on the guidance (of Allah)
12. Or enjoineth piety?
13. Hast thou seen if he denieth (Allah's guidance) and is forward?
14. Is he then unaware that Allah seeth?
15. Nay, but if he cease not We will seize him by the forelock-
16. The lying, sinful forelock-
17. Then let him call upon his henchmen!
18. We will call the guards of hell.
19. Nay! Obey not thou him. But prostrate thyself, and draw near (unto Allah).[2]

This was the first of many revelations, all of which Muhammad repeated word for word to his wife and relatives, who became the first believers. Though beset by some self-doubt, he came to believe he was a true *nabi* (Ar., prophet) and *rasul* (Ar., apostle) of Allah, the one and only true God.

Muhammad's attempts to establish these revelations as bona fide messages from God with his contemporaries were not very successful. His emphasis on one god and a coming judgment were disturbing enough. But his opposition to the polytheistic shrines, so profitable for Meccan life, and his claim to authority and leadership as the final prophet aroused opposition. The few converts he gained included his wife, his cousin Ali, and Abu Bakr, a relative. Some from among the poor also accepted his message. The opposition to Muhammad's teaching was not only religious but social in that Muhammad departed from ancestral tradition and rejected the *sunna* of the tribes and their clans. Muhammad's teachings, if accepted, would necessitate a radical revision of traditional society.

Over a ten-year period, during which the revelations continued, the opposition hardened until he and his Hashimite clan were restricted to a sector of the city by official ban. He tried to arrange a protective alliance with officials of the mountain city of Taif and Bedouins residing near Mecca. But the death of his wife (C.E. 619) and other reversals led inevitably to the *hijra* (Ar., flight) in 622 to Yathrib (later named Medina in honor of the prophet) some three hundred miles to the north.

Muhammad's Success in Medina

Muhammad's success in Medina had something to do with the pre-existing social unrest there caused by blood feuds between two competing tribes. During his final two years of struggle in Mecca he was invited to arbitrate this dispute, since he had established

Stamp, issued by the Indian government in 1979, commemorating the beginning of the 15th century A.H. (After Hijira). About 80 million Muslims live in India making it the third largest Muslim country in the world.

himself as a person of power and moral integrity. He succeeded in quelling the local feuds by political maneuvering, personal charisma, and support for his religion, which provided a new focus of loyalty rather than that of blood and clan. The Jewish community of Medina had introduced monotheistic ideas that prepared the warring tribes to be more open to Muhammad's views, and hence Quranic passages from this era are generally hospitable toward Jews. Scholars claim to see a hardening of his attitude toward Jews in later *sura.*

At first Muhammad's influence and power was quite limited among the new *umma* (Ar., community of faith). But Muhammad's eight years in Me-dina saw the erection of the first mosque (from Ar., *masjid*, place of prayer), the acceptance of Islam by the general populace, and periodic skirmishes to supply his growing army through caravan raids. This led them to occasional clashes with forces from Mecca. During a major conflict in C.E. 624, called the battle of Badr, Muhammad showed his hand as a skilled organizer and warrior. After attempts at treaty, a final victory over Mecca was won in 630, which established his unquestioned power in the two cities and among allied tribes in the countryside. He returned that year in conquest, ordered the removal of shrines to the deities, and consecrated the Ka'ba (a black-stone, cubelike shrine) to the worship of the one god Allah. But Muhammad's career as prophet and ruler lasted only two years, as he died in 632. His achievements may be summarized as follows. First, he brought a new religion complete with new ethical and monotheistic concepts to the pagan people of western Arabia. This religion was centered on a book which was the infallible guide to thought and conduct. Second, he succeeded in establishing a new empire of united—and well armed and organized—Arab tribes committed to the will of Allah. Third, he provided a missionary incentive for his followers to spread their control over others in the outlying areas.

Muhammad and His Successors

There is some indication that certain prominent men did not expect Muhammad to die at all. His death was a crisis for the community, for Muhammad had not chosen a successor nor appointed a council of advisers in accordance with the normal dictates of tribal politics. He had claimed a unique and exclusive authority for himself as the final prophet of Allah. The usual pattern would have been the appointment of a new tribal chief, but without a council it was necessary to take direct action. Three men took the situation in hand and forced Abu Bakr, an early convert and trusted companion, on the community as the sole successor to the prophet. Bakr was given the title of *caliph* (Ar., deputy, successor), since his task was to pass on the heritage of the prophet.

Abu Bakr

Bakr (ruled C.E. 632–34) was faced with a difficult situation. Some Arab tribes that pledged allegiance to Muhammad did so only to him personally. At his death, they felt the covenant was dissolved and were not about to give support to Bakr unless compelled to do so. He dealt with this situation by commanding an expeditionary force that subjugated tribes in Arabia and southern Palestine thus firmly establishing his power on the foundation of Muhammad's earlier success. Bakr was motivated to undertake this partly because Muhammad, immediately prior to his death, had announced his goal of extending his movement to the farthest reaches of Arabia and Palestine. Bakr also clashed with Roman and Persian garrisons and established communities of converts in Persia (Iran). He died in 634 after only two years of his califate.

Umar

Before his death Bakr nominated Umar, who ruled from C.E. 634 through 644. He has been called the most brilliant of the first four leaders, who are sometimes called "The Rightly Guided Caliphs." Umar followed up on Bakr's policies of conquest. On the northwest was a Christian tribe called Bani Ghassan and on the northeast was another somewhat Christian tribe called Bani Hira. These had been subsidized alternately by Persians and Byzantines to act as buffers between each other, as they were often engaged in struggles to gain advantage. These Christian tribes did not have much love for the Byzantines, who forced, from their perspective, a brand of Hellenized Christianity on them in the belief their monophysite and Nestorian beliefs were only half-Christian. The tribes also served as a sort of cushion to absorb rising Arab expansionism. Subsidy from Byzantium and Persia was gradually withdrawn due to dwindling resources. This coincided with renewed Arab advances under Umar, and thus the tribes willingly accepted Arab rule and even joined them in the conquest of Persia. There is evidence that Christians at first viewed the Arab expansion as primarily a political and not a religious movement. Persia was brought into the Arab orbit largely through Christian cooperation.

Umar then turned his attention to the northwest and Syria. At that time Syria was a province of the Byzantines, whose capital had shifted to Constantinople. These Roman rulers were mostly Greek and not Latins from the West. Hereclius, the emperor, fought against the Muslims in Syria but lost partly because the Christian Syrians would as soon have Arab rulers as Greek rulers. The Byzantine rulers had persecuted their Christian coreligionists because they were Syrian Orthodox (Jacobites) who were not in full communion with Byzantine's official church, the Roman Catholic.

In Persia, Syria, Egypt, and other subjugated lands, administration was mostly in the hands of non-Muslims who ruled by permission of their Arab conquerors as long as they paid assessed taxes. In the early decades of the Islamic era Arabs would leave home for conquest and return. Later, Arabs stayed to occupy, intermarry, and control. Non-Muslims were sometimes forced to convert at the point of the sword but more often they could maintain their religious affiliation by paying *jizya* (Ar., poll tax), exempting them from service in the military.

Uthman

Umar was assassinated in C.E. 644, which indicates the existence of a power struggle. Uthman (ruled 644–56) appears to have been a weak ruler who made the mistake of favoring one clan of Muhammad's Quraish tribe over the others. Uthman was of the Umayyad clan, which he favored over the Hashim clan to which Muhammad and his son-in-law Ali belonged. Clan and internecine tribal politics led to Uthman's murder in Medina. His death is seen by some as the beginning of the unraveling of Arab solidarity.

Ali

Ali (ruled 656–61) was the cousin and son-in-law of Muhammad and was present at Uthman's assassination. Being of the Hashim clan, he and his clan were resented and blamed by the Umayyads for the death of their leader Uthman. The Umayyads were well established in the administration of the far-flung empire as Uthman had shrewdly appointed only his relatives as rulers and administrators of distant colonies. Once in power Ali sought to replace these with members of his own clan and was largely successful. However, ibn-abi-Sufyan, the governor of Syria, refused to give up his post to Ali's new appointee and raised an army to defend himself. After a protracted struggle the Syrian Arabs defeated Ali. While attempting to regain control of his own disenchanted troops Ali was slain enroute to worship at a mosque in his recently established capitol at Kufah in Iran. The period of the "Four Rightly Guided Caliphs" had come to an end.

The Islamic Empire Spreads

The governor of Syria who successfully resisted removal was Muawiya. He succeeded in making Syria the new center of Islamic culture and the main power in extending Islamo-Arabic conquest during the period from 661 to 750. In 711 Muhammad bin Qasim made his first foray into the distant land of India, which was destined to become a great Islamic nation from the twelfth to the sixteenth century. During the same period Muslims pushed along the northern African coast, from which they passed to Europe. Tariq, governor of northwest Africa, landed seven thousand men at Gibraltar and began the conquest of Spain. He seized the cities of Seville and Merida, conquered most of the Spanish peninsula, and moved across the Pyrenees into southern France. This northward movement was checked by nobles called Franks, who under Charles Martel defeated the Muslims at the battle of Tours (Poitiers) in 732.

The Umayyads of Syria were succeeded by the Abbasids, who moved the center of Islamo-Arabic power from Damascus in Syria to Baghdad in Iraq. Each of the conquered peoples began in succession to declare their political independence: first in Spain, then in North Africa, and even states as close as Persia. Their common religion gave them a sense of unity while at the same time allowing them to exist as separate political powers.

The Quran and Its Doctrines

The Nature of the Book

The Quran (Ar., recitation, reading) is the full and final revelation of God's will given through Muhammad in Arabic over some twenty years and contains all essential truths from God. It contains 114 *suras* arranged in descending order of length so that the shortest is the last. The exception to this, Sura 1 is used in daily prayers:

Praise belongs to God, the Lord of all Being
the All-merciful, the All-compassionate,
  the Master of the Day of Doom.
Thee only we serve, to Thee alone we pray
  for succor.
  Guide us in the straight path,
the path of those whom Thou has blessed,
not of those against whom Thou art wrathful,
  nor of those who are astray.[3]

Muslims believe Muhammad arranged and organized the Quran along logical and chronological lines.

However, this does not contribute to nor detract from the message, which is wholly the work of God and infallible in every way. Since Muhammad was illiterate, others wrote down what he recited. Traditions vary as to when the Quran was placed in its present form, but it was probably sometime during the period of the "Rightly Guided Caliphs," that is, by the end of the first century A.H.

The memorizing, recitation, writing, reading, and hearing of the Quran is considered an act of piety and a spiritual ·experience. Since its messages are the very words of God they are to be received with faith and submission. The Quran profoundly elevated the importance of the Arabic language, since it was regarded as the very speech of God. A full understanding of it requires facility in that language. Al Shatibi (d. C.E. 1389) said: "Whoever therefore seeks to understand the principles and purposes of the Sharia [Islamic religious law], . . . must take the Quran as a constant companion, friend, and instructor. . . . He should therefore instruct himself in the Arabic tongue in order to train himself in the understanding of it."[4] Two highly recognized renderings into English are by M. M. Pickthall, *The Meaning of the Glorious Koran*, and A. J. Arberry, *The Koran Interpreted*.[5]

The Quran is about four-fifths the length of the New Testament. Its chapters are entitled according to a word found in the text which often seems incidental to the main thoughts of the *sura*. Examples of chapter titles are "The Bee," "The Spider," "The Cow," etc. The chapters are not linked

Leaf from 10th or 11th century Quran. The Quran is believed to be the very words of God to Muhammad the final prophet of God. The Nelson-Atkins Museum of Art. Kansas City, MO.

by a story or narrative as are the biblical gospels. Chapters from the Medina period and those from the Mecca period are discerned by scholars of the Quran. Some compare the function of the Quran in Islam to the place of Jesus in Christianity. Both are claimed by their respective traditions to be the full revelation of God. But Christians who believe the Bible is itself infallible revelation and not just a fallible creation of the early church can easily understand that the Bible is the Christian counterpart to the Quran. A famous theologian, al Shatibi (d. C.E. 1389), said, "There is no path to God except through it, no salvation without it and no holding to anything that diverges from it."[6]

Followers of Islam believe the Quran derived from a heavenly original called the "Mother of the Book." This was the prototype of the Quran given through Muhammad and which the Quran duplicates exactly. There were many periods of time in human history prior to Muhammad when the Quran was given to humankind through faithful prophets. Unfortunately, these earlier revelations failed to survive in their original purity due to human carelessness and evil. The idea of a book existing eternally in heaven with God has caused some Muslim scholars difficulty because the issue arises: If there are two things eternal in heaven (God and Mother of the Book), then there is something eternal besides God. This threatens to destroy a basic belief in the unity of God; that is, that he is absolutely unique and nothing can be compared to him nor be his equal. Yet if Mother of the Book is eternal, something else is eternal besides God.

The Message of God Prior to Muhammad

The message of God had been revealed to other prophets prior to Muhammad. Some claim as many as one hundred thousand prophets have received the message in a way similar to that of Muhammad. The truth was given and a book resulted. In every case the message and content was the same. The first of these prophets was Adam, and he was given a book to guide his life and prevent careless and wicked ways. But succeeding generations corrupted the truth and the message was distorted. In an act of mercy other prophets were given a revelation for their generations, but the cycle repeated itself as corruption followed corruption. Always God faithfully repeated the message to a prophet, but invariably humankind fell into degenerate ways with the inevitable corrupting influence on the message. To Moses the Torah (Pentateuch) was given; to David the psalms; to Jesus the *Injil* (Ar., Gospels). These are names of the messages from God to prophets at various periods of history. The names of other prophets include Salih and Hud.

All prophets received a message identical to that of the Mother of the Book and the Quran, though somewhat incomplete. All but the Quran have either been corrupted or lost altogether. Thus the Old and New Testaments share two defects from which the Quran is free. Having been revealed at earlier stages in humankind's spiritual development when human beings were incapable of receiving the full truth, they are incomplete. Further, the unfaithfulness of

sinners has led to corruption in the Bible's transmission, a fact that explains the discrepancies between the Bible and Quran in parallel accounts. The Quran is exempt from these two limitations and thus is the highest, final, and infallible revelation of God's will. Sura 2 makes this point where it says: "There is no doubt about this book."

Because the Quran is a replica of the eternal Mother of the Book, it too is eternal. About the third century A.H. Islamic theologians raised the Quran to this level saying it was uncreated and coeternal with God—not the ink and paper but the message, words, and ideas. The eternity of the Quran is proved by the fact that Muhammad was illiterate and could not compose the book himself. With belief in such a claim it is a small wonder Islam has the absolute loyalty of its adherents to its teachings. An exegesis of the text is to provide humanity with guidance in every conceivable human and social problem when coupled with the *sunna* (custom) of the prophet and the early community. Because of its sacred character it is never placed on the floor nor positioned in contact with things impure. It vies with the Bible as the world's most memorized book.

The Quran on the Idea of God

The belief about God is simple: there is one God and Muhammad is his prophet. This is encapsulated in the *shahada* (Ar., witness), sometimes called the "two words": "There is no God but Allah and Muhammad is his prophet."

Thus Muslims are strict monotheists who rejected and continue to reject any polytheistic beliefs. Further, this God is an infinite and transcendent being who is Creator and final Judge. He is high above all creatures and beyond their imaginations. As he is infinite he is beyond all representations in statue, picture, or mental image. Other so-called deities are but figments of humankind's wayward imagination. Such ideas are not only false but damnable because they prevent knowing and doing the will of the one true God. People are not to bow down to images nor worship them. Neither are they to look to them for help or even think about them. God alone is God; he has no equal nor is there anything like him. There are many verses like the following: "Say, God is one, the eternal God; begetting not and unbegotten; none is equal to him" (112:26).

This may not seem to modern Jews and Christians to be the revolutionary message it truly was in its earliest setting. But as Islam appeared in Arabia and spread through Africa, the Near East, central Asia, India, China, and Southeast Asia it encountered and rebuffed entrenched beliefs in many gods and spirits. In these settings its message was radical and revolutionary.

The belief in one God has many ramifications. First, the oneness or unity of God means a numerical unity. There is only one God and not two or more. All who hold to belief in another god commit the sin of *shirk* ("associating"), which is the confusing of the nongod with the truly God. So far as Muslims understand, Christians commit this sin because they believe in three gods: God the Father, God the Son, and God the Holy Spirit. The Hindus are even more offensive with their thirty-three million gods. Second, the unity of God means one religion or one true religion. If God is one, then there is one truth about him and one proper way to worship. How could truth about God include conflicting claims? If there is one God and one prophet, there is also one religion.

The unity of God means even more than this, however, for it means God is unique in nature and absolutely unlike anything. God is not like humans. He has a character and nature of his own which is not comparable with nor shared by humankind. This is why God cannot be depicted by images, icons, and statues. This austerity is reflected in the utter simplicity of Islamic architecture. The beauty of Islamic structures is found in their linear scallops and domes, arabesque floral motifs and calligraphy. But images are totally absent. God has qualities such as eternality, infiniteness, justice, mercy, love, power, and sovereign will. But these are not to be separated out as different parts or aspects of God. Rather God is an indivisible unity.

Belief in the radically simple nature of God is what makes Muslims concerned when they hear Christians speak of Jesus as the Son of God. There are several verses in the Quran which are apparently specifically directed against Christians and teach that God has no offspring because he is not like humans and does not have children. It is therefore not possible for there to be a "Son of God." Naturally, in talking with Muslims, Christians would be wise to avoid such offensive terminology until clear understanding can be achieved.

Since God is one in his nature he is alone or solitary in his will. While the God of biblical faith not only shows his will but also his very self, the same is not true of Allah. Though his will is known through the Quran he is above all limitations. The fact that he has habitually acted in merciful and compassionate ways is no guarantee he will always act in those ways in the future. God is transcendent above all, including those qualities which are seen from a reading of the Quran. "No man knows anything of God's knowledge except such as He may reveal" (2:77). God as he is is not known—only his will is known. Even this is not entirely dependable as he is not limited by the habitual attitudes of the past. His unity means he is unbounded and totally free of limitations of all kinds.

The doctrine of the unity or oneness of God leads to belief in God as Creator. Muslims affirm that God created the cosmos, the world, and humankind. When discussing creation Muslim thinkers reason from belief in God's unity. First, it is obvious that persons do not change themselves from state to state. People change, yet they do not do so intentionally or deliberately. Examples are the process of aging or the swings of moods and emotions. People cope with change but cannot claim they effect it. Thus it can be seen that things do not change by choice. There must be a power that brings about change. There must

be a Mover and for Muslims this Mover is Allah. The Creator creates the cosmos and sees to its orderly function by his will. And as there is order in the creation, this testifies to the unity of God. The creation would collapse if this Creator were not essentially one, for the Quran says: "If there were other gods besides God, heaven and earth would dissolve in chaos."(Quran 21:22) Why? If there were more than one god there would be two creators, and if there were two creators, each would have designed the creation differently. Conflict and disharmony would result rather than the order we perceive. Or, if one wishes to preserve the idea of natural order while affirming two gods, one god would have to be the lesser. If there were two creators the wishes of one would have to be subordinated to the wishes of the other so that the former would thereby cease to be god. One cannot be God and be inferior to another being.

The Quran on Judgment

Throughout the Quran there is an ominous theme: judgment is coming for all the indifferent who are now jesting and laughing so carelessly. It is depicted as something not remote in the future but impending and imminent. It is never indicated when this judgment day will come since Allah alone knows. No one, not even the Prophet, can say when it will happen.

The earliest *suras* describe the great day of judgment not with detailed sequence but in broad outline. First, a horrible natural catastrophe will happen and a thunderclap will usher in judgment. A trumpet sound will call people before their Judge. The earth will be shaken by a terrific earthquake and mountains will fall. The heavenly vault will totter and break showing gaping fissures. The edges of the disc of the sun will bend together and the moon will split apart and be darkened. The stars will be extinguished and fall to the earth.

At the first sound of the trumpet all living persons except the few elect will fall stunned to the ground. At the second sound all will arise and the dead will emerge from their graves. This resurrection will occur in a twinkling of an eye. Behind the heavens which have fallen down or been rolled back, the throne of Allah will appear borne by eight angels. The heavenly hosts will stand ranked in columns and all people will gather before the throne. The good will be placed on the right and the wicked on the left. The trial commences.

Sinners will be treated with the strictest justice. Justice will be handed out on the basis of notes recorded in the Book of Deeds. No person can deny his or her sins. The prophets will be called forth and will testify that they faithfully proclaimed their messages of warning. Thus no one will be able to make the excuse that he or she was not warned. Sinners will seek in vain to put the blame on the *jinn* (seducing and misleading spirits) who have enticed them into idolatry (*shirk*).

After judgment has been passed and with Allah watching carefully to see that no soul receives an unjust sentence, the angels come to execute punishment. The sinner is seized, bound with chains, and dragged away amidst scourgings and blows. Under the command of the archangel Malik, the guardian of hell, the unfortunate are tortured in hell, where they must drink boiling water, wear garments of fire, and suffer their limbs crushed with iron clubs.

The Quran takes pains, on the other hand, to describe the joys of the redeemed in paradise. Paradise is situated "on high," but whether this is in heaven or on earth like a renewed Garden of Eden is not clearly stated. It is a lovely place, filled with refreshing streams, where leafy bowers provide shade. The redeemed lounge upon divans and cushions and are clothed in festive garments of silk and brocade. Gorgeous trees such as pomegranate, banana, and palm give fruit to the blessed. Youths as handsome as pearls walk about serving a delicious drink that does not lead men to foolish acts nor cause dizziness nor headache. For entertainment and in marriage, they receive "black-eyed houris," whom Muhammad stated are virgins especially created by Allah. Later commentaries depict these desirable maidens as having been the dutiful wives of redeemed on earth. In short, the bliss of heaven is as pleasurable as the tortures of hell are painful. The Quran says: "But for the godfearing is a blissful abode, enclosed gardens and vineyards; and damsels with swelling breasts, their peers in age, and a full cup. There shall they hear no vain discourse nor any falsehood. A recompense from thy Lord— a sufficing gift" (78:31–36).

The belief in the last day of judgment is an important part of Islamic faith. The future life with its judgment underlies all other themes. Believers should not only believe in the last day but they should fear it. One should fear both the judgment and the Lord of the judgment. "They who fulfilled their vows, and feared the day whose woes will spread far and wide" (39:24). "Believers are they who tremble in fear before the Lord" (17:109). The fear the believer experiences is due to the fact that the final outcome in the afterlife is not known. Not even the Prophet knows whether he and his followers shall escape. Fear, therefore, is no occasional mood which grips people temporarily while otherwise they are confident of their status. It is not a mood which should be banished. Fear is the natural and basic attitude of piety. The pious person should be afraid. Only the damned are free of fear. For Muslims faith has its corollary in fear not assurance.

The Quran and Jesus

The Quran has great respect for Jesus and gives him a higher place than any other prophet save Muhammad himself. He is called Son of Mary, Servant, Prophet, Messenger, Word, Spirit, and Messiah. The annunciation to Mary and the birth of Jesus are alluded to in Sura 19. Whether Jesus' birth was normal or miraculous is not clear in the Quran. One modern Muslim commentator indicates that the popular conception is that it happened in the ordinary way. The ambiguity of the passage, however, leaves the question unsettled. The miracles of Jesus are mentioned, including his healing of the sick, cleansing of lepers, and raising of the dead. There is a reference to the Last Supper as a table of food from heaven. Concerning

Jesus' death Allah says: "O Jesus, I am going to bring thy term to an end and raise thee to myself" (3:48, 55). Another passage alludes to the Resurrection and Ascension (4:154–59).

To Be a Muslim: Five Pillars

To be a Muslim means surrender to the will of Allah generally, and to all laws guiding life specifically. Five duties demonstrate submission to Allah and are sometimes called the "Five Pillars of Islam." These duties may or may not have been required in Muhammad's own day, but subsequent practice has made them *ibadat* (Ar., obligations owing to God). They are *shahada* (Ar., the witness), *salat* (Ar., prayer), *sawm* (Ar., fasting in the month of Ramadan), *zakat* (Ar., almsgiving), and *hajj* (Ar., pilgrimage to Mecca).

The Witness (shahada)

The *shahada* states: "There is no god but God and Muhammad is his Prophet." Muslims must confess this simple creed and hence, as in many other religions, embrace a rigid doctrine from which there can be no departing. The doctrine to which Muslims witness is only seven words and fifteen syllables in Arabic. It is probably the shortest creed in the world and has possibly been repeated more often than any other. Its brevity and conciseness are such that it has not been altered in thirteen centuries. Tradition has it that the Prophet said, "Whosoever recites this creed shall receive rewards equal to the emancipating of ten slaves and shall have one hundred good deeds put to his account and one hundred of his sins shall be blotted out, and the words shall be a protection from the devil."[7]

Mosque, Penang, Malaysia. Mosque architecture in Islamic countries may take on a variety of styles including the ultra modern appearance of this mosque built by the Malaysian government. J. Lewis

The creed is not only orally affirmed but is inscribed in numerous places to remind the faithful. It may be found on banners and doorposts, and appears on all the early coins of the *kalifas*.

When anyone is converted to Islam he or she is required to repeat this formula. A valid conversion calls for the following. First, the formula is to be repeated aloud at least once in a lifetime and the more often the better. Second, the meaning must be understood for the affirmation to be legitimate. No mechanical recitation is effective. Third, it is to be believed in the heart without reservation. Fourth, it must be professed until death.

Finally, it must be correctly recited using the proper words in their order.

Ritual Prayer (salat)

Prayers in Islam are a central and ever-present experience for the believer who performs them according to the prescribed schedule and rigorous requirements of purity. Called *salat* (Ar.; *namaz*: P.), they constitute both an expression of devotion and a sign of surrender to God. Though the Quran appears to call for *salat* only three times a day, both custom and law dictate five times: sunrise, noon, afternoon, sunset, and night. The prayers need not be done in a mosque and may be said individually while alone, although it is thought best when they are done with a group. Congregational prayers at the mosque on Fridays after 12:00 noon are attended by mostly men and are usually accompanied by a sermon from an *imam*. Prayers are also an important part of two festivals: Id al-Fitr and Id al-Adha. The former marks the end of Ramadan and the latter commemorates Abraham's willingness to offer his son Ishmael in obedience to God. The festivals of Id are held out-of-doors and usually attract virtually the whole Islamic community. From the minarets atop mosques of Islamic communities the 4:30 A.M. call to prayer may be issued by the *mu'azzin* in a loud voice or, more likely, over a loud speaker, saying, "God is great. God is great. Come to prayer. Prayer is better than sleep." Prayers in the mosque commence upon issuing a second call.

The first requirement of prayer is that it be performed facing the right direc-

197

Jama Masjid in Delhi, India. Begun under Shah Jahan and finished by Aurangzeb after 1660 C.E., this mosque is the largest in India and one of the most famous in the Islamic world. J. Lewis

tion, which is toward the Ka'ba in Mecca. Thus Muslims in Tunisia face east, Tanzanians face north, Pakistanis and Indians face west, and those in Turkey and the Soviet Union face south. Because of this requirement private houses as well as mosques all over the Muslim world are frequently laid out with this orientation. If one is on a journey a compass may be used to determine the proper direction for the posture of prayer.

The second requirement is ritual purity. *Salat* may be validly performed only when the worshiper is in a state of purity. Therefore, unless one is out in the streets, prayer is always preceded by a bath, or if water is not available then gestures symbolically suffice. The degree of impurity may determine the extent of washing, as does the availability of water. This requirement is the reason why every mosque has a pool or tank of water within the precincts.

The word mosque means "place of prostration" indicating the primary function of the mosque is prayer. The worshiper begins by facing Mecca with hands crossed in front and as the

prayer proceeds many postures are assumed from bowing, to kneeling, to kneeling with forehead to the ground. Prayers can begin only after the *azan* or "call to prayer" is issued by the *mu'azzin* or "crier" for the congregation to assemble:

God is great! God is great! God is great!
  God is great!
I bear witness that there is no god but
  God!
I bear witness that there is no god but
  God!
I bear witness that Muhammad is the
  Apostle of God!
I bear witness that Muhammad is the
  Apostle of God!
Come to prayers! Come to prayers!
Come to salvation! Come to salvation!

After assembling, the prayers follow a set form varying only slightly from sect to sect. All liturgies of prayer, which must be in Arabic, include the shahada as well as the recitation of certain select portions of the Quran such as Sura 1.

Praise be to God, Lord of all the worlds!
The compassionate, the merciful!
King of the day of reckoning!
Thee only do we worship, and to Thee only
  do we cry for help.
Guide Thou us in the straight path,
The path of those to whom Thou hast been
  gracious;
With whom Thou art not angry,
And who go not astray. Amen.

One of the many other prayers uttered is the *Tashahhud*:

The adorations of the tongue are for God,
  and also the adorations of the body, and
  alms-giving!
Peace be on thee, O Prophet,
  with the mercy of God and His blessing!
Peace be upon us and upon God's righteous
  servants!

O God, have mercy on Muhammad and on
    his descendants,
  as Thou didst have mercy on Abraham
    and on his descendants.
Thou art to be praised, and Thou art great.
O God, bless Muhammad and his descendants,
  as Thou didst bless Abraham and his
    descendants.
Thou art to be praised, and Thou art
  great![8]

After these memorized prayers personal and private petitions are allowed, but they are not common. The slightest departure from the rule of purification, proper postures, or required method of prayer nullifies its effect and the worshiper must begin again. Special prayer times are obligatory at an eclipse of the sun or moon and on other major annual festivals.

Prayer is not so much a conversation of the individual with God as it is the demonstration of surrender and a proper act of worship. On Friday, which comes closest to being the most holy day of the week, prayer at the mosque with the congregation is required. The mosque has a *mihrab* (orientation niche in the wall), which marks the direction to Mecca, and hence prayers are said facing the *mihrab*. To the right of the *mihrab* is the pulpit, which is usually elevated a few feet and ascended by a flight of stairs. A lectern may flank the pulpit on which the Quran is placed. Prayers are led by the *imam* (leader), who may be the officially recognized and trained *mullah* (master of theology; variation of Ar., *mawla*) or a respected leader in the community. The *imam* performs the postures and recites the prayers, which others follow simultaneously.

Women are not usually in attendance at Friday mosque prayers, but when present they are either at the side or rear and in some cases cloistered. Some Islamic communities provide for full participation of women behind a curtain at one side. A balcony may be used in some cases from which women may see and follow the *imam* but remain unseen by those below. Friday prayers involve no music and no offering. A sermon may or may not be a part of the service.

Almsgiving (zakat)

The devout are required to give *zakat*, which is of two kinds. There are obligatory alms in the amount of two and one-half percent annually to help the poor, the needy, and the sick and to promote the cause of God. This tax is calculated on the basis of annual income and property values, although a minimum amount is considered exempt. Though this requirement is still on the books, the emergence of state taxes in modern Islamic states has effectively relaxed this requirement. Still, the devout may hold to it, and some fervent Muslims are calling for a return to it. A second kind of alms involves voluntary gifts to the needy. The walkways leading up to mosques on Fridays in the Islamic world are often lined with beggars waiting to receive the coins of worshipers. The needy thus provide the faithful an opportunity to perform a required duty.

Much has been made in modern times of the social concern for the poor and needy mentioned in the Quran. But a careful reading of the Quran shows little deep concern for the poor as a motive for almsgiving. The giving of alms is not an attempt to abolish poverty. Alms are given for Allah's sake because they are pleasing to him, or they are given for one's own benefit as a sort of "purging" of the soul to aid in eradicating the effects of sins committed. Alms also help prevent the accumulation of wealth, which can be a damning burden on the day of judgment. It also stores up good works.

Fasting on Ramadan

A daytime fast is obligatory during the entire ninth month, Ramadan, for all healthy Muslims who have reached puberty. During the daylight hours no food nor water may be taken in. But when night time approaches, the hungry, thirsty, and tired Muslim population, whether in Cairo or Baghdad, eagerly awaits the official moment when they may take a snack of milk, dates, yogurt and fruit as well as great quantities of liquids. Later in the evening they will take a full meal and some will have a pre-dawn meal to sustain them through the day.

Paradoxically, Ramadan is a time when many Muslims eat more and better food than at any other time. They also do more visiting of one another. It is a special time of the year in which one is to show virtue, sincerity, kindness, and interest in others. One is to obey the commandments more carefully. Of course one cannot eat or drink anything during the day and one should not smoke either. The meat shops are open every day rather than the traditional three days. Shops in Bombay which cater to Muslims extend their evening hours, as people

go out into the streets strolling, visiting, and purchasing things for others and their families.

Ramadan is the sacred month in which it is believed the Quran "came down." Every healthy Muslim who is in full possession of his or her faculties is to fast for the entire day, beginning with first light and ending with last light. In Islamic countries radio stations announce the precise moment the month of Ramadan begins and ends as well as the daily fast times. In earlier times the daily signal to begin was the moment when it was possible to distinguish a black thread from a white one. During this time nothing, including one's saliva, is to be ingested if it can at all be avoided. Since Ramadan is a month in the lunar calendar, it rotates periodically through the seasons of the year. When it falls during the cooler season it is not so oppressive. However, when it occurs during the scorching summers of Islamic lands it is a very real ordeal for those who must remain active during the day. Mercifully, during the height of summer seasons outdoor activities are greatly reduced while people occupy themselves indoors.

Fasting, it is said, makes one think of God and is itself an act of dedication to God. Further, it underscores humankind's dependence on God. Man, says the Quran, is as frail as the rose petal. Nevertheless people assume airs and are pretentious. Fasting reminds them vividly of their essential frailty and dependence. Throughout the month many spend much of each night in the mosque, where the Quran is recited. In thirty consecutive evenings the entirety will be given. Great honor is accorded those who know all or portions of the Quran from memory. Voluntary fasting on certain other days is also very common as Muslims imitate the Prophet's example. The famous theologian al-Ghazali recommended fasting on the first, middle, and last days of the month.

Water purification prior to Friday Prayers at the Jama Jasjid, Delhi. An essential preliminary to prayer is to purify oneself at the water tank found in the precincts of every masjid. J. Lewis

The Hajj

Mecca is one of the last of the forbidden cities of the world because only Muslims are permitted entrance. At least once in the lifetime of every healthy adult of either sex, all who have the means are to make a journey of piety to Mecca. Thus, during the designated period (the last month of the year, Dhu-al-Hijja) thousands of faithful find their way to the city arriving by sea, air, and land in the Kingdom of Saudi Arabia. In an average year they number nearly two million. In 1965 a group of Senegalese set out in January for a 3,400-mile walk across the African desert to the Red Sea. At the port city of Jeddah

flights land every five or less minutes around the clock during Dhu-al-Hijja, where in normal times only two dozen per day land.

The pilgrimage takes several days. First, one must assume the official dress of a pilgrim before entering the sacred city. Second, the pilgrim must prayerfully circumambulate the Ka'ba seven times, in a clockwise manner. The Ka'ba is a cube-shaped structure, neither temple nor shrine, some fifty-five feet high and draped with velvet, which covers the black stone set in one corner. Those who get close enough to kiss or touch it are fortunate, given the throngs at peak times. The third step is to overnight in Mina, some four miles east of Mecca, in preparation for the next step, which is to pray on a nearby mountain in imitation of the Prophet. The fifth step is to overnight at Muzdalifah near Mina. The sixth step involves three days of ceremonies at Mina, including the Id al-Adha, or "Festival of Sacrifice," commemorating and reenacting Ishmael's miraculous deliverance when Abraham was about to slay him as God had commanded. After this and other ceremonies the pilgrims return to Mecca and the Grand Mosque to circumambulate the Ka'ba seven times with prayer. Many pilgrims also visit Medina, where Muhammad is entombed, before returning to their places of origin.

The Sunni and Shi'a Denominations

There is a saying popularly believed to come from Muhammad which says: "My community will divide into seventy-three sects of which only one is

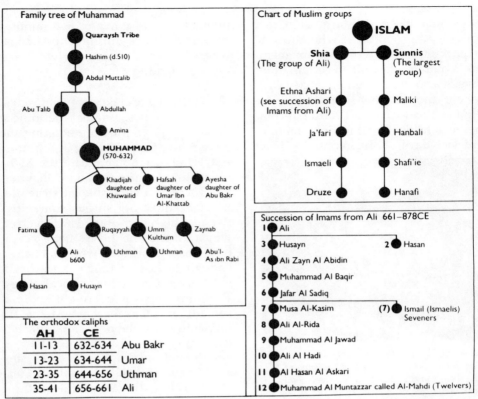

Family tree of Muhammad

Quaraysh Tribe

Hashim (d.510)

Abdul Muttalib

Abu Talib — Abdullah

Amina

MUHAMMAD
(570-632)

Khadijah daughter of Khuwailid — Hafsah daughter of Umar Ibn Al-Khattab — Ayesha daughter of Abu Bakr

Fatima — Ruqayyah — Umm Kulthum — Zaynab

Ali b600 — Uthman — Uthman — Abu'l-As ibn Rabi

Hasan — Husayn

The orthodox caliphs

AH	CE	
11-13	632-634	Abu Bakr
13-23	634-644	Umar
23-35	644-656	Uthman
35-41	656-661	Ali

Chart of Muslim groups

ISLAM

Shia (The group of Ali) — Sunnis (The largest group)

Ethna Ashari (see succession of Imams from Ali) — Maliki

Ja'fari — Hanbali

Ismaeli — Shafi'ie

Druze — Hanafi

Succession of Imams from Ali 661–878CE

1 Ali

3 Husayn — 2 Hasan

4 Ali Zayn Al Abidin

5 Muhammad Al Baqir

6 Jafar Al Sadiq

7 Musa Al-Kasim — (7) Ismail (Ismaelis) Seveners

8 Ali Al-Rida

9 Muhammad Al Jawad

10 Ali Al Hadi

11 Al Hasan Al Askari

12 Muhammad Al Muntazzar called Al-Mahdi (Twelvers)

© DIAGRAM

This chart shows the family tree of Muhammad and his first four successors or caliphs, all of whom were related by marriage. They are known as the rightly guided caliphs because they ruled before the Sunni-Shia split in Islam. Religions on File

correct." If the Prophet said this, he underestimated the divisions in Islam, for throughout history many more than that have emerged. Hence, Islam is nearly as divided as Christianity. Two major branches are the Sunni and the Shi'a, which some compare to Catholics and Protestants. Just as Protestants and Catholics have subgroups or sectarian movements, so it is with the Sunni and Shi'a.

The Sunni claim to represent orthodoxy and hence present themselves as true Muslims. They speak of themselves as "the people of established custom [*sunna*] and the genuine community." They indeed claim to be the true representatives of Islam whose beliefs and practices correctly preserve the original faith established by Muhammad and his early followers. The Sunnis are said to be the traditionalists of Islam because they base their system on the "custom" of pious men from the beginning. The Shi'a origins date from the Fourth Caliph, whom they believe was the only proper descendant and preserver of the faith.

The Sunni distinguish themselves from the Shi'a, yet they will tell you that in most matters of faith and practice they believe and practice alike. The Shi'a will say the same about the Sunni. In most respects each regards the other as a brother Muslim. Yet throughout history and in modern times pious practices, mixed often with politics, have led to clashes and bloodshed. The differences between them lead to separate mosques, separate organizations, and unique practices and beliefs. In the past Islam has not acted—and does not act today—like a unified religious body. Even within separate nations Islam's many branches are organizationally distinct, though greater cooperation may be found in Islamic states or countries where Islam is a majority religion.

Historical Background to Division

In order to understand the differences between Sunni and Shi'a we must go back to the first century A.H. Shi'a as a separate branch began at the time of the Fourth Caliph. After Muhammad's death the first three successors were Abu Bakr, Umar, and Uthman, all of whom were related to Muhammad by marriage. The Fourth Caliph was Ali, who was related to the Prophet by both marriage and blood since Ali was Muhammad's cousin as well as son-in-law. The Shi'a trace loyalty to the Prophet through Ali, whom they believe the Prophet designated as his successor on the occasion of his "Farewell Pilgrimage." They also cite certain verses in the Quran. The Sunni trace their connections to the Prophet through the community ruled by Abu Bakr, Umar, and Uthman.

When the Third Caliph, Uthman of the Ummawi clan, was assassinated,

Ali tried to put his relatives in administrative positions throughout the expanding Islamic empire. Ali's appointees arrived in Damascus to take up their work but were not accepted. An armed struggle took place and the appointees of Ali were themselves assassinated. Ali's second son, Husayn, gathered a following and took up the fight against the Ummawi usurpers but was surrounded and cruelly murdered on a battlefield in present day southern Iraq along with innocent family members. The date was C.E. 680, or 10 Muharram A.H. 61.

That did not mean the end of the Ali movement, who now called themselves shi'a (Ar., followers or partisans). It did mean, however, that the Shi'a lost out in the attempt to retain political control of the empire. They continued to claim to be the proper and correct ones to lead the faith, since Ali and his descendants were the Prophet's intended successors.

The assassination of Husayn on the battlefield is commemorated annually by the Shi'a and is one of their distinctives. Husayn is considered a martyr and his assassination has introduced elements of martyrdom, sorrow, and suffering of the just at the hands of wrongdoers. Husayn set the example for Shi'a who idealize one who sacrifices himself in the service of Allah and the Prophet. An annual festival on the tenth of the month of Muharram commemorates Husayn's death and has served to interject an emotional fervor found among Shi'a that is not found elsewhere. During this festival the story of Husayn's death is dramatized by preachers, narrated by storytellers, and depicted in passion plays called *taziyahs*. Parades are organized and processions act out certain details of the historical event. During the parades some believers may join the procession beating their breasts, wailing, and inflicting bodily punishment on themselves. Their mourning is thought to purge the soul. The sorrowful element is mixed with joy and rejoicing, however, for Husayn's example gives guidance to the community. The mourning is also for leaders of Shi'a who, like Husayn, have had to suffer for their beliefs. The passion plays may last for days as the history of these martyrdoms is depicted.

Sunni Distinctives

The Sunni recognize four orthodox schools of law (Ar., *fiqh*) not generally recognized by Shi'a. *Fiqh* refers to a code of behavior governing all of life and faith and providing guidance in every area of life. Several codes or "lawbooks" emerged in Islamic history with some communities following some and others preferring other *fiqh*. In most regards these lawbooks are quite similar. The greatest variation arises in the area of the theory of law because Shi'a depend on the *imam* and his guidance to help the doctors of the law solve legal problems. There is much less dependence on the *imam* in Sunni jurisprudence.

The major difference theologically between the two groups is that the Sunni have rejected the allegedly excessive rationalism of the Shi'a. A theological dispute in the early centuries centered on the question of the free will of man. The Mutazilah theologians, who affirmed greater freedom

for man, were repudiated by Sunni, who upheld a stronger statement about the finality of Allah's will.

The Shi'a and the Doctrine of the Imam

All Muslims refer to their *imam*. The word means "leader" but it is used in several connections. First, it may be used of a mosque leader who may be untrained or educated as a "pastor." Second, it may be used respectfully of a learned man who, though not a congregational leader, is worthy of great respect. Sunnis call the founders of the four schools of law upon which they draw by the name. But *imam* has another meaning for the Shi'a. At Muhammad's death his role as ruler and religious guide fell to his successor and descendant, Ali. He was the rightful *imam* in their view and held that position briefly. When Ali died and Husayn was assassinated, divine guidance continued to be given through their descendants, who were *imams* or "leaders par excellence." These were to "guarantee protection and continuing implementation of the Islamic message" as well as to provide authoritative interpretation of the Quran. Each *imam* was to nominate the most worthy successor from among his relatives.

The importance of the imamate through Ali can be judged by the fact that Shi'a add to the *shahada* a phrase that declares Ali the commander of true believers and "the Friend of God."[9] By including Ali in this way the Shi'a perpetuate faith in their line of *imams*.

The Imamiyya Sect of Shi'a

This group, which goes by different names, one of which is Ithna Ashari-ya, are called "The Twelvers" for their belief that the lineage of their *imams* ceased after the twelfth *imam*. The twelfth in the line of the *imams* mysteriously disappeared and supernaturally gives guidance to the community through representatives who have direct access to him. It is also believed there is a hidden *imam*, called *madhi*, who will come at the end of time.

Meanwhile, the learned men of the community act as interpreters of the divine will. The Shi'as of Iran make up more than ninety percent of this sect, and Iraq's Shi'a are more than fifty percent "Twelvers."

The Sabiyya Sect of Shi'a

This group is called the "Seveners" for their belief that at the seventh *imam* the imamate was fixed in a particular family from which the present Aga Khan is descended. As viewed by other Muslims, this group has been quite radical in their views. Throughout history they have fostered secret societies in their effort to spread their creed and community. They engaged in revolutionary activities against the established Muslim rulers, using terrorism as one of their tools. They were successful in establishing themselves in Egypt, and the Fatimi dynasty of Egypt (C.E. 969–1174) rose to power through their activities. This was a brilliant era of Muslim culture resulting in the founding of modern Cairo and the al-Ashar University there. Also called the Ismailis (in India), they have flourished wherever Indian nationals have immigrated. Sometimes called Batiniyah (hidden), they profess an esoteric teaching open only to those who have gained initiation into their secret knowledge. They are exclusive in worship and often looked on with disgust by other Muslims. On one occasion a well-informed and educated Indian Muslim belonging to another denomination said of them: "Ten years ago we would not have even considered them Muslims and even today the Seveners are only one percent Muslim!"[10]

The Sufi Way

The Arabic word *sufi* is traced by some to the word *purity* and by others to the word *wool*. If the former is correct it would identify one theme in the movement, which was withdrawal from the world and worldly ways. If the latter, it refers to the early ascetics of this movement whose preference for coarse garments made of white wool became standard dress. These ascetics were driven to withdraw from ordinary society in protest of the worldliness of the Ummawi princes in Damascus. Others were searching for a direct experience of God beyond the customary duties of everyday religious requirements.

Islam is a religion of law and duty. By means of *sharia* (law) all Muslims know exactly what is expected of them in order to show obedience and surrender to God. The law books leave nothing to imagination or speculation; they were written to eliminate personal uncertainty and community controversy. The Law never entirely achieved that goal, but for most Muslims it has provided guidance for life that is comforting. One knows what God and the community expects and the expectations are within the reach of all. When a former Muslim was asked, "What was the most satisfying aspect of Islam for you personally?" the response was: "The guidance of law provides the greatest satisfaction."[11]

Sufi Mendicant. Jama Masjid. Delhi. The plaque hanging from his neck, a portion of sura 21:87 reads: "There is no God but thee, glory to thee. I was indeed among the unjust." J. Lewis

But a life ruled by law had a negative effect for some. It laid down clear rules requiring some matters and forbidding others. But the law also made it possible for one to follow the religion mechanically without meaning. One could do one's duty without having any feeling about it. Religion could become quite devoid of faith, love, or even fear. In the view of some, religion had become too much a matter of external ritual, lacking entirely in personal experience. While such did not bother many, it caused dissatisfaction to a few. These are some of the factors in the rise of a movement called Sufism in Islamic history.

Sufism began in the first century A.H. and by the sixth century A.H. it had a strong presence everywhere in Islam. Since that time it has declined considerably although it has a left its imprint on Islamic life today through Sufi literature and *pir* (Persian, saint) reverence. The African nation of Sudan has perhaps the most vital Sufi community in the world today.[12]

Encouragements in the Quran

While many reacted to the formalism and worldliness of Islamic rulers, others found in the Quran encouragements for a personalistic encounter with God. The formalists tended to see the worship of God only in terms of performing the prescribed duties. But the Quran says, "Whether ye turn to the East or the West, there is the Face of God."[13] And again it says "God is nearer to thee than thy jugular vein."[14] Somehow God was within, and if that were the case then by introspection and inner-directed experiences one could find him. Sufis found certain other passages in the Quran stimulating, such as Sura 24:35f:

God is the Light of the heavens and the
    earth;
the likeness of His Light is as a niche
    wherein is a lamp
    (the lamp in a glass,
    the glass as it were a glittering star)

kindled from a Blessed Tree,
an olive that is neither of the East
    nor of the West
whose oil wellnigh would shine,
even if no fire touched it;
    Light upon Light.[15]

The passage is ambiguous. What does it mean? Sufi seekers could find in it a meaning cordial to their concerns. Certainly it has the idea of a light (God) that shines and burns within a lamp (man). Some Sufis described their experience of God in terms of an intense light and a burning fire. Some Sufi believers not only derived support from these special passages but regarded the entire Quran as an allegory of the soul's quest for union with God. Beneath the obvious meaning there was a hidden meaning known only to a select few who had a special knowledge revealed by God.

The Life of the Prophet

Sufis looked also to the life and practice of the Prophet for inspiration. He was given to habits of meditation, fasting, and prayer according the *hadiths*. He was self-denying and disciplined. Further, there was a noncanonical story of his miraculous night journey from Mecca to Jerusalem, and another of how he ascended through the seven heavens to meet face to face with God before the throne. The Sufis interpreted this to mean that the soul could rise, through prayer and meditation, into the very presence of God to be united with him.

Sufi Orders

Throughout history various Sufi orders or brotherhoods have emerged. One such was organized by Jalal ad-Din Rumi (C.E. 1207–73), who established an order known as the "whirling dervishes" for their ritual practice of whirling while repeating the name of God. Up to this time there were loosely organized communities of Sufis with no agreed-to rules or lines of authority. From this time forward many orders emerge ruled by a *sheikh* who led in discipline and spiritual exercises. Often the *sheikh* was born of a wealthy or respected family but had undergone a spiritual transformation qualifying him to gather followers. A successor would be appointed to the master sometimes from within the clan or family. An order might be loosely or tightly organized and with or without buildings. Shrines of masters were often erected which became centers of Sufi activities, especially on the *urs* (A., death anniversary) of the *sheikh*. Communion with the saint was believed possible and desirable because he was closer to God and able to gain favors from God. Methods of communion with God and achieving union with him included *dhikr* (Ar., remembrance by repetition) accompanied by certain physical exercises, as though the devotee were drawing the name from parts of the body. Music played a part in expressing devotion to God and frequently accompanied *urs* in India and elsewhere.

Stages of Progress

Sufism speaks of advancement in the spiritual life as a ladder or staircase leading to heaven or a journey toward heaven by a *salik* (Ar., traveler). Sufi doctrine is intended to guide the traveler in the attainment of a perfect knowledge of God through certain progressive steps often guided by a master.

The first step has as its object the purification of the soul through repentance, abstinence, renunciation, and voluntary poverty. Repentance is first and involves the awakening of the soul from the slumber of indifference to an awareness of evil ways. Rabiah (C.E. 717–801), a famous Sufi mystic, taught that sin was hurtful to the soul because it caused separation between the soul and its Beloved. She taught that true heartfelt contrition was essential for repentance, but that fear of punishment was an unworthy motive for repentance and could not produce it. In fact, repentance could only happen when divine grace enabled one to repent. God alone could so touch sinners that they would turn from and forsake their evil ways.

A second step toward the goal of union with God was to experience a variety of states of emotion ranging from fear, hope, longing, and intimacy to tranquillity and certainty. These emotional states are induced by God in the heart, and when authentic humanity is unable to repel them when they come nor retain them when they depart. The traveler is to traverse all the states of experience that God is pleased to send.

A third step is sevenfold and consists of the following, which lead to ultimate union with God.

1. Service—One is to obey the laws of Islam and serve God.

2. Love—There is a divine influence that inclines the soul toward God.

3. Renunciation—Under divine love all worldly desires are expelled from the heart.

4. Knowledge—The candidate contemplates the nature, attributes and works of God.

5. Ecstasy—There is an experience of mental excitement produced through contemplation of the only existing reality, God.

6. Reality—The heart is now illuminated with the true nature of God.

7. Union—In union with God the mystic sees God face to face.

The Sufi desire for union with God resulted in a variety of religious experiences. For some it was an intense personal devotion to God described as a lover. But others sought a union with Allah not altogether unlike the nondual experience of the *Upanishads* in which the distinction between the Sufi and Allah disappears.

Islam in the Modern World

In nearly every Islamic community individuals can be found who are friendly with outsiders and eager to make the acquaintance of non-Muslims. Others want little or nothing to do with them. The reasons, in part, are bound up with the reformed and revivalistic tendencies found today in the Islamic community.

Since the thirteenth century Christian thinkers have had to come to terms with critics of its doctrines. The rise of rationalism and the scientific method in the seventeenth century coupled with the emergence of German higher criticism in the following two centuries forced the Christian community to defend its cosmology, its supernaturalist views, and its doctrine of Scriptures. Rationalists, humanists, and materialists pressed Christians to explain how their worldview was viable in the face of what secularists believed were adequate or superior explanatory theories.

By contrast, until the nineteenth century Islam was, for the most part, insulated from similar hostile challenges. The schools of literary criticism that challenged beliefs in the Bible had no counterpart in Islam, which had a largely unexamined and unquestioned belief that the Quran was the veritable Word of God. However, Western colonial conquests and Christian missionary endeavors in the nineteenth and twentieth centuries resulted in a frontal assault upon Muslim life and thought. These movements forced Muslim thinkers to defend their faith and come to terms with the criticisms and intentions of colonial imperialism and the Christian church.

As late as the seventeenth century three great Islamic empires kept Muslim culture intact and vital in the lands of present-day Iran, Turkey, India, and Pakistan. Emperor Shah Abbas (C.E. 1588–1629) created a strong central government for the Safavids in Iran who had earlier declared Twelver Shiism (Ithna Ashari) to be the official religion. The Ottoman empire, based in Turkey and the Mediterranean, was an influential power which in C.E. 1683 laid siege to Vienna. They were turned back only by the combined powers of European princes. Until overthrown by a democratic revolution in the 1920s, the Ottoman Empire was a strong center of Islamic life and practice.

The Mughal empire in India had its last strong ruler in Aurangzeb (ruled C.E. 1658–1707). Thereafter infighting among the successors to the throne together with the rise of the Hindu kingdom of Shivaji (?–1680) brought decline to the Muslim civilization and power. Many Indian Muslim intellectuals came to the realization that Islam could no longer hope to rule India as it once had. While this was deeply depressing for some, others looked for ways of coming to terms with the new political and intellectual factors impacting their world. Indian Muslim reactions to the modern world symbolized the range of responses being experienced all over the Islamic world. Some Muslims actively sought to recover their lost political control and devoted themselves to convincing the Islamic community of the need to work together toward that end. They were convinced that the golden days of the past could yet be recovered. This general position may be called the view of the revivalists. Shah Waliyullah (1703–62) is an example of this. In the twentieth century Ayatollah Ruholla Khomeini of Iran is the clearest exponent.

But others sought ways to remain true to Islam while coming to terms with views prevailing in the Western world. Those who encouraged Islam to accept and coexist with the new political, social, and technological realities while still upholding Islam might be called the modernists. An individual who exemplified this in nineteenth-century India would be the intellectual Syed Ahmad Khan. In the twentieth century, Saudi Arabia is an example of a nation seeking to preserve its Muslim heritage while incorporating what it deems noncorrupting into its national life (see inset).

> For over a half century Saudi Arabia and the United States have worked together to develop a special relationship. One based upon not only common interests, but also the bonds of trust and understanding. . . . Helping the people of both countries to understand each other better has always been a top priority. . . . Islam is the vital force that guides and sustains all Muslims in every aspect of their daily lives. . . . Today, Saudi Arabia looks forward to even more fulfilled dreams with the United States.
>
> —From a four page advertisement by the Saudi government placed in the magazines *Newsweek*, *Insight*, and *Time*, July 31, 1989.

The struggle between these two factions in Islam, that is between the revivalists and the modernists, is said by some scholars to be as significant as the religious, political, and ideological conflict that faced Europe in the sixteenth century when Catholics and Protestants vied for control. From time to time Islamic brother fights Islamic brother in pockets of fratricidal war reminiscent of the religious wars that decimated Europe in the seventeenth century.

Revivalist Muslims Today

Revivalists are also called fundamentalists since they think of themselves as returning to Quranic practices and ideas which others have given up.

What are some examples of modern-day fundamentalists and what characterizes them? While the present Iranian state may be an extreme example of the revivalist position, it is also one of the most well known.

What are some of the characteristics of Islamic fundamentalism? In a general way it can be said that fundamentalists are ignorant of and indifferent or hostile to Western culture. Some Arab leaders in the past and present have felt the need to understand and even incorporate ideas from the West which were not in conflict with Islam. But the fundamentalist view is that Western culture is decadent in its irreligion, music, lyrics, art, dress, social manners, profane communication, literature, and values. Most of all, the West fails to worship God and follow the will of God. The Western world, as viewed by the late Iranian *mullah*, Ayatollah Khomeini, is a world that is empty, worn, unworthy, and corrupt.

Fundamentalists have a revived sense of their own superiority in cultural matters. Whereas some Muslims have aped the West, such as the former shah of Iran, fundamentalists believe in themselves and in their own culture. There is a renewed awareness of Islam's resources to meet the needs of society today. Iranians would rather be first-rate Iranians and Palestinians first-rate Palestinians than second-class Frenchmen or second-rate Americans. Consequently there is a passion for Islam and a deep-seated belief in the superiority of the Muslim way of life.

A third mark of fundamentalism is a

penchant for conformity to the habits and ideas favored by the leaders of the movement. The individualism found in the West is regarded as symptom and cause of the moral decay there. Conformity to the Islamic way is the sure antidote to such harmful personal freedom. Education, both formal and informal, is designed to promote hatred for that which is non-Islamic. Political indoctrination begins very early and is unrelenting. There is an approved Islamic look in the case of the Iranian-style fundamentalism. For men the Islamic look includes beards, fatigue jackets or windbreakers, and no long hair. There are approved slogans on the lips of the populace, who accuse their enemies of hypocrisy and the United States of being "the Great Satan." Opposition to their enemies is woven into every facet of life and even moderate Muslims, who are not supportive of their programs, are objects of intimidation and coercion.

Finally, there is a sincere belief that all aspects of the state including economics, finance, education, social services, and international relations are best guided by the ideals and principles of the Quran and *sharia* as interpreted by the elite religious leaders.

The Quintessential Revivalist: Iran's Khomeini

Probably the most famous revivalist of recent times was the Shi'ite *Imam*, Ayatollah Ruholla Khomeini. In the late 1970s and 1980s he was the unquestioned leader of most of Iran's thirty-six million people who planned and directed the overthrow of the empire of the shah of Iran. His name, Ayatollah means "sign of God" and is an auspicious title conferred on about fifty other Iranian *mullahs*. There is no formal criteria used, but when a large number of the faithful decide to call a leader by this term it is conferred as an honor.

Khomeini was known for being an ascetic, a theologian, and some knew him even as a mystic. He once taught theology in one of Iran's Muslim seminaries, though he was not regarded as the most brilliant Shi'a theologian. What characterized Khomeini most was the way he personally embodied that element for which the Shi'a have become most well known—the passion for martyrdom.

In 1964 Khomeini was arrested by the former shah, then driven into exile, first to Turkey and then Iraq. In Iraq he wrote sermons and printed tracts against the idolatrous shah. He began to call for a return to an Islamic republic based, in part, upon the ideas of Plato's *Republic*, which advocates the rule of the many by the ideal man. Naturally, Khomeini thought of himself as that man, though he was content to let his followers make that suggestion.

When Khomeini returned to Iran on February 1, 1979, it was to step into a vacuum left by the former shah, whose repressive measures had caused deep anger and resentment among the people. They were ready for a return, as it were, to a more authentic Islamic future. When he stepped off the Boeing 747 that brought him to Iran, supporters called out "The Holy One has come." Cassette recordings of his antishah, anti-West, anti–United States sermons

Alleged hair of the Prophet. Jama Masjid, Delhi. The attendant will also show visitors a gigantic footprint of Muhammad etched in marble. Some modern Muslims regard much of this with skepticism. J. Lewis

never discouraged this has angered many of the *mullahs* in Iran, though it would be dangerous to give public expression to that sentiment.

During the celebration of Muharram in December of 1979 the new constitution was instituted and provided for an elected president and a parliament. But it placed above them a "guardian council" of devout, at the head of which was to be the leading theologian of Iran. This theologian must approve of the president, may veto any act of government, and is commander of the armed forces. Thus Iran, under Khomeini, became a theocracy with himself as the chief instrument of God to bring about justice and the glory of Allah. This is strikingly close to the program of Shi'a's hidden twelfth *imam*.

The Modernists

The modernists, of which there are many shades and differing outlooks, generally call for a rethinking of the blind dogmas of the past. Mostly, modernism calls for a careful examination of the closed-mindedness of the past toward modern knowledge and understanding of the world and humanity. There was a feeling that a restatement of Islamic beliefs could profitably sift the superstitious and miraculous accretions that had, through the centuries, been added to the pure faith.

An Early Indian Modernist: Syed Ahmad Khan (C.E. 1817–98)

By the time Syed Ahmad Khan was born, British power had spread in his native land of India from the Himala-

sold like pop music in the bazaars. His speeches spoke of what a "joy" and "honor" it would be to die in a war with the United States. This martyrdom theme arises naturally from the history of the Shi'a movement, who believe their martyred heros, Ali and Husayn, were unjustly and cruelly killed in a struggle to uphold the truth.

His return to Iran has elements of the messianic ideas found in Shi'a's history as well. The twelfth *imam* in the lineage of Shi'a disappeared in C.E. 940 and subsequently the "Twelvers" have believed he is in hiding but will return to purify religion, deliver the oppressed, and institute God's justice on the earth. While the Ayatollah never claimed to be the hidden *imam*, others have used the term suggesting that he is. The fact that the Ayatollah yas to the southernmost parts of the subcontinent. In 1857, as a result of the Sepoy Mutiny, the government was transferred from the East India Company to the British Crown. The ideas and the culture which the British brought with them were rejected by most Muslims. While the Hindu community seemed eager for new ideas, if only to show how their own texts and traditions were as good or better than them, the Muslims looked on scientific and modern thought with disgust, indifference, or contempt. The Muslims tended to look backward to the glories of the past, while the Hindus were more open to the ideas of the outside world.

Muslim skepticism and reaction to modernization in India was first challenged by Syed Ahmad Khan. He sought to awaken Islam to its need to rouse itself to accept a new day. He advocated that Islam take a progressive and realistic view of its place in the new India.

He was born into a noble family in Delhi and received a traditional Muslim education. He was then employed in the service of the East India Company and remained loyal during the Sepoy Mutiny, recognizing that Muslims who fought against the British could not succeed. It was his growing conviction that Muslims should not attempt to turn back the pages of history and attempt to rule India again. The British were in India to stay and the wisdom of the hour was to make the most of the situation. He began to write voluminously with two audiences as his target. To the British he proposed that Muslims could be trusted and loyal subjects. To his

Muslim brothers he proposed they cease dreaming about the past and enter with goodwill into the life of India. "Sir Syed's aim was to produce a progressive, educated, well-informed Muslim, capable of success in the modern world without anyway forswearing his loyalty to the tenets of Islam."[16] Without compromising the values of his culture or the fundamentals of his faith he sought to assimilate Western thought and ways.

In achieving his own synthesis he had to reinterpret many Islamic beliefs. He first of all rejected those things that he judged were not scriptural that had been added to the faith in the course of the centuries. Second, he returned to the Quran, interpreting it in the light of modern needs, concerns, and beliefs. His reinterpretation of the Quran was rationalistic and played down the supernatural, which angered the traditionalists, who called him and his followers *necharis* (believers in nature). In spite of opposition, his modernized views of the Quran and its teachings came to be accepted in time by many in India and abroad.

Islam in North America

Islam in North America prior to 1950 existed in few communities and was relatively unnoticed. While there is evidence that Islamic believers existed among Afro-American slaves in the nineteenth century, it was immigrants from Syria and Lebanon who kept Islamic traditions alive until the mid-twentieth century. At that time, under liberal immigration policies, newcomers from the Middle East and Asia swelled the numbers; it is now estimated there are some three million followers, half originally from about sixty different countries and about half black American.[17] Less than ten percent, however, are affiliated with any of the six hundred organized mosques, and thus Islam's followers in North America are adrift in a secular world and are still paid little notice by the other major religions.

A Muslim Becomes a Christian*

My Life as a Muslim

I was born in 1947 at Mounath Bhajan, District Azamgarh near New Delhi, India. My father is a cloth merchant who weaves carpets and sells Banarese *sarees*. He was born into the "Ansari" caste, which is the weaver caste. As such, I grew up working alongside him and was able to join the ranks of carpet weavers for employment. I have three brothers and four sisters, though only seven of us have survived. All are married. I am married and have one child.

Our family belongs to the Sunni sect of Islam. I will have more to say about the Sunni later. According to their rituals, I was circumcised at an early age as a mark of belonging to the sect. I studied in Arabic and Urdu medium *madrasas* (schools) in North India. Most of the time as a student I lived in hostels smoking the *hooka* (a water-

cooled pipe) and spent my free time talking on current topics of interest with other students and people in homes and marketplaces.

If you were to ask me who was the greatest influence in my life I would have to say it has been my father. As a Hafiz Quran, (one who has memorized the text of the Quran), he has the distinction of having committed the entire Quran to memory in the Arabic language. He is highly honored for this feat, which is not easy since Urdu and not Arabic is our mother tongue. He would often question me about my lessons and my knowledge. He was the most devoted person I have ever known. This contrasted sharply with my brothers, who never prayed except for going to the mosque on Fridays.

I had no doubts about the faith whatsoever through my school days and even in seminary, until I met Bishop Nazir. The name Nazir in India indicates an Islamic family. Obviously he or his family had become Christians and, though often many converts from one religion to another seek to bury their family past by changing their names, he did not.

I remember very clearly the circumstances under which I met the Reverand Nazir and one of his associates, the Reverand Talibuddin. I was in New Delhi working as a carpet weaver and repairman, since I had not yet been placed as the *maulvi* (a learned

*This story, told by a recent Muslim convert to Christianity, was recorded in 1985 by Dr. Fred Schelander, Christian and Missionary Alliance missionary in Maharashtra State, India. The Reverand Paul Shah of Bhusawal did the translation.

man; a graduate in theology) of a particular *masjid* (mosque). I happened to be passing by the Reverand Nazir's church with one of my carpets when he called out to me and asked if I would look at some carpet in the church that needed repairing. I had two thoughts. Here is a chance to make some money and an opportunity to win back a brother Muslim who has strayed from the religion of his early days. I had no doubt that a Muslim was the best of all persons, so why wouldn't he want to reconvert? I will return to this encounter later.

I felt qualified to do the work of a *maulvi* because I lived as a Muslim in surrender to Allah. Let me tell you how I thought of the Islamic faith and the training I had in it before I converted.

The Muslim Faith as I Experienced It

A Muslim is one who follows Islam, which means God rules the world. Allah is *wahadahu la sharik*. That is, he is one who has no parts. What can I say of Allah? After all, I do not understand Allah. Allah is too great to be understood. It is Allah who understands me; I do not need to understand Allah. And as for the Prophet of God, none has the right to discuss the greatness of the Prophet or compare one prophet with another. According to Islam, all the prophets are one; there is to be no comparison. God has sent them all, so we are not to decide which prophet is superior and which is inferior. Each has been sent in his own time by God.

I was faithful in all the duties expected of me. I performed regular prayers. Let me tell you about prayer. If you were to ask me if I prayed while I was a Muslim, I would say that there is no prayer in Islam. You will be surprised at this, but I must honestly say that the only one who prays is the *peshimam*, or the one who conducts the *namaz* in the mosque. He will pray in the Arabic language and everybody will follow him. We pray what he prays. If prayer is "saying prayers" then we prayed. But if you mean prayer from the heart, then I must say there is no personal prayer among us.

I also was very respectful toward the saints. In the Islamic community *pirs*(saints) are found. These are considered spiritual mediators to reach God. They are called *vaisilavai* or "the mediators to God." Also, a saint may be called *sahib habr*, or the "master of the grave," which is a respectable way of addressing him. It is believed that these holy men, though deceased, can give certain blessings and gifts of their own because they are so near to God. Their prayers are better than those of ordinary Muslims. Another name for them is *peshazgar* meaning "the one who keeps away from certain things." What that means is that they prevent any unfortunate things from happening to those who pray to them. Those who visit the grave site or shrine expect a blessing for their family. And anyone who goes on a long pilgrimage to visit a famous shrine will receive a truly great blessing. We have many very famous shrines of *pirs* in India from north to south and from east to west.

As a Muslim I was naturally committed to the teaching of the Quran. The main teaching of the Quran is this: "God is one." This is the greatest teaching of Islam. The next to it is love to man. There are five duties: (1) *kalme*, or *shahada*; (2) *namaz*, or prayer (*salat* the number of times for prayer is not given in the Quran, only in the *hadiths*); (3) *roze*, or *ramazan*; (4) *zakah*, or alms; and (5) *hajj*, or pilgrimage.

The *shahada* has two parts: the first part means I witness that God is one and the second part means martyrdom in the way of God. Those who die in the way of God are not to be called dead bodies.

As I said before, I belonged to the Sunni sect of Islam. In India the main two denominations are Shi'a and Sunni. Once upon a time they had a lot of arguments and quarrels between them. That doesn't happen any more because they are entirely separate organizations. They agree that no one should convert from either group to the other. On the surface there are no conflicts. Of course, there are many sects among the Sunnis.

The Sunnis divided into two main schools of thought in the last two or three centuries. One is called Dar-ul Ulum-Deoband. Its theological *madrasa* was established by Kasim Nanotair to train *maulvis*. The *madrasa* is at Deoband in district Saharanpur in Uttar Pradesh. Nearly three thousand students were studying there two years ago when I was there. They believe in one God and nothing else. They reject *pirs*, or mediators, and the burning of candles or incense to them. In their view, the saints cannot help us—only God can. The second school

is the Bareilly school founded by *Maulvi* Ahmed Allah. This is the largest Islamic theological college in India. He believed that to reach God you need *pirs*. According to him Allah likes to hear the requests of *pirs* on behalf of their followers. There are many Hindu converts to Islam in this school.

How does the Sunni sect regard the Shi'a and vice versa? A person in one sect is not permitted in the mosque of another sect. The *maulvis* and *peshimams* of one are not accepted by the other. A *maulvi* from the Deoband group is not permitted in the Bareilly *mosque*. Muslim sects have nothing to do with each other except when confronted by non-Muslims. Then they all join together.

My Training and Life as a Maulvi

I decided to become a *maulvi* for one reason—to serve my community and religion. I got my training in many, many places. First of all, I trained at home where I got the fundamental knowledge. Then I went to Mubarkpur where I studied in the Arabic university there. Then I went to Banaras where I studied in the Hamedia University. From there I moved to Muradabad Jaunsye Naimiya and after that to Balie Rash dul Ulum. All in all I studied thirteen years.

Our daily study schedule was from 8:00 A.M. to noon and from 2:00 P.M. to 4:00 P.M. There were no special classrooms. The curriculum plan was to learn one book at a time. Whenever one book was complete then another book was taught. No one was promoted ahead of anyone else. All stayed together until the work was completed. The book we studied was the Quran, but we approached it topically on the subjects of law, medicine, social work, apologetics, exposition of scripture, and language. In this way the topics studied are those found right in the Quran itself.

In some cities there are four to six *madrasa*, each with one hundred to three hundred day scholars. In Banaras there are nearly fifteen *madrasas* and in each there are at least five hundred students. The hostel where students live doubles for the classroom. Each person after class will spread his bed on the floor and that will be his sleeping place. The students will receive financial support from local people who consider the students to be "guests of God." Some rich people will undertake to provide food for five persons per day. They give support by the gift of grain and the utensils to make food.

The duties of the *maulvi* include explaining *sharia*, or Islamic personal law. The law of Islam deals with matters of who should get what part of the family property when it comes time to divide it. That is, it deals with matters of inheritance. The *maulvi* is the *muft* or "giver of the judgment." In case of divorce he is the one who is supposed to give *fatwa*, or the religious judgment. In matters of divorce he must render an interpretation and give a legal opinion as to whether the proposed divorce is valid or invalid. He is the one who approves certain other matters as well. He decides what to do according to the Quran or *hadiths*. Furthermore, the *maulvi* is

supposed to teach in a *madrasa* where others are trained to become *maulvis*. He is regarded as the most religious man in the community. He must pray five times a day. When he is invited he will give discourses on certain subjects as per the needs of the community. On Fridays he will preach and afterward he might be given a little gift by the congregation as a token of love. The goal of the *maulvi* is to serve the people and to serve Islam.

Conversion

I need now to return to the question of conversion, because that is why I am telling this story. You may remember that I expected to convert the Reverand Nazir. If a person says, "I want to become a Muslim," it becomes the duty of the one who hears this to convert him without delay. The way to convert is for him to repeat the *kalama* "God is one and Muhammad is Prophet." If for some reason he delays the *kalam* and he dies, he dies a *kafir* (unbeliever). The one who bears responsibility for his dying as an unbeliever is the one who caused the delay. To convert there is no need of a ritual bath. If he has given *kalama* then he is officially a Muslim. Then he will be taken to the mosque and asked to pray along with other people, repeating the prayers and gestures with all others. At the mosque people will tell him to do as they do in worship. He may not know how to pray or do the gestures, so naturally he will need to follow the *imam*. As to circumcision, normally he will be required to be circumcised. Barbers are specialists in this and they are ordinarily paid twenty-to-twenty-five rupees for the act. If the convert himself does not have enough money, some one from the Islamic community will pay.

I will mention a real case. One pundit named Madan Lal, a Brahman, became a Muslim. What precipitated his conversion was this. His daughter-in-law had died and as a Hindu she had to be cremated. He said this about the ceremony: "Before her death I had not seen even her little finger exposed." But when she died her body was set on fire at the cremation grounds, and when the clothes burned off her all the public saw her naked body. This was so humiliating he said: "I do not want to be a part of a religion that allows such a thing." Both this man and his wife left the Hindu religion and became Muslims.

It has taken me a long time to get around to telling you the rest of the story about my conversion. But I felt that you needed this background to understand my experience. I met Bishop Nazir when I was working to repair the carpets in the presidential palace in New Delhi. The church is opposite the presidential residence. I had the carpet design from the presidential palace in my hand and the bishop had seen it and wanted to know if I could repair the church carpet. I agreed to work on it. I then learned that he had a Muslim name, so I knew he was from an Islamic background. I wanted to explain to him about Islam and bring him and his family back to Islam.

The two pastors invited me to visit them after I had repaired the carpet. Through Bishop Nazir I took my first steps toward becoming a Christian. Later on I had stayed overnight with

many Christian pastors in Punjab and other places. My many business contacts with people of different backgrounds helped me learn several languages, though I knew Urdu, Persian, and Hindi best. On one occasion when I was living with Christians, there was a baptism and I decided to take baptism, too. But I didn't know much about it. I continued to live with the Christians but I had many questions. I was disturbed by the behavior of Christians and totally upset by their lives. The leaders were not better than Muslims so far as I could tell, and some were engaged in drinking and immoral activities. You might say I became a backslider and returned to Islam. Yet the lives of Christians disturbed me, and when I criticized them they didn't like it and regarded me as a nuisance. I don't want to blame them, but in many ways they were the cause of my backsliding. In fact, I became a hater of Christians and decided to return to Islam.

About this time my travels took me to central India. I had friends in Bhusawal, Maharashtra, who were former classmates of mine serving as *maulvis* there. I decided to stay with them for a while. On one occasion I entered into discussion with the pastor of the Alliance church and Christians there, hoping to harm them and take vengeance.

I met the pastor of the Alliance church in this way. I was just strolling on the streets of Bhusawal when I saw a sign board with the message "Come unto me all ye that labor and are heavy laden and I will give you rest." I decided to accept this invitation and the pastor, the Reverand Paul Shah, invited me into his home. I told him I wanted to argue with him about Christianity. He said that was all right if that was what I wanted to do.

The truth is, I was angry with Christians for what I felt were mistaken beliefs and behavior. I wanted to take my revenge, so I met with him along with two of my *maulvi* friends. He said he was once a Muslim, a thing I had guessed from his name. He answered many of my questions. Pastor Shah told me there was a great difference between nominal Christians and true, believing faith in the heart of the real believer. Then I found that in every church there are both nominal and real Christians. After talking to him I was convinced I should take baptism again.

There were many Christian influences leading to my conversion—some good, some not so good. But I must say that in a way the Quran is the book that led me to Christ. In the Quran there are so many things one is not to do. It is full of orders and taboos. Once Muhammad told his daughter Fatima that even if you commit sin still none will save you, even though you are the daughter of the Prophet. If all are sinners then there is no escape and forgiveness for them. Heaven will be an empty place. There was no forgiveness in the Quran. Naturally, I was puzzled and confused. Still, I liked the Quran. But I insist that there is no forgiveness to be found in Islam, though it helped me to understand that there is need for the sinner to find forgiveness, since all are sinners. In Christianity there is forgiveness of sin. But not only that, there is power whereby you

are able to live the life of victory. While forgiveness is what you get from God through the Gospel, there are real disadvantages of being a Christian. I have lost everything. All of the things and persons of the past are now gone. I have suffered the loss of every past social and family connection.

What, then, is the principal difference between the Christian faith and Islam? In Islam you have to give an account of your deeds. All you have done. But the Bible says that all are sinners and none are sinless. All the prophets of Islam spoke of the righteous path. Christ not only spoke about righteousness, but he is the one who can give one forgiveness and lead to the path of righteousness and salvation. We are sinners, but we have the support of his mercy and merciful forgiveness. Apart from forgiveness of Christ, I do not find any special difference between the teachings of Christianity and Islam.

And what about Allah in my mind and life as a Christian? Allah is always on my lips. For years it has been so. And that seems right to me since most of the Arabic names of God used by Muslims are used by Christians, too. I find them meaningful to use in my prayer life.

A final word about dialogue between Muslims and Christians. Any conversation with Muslims must be in the Urdu language. Muslims are attracted by the use of that language, which is the mother tongue of most Muslims in India even today. Discuss and talk on the themes of Islam. A person should know that I am a Christian and yet the talk should, at least at first, center on Islamic themes. He knows so little of our faith. But if you show real interest and knowledge of Islam, he will be drawn in and interest will be created. Don't discuss any of the faults or weaknesses of Islam, nor speak ill of Muhammad or the Quran. Speak to him of Jesus and his stories and miracles. They are described in the Quran, and he would be very much eager to know what more is said of this in the *Injil* (the Gospels). He must not feel that he is neglected. He should feel the difference in his life, both spiritual and physical. If he becomes a true convert he should not mix with nominal Christians until he is really strong in the faith.

Discussion

1. Compare and contrast the similarities and distinctives of the Sunni and Shia denominations of Islam.
2. How would you answer the question: "Do Muslims worship the same God as Christians?"
3. Muslims regard Christians and Jews as "Kithabia" or "People of the Book (Quran)." What does this mean? In what way might Christians regard Muslims as "People of the Bible?"
4. What characteristics of Muslim "revivalists" or "fundamentalists" can be observed in today's Muslim world?
5. Discuss the problems the Apostle Paul faced in his transition from Judaism to Christianity. What problems would be the *same* for a Muslim convert to Christianity? What problems would be *new*?

Notes

[1]Bernard Lewis, *Arabs in History* (London: Hutchinson's Univ. Library, 1950), 27; most of the geographical information in this section comes from Lewis.

[2]Mohammed Marmaduke Pickthall, *The Meaning of the Glorious Koran* (New York: Mentor Books, 1953), 659–60.

[3]David S. Noss and John B. Noss, *Man's Religions*, 7th ed. (New York: Macmillan, 1980), 511.

[4]al Shabati quoted in *The Great Asian Religions: An Anthology*, compiled by Wing-tsit Chan, Isma'il Ragi al Faruqi, Joseph M. Kitagawa and P.T. Raju (New York: Macmillan Pub. Co., Inc., 1969), 366.

[5]Mohammed Marmaduke Pickthall, *The Meaning of the Glorious Koran* (New York: Mentor Books, 1953); A. J. Arberry, *The Koran Interpreted* combined in one volume (New York: Macmillan, 1955).

[6]al Shabati quoted in *The Great Asian Religions: An Anthology*, 336.

[7]Samuel R. Zwemer, *Islam: A Challenge To Faith*, 2d rev. ed. (New York: Laymen's Missionary Movement, 1909), 102.

[8]Thomas Patrick Hughes, *A Dictionary of Islam* (Clifton, New Jersey: Reference Book Publishers, Inc.: 1965), 465–66, 468.

[9]Robert F. Weir, gen. ed., *The Religious World: Communities of Faith* (New York: Macmillan, 1982), 331.

[10]Author's conversation with a Muslim lawyer in Yavatmal, Maharashtra, in 1980.

[11]Refer to "A Muslim Becomes A Christian" at the end of this chapter.

[12]This according to Lionel Gurney of the Red Sea Mission; interview with the author at Yavatmal, Maharashtra, India, in 1980.

[13]Sura 2:109.

[14]Sura 50:16.

[15]Arberr, *The Koran Interpreted*, 50-51.

[16]Wm. Theodore de Bary, ed., *Sources of Indian Tradition*, Vol 2. (New York: Columbia Univ. Press, 1958), 189.

[17]Yvonne Y. Haddad, "Muslims in America: A Select Bibliography," *The Muslim World* 76, no. 2 (April 1986): 93.

Part Four

Religion in India, China, and Japan

8 Religion in India

Ruins of Mohenjodaro. Prior to the arrival of the Aryan invaders, a complex and sophisticated civilization occupied the Indus Valley. Very few artifacts of proven religious significance have been found.
Mary Wilder

Religion and the Indus Valley Civilization

The study of religion in India customarily begins with the prehistoric Indus Valley civilization dated from 2500 to 1500 B.C.E. The archaeological remains of this civilization are widely scattered at hundreds of sites spread through present-day Pakistan and northwestern India. The most notable sites are at Mohenjo-daro and Harappa in the Indus River valley in Pakistan, though recent finds in Lothal, India, have attracted interest since the late 1970s.

This was a Bronze-Age, literate, and advanced urban civilization extending from present-day Bombay to the Himalayan foothills in the north and from the environs of New Delhi west through Pakistan. Their cities were remarkably well planned as seen at Mohenjo-daro, with symmetrical and perpendicular street lines, houses of standard brick size, excellent drainage, standardized weights and measures, and a heated public bath. No clearly identified temple has been found.

The exact identity of these people and the nature of their ethnic origin and language is disputed. Some scholars identify them as early ancestors of the Dravidian peoples, whom they believe were compelled to resettle to the east and south by the advancing Aryan invaders. These invading Aryans and their religion begins the formal study of Hindu traditions.

Evidence can be cited that the Indus Valley people were Dravidians and includes pottery distribution patterns, references in Aryan literature, and later inclusion of Dravidian vocabulary in the language of the Aryans, which was Sanskrit. However, this view has not gained universal acceptance. This question will probably not be answered until scholars are able to decipher the Indus Valley script. This remains one of the important tasks to be accomplished by Indologists and linguists.

The artifacts of the Indus Valley people are of special interest to the study of religion because of their similarity to later Indian religious iconography and for the ritual activities they appear to imply. Soft-stone impression seals, whose original use is not clearly established, were found and can be viewed in many museums including the National Museum in New Delhi. Most are about two inches by two inches and are artfully carved with a variety of known and fantastic animals such as bulls, tigers, rhinoceroses, deer, elephants, unicorns, and multiheaded beasts.

The human form, found on five of the more than three thousand seals, is shown in a yogic sitting position similar to that used by later practitioners of seated meditation. One seal has been dubbed "proto-Shiva" due to associations with the Hindu god Shiva (also Siva), which emerges in Hindu literature only about 100 B.C.E. some fifteen or more centuries later. The yogic figure does have some remarkable similarities to later Hindu practices, as pointed out by some Indologists. A three-pointed hat (or possibly horns) rests on the head of a figure with three faces and is surrounded by an elephant, rhinoceros, tiger, and buffalo. These features have been interpreted as corresponding generally to the Hindu deity Shiva, whose sign is a trident, sometimes has three faces, and is lord of beasts and *yogis*.

A mother-goddess cult has been inferred from the inches-high, baked-clay, female figurines found. Though their execution is crude enough to be either child's play or of the nature of toy dolls, the wide hips and prominent breasts have suggested a type of fertility cult. The later Hindu mother goddess Shakti (also Sakti; Skt., power) is connected with this in the opinion of some.

Circular, donut-shaped stones found among the Indus ruins are similar in shape to the *yoni* (Skt., womb) used by Hindus much later to represent the female regenerative organ. Protruding from this is a cylindrical limestone shaft or cone similarly reminding one of the *lingam* (Skt., phallus), symbol of the male sex organ later used iconically for Shiva, the so-called lord of creation and destruction.

On the basis of the above it has been inferred that the Indus Valley people worshiped animals, practiced seated meditation or had deities that did, were involved in mother-goddess fertility worship, and had a kind of phallic symbolism. This, however, is a conclusion that cautious historians are reluctant to make. The visual similarity of images found on Indus Valley artifacts to later Hindu practices cannot alone establish a connection between the two. There must be some written corroboration from the Indus script.

The unlocking of this mystery must await potential clues that could come from decoding the short inscriptions found on the soft-stone seals. Since no written texts have been found, the writings on the seals are our only hope of resolving scholarly differences.

The language of the Indus people used pictographs and alphabetical signs of more than 250 characters. Dr. R. S. Rao, archaeologist and linguist of the Archaeological Survey of India (retired), has studied the script and concluded it is non-Dravidian. By using known Semitic alphabets, he theorizes the Indus Valley people, who were contemporaries of the Sumerian and Mesopotamian cultures, were the first to invent the alphabet and passed that epochal invention on to their neighbors to the west. His conclusion is that their language belongs to the Indo-European family of languages.[1]

However, A. L. Basham takes a different view and endorses the position of Catholic Indologist Father Heras, who held that the language was indeed Dravidian and its people were ethnic and linguistic ancestors of the Tamils of South India.[2] Until the seal scripts are convincingly decoded it is not possible to answer the question of the religious beliefs and practices of the Indus people with any certainty. The danger of concluding too much from nonverbal data is the point of the following comment:

> What can be known of the religion of the Indus Valley people is very meager indeed. No written records of a religious nature have survived, and it is very chancy to reconstruct religious beliefs on the basis of artifacts alone. For example, at Columbia University in New York, at the top of imposing steps and in front of a great domed building stands a magnificent marble statue of a woman draped in flowing robes. On the pedestal of the statue is the inscription "alma mater." If New York should be buried and all written records lost, and if future archaeologists should dig it up again, it would be easy for them to reconstruct all this as a sacred place where a great mother goddess was worshiped by a coastal people.[3]

The Aryans and Their Religion in the Vedic Period

At an undetermined time before 1500 B.C.E. the Aryans, a seminomadic pastoral people, migrated eastward from their pastoral homes in central Europe and began a series of encroaching waves of contact and conquest in the Indus Valley. These warring nomads brought with them oral traditions which they later reduced to religious texts, as well as practices that were to become known as distinctively Hindu.

Earlier migrant waves had occupied present-day Iran and permanently marked that region with similar beliefs, resulting in a religion called Zoroastrianism. These Aryans were fair of skin and spoke a language, Sanskrit, related to Indo-European languages such as Latin and Greek. The name Aryan means "noble" and serves to indicate their self-esteem and pride.

There is good evidence the Indus Valley civilization had been previously shaken by a series of disastrous

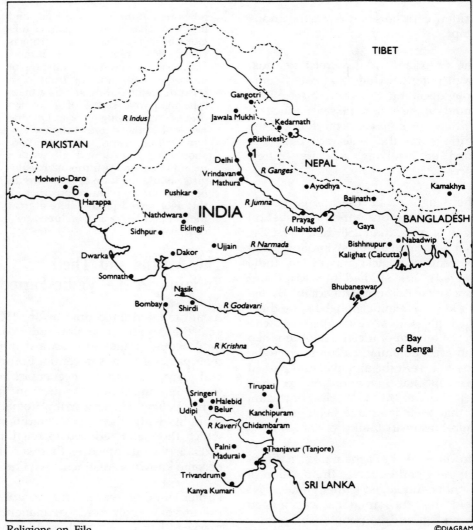

Religions on File   ©DIAGRAM

floods. This drove the inhabitants out of earlier population centers to newer homes before the invading Aryans arrived. Around 1500 B.C.E. the Aryans attacked, conquered, and occupied the Indus Valley area. Little is known about the nature of their material culture except that in contrast to the Indus people, they were inclined to village life rather than city dwelling.

Artifacts of the early Aryans are virtually nonexistent. However, important aspects of military, social, political, and religious life are known to us through their religious literature, the Vedas. The word *veda* means, literally, "knowledge" and refers to a body of religious literature written over several centuries and consisting of four parts. Known also as the four Vedas, they consist of the *Samhitas*,

Brahmanas, Aranyakas, and Upanishads. The following chart suggests probable dates and chronological sequence and also indicates how the Samhita comes first in each collection, followed by other texts, the last of which are the Upanishads.[4]

exclusive of the Upanishads, or when referring to the entire collection of texts diagrammed below. All are considered shruti (Skt., that which is heard; also sruti). It is believed the rishis (Skt., one who knows) hear, or better intuit, the sound of eternal

THE FOUR VEDAS: A CHRONOLOGICAL CHART
(approximate dates)

	1500–600 B.C.E. SAMHITAS	1000–600 B.C.E. BRAHMANAS	1000–600 B.C.E. ARANYAKAS	600–300 B.C.E. UPANISHADS
1500	Rigveda	Aitareya Kausitaki	Aitareya Kausitaki	Aitareya Kausitaki
1000	Samaveda	Pancavimsa Chandogya Talavakara		Chandogya Kena
800	Yajurveda	Taittiriya	Taittiriya	Taittiriya Katha Svetsvatara
		Satapatha	Brihad	Brihadaranyaka Isa
600	Atharvaveda	Gopatha		Mundaka Prasna Mandukya

In the above chart the horizontal dates refer to the periods during which the various commentaries—the Brahmanas, Aranyakas, and Upanishads —began to be appended to the Samhitas. For example, through the years the Brahmanas were appended to each of the Samhitas and in turn the Aranyakas were appended to that series and lastly the Upanishads were appended. Thus each of the four Vedas consist of Samhitas, Brahmanas, Aryanyakas, and Upanishads. The vertical column on the left indicates the dates for the earliest text in each of the Samhitas. It should be pointed out that Hindus may use the term Vedas with a variety of meanings: when speaking only of the four Samhitas, when referring to everything

truth and, through personal spiritual purity, reproduce it just as an echo reproduces an original sound or an image is reflected on a clean mirror. The Vedas are not considered revealed by God as the Bible is in the Christian faith, since the truth is impersonal. Other texts of great respect may be called smrti (Skt., that which is remembered) and have the force of sacred commentary.

Samhitas

The Samhitas, or "collections," contain the earliest Hindu texts written over several centuries by many authors and comprising four books: the Rigveda,

Samaveda, Yajurveda, and *Atharvaveda.* The oldest of the collections, the *Rigveda,* contains 1,082 hymns divided into ten chapters for use in the sacrificial ritual and contains praises to scores of deities. The last chapter contains later and somewhat speculative ideas suggestive of themes which are later developed in the *Upanishads.*

The *Samaveda,* written somewhat later, generally includes little that is not already given in the *Rigveda.* The *Yajurveda* mixes hymns for the sacrifice with ritual explanations, indicating sacrifices had become subject to a variety of interpretations and even speculation. The *Atharvaveda,* unlike the other three, deals not with sacrifice but provides *mantras* (sacred verbal formulae) to control and manipulate the spirit world, including such things as spells and incantations to insure health, protection, success, and advantage.

Brahmanas

The *Brahmanas* are a separate prose production but are attached to various of the *Samhitas.* For example, the *Shatapatha Brahmana* (*Brahmana of a Hundred Paths*) is attached to the *Yajurveda,* and both the *Rigveda* and *Samaveda* have important *Brahmanas* appended to them. The *Brahmanas* contain commentaries on and interpretations of the sacrifices with new and important developments. As the sacrifices had become more complex, formulae were codified by the priests to aid in the recall of the procedure. Furthermore, texts indicate that the increased importance of the sacrifices caused discussion about the meaning and significance of ritual. The *Shatapa-tha Brahmana* tells of a creator deity, Brahma, who arises out of the sacrifice. In Vedic teaching Brahma, who replaces earlier creator deities Prajapati and Purusha, creates the gods but is inferior to them.

Performance of the sacrifice was becoming very technical and expensive. The priestly class, existing to aid in such matters, had begun to divide the responsibilities and specialize in order to correctly supervise the ritual. The Hotr priests pronounced selected verbal formulae appropriate to the sacrifice performed. The Advaryu and his assistants assembled the materials necessary and actually executed the various steps of the sacrifice. A third class of priests, the Udgatri, were musicians who chanted or sung the Vedic hymns according to a seven-note scale. A fourth category of priests stood highest of all and had oversight of the entire ritual. Called Brahmans (also Brahmins), they knew what to do in case of an error and hence were indispensable.

The Brahman class since earliest history has been held in high esteem in Indian society and continues to receive great respect. The word Brahman can refer to "sacred action or power" and is the root behind Brahmanas, texts which detail the sacred action to take when sacrificing. But it can also refer to those persons who know what sacred action to take, that is, the Brahman priests who personify right actions. These are called *brahmin.* A separate word is the word *Brahman,* which refers to highest reality. It is sometimes conceived of as Supreme Personal God as in the *bhakti* devotional systems, or as an impersonal nondual principle as in Shankara's Advaita Vedanta system of thought.

The *Brahmanas* also continue a vein of speculation found at the end of the *Rigveda*. No one unified position is given of cosmic and human origins in these speculations, but several conceptions are presented. These include the view that the world simply arises mysteriously out of cosmic chaos or results from a cosmic sacrifice. The *Brahmanas* introduce the idea of the increasing importance of the priestly class; they indicate that the skill of the priests is what makes the sacrifice effective, as much or more than the gods themselves.

Aranyakas

The Aranyakas ("Forest Texts") generally date later than the *Brahmanas*, just as the *Brahmanas* postdate the *Samhitas*. They are called forest texts because they advocate retirement into the forest for meditation on the sacrifices. They question the value of formal sacrifice and suggest instead a symbolic meaning that is to be preferred to the very act itself.

Upanishads

The last literature added to each of the Vedas is the *Upanishads*. These texts preserve dialogues between a *guru* (teacher) and truth-seeking disciples on a variety of topics. As a class, these texts consist of fluid speculation on human and cosmic origins, the relation between Brahman and *atman* (the individual self or soul). The knowledge of the *Upanishads* was restricted to the few who had *gurus*. Indeed, the very name *u-pan-i-shad* means "to sit

near to," indicating a close and dependent relationship between teacher and

---

Brahma
a creator deity with supreme power associated with Prajapati and Purusha in Vedic literature. Later associated with Vishnu (sustainer) and Shiva (destroyer) in the Trimurti.

Brahmanas
Vedic texts detailing sacrificial formulae.

Brahman
1. cosmic sacred power making sacrifice effectual;
2. in the Upanishads the ultimate reality behind all things identical with Atman; also sometimes considered a personal god, Isvara.
3. those endowed with sacred power who served as priests and conservers of Vedic truth; the highest caste among Hindus (sometimes "Brahmin" to distinguish from other meanings).

---

disciple.

The *Upanishads*, often reduced to thirteen "important" ones by some scholars, pick up on questions found as early as the later rigvedic hymns. The following is a late rigvedic hymn (10:129; 6–7):

> Who knows for certain? Who shall here
>   declare it?
> Whence was it born, and whence came this
>   creation?
> The gods were born after this world's creation:
> Then who can know from whence it has
>   arisen?
>
> None knoweth whence creation has arisen;
> And whether he has or has not produced it.
> He who surveys it in the highest heaven,
> He only knows, or haply he may know
>   not.[5]

This hymn would suggest that, since creation predates the deities, some other reality may be responsible for it; whatever it is, perhaps even the deities themselves owe their origin to it. But one is left only with uncertainty, and one senses a twinge of skepticism. Elsewhere, the *Upanishads* explore other possible explanations for the nature and origin of the primeval first principle. Two prominent ideas are Brahman and *atman*.

Rigvedic Religion

The *Rigveda* indicates that sacrifices to the deities were performed in domestic or out-of-doors settings by the head of the house. Usually this was done without the assistance of the priestly class, which, though present, was not as involved as it later became during the period of the *Brahmanas*.

Domestic rituals were performed two or three times daily around the cooking fire or at a fire started for ceremonies. Agni (Skt., fire), the god of fire, was the most prominent deity, but others were also praised. Materials used were libations of milk and soma juice; clarified butter; cereal cakes; fragrant items such as sandalwood, flowers, and perfume; food items; and meat from a sacrificial animal. The ceremonies were restricted to the family, though some sacrifices were of a public nature in the open air. The Rajasuya sacrifice was social-political in nature, as it celebrated and solemnized the rise of a new king. The Ashvamedha, or horse sacrifice, was made by a ruler who would release a horse to wander. Wherever the horse went was then claimed by the ruler's warriors, who followed the horse. At the end of from one to three years the horse was then presented to the deities in exchange for their blessing in an elaborate ceremony attended by the noble and common alike.

Gayatri Mantra

A Rigvedic prayer offered by many Hindus today:

"Let us meditate on the desireable splendor of the Sun God, Savitri. May he stimulate our thoughts."

The deities praised by rigvedic society included the following, which may be organized into the earthly, atmospheric, and deep-space realms. Earthly deities include Agni, the god of fire, who consumes the sacrifice. He is also regarded as the priest of gods, as he is the one who bears the sacrifice with its accompanying petitions to the realm of the gods. In this role he is called "he whose mouth is a spoon," or "butter backed," as clarified butter was spooned into the fire during the ritual. Like all Vedic deities he was viewed as one who, if properly fed and provided for, would reciprocate by granting the petitions for the good life that were presented by rigvedic man: length of days, wealth, health, many sons, success in battle, and upon death, life with the gods. Soma is the god of the intoxicating drink that was ritually consumed by participants and presented to the deities— most likely made from a mountain-grown hallucinogenic mushroom of the upper elevations—Soma can refer to the plant, the deity, or the drink offered to the deity. He was central to sacrifice, and some libation with soma juice was usually made by pouring it out on the grounds where gods were in attendance. Soma as a liquid was analogous to rain; hence, Soma the deity was lord of rivers. But Soma was also identified with storm, sun, and fertility. This diversity indicates the absence of rules to contain the associations of deities in the *Rigveda*. Agni and Soma appear to be the prominent deities for rigvedic society. Along with Indra, three-fifths of all hymns are addressed to them.

The atmospheric deities are sky or midspace deities. Indra, the sometimes violent and soma-intoxicated god of the storm, is also patron of the warrior class. He is locked in cosmic battle with Vritra, a demon, who withheld rain and the prosperity that was impossible without it. With his *vajra* (thunderbolt) he defeats Vritra, thus restoring prosperity and reinstating cosmic order. Indra is addressed in one-tenth of all hymns. Some see in Indra nonmythical echoes of a real warrior king who battled *dasyas*, dark-skinned opponents of the Aryans. Indra is presented more anthropomorphically than the other gods and has fair hair and a beard and at birth emerged miraculously from his mother's side. While Indra was a deity worthy of worship according to the *Rigveda*, he was made a demon in the pantheon of Aryans who settled in Iran about the same time their cousins invaded the Indus Valley. Maruts, deities associated with Indra, control or personify thunder, lightning, wind, and rain while riding golden-wheeled chariots across the skies. Rudra, father of the Maruts, is celebrated in only three hymns and hence is of minor importance. He was the mountain-dwelling, storm-sending deity who was feared and entreated by worshipers to be "auspicious." The word for auspicious is *Shiva*, and for this

reason Rudra is connected with the deity Shiva, who appears much later. Rudra has his benevolent side as well, and this corresponds with Shiva, who is known as Sustainer and Destroyer.

Deep-space deities include Varuna, who is of considerable importance to the rigvedic people. He was ruler of the natural and moral law and had the title of universal ruler (*swaraj*), which is shared only with two others: Agni and Indra. That the relative importance of the deities cannot be measured by the number of times they are found in the texts is substantiated by the fact that Varuna is mentioned in only about thirty hymns. He dwells in upper space, from which he beholds the moral deeds of humankind and inflicts diseases and punishments upon those who lie and misbehave. He is omniscient, knowing all which humans do, think, or plan. To the penitent Varuna is gracious. In every hymn to Varuna there is a prayer for forgiveness of sin. Sin can be either a ritual error or a moral misstep. Rigveda 7:86; 4–5 says:

> What has been that chief sin, O Varuna, that thou desirest to slay thy praiser, a friend? Proclaim that to me, thou that art hard to deceive, self-dependent one: thee would I, free from my sin, eagerly appease with adoration. Set us free from the misdeeds of our fathers, from those that we have committed ourselves.[6]

Two words connected with Varuna are important for later developments. He is not only moral ruler but sustainer of the natural order (*rta*). Rta (Skt., order, cosmic law, truth) was a universal principle producing regularity in nature and guarding against chaos. This idea of a lawfulness in the world included the human realm from birth to death. *Rta* is thought at some point to be linked to the idea of *karma*, which appears later to explain the lawful relation between human deeds and their subsequent physical and moral outcomes. *Karma* said every act, thought, and attitude had its consequences in this life or the life to come for good or bad. It is assumed in the *Upanishads* though not found in the *Rigveda*. A second word is *maya* (Skt., occult power), by which Varuna ruled his cosmic dominion. He had uncanny power and crafty skill causing the sun to traverse the sky and the seasons to be regulated. The word *maya* takes on vastly different meanings later such as in Shankara's Advaita Vedanta, where it means "illusion"—referring to the world as real when, in fact, it is illusory to think it so.

The *Rigveda* elevates a few deities to supreme ruler status but in no sense does any one of them receive a status of unrivaled and unqualified Supreme Deity. The rigvedic hymns assign attributes and honorific titles of one deity to others on the occasion of their worship without any explanation or concern about contradiction. How can this be explained? Perhaps a clue is found in the fact that worshipers sought to attain their petitions by flattery, cajolery, or any effective means. To say the most impressive things possible seemed proper since it was so practical. One scholar says:

> Either the particular god of the moment is made to absorb all others, who are declared to be manifestations of him; or else, he is given attributes which in strict logic could only be given to a sole monotheistic deity. Thus various Vedic gods are each at different times declared to be

creator, preserver and animator of the universe, the sole ruler of all creatures, and so on. Such hymns, considered separately, seem clearly to imply monotheism; but all they really imply is a ritualistic henotheism. As each god comes upon the stage in the procession of rites, he is impartially granted this increasingly extravagant praise until everything that could be said of all the gods collectively is said of each of them in turn, individually.[7]

The term *henotheism* has been accepted by scholars to describe this practice of applying the characteristics of one or more gods to the one who, at the moment, was in the mind of the hymn writer or singer.

One final deep-space deity is Vishnu (also Visnu), who in the *Rigveda* is of secondary importance, being mentioned in only six hymns. But in post-Vedic times he becomes prominent as a deity of devotion. In the Vedas, however, he is known for three giant steps by which he traverses the world. This is usually interpreted to refer to the sun in its three positions at dawn, high noon, and dusk. He is also a friend and ally of Indra in their common battle against Vritra.

Religious Concerns in the Upanishads

Brahman in the *Upanishads* refers to the eternal reality or power in the universe upon which it depends. It is viewed as infinite and endless; real yet incomprehensible. There is no consistency of ideas for, though it is sometimes described with personal theistic qualities, there is a preference for impersonal terms. The majority of passages seem to indicate Brahman is an impersonal reality unknowable except by an experience best described as direct perception, unmediated knowledge, or intuition.

The *atman* (Skt., soul) is the individual soul or perhaps the soul of the universe. More importantly, it was thought of as that reality within the person giving consciousness of individuality. It is the inner or subjective "I" which is self-existing, immortal, and full of being. The human being participates in or possesses *atman*, which is nonobservable and unseen. It is associated with mind, breath, light, and space and is the very life force of all things. It, like Brahman, with which it is associated, is often viewed as impersonal and in that mode may be best identified as "that" or "it."

In the *Chandogya Upanishad* a long dialogue between a man and his son over the nature of reality concludes by saying the essence of the universe (Brahman) and the essence of the individual self (*atman*) are identical. The father, Aruni, expressed this in lines that have become a classical expression of nondualism: "That thou art" (*tat tvam asi*).

What was the value of seeing reality in this way? We can only note that in the later Vedic period a notion arose that saw life in very negative terms. Life was not good in contrast to life's outlook in rigvedic times when things were good. Life was full of suffering. It was accepted that life is *samsara* (Skt., wandering) or an endless round or cycle of births and deaths. Reincarnation, not known in the *Rigveda*, is now accepted fact. It is assumed one would return after death to live a span

of life in some form. Returning repeatedly to this world was thought to be a painful thing.

A law which governed the process of life and rebirth was called *karma* (Skt., deed, work). Meaning also "action," it referred to an inexorable law governing human action which said that every act, word, or thought had its consequences for good or bad either in this life or in the world to come and probably both. For example, according to the *Chandogya Upanishad* pleasant conduct results in rebirth from a pleasant womb, but unpleasant conduct brings rebirth as a dog or a pig. The unfortunate might continue indefinitely in these rounds of birth and death. But by far the better thing was to end *samsara* through *moksha* (Skt., liberation; also *moksa*). *Moksha* in the *Upanishads* is a direct perception into the true nature of things. It is the knowledge of the nondual nature of reality. This special knowledge, regarded as the special possession of a few, said that suffering and *samsara* will end only when one comes to accept that the self within is identical with the self without. In other words, one must realize that *atman* and Brahman are the same and not different. Brahman is *atman*. To come to this knowledge would mean deliverance or release from *samsara* and one would achieve *moksha*.

Such knowledge was of a special kind and did not come easily. In fact, austerities, physical deprivations, ascetic practices, and self-denial were essential to overcome wrong perceptions and promote understanding. Meditation was helpful. The assistance of a teacher or *guru* was needed by whom one could gain knowledge of reality and the key to its mysteries. It was impossible to grasp the radical oneness of all things by formal study, discussion, and philosophical or theological inquiry alone. One needed an intuition into special truth, the kind of which ordinary knowledge was only preparatory. Thus in the *Kena Upanishad* (II.3) we have the following teaching about the knowledge which is liberating.

> It is conceived of by him of whom It is
> not conceived.
> He by whom It is conceived of, knows it
> not.
> It is not understood by those who under-
> stand It.
> It is understood by those who understand It
> not.[8]

This teaches enigmatically that there are two fundamentally different kinds of knowledge. One is logical, discursive, and ordinary operating by means of verbal and logical distinctions. Such knowledge is on the lower level but does little to aid in escaping *samsara*. It is merely preparatory, at best, for the highest knowledge. This knowledge rises above logic and language and in true, contentless knowledge one escapes *samsara* and *moksha*, suffering and joy, by experiencing the identity of *atman* and Brahman. Rising above all distinctions, reality appears nondual and liberation is attained.

The *Upanishads* have more than one theme and are not as explicit and unambiguous as the above explanation might suggest. They contain many different and even conflicting streams of thought. Skepticism, theism, materialism, and nondualism intermix and compete. The nondual theme is strong in the *Upanishads* but

was not systematized until the appearance of the prodigious thinker Shankara (also, Sankara; b. C.E. 722), who developed Advaita Vedanta (Skt., nondual knowledge).

Religion, Society and Ritual

Religion and Society in the Later Vedic Period

The *Upanishads* witness to a stream of thought emerging among a group of people who thought pessimistically about this life and accepted *karma* and *samsara* as good reason to long for *moksha*, the unitary experience of Brahman.

But it seems clear that the common people did not generally accept withdrawal from the world nor view life so negatively. They accepted a division of life for men called *ashramas* (Skt., stages; also *asramas*), which at a midlife period permitted men to devote more attention to transworldly affairs. The four *ashramas* are mentioned in *shastras* (valued ancient texts), where they are help up as an ideal for the upper three castes. These *ashramas* are: studenthood, householder, forest dweller, and ascetic. They are still regarded by some modern Hindus as options to be exercised.

The stage of studenthood begins with the *upanayana* rite described earlier in this text. By this ritual the youth is admitted to the formal study of the Vedas under the guidance of an *acharya* (Skt., teacher; also, *acarya*). The boy is to remain celibate while undertaking initial studies and is given the name *brahmacarin*. The householder stage (*grhastha*) begins with marriage and consists of establishing family and status in society. The *Laws of Manu*, dated from 200 B.C.E. to C.E. 200, contain detailed instructions about daily rituals, diet, and activities for each of the *ashramas*. As householder it was legitimate to aim at a life of pleasure and worldly success. While some moved beyond this, many did not and were content to pursue a life of comfort. The *Laws of Manu* do seem to encourage pursuit of the third stage, the forest dweller (*vanaprastha*). The individual may not literally retire to the forest, though this was indeed often what happened. He may merely vow to withdraw from sexual activity and worldly concerns while living in society periodically. The ascetic (*sannyasin*), or fourth stage, is an extension of the third. To pursue this, one seeks to live without attachment to possessions or family while meditating on or searching for *moksha*.

Those who did not aim for *moksha* would continue daily household rituals described in the *Gryha Sutras* (600?–300 B.C.E.) These *sutras* (Skt., texts) contain no mention of the ideas of *karma* and *samsara* so common in the *Upanishads*, and yet they are contemporary documents. This would tell us that Hindus in the later Vedic period followed and practiced a diversity of concerns just as they do today.

Social Classes and Vedic Religion

The *Rigveda* speaks of four *varnas* (colors) resulting from the dissection of Purusha, or cosmic man. These *varnas* are the four major caste divisions of ancient India which have

been expanded over time into three thousand or more castes in modern times. This social hierarchy, in descending order, consists of Brahmans, Ksatriyas, Vaishyas, and Shudras. The superior status of Brahmans seems to come from their role in supervising the Vedic sacrifices; their superior social standing has continued into modern times. Ksatriyas (warriors) were next in standing and Vaishyas (producers: merchants, farmers) were third. Only these first three ranks could aspire to Vedic knowledge and ritual. Shudras were not admitted to the ranks of the "twice-born," nor, of course, were other communities such as tribal people, who were considered beneath even the Shudra, the servile class. Those without caste were given degrading names such as "untouchables," "unseeables," or simply "outcastes." Mahatma Gandhi sought to give these noncasted people some social self-respect by calling them *harijans* (Skt., children of God).

The Origin of Castes

"One fourth of the Supreme Being constitutes all beings, while three fourths of him are immortal and stand above. With the one fourth below, he extended on all sides into the animate and the inanimate . . . . His face became the Brahman. His arms were made into the Kshatriya, his thighs became the Vaishya; from his feet the Shudra was born. The moon was born from his mind, the sun from his eyes, thunder and fire from his mouth, wind from his breath."

—Rigveda X,90

While a simple four-division caste system dates to Vedic times, Indian society early stratified and subdivided into hundreds of additional castes that had their own characteristic taboos and requirements in the areas of rituals, occupation, diet, marriage, and other minutiae. Where one stood socially in relation to others was often explained with reference to the law of *karma* and its inexorable operation. Striving for higher caste status or attempts for upward mobility could easily be criticized as inappropriate according to this system. Where, when, how, and who one was born was a matter of one's just deserts. This worked both positively and negatively. The upper castes could defend their status as deserved while justly suppressing lower castes as having their proper rewards. The lower one's caste, the fewer the benefits, and the more negatively the caste system is generally perceived. The modern Indian secular state has constitutional and legislative prohibitions against caste discrimination in civil employment and social services such as education and health. Quotas for noncaste people, called "Scheduled Castes" in the Indian constitution, are set by the government to guarantee employment and educational opportunities in medical colleges, law schools, and universities. However, caste discrimination still exists in most regions and continues to determine the bounds of social relationships to a significant degree.

Vedic Rituals Past and Present

There were once as many as forty or more *samskaras*, rites of passage purifying and/or protecting one during life events of critical importance. Many ancient *samskaras* are no longer ob-

served in modern times, while others have been reduced in scale or ritual complexity. There are ceremonies at conception and birth (*garba samskaras*), naming of the child (*namakarana*), eating of first solid food (*annaprasana*), initiation to Vedic study for boys (*upanayana*), engagement, marriage, death, and postdeath.

The *shraddha* (Skt., death) ceremonies attending death, like all others, vary somewhat by caste, region, and circumstance. However, the following is common. If death is imminent, special steps may be taken to assure the best possible position in the after-death period. Some may take the dying to a sacred stream or, if possible, to the Ganges River to die. The body will then be wrapped and perfumed in preparation for cremation in the open air of a rural community or at the public Hindu burning grounds. Cremation is usually within twenty-four hours. The procession will bear the body on a pallet, covered with garlands of flowers and led by the chief male member of the household. The funeral pyre will be constructed according to ritual requirements. The head of the funeral delegation will light the fire and when it has consumed the body and the ranking male has circumambulated counterclockwise four times the ashes will be gathered and thrown into a sacred river or otherwise properly scattered. A period of ritual impurity varying from eight to thirty days affects all mourners after the cremation. Then, after appropriate purification, the relatives perform *shraddha*, which affects the destiny of the deceased. Brahman priests may be invited to invoke the help of deities and assist in *puja* (worship accompanied by acts of devotion) to the ancestors and deities. The family representative will serve food to the Brahmans as though they are representatives of the deities, after which small balls of rice will be given to the assembled guests. Rice and other things of use to humans may be presented to the dead. A final prayer like the following may be offered:

O Fathers, go away by the somber ancient paths, after bestowing on us wealth, and endow us here with auspicious prosperity and valiant sons.

The Brahman priests may conclude the ceremony with this prayer:

If the ancestors are in the world of gods, they are gratified by the food offered in fire, if they are in the world of ancestors, they are gratified by the dinner given to the Brahmans; if they are in hell they are gratified by the rice-balls offered on the ground.[9]

Period of Classical Diversity: New Religious Movements

Jains

Jains and Their Contemporaries

It may not be possible to determine when the Jain religion began because Jain tradition traces its origins to eternity past. Jains believe a series of twenty-four *tirthankaras*, or "guides to crossing the river," go back to the beginning of time. The last two seem to parallel roughly the late Vedic period corresponding to the formation of the *Upanishads* (600–300 B.C.E.).

Parshva and Mahavira

Jain Deity. To outsiders, rituals occurring at Jain temples are hardly distinguishable from those found in Hindu temples. J. Lewis

Parshva was the twenty-third *tirthankara* and may have been a historical person. It is generally conceded that historicity is more likely the case for his successor, Mahavira ("Great Hero"). Mahavira may have been contemporary with Gotama around 500 B.C.E. If this is so it is probable that Mahavira was faced with the same diverse options for solving religious issues as was the Buddha. Whether he was an innovator or more of a transmitter of past beliefs from his community we cannot tell.

Jain traditions about Mahavira are as full of miraculous deeds and special circumstances as those of the Buddha. According to Jain literature, Mahavira was born with the name Nataputta

Vardhammana in the area now called Bihar in modern India. Like the Buddha, he was reared in great luxury and given ample opportunity to have all the pleasures of the world. He married and had a daughter but was challenged by a monastic community who followed Parshva. Wishing to follow the ascetic life of these monks, he nevertheless recognized that his duty to his parents and family came first. After his parents died and with family consent he, like the Buddha, set out in search of truth under the guidance of the followers of Parshva. After learning all he could from them, Vardhammana launched his own search, which was marked by extreme renunciation and acceptance of the ideas of rebirth, the painfulness of life, and *ahimsa* (Skt., nonkilling) toward living things. Though much more is involved, three ideas are the hallmark of Jainism: *ahimsa*, asceticism, and the *jiva* (Skt., soul), which exists in all things.

So intent was Mahavira on finding escape from life's sufferings and from attachment to the world that he refused to wear clothes, which caused others to make sport of him. After twelve years of searching and wandering, it was beside a sal tree in seated meditation that he reached *moksha*. *Moksha* is used by many religious movements and means simply "liberation," or release. Upon his death he went, as do all Jains who succeed in attaining the experience of *moksha*, to the *lokakasha*, "top of the universe," to be forever untouched by worldly cares.

Jiva and Ajiva

Mahavira accepted ideas which were widely diffused in society in his day.

These include beliefs found in the *Upanishads* and the *Tipitaka* (Pali, lit. three baskets; Buddhist scriptures) that life is full of pain, that self-denial and negation has value for spiritual progress, and that attitudes toward the *atman* are crucial for attaining *moksha*. The *Upanishads* taught that the *atman* was permanent and identical with Brahman. Each person was essential *atman* and *moksha* resulted when one came to a full recognition of this. The Buddha took a position opposite to the *Upanishads* by holding that there was no permanent *atman* nor any permanent Brahman. Ideas of a permanent *atman* or Brahman were illusory and led only to further suffering.

But Mahavira held beliefs that were different from either the *Upanishads* or the Buddha. In his view there was not one *atman* as taught by the *Upanishads*, but all the world consists of an infinite number of separate *atmans*, each of which he called *jiva*. Reality consists of a second category, the *ajiva* (Skt.; nonliving, material, nonsoul), which is the material context for the *jiva*. Both the *jiva* and *ajiva* are eternal, although the *jiva* is that which is principally valued. *Jiva*, or soul, is harmfully enmeshed with the *ajiva*, though this is not the way it should be. What causes this? The answer lies in the Jain concept of *karma*.

Karma

Wrongful acts cause karmic matter to penetrate and weigh down the *jiva*, making it impossible for it to rise to the top of the universe where it naturally seeks its rest. *Karma* is harmful matter that penetrates, infects, and clings to the *jiva* and prevents it from

Jain Bird Hospital, Delhi. Care for sick and injured birds is rooted in Jain belief that animals also have eternal souls (jiva). J. Lewis

attaining liberation. This is the universal and inescapable problem confronting humanity. *Karma* that clings to the *jiva* not only prevents *moksha* but determines the individual's existence in the next life. Harmful words, deeds, and thoughts result in being born into lower forms of life such as a bug, worm, dog, monkey, horse, or woman. These and all other forms and levels of life are arranged in a hierarchy of value and all have an eternal *jiva*. Jains are vegetarians and observe *ahimsa* (non-killing) since all life entities have *jiva*. Technically, even vegetable life has *jiva*, but as it is trapped in an extremely low level of *jiva*, or matter, it is not as serious to eat such things. The monk who is serious about pursuing *moksha* might regard full abstinence of food, or starvation, as the final solution for avoiding harmful karmic acts. Such an extreme measure is not to be pursued ill-advisedly and is not required for a Jain to reach *moksha*.

Monastic Life

Individuals who take up the monastic life set out in pursuit of a goal Jains admit few attain. Monastic pursuits are essential, however, since it is believed that the only way to purge karmic matter from the soul is through self-denial of comforts and usual pursuits of life. The vows monks take reflect this and are five in number:

1. The vow to avoid the killing of living begins by being circumspect in diet and daily activities such as where one sits or walks so as not to take life, even unintentionally.

2. The vow to speak the truth both in motive and in actual word.

3. The vow not to take what does not belong to one nor to permit others to do the same.

4. All sexual activity is renounced.

5. All attachments are given up.

While these rules are embraced by monks, another code, less demanding in some ways but fully in the spirit of the above, was provided for laypersons. This code incorporated the first three but not the last two of the aforementioned vows. For laypersons it was enough to require chaste behavior and observe designated times of abstinence and self-denial.

Jain monks can be seen in either Jain temples or homes instructing the faithful, an activity not regarded as karmic matter–producing. Women may also take up the monastic life, but must first be reborn in the next life as men to actually achieve liberation. Upon liberation all *jivas* residing at the top of the universe are identical while remaining separate. They are not one as in the *Upanishads*. *Jivas* are of infinite number though identical in nature when free of karmic matter.

According to Jain doctrine, *tirthankaras* cannot help the monks, nor can deities of any kind. The completion of karmic matter burnoff can only be accomplished by a final act of starvation, though this is not to bypass completion of all the vows whereby one breaks with all attachments.

Community Diversity Since Mahavira

It is a startling sight to see a Jain monk at a temple or festival without clothes. The nonwearing of clothes was an issue that first divided the community. One group affirmed the legitimacy of wearing at least a single white garment and have been called the "white-clad" liberals, or Shvetambaras. The other major group is called Digambaras, or "sky-clad," referring to their approval of no clothes whatever following, in their opinion, the example of Mahavira himself. Originally the former group was associated with northern India, where it could be very cold, whereas the Digambaras claimed strength in the temperate south. Jains are dispersed now throughout India, although they are often found in major centers of business, especially in Gujarat state north of Bombay. The Jain emphasis on *ahimsa* has led away from fishing or farming and into business and clerical occupations. A third Jain community is called the Sthanakavasis; they differ from the others in permitting neither temples nor idols.

Jain Worship Today

Wherever there are Jain temples images are found and appear to the outsider to receive the same kind of worship, or *puja*, Hindus give their deities. Incense is burned, garlands of flowers bedeck images, and prayers are addressed to the images, many of which are famous Jain leaders of tradition and history. While Jains see themselves as different from other religious communities, they are generally regarded by Hindus as little different from themselves and are classed by the Indian government in the same religious category as Hindus for the sake of political representation.

Tipitaka Buddhists

Sometime around the fifth century B.C.E. a movement began in India that grew and spread around the teachings of one who was given the title Buddha, which means "the enlightened one." Today there are about three hundred million Buddhists in the world, though less than two million are found in India, the birthplace of the movement. It became a missionary religion that spread through Asia, and large numbers are found today in central Asia, Nepal, Taiwan, Hong Kong, Korea, Japan, Mongolia, Tibet, Burma, Thailand, Cambodia, Laos, Vietnam, Indonesia, and Sri Lanka.

Two words are often used to describe this movement that, from the standpoint of history of religions, are less than satisfactory. The movement is sometimes called "heterodox" or "unorthodox" to contrast it with the Vedic teachings, from which it differs considerably. These terms are unfortunate since they are usually employed in a context of discussing Hindu developments and imply that Hindu traditions are in some sense an "orthodox," correct, or acceptable position on religious doctrine. "Unorthodox" implies that Buddhists hold incorrect religious views and are therefore "heterodox." For the historian of religions to accept such language would be to patronize the one (Hindu) and be insensitive to others (Jains, for example). In this study we will not use these words, as they can easily lead to misunderstanding and are thus inappropriate.

Another term, *Buddhism*, is misleading and, despite its frequent usage in

some scholarly studies, will not appear in our studies. Wilfred Cantwell Smith has urged the word be dropped because it erroneously connotes a single religious system with a unified pattern of beliefs and practices, when in fact there have been and continue to be scores of Buddhist communities whose beliefs and practices vary widely and sometimes conflict sharply. To refer to them with one catchall word, *Buddhism*, is to imply uniformity when, in fact, there is great diversity and contrast. It is necessary, when speaking historically and hence descriptively, to distinguish the many Buddhist groups from one another. A variety of factors have contributed to the proliferation of Buddhist groups, among them loyalties to different texts and different authorities on the interpretation of these texts.

One Buddhist community appearing very early which gained in strength and influence was called Theravada; its canonical scriptures are the *Tipitaka* written in the Pali language. Theravada means "the elders," or "the way of the elders" and was only one of more than eighteen different groups competing for followers from 500 to 200 B.C.E. Gradually the Theravadins established strong communities across India and Nepal and abroad in China, Sri Lanka, Burma, Thailand, and Cambodia. The community remained strong so long as it had imperial support, but it tended to languish without it as in India where it fell into disfavor and demise at the end of the first millennium C.E.

What follows is a description of the Buddha and his teachings as held by the Theravadins. No writings of the

Buddha himself exist, and the extensive oral period preceding the recording of the *Tipitaka* makes it impossible to verify historical details about him or to be certain the texts accurately reflect his teachings. Theravadins, of course, believe they do.

The Life of the Buddha

The Pali name of this influential religious figure was Siddhattha Gotama. He was born into a noble family and upon reaching enlightenment was honored with the title Buddha, meaning "the enlightened one." Traditional dates for his life are from 563 to 483 B.C.E. Both the *Tipitaka* and later materials such as the *Jataka Tales* give biographical material about him, though much of it is legendary or embellished. The following is usually accepted as a general outline of his life.

Since his father ruled the small kingdom of their Sakya clan near the Indo-Nepal border, Prince Siddhattha grew up accustomed to luxury and comfort. In time, he married and had a son. There are stories about the miraculous birth of Siddhattha and reports of prophecies about him becoming an ascetic who would leave all to search after truth. He lived at a time when many were seeking answers to ultimate questions as witnessed by the *Upanishads* and the emergence of the Jain community.

His regal setting contrasted with that of the common people, and according to legend he was shocked into coming to grips with life by experiencing the so-called four passing sights: an aged man, a diseased man, a dead body, and a hermit truth-seeker. These living examples of change, suffering, decay, and desperation profoundly disturbed the prince, who is reported to have said: "I also am subject to decay and am not free from the power of old age, sickness, and death." Accordingly, he determined to set out in a search for life-and-death answers. Though not without struggle, he decided at the age of twenty-nine to renounce his birthright, leave his family, and take up the ascetic life. Shaving his head and beard, he believed that unencumbered in this way he would have the best chance of finding answers. This turning point, called The Great Renunciation, marks the beginning of the Buddha's career.

During six years of wandering across northeast India he sampled teachings of many *gurus* and practiced meditative techniques. He considered the doctrine of the unreality of things taught by *Kalama*, (an Indian guru), but this and other options were not satisfying. Ascetic practices nearly cost him his life. Finally, while sitting under the pipal, or bo tree, called by Buddhists reverently the Bodhi (enlightenment) tree, he achieved a breakthrough of understanding. He was resisted in this by an evil demon, Mara, who first tempted then threatened him, trying to dislodge his resolve. All of this is richly elaborated in Buddhist literature and lavishly depicted in sculpture, painting, and bas-relief art in places like Sanchi and Ajanta in India. After his enlightenment he sought five companion ascetics who had rejected him earlier for his stand against their excessive deprivations and preached to them a sermon containing the (skt., truth; P., *dhamma*) *dharma* which persuaded them to be his first converts. This is called the Deer Park sermon given at Isipatana near Banaras in India.

Gradually the number of his followers increased to include three whose names became famous through their association with him: Sariputra, Ananda, and Devadatta. By the time of his death at eighty, numerous communities in northern India had been established, and the Buddhist tradition had been launched to become a major force in the life and thought of southern and eastern Asia.

The Tipitaka

It is now time to look more closely at the *Tipitaka* and the questions it poses. The *Tipitaka* in its Pali version contains nine sections arranged in three major collections. The material includes prose discourses, poetic verse, tales of the Buddha's life, miracle tales, and discourses to delight through question and answer.

The first collection of the *Tipitaka* is the *Vinaya Pitaka*, which has five parts dealing with discipline and life in the *sangha* (monastery). The *Patimokkha* gives 227 rules governing life for the community of *bikkhus* or *bikkhunis* (monks and nuns). These rules were recited in their entirety at the twice-monthly meeting coinciding with the new and the full moon. One could be expelled from the *sangha* for sexual misconduct, theft, murder, spiritual pride, ignorance, or striking a superior.

The *Sutta Pitaka* contains the teaching of the Buddha, is illustrated profusely with stories, and is the second main collection. *Sutta* (P.; Skt., *sutra*) means

"thread": the text is likened to a string linking jewels of truth. The first four parts, or *Nikayas*, contain teachings or discourses of long or medium length and show evidence of a gradual development of ideas by its writers, who were writing at least two hundred years after the Buddha. The fifth *Nikaya* contains past lives of the Buddha and other ideas making the Buddha a semidivine and cosmic figure. Such ideas are counter to the general view of the Buddha in the *Tipitaka*, where he is human or, at most, superhuman. Select passages from the *Sutta Pitaka* formed the nucleus of a small book that is as significant to them as the book of Romans is to many Christians. Totaling 423 verses arranged in twenty-six chapters, the *Dhammapada* summed up the Buddha's teaching and was widely circulated.

The *Abhidhamma Pitaka* (*The Basket of Doctrinal Subtleties*) contains scholastic details, and with its emphasis on definitions and minor points it seems to be of more academic interest than the other two. Found within it is the *Kathavattus*, which argues against and refutes several competing Buddhist groups such as the Mahasanghikas, whom the Theravadins considered heretics.

Tipitaka Doctrine

What do the *Tipitaka* scriptures indicate about the religious goal and the means to achieve that goal? According to the *Tipitaka*, the Buddha accepted ideas current in India during his days, such as life being characterized by suffering, the law of *karma* (Skt.; P., *kamma*), reincarnation, seated meditation, and limited austerities for those who seek truth. But the Buddha conceived the human problem differently from his contemporaries. His views can be summarized under the following characteristics of human existence.

Anicca

All existence is impermanent and changing. This is the teaching of *anicca* (P., transience), and is the first mark of existence. Nothing remains enduringly the same; everything is subject to decay and change. Any view maintaining there is something permanent, lasting, unchanging, or static is misinformed or ignorant. A dominant view found in the *Upanishads* is that *atman* and Brahman are permanent, lasting, identical, and unchanging. This is denied in the *Tipitaka* and hence the Buddha is making a radically different proposal. There are references in the *Tipitaka* and *Dhammapada* to deities, but even these are subject to change, being neither eternal nor immutable. All aspects of reality are marked by the principle of change. This is a starting point for understanding the doctrine of the *Tipitaka*.

Dukkha

The second mark of existence is that all of life is suffering. It was commonly accepted in society of the Buddha's time that life was flawed and marked by pain. The ills of old age, sickness, and death are the obvious ones and easiest to understand. But *dukkha* is much more than this. *All* of life is suffering, misery, hurt, and pain, including those experiences that appear at first to bring pleasure and satisfaction. What causes this suffering is the failure to understand and accept the first mark of existence—*anicca*. To regard things, persons, experiences, gods, and all facets of life as permanent or lasting when in fact they are transitory and quickly fleeting leads to pain. It is not that there is suffering now and again, but that, properly understood, all of life is suffering. The person one loves, the pleasures one enjoys, the gods one turns to are all transitory and changing. To think there is something one can lastingly cling to, possess or keep, leads to suffering. Why? Because whatever is the object of affection or grasping slips away since its basic nature is impermanence.

Suffering encompasses the entirety of life from birth to death; it is not some occasional setback or disappointment. Some commentators classify *dukkha* in three categories: (1) unconscious suffering—where the person is as yet unawakened to the reality of pain and its cause; (2) manifest suffering which is consciously experienced as mental or physical suffering; and (3) delayed suffering which refers to thoughts, actions, and words which, through the law of *karma*, causes later suffering.

Anatta

The third mark of existence is *anatta* (P., nonsoul). This is an extension of the doctrine of the transitory nature of things to include the *atman* itself. As there are no permanent things, there is no *atman* either. To believe there is a single permanent self, as the *Upanishads* taught, or to believe there are many *jivas*, as the Jains do is a most serious blunder. For if there were a permanent *atman* there would be something one could cling to that would not disappoint. But there is no *atman* any more than there is anything else that is lasting and continuously the same. *Anatta* strikes a final blow at the very center of grasping, clinging, and attachment which is the self, ego, or *atman*. Just as there are no lasting things to grasp, so there is no lasting self to do the grasping. When it is understood that there are no things to grasp and no self to grasp them, then one is close to liberation.

The *atman* like all things is dependent, derived, and changing. It is the result of the constantly shifting *skandhas* (Skt., heaps), which are five in number. Four are immaterial and one material:

Rupa—physical or material form
Vedana—feelings
Samjna—perceptions
Samskaras—volitions
Vijnana—consciousness

These *skandhas* are always changing under the influence of *karma* and, as such, there exists no entity that endures the same from moment to moment. It is gross ignorance to think otherwise and a serious cause of suffering.

A doctrine which helps to understand the above is *paticcasamuppada* (P., dependent origination). This teaches that nothing exists that is not dependent on something else. If there was something independent, underived, or "uncaused," then this would be permanent, a position which the *Tipitaka* denies. Dependent origination, outlined in the *Tipitaka*, usually has twelve parts and can be thought of as a wheel with spokes. To demonstrate how all existence is dependent the following causative links are identified.

1. Ignorance (*avijja*) results in volitional activities.

2. Volitional activities (*sankara*) leads to consciousness.

3. Consciousness (*vinnana*) links one to name and form.

4. Name and form (*nama-rupa*), in other words, mind and matter, leads to the operation of six senses.

5. The six organs of sense (*salayatana*) leads to contact with objects of the senses.

6. Such contact (*phassa*) leads to sensation.

7. On sensation (*vadana*) depends craving.

8. Craving or desire (*tanha*) results in attachment.

9. Attachment (*upadana*) causes existence or becoming.

10. Becoming (*bhava*) leads to birth.

11. Birth (*jati*) brings about old age, death, suffering, misery.

12. Old age and death (*jaramarana*) in turn result in ignorance.[10]

Ignorance is often put in first place, since entering into existence at all is caused by ignorance. But if ignorance were to cease then there would be no *karma* and correspondingly no consciousness, name, form, etc. If one can at some point break out of this cyclic process, then one can end the rounds of birth and death, or *samsara*.

Dependent origination applies *anicca* by showing that nothing is self-existent and hence everything is derived and if derived then nonpermanent. It serves also to show how *anatta*, the doctrine of nonsoul, is justifiable, since it comes into existence, if indeed it is proper to say this, by a process and never stops being of the nature of process. It is never static, complete, whole, or truly permanent. The *Tipitaka* teaches rebirth without reincarnation. By indicating that becoming is the nature of all things and that there is never any continuity from one moment to another, it is inappropriate to speak of anything carrying over from one moment to the next or from one life to the next. The *atman* is not enduring from moment to moment nor, by extension, from one lifetime to another. The term *reincarnation* is rejected in favor of the term *transmigration* since the former wrongly suggests a continuous *atman* while the latter supports the idea of change.

Buddhists have been criticized for their doctrine of dependent origination and other related doctrines, especially in the area of ethics and moral responsibility. If *anatta*, or nonsoul, is true then a "person" is never the same from moment to moment. From moment A to moment B we move from person A to person B. According to *karma*, acts done at one moment inexorably bear fruit at another. But since the *Tipitaka* teaches a kind of multiperson existence, a question of fairness arises. Is it fair for the bad *karma* of person A to fall on person B? According to the *Tipitaka*, the consequences of all acts fall on someone else. Where an evil act is done, is it fair for evil consequences to fall on anyone other than the person responsible? Is this not a gross injustice? Buddhists are prone to turn aside from answering this problem directly. They prefer to point out that it is imperative for individuals to act responsibly and realize how their lives affect others. Hence, the need to live for others. What is a serious ethical problem as seen by nonbelievers thus becomes for believers an occasion to appeal for ethical conduct. Neverthe-

less, the problem remains for Buddhists to answer.

The Religious Goal

One cannot talk about the religious goal without talking about the human dilemma as the *Tipitaka* sees it. The problem according to the *Tipitaka* is ignorance of the true nature of things as summarized in the three marks of existence. More precisely, it is to be ignorant of or indifferent to the consequences of craving. Craving in the *Tipitaka* also means grasping, lusting, attachment, or desire. Desire or attachment opposes two of the fundamental teachings: that there is some permanent thing to possess and a lasting self to possess it. But since all things are in process and will soon pass away, what one thought to have, hold, possess, or use is taken away and suffering is the result.

The religious goal is to so radically accept the true nature of things, and to part so fully and finally with craving, that *samsara* is broken and suffering is at its end. The word for this experience is *nirvana* (Skt.; P., *nibbana*). This is not a place to which one goes but an experience which is not fully described in the *Tipitaka*. It means literally "blowing out," but not so much of existence as of craving. When craving and desire are absolutely at an end, ignorance is removed, the cycle of dependent origination is broken, the "heaps" do not reconfigure under *karma's* law, and the religious problem posed by the *Tipitaka* is resolved.

What happens to the soul at death? Such an ignorant question was often asked the Buddha, according to the texts. It is a question he never answered directly. He preferred to use illustrations. Citing the case of a burning candle, he asks where the flame goes when it is extinguished. "Does it go somewhere when it is out?" The answer is that it does not. It simply ceases to exist, which is exactly the case with the individual.

Nirvana can be achieved in this life, and not just upon death. But why does the body continue if *nirvana* is achieved? The answer is that the fruit of past *karma* has been born and will continue until it has played itself out. But because of release from *samsara* no new karmic fruit is forthcoming. Upon death the "heaps" disperse not to regroup.

Attaining *nirvana* is a long, arduous ordeal at the end of many lifetimes of striving. It is usually not thought achievable without entering the monastic community to take advantage of all the Buddha taught and himself practiced in pursuit of enlightenment.

The Means to the Religious Goal

Those who wish to seriously pursue the goal cannot do so amidst a world which so easily distracts. The Buddha's disciples established communities sheltered from ordinary society called *sanghas*, or monasteries. Both men and women were welcome, though generally nuns were few and were strictly segregated. The *bhikkhus* and the *bhikkhunis* both had the following aids toward pursuit of the goal: study of the Buddha's teachings, meditation on them, self-denial, and ethical practices.

The Sangha

Upon entering the *sangha* one vowed to keep its regulations as recorded in the *Vinaya Pitaka*. These rules were restated every two weeks at the Uposatha ceremony. Some of the rules mandated simple living and dependence on others for food. Thus monks begged from nearby communities, usually in the forenoon. This served a twofold purpose: monks were taught to limit ego esteem as a step to the full acceptance of *anatta*, and laypeople were provided opportunities to gain good *karma* useful in progress at some distant time toward *nirvana*. Few things were as meritorious as aiding monks in their spiritual journey or assisting in the support of monastic institutions and the erection and beatification of their facilities.

Meditation was practiced as a means of understanding and internalizing the teachings of the *Tipitaka*. Excessive and life-threatening austerities were discouraged in keeping with the experience of the Buddha himself. Meditation used a variety of techniques that aided in minimizing distractions and erroneous thoughts so that one could concentrate on the experience of the truth.

The Buddha taught the "Noble Eightfold Path" as that which all followers must accept.

> What is the Noble Truth of the Path that leads to cessation of suffering? —It is just the Noble Eightfold Path, consisting of right outlook, right resolves, right speech, right acts, right livelihood, right endeavour, right mindfulness and right rapture of concentration.[11]

Ancient Buddhist Sangha at Ellora, Maharashtra. Cut into the side of a mountain, this provided refuge for monks at Ajanta, Maharashtra during the monsoon. J. Lewis

As monks progressed in understanding, higher and higher levels of ethical performance were expected. This can be seen with respect to the *Brahmaviharas*: (1) *Metta* or loving kindness; (2) *Karuna* or compassion; (3) *Mudita* or sympathetic joy; (4) *Upekkha* or equanimity. As one progresses one moves closer to attaining the highest level or equanimity. This means one is able to see things without partiality, calmly and with an unattached mind. It is to have no desire at all or at least no harmful desire and enter what might be called moral neutrality. One does not seek a course of action as that might suggest a preference and that would be an evidence of attachment. But neither does one refuse a course of action nor oppose one since that too would show a kind of preference.

For the monk, four levels of rank are distinguished: (1) The *sotapanna* is one who has just "entered the stream,"

virtually a novice monk. (2) The *sakadagamin* has progressed so far that he is a "once-returner," needing only to be reborn once more before receiving enlightenment. (3) The one who is certain to get enlightenment in this life and will not be reborn before *nirvana* is the *anagamin*. (4) The ideal is the *arhant* (P.; Skt., *arhat*), who has already achieved *nirvana*. The *arhant* alone is fully liberated. No unmistakable evidence for the last three stages is described, but since it is presumed that superior spiritual achievement is mutually recognized, no formal criteria are needed. There are numerous warnings in the *Tipitaka* against false claims and spiritual pride, however.

Buddhists Outside the Sangha

We have already seen that if one wishes to be serious in reaching the religious goal it is necessary to leave behind the ordinary life in society.

Buddhists outside the *sangha* accepted the doctrines of the Buddha to the

Ancient Sangha cells for Buddhist monks at Ajanta, Maharashtra. J. Lewis

best of their understanding. But often this lagged behind orthodox teaching considerably. The common people of the past and in Buddhist lands today integrate pre-Buddhist and non-Buddhist ideas freely, so much so that dealing with the spirit world is a major part of their lives. The belief system of ordinary Buddhists in Sri Lanka, for example, contains a mixture of astrology, magic, sorcery, and exorcism ceremonies. Fear of spirit attack constantly plagues some, and many believe that demons and deities are all around and potentially dangerous. The belief in *karma*, basic Buddhist ethics, respect for the Buddha, and support of the *sangha* and its programs are central points of continuity with Buddhist doctrine.

Lay involvement in support of the *sangha* was essential for it to thrive, and in return its benefactors could expect to collect handsome accumulations of good *karma*. The *Dhammapada* indicates great rewards for pious support of the *sangha* and equally excellent rewards for acts showing devotion to the Buddha. The *Tipitaka* teaches that the Buddha was a mere man whose greatness lay in his discovery of a way to escape life's suffering. But there is evidence also that some were giving him a status approaching the superhuman and even the semidivine. Lay attitudes could be expected to run the range from admiration of this spiritual giant to outright worship. Later Buddhist texts emerge to prove there were communities that elevated him to a deity not unlike the deities of Vedic and post-Vedic Hindus. In all probability some in the Theravada laity embraced such conceptions, though it was not, strictly speaking, in agreement with their religious texts.

A popular activity for Buddhists of the Theravada community was to circumambulate a *stupa* (Skt.; P., *thupa*). The *stupa* was an earthen mound for burial of important persons in the pre-Buddhist era. Buddhists made it a place of devotion and meditation by placing in it articles or remains of the Buddha or his close associates. The so-called Great Stupa of Sanchi in the state of Madhya Pradesh, India, was erected in the first or second century B.C.E. and served to accommodate the interests of lay and monastic followers. To reverently walk around its perimeter while thinking on the Buddha's teaching or some other worthy thought was very meritorious.

If early generations of Theravada believers were like their modern counterparts in countries such as Sri Lanka, Burma, Thailand, and Cambodia, they would have continued practices and beliefs not in conflict with the *Tipitaka* but which enabled them to deal with the realm of spirits and evil forces. The *Tipitaka* recognizes the existence of an evil spirit world but provides little or no instruction on how to cope with it. Present Buddhist societies in these countries have many beliefs and prescriptions that enable them to defeat malevolent powers. We may presume that the earliest Theravada community did as well. Certainly there are no prohibitions against such beliefs.

Diversity Among Early Buddhists

Bodhisattva: Mahayana Ideal

At least eighteen competing Buddhist groups existed side by side in the early centuries in India. Many died out; some, like followers of the *Tipitaka*, survived to modern times while still others were absorbed by similar communities.

It has been customary to divide Buddhists into two main parts: Hinayana and Mahayana. Hinayana (Skt., small vehicle) refers to the followers of the *Tipitaka* community who place emphasis on each individual seeking and achieving his or her own enlightenment. That name was given to them by the Mahayana (Skt., great vehicle) school and implied a criticism since Mahayana claimed to possess the more noble goal of the enlightenment of all beings. Hinayana prefers to go by the name Theravada (P., the way of the elders). The names Hinayana and Mahayana are useful only to distinguish an early division historically and ideologically, but lack precision beyond these generalizations.

Mahayana arose in the period after 100 B.C.E. and generated a large number of followers, texts, and schools that had a continuing following in Tibet, China, Japan, and the Chinese colonies of Korea and Vietnam. Mahayana groups and the texts associated with them have three distinguishable but often intertwined emphases: *prajna* (Skt., wisdom), *bhakti* (Skt., devotion), and *tantra* (Skt., occult). The wisdom texts emphasize nonduality and gave rise to many schools, two of which we shall examine, namely Madhyamika and Yogacara. Then there are texts presenting Buddhas and *bodhisattvas* as eternal gods with grace and power to deliver to paradise those who have faith. Finally there are tantric texts.

The Bodhisattva

Found in virtually all Mahayana texts is the *bodhisattva*, who, because he has arrived at the threshold of enlightenment, is the spiritual ideal toward which humans should strive. In later Mahayana texts he is more than human or superhuman and is presented as divine savior fully worthy of worship. The *bodhisattva* served as a reminder of the religious end, *nirvana*, toward which seekers should strive. But he was also a means for those seeking enlightenment, as they could be helped by acts of devotion to him. Though Buddhas are still preeminent in these texts to teach and inspire, the *bodhisattvas* have a lofty status for their spiritual achievement.

The word *bodhisattva* means literally "enlightenment being" and in Hinayana texts referred to a human or transcendent being who was destined to achieve enlightenment. But in Mahayana texts such as the *Astasahasrika-*

Prajnaparamita sutra (*The Perfection of Wisdom in Eight Thousand Lines*, first century B.C.E.) it signified one who, though qualified to step into *nirvana*, refused to become a Buddha, alone preferring to delay the final step until others could join. This thought, not found in the *Tipitaka*, permeates all Mahayana texts.

It was an ancient belief that Buddhas were rare. Those who achieved enlightenment did so by their own herculean efforts, which were effective for themselves alone. The Mahayana texts suggested these older ways were no longer valid and presented the idea that enlightenment was for the many and not just the few. The *bodhisattva* was the key to this fulfillment. All those who desired so could arrive at the status of a Buddha by practicing the spiritual disciplines of a *bodhisattva* over many centuries. The *bodhisattva* became the spiritual hero, model, and teacher for the qualities of compassion, mercy, and unselfishness which contrasted with the *arhant*, who, in some texts, was criticized for seeking only his own enlightenment.

Some *bodhisattvas* are famous in the texts for teaching the doctrine of Mahayana. Manjusri, a *bhikkhu*, taught a text of eighty thousand lines. Maitreya, the future Buddha, is said to have taught wisdom *sutras* to ancient scholars. Avalokitesvara reigns in a transcendent paradise from which he dispenses grace and mercy. *Bodhisattvas* are central in the three schools of Mahayana thought and practice treated below: Madhyamika, Yogacara, and Bhakti.

The *bodhisattva* career was in some ways not different from the *pratyeka-buddha* (a self-enlightened one who does not teach others) and *sravaka* (having the benefit of the Buddha's teaching and the *sangha*). Like them, he accepted the necessity of breaking with craving through understanding the truths of nonego and transitoriness, the practice of virtues, and meditation on the truth. But unlike the *sravaka*, he was not obligated to enter the *sangha*. And in contrast to both, he pursued the task of aiding all beings in achieving their own enlightenment, even though this might last an indefinite or even infinite period of time. The *bodhisattva* is described in the *Astasahasrika–Prajnaparamita sutra* in this way:

> Doers of what is hard are the bodhisattvas who have set out to win full enlightenment. Thanks to the practice of the six perfections, as described above, they do not wish to attain release in a private Nirvana of their own. They survey the highly painful world of beings. They want to win full enlightenment, and yet they do not tremble at birth-and-death.[12]

The goal was no longer the earliest possible solitary experience of *nirvana*, but the cessation of suffering of all suffering persons through the benefit of his spiritual merit and progress. Distinguishing the *bodhisattva* from the *arhant*, *pratyekabuddha*, and *sravaka* was the vow taken to save all suffering creatures. This elevated him to a superior standing in the Mahayana texts. The vow of the *bodhisattvas* in the *Astasahasrika* marked him as worthy of great merit and respect for his qualities of self-sacrifice, compassion, and pity. The *bodhisattva* was later elevated to the status of a god in texts such as the *Sukavativyuha Sutra*. Note the qualities of mediation and saviorhood in this vow: "We will become a shelter for the world, a refuge, the place of rest, the final relief, islands, lights and leaders of the world. We will win full enlightenment and become the resort of the world."[13]

Skill-in-Means

A common teaching device of Buddhas and *bodhisattvas* is the use of *upaya* (Skt., skill-in-means, skillfulness of device). When teaching the ignorant or those whose spiritual perception is immature, it is necessary to be skillful in the methods used to advance them toward enlightenment. It is foolish to present truths that they are incapable of understanding. Sometimes translated "tactfulness," *upaya* deals in the use of fictitious or contrived stories and doctrines as a platform from which to move on to higher and more complete truth. In the *Saddharmapundarika Sutra* (*The Lotus of the True Dharma*), Sariputra, the receptive and teachable disciple of the Buddha, is informed that Hinayana disciples who have pursued *nirvana* for themselves are in error and need correction. That is, the vehicles of the *arhant*, *pratyekabuddha*, and *sravaka*, though indeed taught by the Buddha, were just preliminary and elementary vehicles to be transcended when they were mature enough to accept the vehicle of the *bodhisattva*.

To illustrate the Buddha's own use of *upaya* a story is told of a company of people on a difficult and long journey. The guide (symbolic of the Buddha), fearful lest the travelers become discouraged and give up, magically conjures up a large city to refresh and encourage them.

> Then the company proceed into the magic city, imagining they have arrived at their destination, and are settled in comfort. When the leader perceives that the company are rested and are no longer fatigued, he makes the magic city disappear, and says to the company: "Come along . . . I only created this past large city for you to rest in."[14]

As there was no city, in fact, to give them rest, a question arises whether the Buddha was dishonest to teach Hinayana and the vehicle of the *arhant* as true, when he later acknowledges them only as preliminary to ultimate truth. The text argues that, since they lead to enlightenment, such deceptive methods are justified. "If I only use spiritual power and wisdom, casting aside every tactful method, and extol for the sake of all living creatures the wisdom, powers and fearlessness of the Tathagata, living creatures cannot by this method be saved."[15]

Buddhist Systems of Thought

Madhyamika

An Indian Buddhist monk named Nagarjuna lived between C.E. 150 and 250 and was associated with a school of thought called Madhyamika (The Middle Way). Gotama's teaching in the *Tipitaka* was also called the "Middle Way" but the two are distinct. Gotama was said to have taught a doctrine midway between the extremes of asceticism and indulgence. Neither starving nor gratification addressed the real issue: breaking with erroneous acts and thoughts which produced *karma* and *samsara*. The middle way, according to Gotama, was to cling to nothing, including these extremes.

In the *Tipitaka*, *prajna* referred to that understanding which experiences the marks of existence that lead to *nirvana*. But in the *prajna* texts it was an understanding of the doctrine of emptiness, or *shunyata*. Two important *prajna* texts are the *Vajracchedika*, or *Diamond Sutra*, and *Astasahasrika Prajnaparamita*. This latter text was circulated in scaled-down versions of as few as one hundred words and in China was called the *Heart Sutra* since it contained only the very heart of the matter. The main doctrine taught in *prajna* texts is that all the constituent elements of reality are *shunya*, or "empty" of permanence. Emptiness or voidness characterized all things and hence, if properly understood, would serve to prevent craving and the suffering that went with it. Even the nature of the Buddha was "empty" and provided no place to lay hold of for grasping.

Nagarjuna was critical of non-Buddhists whose affirmations of an enduring self were grossly in error and disproven already in the *Tipitaka*. But he was also critical of ideas derived from the *Tipitaka* which appear to accept a residual permanence due to a misunderstanding of *paticcasamuppada*.

To correct false notions of dependent origination he argues that it is not just that every thing depends on causes and hence has no independent existence, but that origination itself is false and due to *avidya* (Skt., ignorance). Nagarjuna used logic to correct the misconception of things coming into existence. First, it is self-evident that things do not originate merely by the perception of them. The perception of a form is not caused by the eye, for there is no contact between the eye and the form. Next, he points out that things cannot cause themselves to exist, for that involves a thing preexisting itself. If a thing exists it cannot come into existence again. Third, there are no causal connections between things, and to prove this one might take an example. Thing B cannot be caused by thing A because A itself has no prior existence. Its nonexistence is argued on the grounds that a thing cannot be self-caused. As there can be no connection between B and A, to claim that there is is not different from claiming anything is caused by anything else. Thus light could be caused by darkness. It is manifest, therefore, that things cannot be caused by themselves nor by other things nor by a combination of these two impossibilities. Fourth, things do not exist without cause, for then all things could arise at any time without rule.

But Nagarjuna was not arguing that nothing existed, for that would be the view of nihilism, which he also rejected. His goal was to make clear that there is no thing on which one can depend or to which one can cling and this includes views of truth and error as much as material objects. The true nature (*svabhava*) of things is *shunyata* (Skt., emptiness) or *shunya* (Skt., void). This view does not affirm the existence of anything, for the nature of things, in his view, is to have no nature. But it does not deny the existence of things either, for the true nature of all things is emptiness.

The claim that emptiness is the nature of things is advanced for the practical purpose of overcoming ignorance and achieving *nirvana*. But in the end, even the view of emptiness itself is given up, and when that occurs enlightenment has been complete. Until then things appear to exist, and as such they are past, present, or future, and as such they have a nature, and as such they are subject to *karma* and rebirth.

One might think that where emptiness is the nature of all things ethical considerations would be unimportant. But ethics have value as a preliminary step since they work against selfishness and self-centeredness. "View as enemies, avarice, deceit, duplicity, lust, indolence, pride, greed, hatred and pride concerning family, figure, glory, youth or power," says Nagarjuna.[16] Moral behavior has additional positive benefits for those who fall short of enlightenment. The ethical life is sure to improve one's standing in the afterlife, according to the laws of *karma*. "Always perfectly meditate on kindness, pity, joy and indifference; then if you do not obtain a higher degree you will obtain the happiness of Brahman's world."[17]

Yogacara

This wisdom school was founded in the third century C.E. and was led by subsequent notables such as Asanga and his brother Vasubandhu (fourth century C.E.). Yogacara (Skt., the practice of yoga) gets its name from the methods used (Yoga-meditation) to clear the mind of false perceptions. It is also called Vijnanavada (Skt., consciousness school), which points out its tendency to emphasize consciousness as the only real. The school is a form of subjective idealism.

The brothers are said to have been born in northwest India in the region of Gandhara where they studied and struggled with a number of Buddhist schools of thought. Both belonged to Hinayana schools before their conversion. Vasubandhu reportedly so regretted his former attacks on Mahayana ideas that he was only narrowly persuaded by his brother from cutting out his tongue. He encapsulated his thought in a short composition of twenty-one verses called the *Vimsatikas*, a preface to his longer treatise on Yogacara. The classical text of Yogacara is usually said to be the *Lankavatara Sutra*.

Yogacara agrees with Madhyamika that all elements are essentially empty but nevertheless teaches the existence of one irreducible reality: the storehouse consciousness. Thus it denies reality to the external world while at the same time defending consciousness as real. It disagrees with Hinayana interpretations of the *Tipitaka* that all things are composed of irreducible constituents (*skandhas*) which converge at one moment only to reconfigure the next. In the mind of Yogacara followers these *dhatus* (Skt., basic elements) cause Hinayana followers to be guilty of a kind of incipient realism. For if there is something that exists with a nature of its own, no matter how small, then there is a point at which one can be tempted to cling and hence suffer.

Yogacara denies that the Buddha ever intended his followers to hold to the existence of even such minute entities, although he did speak of them. Why did the Buddha speak as if there were such things? Yogacara answers that he did so for the sake of communicating with those who could not understand without reference to some such entities. This is an instance of *upaya*, or "skill-in-means." The Buddha used any device available to assist the student in progress toward the truth.

The mind as it truly is lacks perception of objects and is called *alayavijnana* (Skt., storehouse conscicousness). In its essence it is without origin, without qualities, and has neither existence nor extinction. There is no subject/object duality and, in fact, there is no reality to the mind itself. It is a mistake to believe anything has reality outside the mind. Yet the experience of the unenlightened person is such that independent reality is typically affirmed. The mistaken notion of the existence of things is due to the activity of the senses on the mind much like the reflection of the moon upon a lake. One sees in the waves the presence of the moon when in fact it is not there. Similarly the senses give the impression of reality, but this is illusory. Once these thoughts are created they persuade the mind of the validity of their existence.

How is it that in the absence of the reality of external phenomena the mind does this? Yogacara answers that the mind (*citta*) is in the habit of endlessly creating the mistaken impression of phenomena. But why should it be in such a habit? According to the *Lankavatara Sutra*, from which Yogacara draws much of its teaching, this is simply the way things

are. *Maya* (illusion) is ultimately the cause of this. But one further explanation is that there is a mechanism at work whereby karmic "seeds" act upon the pure mind, which is "perfumed" with images that are brought to it by the senses. Just as an item may take on the odor of perfume that does not properly belong to it, so the karmic senses have a capacity to register on the mind entities for which there is no reality.

Numerous problems were posed by the opponents of Yogacara. One put his question to Vasubandhu this way.

> The existence or non-existence of anything is determined by means of proof. Among all means of proof immediate perception is the most excellent. If there are no external objects, how is there this awareness of objects such as are now immediately evident to me?[18]

Vasubandhu responded by likening the awareness of external objects to things experienced in dreams. While dreaming, objects perceived seem real, but upon awakening they are known to be illusory. So it is with the false perception of things. The *Lankavatara* puts it like this:

> It is as if some man, asleep, dreams of a country, full of women and men, elephants, horses . . . rivers and lakes. In his dream he enters the women's apartments of the king's palace, and then he wakes up. Awake, his memory runs back over the country and the women's apartments. It would not be an intelligent thing to do for this man, to go in his memory through the various unreal experiences which he had in his dream, or would it? In the same way, the foolish common people bitten by false views and under the

influence of the heretics, do not realize that what is seen by their mind is like a dream.[19]

Another objection runs like this. If things exist in the mind alone, how is it that several persons can testify to having experienced the same phenomenon? When three people all look at a cube and describe it as to height, length, and depth, how is it, if mind alone is real and the impressions therein, that there is such agreement between the three as to the dimensions of the cube? Why should there not be significant variance between the reports? What accounts for this uniformity? In answering this Vasubandhu reaffirms the false appearing of seemingly external objects but offers only an illustration which does not truly explain. But in the end Yogacara does not expect understanding from those who are not enlightened.

What is the way out of ignorance? The beginning is to hear the truth and begin to act on it. This leads to "seeds of enlightenment," which begin a long series of disciplines leading ultimately to bodhisattvahood and the experience of *tathata* (suchness) or *samata* (sameness), which is the goal. Liberation comes when the individual mind is purged of all that distorts and prevents the realization of storehouse consciousness or pure mind. Yogic techniques are employed to aid in this process. In an attempt to speak meaningfully of storehouse consciousness, the impression is given that it has some reality to it. It is spoken of as the matrix from which the Buddhas came as well as the Buddha-nature itself that is found in all beings.

Asanga's writings are a complex scholastic study of the mind and an ancient example of efforts to understand its operations. Vasubandhu's attempts to argue that there can be knowledge without a knower, thoughts without one to think them, and perceptions without a perceiver were convincing to many and resulted in the school being subsequently established in both China (Wei Shih) and Japan (Hosso).

Buddha Bhakti

The Theravada scriptures contained some ideas which were not always fully consistent with the main picture of the Buddha as a mere human being—one whose great achievements were worthy of respect but not worship. Certain passages in the *Abhidhamma Pitaka* indicate Gotama was only one of many Buddhas. Written later than many parts of the *Tipitaka*, it stated there were as many as twenty-four Buddhas who existed in other ages. Gotama himself was one of these and was reborn to earth from a previous existence in which he was perfect, omniscient, and sinless in his Tushita heaven. It taught that Gotama was to be followed by a future Buddha called Maitreya, who was to come at the end of the age. Thus the Theravada scriptures contain ideas, which when fully developed and combined with related notions ultimately led to the establishment of competing groups.

Details of the rise of diverse views about the Buddha and his teachings are not fully known. Some suggest that in the fourth century C.E., following the Second Council of Buddhists at Vaisali, a group called the Mahasanghikas were excluded from the main body because they emphasized the doctrine of many Buddhas.

Bhakti (devotion) to Buddha looks upon the Buddha as a transhistorical deity with power to save. A heavenly abode was promised for the faithful and was graphically depicted in newer texts, while the original goal, *nirvana*, was often obscured. Occult themes were combined with devotional attitudes to the Buddha. This added magical and animistic practices, which sometimes prevailed in popular piety. Thus Mahayana refers generally to a variety of attitudes toward the Buddha that are somewhere on a continuum between two poles. At one extreme were those who accepted some form of *prajna* by which the Buddha himself is transcended, and at the other extreme were those who worshiped the Buddha as a deity.

Buddha *bhakti* thinks of the Buddha differently than the Tipitaka does. In the latter the Buddha is not divine and neither he nor other humans nor heavenly gods and powers could do what the individual alone could do. The Buddha's teachings could assist in reaching *nirvana*, but the Buddha could not directly affect one's progress. This view is one of salvation by self-power. All depends on the individual and one's determination to experience *nirvana*.

But in Buddha *bhakti* salvation is bestowed by the grace of the divine Buddha and is a matter of other-power. The Buddha's superior achievements not only gained *nirvana* for himself but also immense merit to

dispense to those devoted to him. Pious acts demonstrating faith and devotion included circumambulation of *stupas*, repetition of his name, and many other acts of worship.

One of the most spectacular archaeological examples in India of how Buddha *bhakti* was added to earlier Hinayana conceptions is found in the rock-cut temple caves of Ellora and Ajanta in Maharashtra. These monumental works were financed by the Satavahana dynasty in the early centuries of the Christian era. The earliest caves contain simple *stupas* without the image of the Buddha. The somewhat later art suggests the Buddha as a teacher worthy of reverence but not an object of divine worship. But at an even later period images were added and sanctuaries (*chaitya*) became settings for the worship of the Buddha.

The Three-Buddha-Body Doctrine

Mahayana literature reflects a doctrine called Trikaya (three bodies) which said there were three Buddha-realities. This doctrine probably arose to accommodate the popularity of devotion to the Buddha. It was taught by the Sarvastivada community, which competed with Theravadins for followers. The first body, Nirmanakaya, refers to the appearance of Gotama on earth as a transformation of a higher Buddha-reality. This appearance was required so that his teachings could be learned by people on earth. He is not the only Buddha, for there are many others in realms which transcend this world. Such a heavenly realm of Buddhas constitutes the second body, the Sambhogakaya (body of bliss). Here the Buddhas exist in transcendent bliss untouched by sufferings and unaffected by the senses. There are innumerable cosmic worlds presided over by infinite Buddhas and *bodhisattvas*. Many Mahayana texts begin with heavenly scenes crowded with myriads of beings attending to the teaching of the cosmic Buddhas. A third body is the Dharmakaya (body of truth), which is the cosmic, unlimited, and absolutely undifferentiated Buddha visible only to Buddhas, *bodhisattvas*, and others who understand its nondual nature-transcending distinctions and discrimination. The Trikaya incorporates all levels of reality: earthly, heavenly, and the nondualistically transrational, thus enabling Buddhist thought to compete with challenges from other religions in the marketplace of ideas. It embraced the broadest range of attitudes toward the Buddha from human, to divine, to cosmic and beyond with great appeal.

Buddha Bhakti Texts

For five hundred years after the beginning of the Christian era, scores of devotional texts were written in Sanskrit. Some of these give details about the miracles and divine acts of the Buddha, such as the *Mahavastu*, which was later incorporated into the *Tipitaka*. It introduces the *bodhisattva* who is compassionate, tranquil, and merciful. The *Mahavastu*, rising out of the Mahasanghika school, urged that *nirvana* was achieved through ceremonial worship of the Lord. Another text, the *Lotus Sutra* (*Saddharmapundarika*), takes a critical position against contemporaries who seek to attain salvation for themselves without being concerned for the welfare of others. It identifies such attitudes as immature and reflecting only the preliminary teachings of the Buddha that

should be exchanged for the higher goal of becoming a *bodhisattva*. Support of the *sangha*, gifts to build temples, and recitation of the name of the Buddha in faith (even if only once) is meritorious and saving. The *Lotus* was influential not only in India but perhaps even more so in China, its colonies of Korea and Vietnam, and Japan.

The *Sukavativyuha Sutra* (*Lotus of the Pure Land*) is another cardinal devotional text that describes *bhakti* practices of the times and was influential in Tibet, China, and Japan.

Bhakti Practices

The *stupa* was originally a funerary mound that lay Buddhists incorporated into their worship between 250 and 50 B.C.E. While *sangha* life satisfied the ritual and ceremonial needs of monks, it appears laypersons modified the *stupa* so as to make it a center for their piety. The hemispheric mound of earth and stone held Buddhist relics and was increasingly elaborated by erecting ornately carved wood or stone railings around it. The support of the nobility and the gifts of the populace provided funds for artists to carve and erect *stupas* such as the Great Stupa at Sanchi in central India and those at Amaravati and Nagarjunakonda in south India.

What function did the *stupa* have in their worship? The carvings found at Sanchi show both individuals and groups engaged in a variety of activities from circumambulation of the *stupa* while bearing incense and flowers to placing votive lamps around its base. The presence of musicians in the carvings shows that music

Great Buddhist Stupa of Sanchi, Madhya Pradesh. 1st century B.C.E. *Stupas contained relics of the Buddha or his disciples and were used for meditation and devotional activities.* J. Lewis

was a part of the rituals. The *stupa* was the setting for festivals held in honor of the Buddha. While for some the *stupa* may have been only a symbol, in time it was elevated to sanctity and circumambulation of it was considered merit-producing. Miniature *stupas* were placed in homes as both symbol and icon. The carved panels found at Sanchi intermix Buddhist and animistic themes indicating perhaps that laypeople were as interested in controlling the spirit world as with things Buddhist.

The idea of a divine Buddha gave all other items of worship value. Though there is no image of the Buddha associated with the earliest *stupas*, it was not long before images were presented to the faithful for worship. The *Mahavastu* describes the worship appropriate to the Buddha to include presentation of flags, banners, flowers, garlands, and incense. Other texts describe the Buddha as having *karuna* (divine compassion) as a savior who saves those who have faith in him. In *bhakti* the Buddha is more than guide, he is giver of salvation. He is more than the one who has found the path, he is the path itself which one gains through faith.

Tantric Buddhists

Tantrism refers to a wide diversity of beliefs and practices of some Buddhists who added magical formulas, occult beliefs, and esoteric exercises to established Buddhist doctrine. *Mandalas* (symbolic diagrams), *mantras* (sacred formulas), and *mudras* (symbolic hand gestures) combined, in some cases, with socially forbidden sexual practices to form traditions that seem only remotely connected to the major concerns of early Buddhist groups. Tantra presents *prajna* as a female principle or goddess. Sexual union with a partner might assist one in pursuit of emptiness. Tantric manuals adopted a coded language clear only to the initiated. The movement profoundly influenced the doctrine and practice of Buddhist traditions in Tibet and to a much lesser extent China.

Hindu *Bhakti*

Theory and Practice

Bhakti is the Sanskrit and modern Hindi word meaning literally "devotion." It conveys the meaning of surrender to and love for a personal deity and is the dominant Hindu attitude toward deities which are said to number 330 million. No one actually knows or has taken the effort to identify them all. However, they fall into the following categories: those having both Vedic and post-Vedic origins or connections; deities popular in specific regions; those confined to local districts or villages; and gods patronized by a particular caste, family, or individual.

Puja refers to acts performed to express one's devotion. These acts may occur anywhere but are usually done in the home, the temple, at outdoor shrines, or during festivals held occasionally or annually. *Puja* may be simple or elaborate, inexpensive or costly, but it is almost always performed in the presence of the deity's image or symbol.

The earliest literary evidence of *bhakti* is in a late *Upanishad*, the *Svetasvatara Upanishad*, where devotion to Shiva is encouraged. The archaeological evidence of *bhakti* practice is somewhat later with second-century B.C.E. inscriptions referring to construction of an enclosure for the worship of Vasudeva (Vishnu). *Bhakti* practices, however, may predate both the literary and archaeological evidence and arise as early as 500 B.C.E.

Most Hindus will frankly admit that they worship several deities. They do not think of them as one god in many forms. Some educated Indians may claim that Hindus as a class are as monotheistic as Christians, but this represents their own religious beliefs rather than that of the masses.

The deity and the icon, whether statue, picture, or symbol, are one and the same in the view of most bhaktists. To worship the image is to worship the deity. Since the deity is personal, *puja* consists of offerings, acts which would please the divine person. Garlands of flowers and incense are common but foods, candies, *ghee* (butter clarified by being brought to the boiling point), fruit, and incense are presented. In temples attempts are made to keep the deity comfortable. Appropriate clothing is provided for either cold or hot weather. Deities may be seen who enjoy the comfort of an electric fan while devotees swelter. For warmth a shawl may be draped over the shoulders. The deity is awakened in the morning by a temple priest, put to rest for a short nap in the early afternoon, and given night rest when temple doors are closed in the evening.

Regular *puja* may be done in the home. An older member of the family may serve as representative for the entire household. A common sight in a Hindu home is the display of several pictures of deities framed and hanging high on the wall in a prominent part of the main room. A garland of flowers may hang from atop each picture, or in some cases the garland may be of sandalwood shavings or colorful paper.

Temple worship is not congregational but provides devotees opportunities to do *puja* when they can and according to their means. A variety of reverent gestures are used and prayers may be silent, semiaudible, or either formal or extemporaneous. Special festivals are held annually to commemorate significant events in the deity's personal history and attract large crowds. Temple priests assist as needed and also function as guardians, since their quarters are usually on the premises.

Shrines to deities may be unprotected in the open, as in the case of stones or large boulders colored with a red-or-ange dye or a cloth flag erected nearby on a bamboo stave. Trees and unusual natural phenomena are possible sites for shrines. In the central India city of Yavatmal, government post office workers found a dead monkey on the office lawn. Bhaktists of Hanuman (the monkey god) gave it a ritual burial and have repeated ceremonies on the death anniversary ever since. A sizeable shrine may emerge there in years to come.

Positioned throughout India are famous shrines and temples which are very old. There are also rivers, such as the Ganges and its headwaters, which are associated with the deities Shiva,

Parvati, and Vishnu and are therefore considered sacred. Cities such as Puri

Temple of Goddess Minakshi. Madurai, Tamil Nadu. Considered part of the family of the deity Shiva, Minakshi's temple dominates the skyline of this South Indian city. J. Lewis

(Orissa), Banaras (Uttar Pradesh), Mathura (Haryana), and Madurai (Tamil Nadu) have famous temples to which devotees travel in sacred pilgrimage. Nearly every state has places made famous for their association with deities and which attract annually great throngs of people. Every twelve years the Kumbh Mela is held at Allahabad on the Ganges and is attended by the largest crowds of all. It is safe to say that millions of Hindus annually make pilgrimages and festivals the highlight of their year, and where travel distance is great it may be one of life's most memorable events.

Bhakti and Grace

Bhaktists accept *samsara*, *karma*, and *moksha*. However, a concept in *bhakti* literature and practice not found in Vedic scriptures is the grace of the deity. In *bhakti* the follower doing *puja* sincerely knows that, unless the god grants his grace, no liberation is possible.

The grace of god and its importance is indicated in the *Narada Bhakti Sutras* (tenth century C.E.):

33. Therefore that alone is worthy of being accepted as the goal by people who are desirous of permanent release from all bondage.

34. Teachers describe in hymns and songs the following as a means of spiritual realization.

35. But that state of supreme love and immortality is made possible only by giving up the objective reality of the world as it appears to the ego-centric intellect and senses, and the consequent renunciation of attachment.

36. By uninterrupted loving service.

37. By hearing and singing the glory of the Lord, even while engaged in the ordinary activities of life.

38. Primarily, it (moksha) is got only through the grace of great souls, or through a slight measure of Divine grace.

39. But it is extremely difficult to come into contact with a great soul and to be benefited by his company; the influence of such a one is subtle, incomprehensible and unerringly infallible in its effect.

40. Nevertheless it is attainable by the grace of God and godmen alone.

This passage indicates an important place for the *guru*, since it is through him that the grace of the deity is mediated. However, it is the grace of the deity that saves.

Bhakti and the Religious Goal

The objective of *bhakti* in the above text is union with the deity and a place forever at his side. However, there are two levels of progress toward that ultimate goal—lower and higher *bhakti*.

Lower *bhakti*, also known as imperfect *bhakti*, is preparatory and is characterized by a desire to obtain some favor from the deity. As such, it is not entirely a selfless or altruistic worship. The devotee may worship to gain help in sickness or trouble. Women may seek help in childbearing or may request a male child. Men may seek help in business difficulties, family problems, or health. Personal requests may be of infinite variety. One who makes progress toward higher *bhakti* gradually and increasingly limits personal desires and surrenders selflessly to the deity.

Higher *bhakti*, also perfect *bhakti*, seeks no benefits from the Lord and is attached to him and nothing else. Practical steps one can take to make progress include listening to the praises of the deity, singing the Lord's praises, meditating on the Lord, and worshiping the Lord as friend, companion, lover, or master.

Higher *bhakti* may conceive of the deity wholly in personalistic terms or may seek a nondualistic union with him. The difference is sometimes illustrated in the following way. When

God is viewed as personal the union with him is like a fish enveloped in water. The devotee is surrounded by the ocean of God's love. But when the goal is a nondualistic union with the deity, it is likened to a drop of water in the ocean. The individual is absorbed into the vastness of God and loses identity. The oneness is absolute and complete.

Vishnu Bhakti

Followers of Vishnu are called Vaishnavites or Vaishnavas. In the Vedas Vishnu was a solar deity, though not a particularly important one. A story in the *Brahmanas* tells how Vishnu tricked a demon king into granting him control over all the space he could cover in three strides. Vishnu looked harmless because he had transformed himself into a dwarf beggar. But after the request was granted Vishnu resumed his cosmic proportions and in three steps took control of earth, heaven, and deep-space. Interestingly enough, Vishnu is not an object of *bhakti* in the Vedas. According to some scholars, it is only in the *Mahabharata*, one of two Indian epics, that Vishnu is presented as supreme god of the universe who receives the devotion of the Satvata tribe.

Vishnu's Iconic Marks

Vishnu usually has four arms, which suggest his extraordinary skill in helping humans. In his hands are symbols of his power and purity: the mace, the discus (a weapon), the conch shell, and the lotus. Other marks may vary but his head is crowned, his face is full and sweet, his garments are yellow, and his feet are blue. Like all deities,

he has a mount and a consort. Garuda, the giant bird, carries him where he bids and Lakshmi, goddess of fortune and beauty, is often at his side. Stories of Vishnu as creator describe him reclining on a cosmic serpent Shesha or Ananta. Marks on the forehead or arm in the form of a U with a vertical line in the middle identify its wearer as a follower of Vishnu.

Avatars of Vishnu

An important feature of Vishnu is his ability to appear in animal or human form. The word *avatar* (Skt., to descend into) is used of Vishnu's many manifestations and has sometimes been likened to the Christian concept of the Incarnation, though there are significant differences. While not found in the Vedas or the *Upanishads*, the term does appear in the *Bhagavad Gita* (4:6–8), a portion of the *Mahabharata*. There Krishna is said to have made many descents into the world. The doctrine of avatars is popularized in the *Puranas*, *bhakti* literature written from the tenth century C.E. onward. Some texts indicate there are twenty-two avatars, but others accept only ten, of which one is future and nine are in the past. The avatars of Vishnu are:

As a FISH (Matsya) he saved ancient man from a devastating flood.

As a TORTOISE (Kurma) he was instrumental in providing nectar for the gods to make them immortal.

As the BOAR (Varaha) he rescued the earth when it was inundated.

As the MAN-LION (Narasimha) he saved a devotee from persecution.

As the DWARF (Vamana) he reclaimed the world from the demon Bali.

As RAMA-WITH-THE AXE (Parasu-rama) he destroyed the Kshatriyas and returned authority to the Brahmins.

As KRISHNA he destroyed the evil king Kamsa and saved the world.

As the BUDDHA he defended Vedic religion by cleverly offering a false system which was embraced by those unfit for the highest truth.

As KALKI, the future avatar, he will come at the end of the era to destroy evil and restore the truth.

Rama, Krishna, and Buddha were already established deities of the past who were incorporated into the doctrine of Vishnu's *avataras* by some who were seeking to broaden the powers of Vishnu and perhaps extend their own influence. The idea of Rama and Buddha as avatars has been championed by some but strongly resisted by others. Again, Krishna's identity as an avatar of Vishnu has been similarly resisted by those who regard him and not Vishnu as the supreme god.

Shiva Bhakti

Names for Shiva include Mahadeva, Nataraja (Lord of the Cosmic Dance), and Ardhanarisvara. It should be recalled that the rigvedic literature refers to Rudra as "Shiva" (auspicious) for his cruel and unpredictable behavior as lord of the storm. Shiva in later *bhakti* literature is viewed as one who understands and has compassion for the difficulties of life, but the darker side of his nature is not forgotten, either. In fact, he seems to inspire more fear and respect than feelings of warmth and companionship. In the later *Upanishads* he is presented as lord of *samsara* and *karma*. Two qualities are at the center of this complex figure:

creative fertility and awesome powers of destruction.

Shiva's Iconic Appearance

Pictures of Shiva show him with blue or grey body having smeared himself with ashes to signify the ascetic life. Rising out of the top knot of hair is a water fountain as indicated in myths that recount how he created the mighty Ganges River and its four headwaters in the Himalayas. At mid-forehead a vertical third eye symbolizes his omniscience, and draping his body or positioned under him when seated is a tiger skin. He is known as "Lord of Beasts." Serpents coiling about his neck reinforce this point and inspire fear. As patron of ascetics he may also appear naked in seated meditation. The ancient Elephanta caves in Bombay harbor were dedicated to him and show him with three faces perhaps in an attempt to incorporate the complexity of his nature and attributes.

His mount is Nandi the bull and his consort is Parvati (also, Uma), about whose relationship to Shiva the *Puranas* have much to say. The lingam, his symbol, is typically seen rising out of the *yoni*. This stone pillar represents the male sex organ and signifies fertility and generative powers. Some *lingams* are stylized and multisided while others are more clearly phallic emblems. Some interpreters may make too much of this while others ignore the sexual overtones of such symbolism. Shiva bhaktists themselves may be acutely aware of the sexual and others, apparently blithely ignorant to it. Shaivites of the Lingayat community in Karnataka wear a miniature *lingam*, while the more widespread sign of Shiva consists of three horizontal bars often marked on the forehead

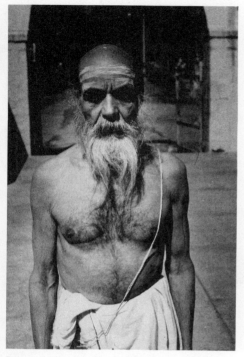

Priest of Shiva with sacred thread marking upanayana intitiation. The three horizontal stripes mark him as a follower of this important Hindu deity. J. Lewis

or arm with a white paste.

Shiva's Family

Deities connected with Shiva might best be thought of as members of his family rather than simply avatars, as in the case of Vishnu. Ganesha is the elephant-headed son of the divine couple whose condition as human-beast was caused when Shiva angrily beheaded him in a case of mistaken identity. His followers throughout history have generally been few, except in central India where turmoil in Maharashtra during the British colonial era led many to rally around him as a symbol of unity. Political gatherings were banned, so the festivals of Ganesha were used surreptitiously for political ends. The Ganapati festival in that state and elsewhere near the end of the monsoon season is widely celebrated and consists of a festive reenactment of events in his life. There is some evidence his popularity is on the increase among low castes where he serves as a symbol of their search for social and economic equality.

One of the largest and most interesting temples in southern India is located in Madurai, Tamil Nadu, and is dedicated to a member of the Shiva group, the goddess Minakshi. Her origins are connected to Pandyan political history where she was regarded as Shiva's consort. A spectacular week-long festival is held yearly in April or May reenacting her marriage to Shiva, who is relegated to somewhat subordinate importance in the celebration. As part of the ceremonies the goddess is taken from her altar of worship in the temple precincts and placed atop a multistory cart with twelve-foot diameter wooden wheels and pulled by ropes through the streets by hundreds of devotees to the delight of the faithful and the interested. Her consort follows in a cart of his own.

Temples and Festivals

While temples dedicated to Vishnu are almost always open to non-Vaishnavites and non-Hindus, it is not always so with Shaivites. A Shaivite temple in Trivandrum, Kerala, restricts temple admission to Hindus and, although the Minakshi temple precincts are open to all, the inner

The wheels of Minakshi's regal chariot in the streets of Madurai, Tamil Nadu. The annual festival commemorates marriage to her husband whose vehicle is seen in the rear. J. Lewis

sanctuary is posted "Hindus Only." *Puja* in Shaivite temples often involves pouring milk or water over the *lingam* and showering it with flowers. The temple priests service a suspended vessel full of liquid over the *lingam*; liquid drips continuously on it. Such liquid has been known to be collected and sold to devotees for therapeutic purposes as "Shiva's seed." A water pool within or attached to the temple precincts serves for ritual purification.

As indicated above, temples may host unique ceremonies. The Shivratri is an all-night festival in the spring celebrating Shiva and Parvati's marriage. It was at just such a festival that one of India's nineteenth-century Hindu re-formers, Dayananda Saraswathi, observed a rat crawling over the icon, prompting him to ask grave questions about image worship. He ultimately rejected belief in many gods and established the Arya Samaj, one of the enduring social and religious reform movements.

Shiva Sects

Although most bhaktists of Shiva are not associated formally with any sect, there are historical movements worthy of note. Between C.E. 800 and 1200 a community in Kashmir explained their doctrine and outlined the proper performance of ritual in manuals called *Agamas*. The Lingayats of Karnataka emerged after the twelfth century C.E. The Tamil people in southern India turned strongly to Shiva worship as early as the seventh century C.E. when inspired by poets like Appar and Samvanda whose *kirtans* (devotional hymns) are sung at *bhajans* (hymn sings). Meykandar provided a theological defense against nontheistic challenges to faith in Shiva in the thirteenth century. The Shaivasiddhanta movement he launched survives today in Tamil Nadu, providing leadership to a vast number of people who defend theism against Advaita Vedanta (nondualism).

Krishna Bhakti

Bhakti to Krishna has two major streams: that which follows the lofty picture of Krishna as the cosmic, supreme, and almighty deity presented in the *Bhagavad Gita*, and the one presented in the *Bhagavata Purana* of the ninth century C.E., wherein Krishna is popularly presented as mischievous child and adolescent playboy lover. The erotic scenes have received a variety of interpretations ranging from frank acceptance of eroticism on one hand to sublime and pure symbol of union with the deity on the other.

Krishna and the Bhagavad Gita

The *Bhagavad Gita* (Skt., song of the lord) is one of India's most popular religious texts since it takes an accommodating view toward several religious positions. In the end it teaches both theism and *bhakti* to Krishna as supreme lord. It is valued by most religious communities including Vaishnavites, followers of Krishna, and Vedantists of many kinds. Some

liken it in importance to the book of Romans for Christians and, though it is *smrti* (valued next to *shruti*), it has nearly the force of *shruti* to many who call it the "Fifth Veda." Most hotels visited by foreigners have two religious books in dresser drawers: the Gideon Bible and the *Bhagavad Gita*.

The *Mahabharata* was composed over many centuries beginning in 400 B.C.E., and the *Gita* was inserted into it sometime around the beginning of the Christian era. The author's immediate concern was to address a pressing problem among the readers of that society. A significant number of persons were leaving their stations in life and abandoning daily duties to pursue *moksha*. This may have resulted from the influence of reading the *Upanishads*. The answer of the *Gita*, after considering various options kindly and respectfully, was that salvation could be attained through unattached devotion to Krishna without foregoing one's duties in life.

The story revolves around a warrior, Arjuna, who faces Duryadhana and his army but is dismayed at the prospects of the battle at hand because some of his opponents are cousins and former teachers. He determines not to fight, although this conflicts with his conventional duty as a warrior. In his dilemma, his chariot driver counsels him and serves the function of reviewing Arjuna's options and, by extension, the options open to all humankind. His chariot driver turns out to be none other than Krishna, the supreme deity, in disguise. In the course of their conversations Krishna examines several religious positions and, in the end, presents a new religious outlook.

The first position he examines is the teaching about the relation of matter and spirit, or that between Prakriti and Purusha (*atman*). Arjuna is given to understand that though all reality, including the body, is pervaded by the *atman* he should not think that to kill the body was to kill the self since the *atman* survives forever and is imperishable. It passes through stages of life but at death discards one body to take on another and is therefore impervious to external changes. This teaching accepts the upanishadic teaching about a permanent *atman* but stops short of accepting its nondualistic emphasis.

The second position is the traditional sacrificial ritual, which Krishna approves, though not with enthusiasm, as a direct means of obtaining one's desires. The sacrifices are permitted, not to the supreme deity, but to cosmic forces and agencies who keep the ordinary course of life running smoothly. Such acts are therefore necessary and good. Krishna is building a case against abandoning one's duties and, since this is one obligation, there are surely others.

There is a third position. It affirms that one can do *karma* (here: work; appropriate action) without any subsequent undesirable consequences so long as one acts with nonattachment. Acts performed without concern for their consequences are virtuous because they are selfless. This view is called *Karma-Yoga*, meaning "restrained acts" or acts undertaken without consideration of personal gain

or loss. The outcome is that socially determined and sanctioned duties are to be performed without introspection or hesitation. Albeit socially conservative and ethically unreflective, this position has an advantage over beliefs on sacrifice that get their desires in the short run but lose in the long run by remaining in *samsara*.

Finally in chapters 7 through 9 and in chapter 12, Krishna casts off his disguise to show himself as none other than the transcendent lord who when worshiped grants salvation by his grace. Verses 6 and 8 of chapter 12 summarize this by saying:

> Those who, laying all their actions on Me, intent on Me, worship, meditating on Me, with unswerving devotion, these whose thoughts are set on Me, I straightway deliver from the ocean of death-bound existence, O Partha (Arjuna). On Me alone fix thy mind, let thy understanding dwell in Me; In me alone shalt thou live thereafter. Of this there is no doubt.[20]

Two other works give additional textual foundation to Krishna *bhakti*. One is the *Harivamsa*, added to the *Mahabharata* about C.E. 300, and the other is the *Bhagavad Purana*. Both claim to provide details overlooked before. The *Bhagavad Purana* describes Krishna's early childhood as one full of mischief and good times and is often depicted in pictures hanging in homes. Further, it tells how Krishna as a youth sported sexually with the *gopis*, or village cowgirls. His love for them and theirs for him is said by some to be a picture of *bhakti* love in parable form.

Krishna Sectarian Groups

In the eighth century in the land of the Tamils, the Alvars (men who have intuitive knowledge of god) launched an intensely emotional movement which accepted all castes and even outcastes, a bold attitude for its time. A somewhat complete account of their beliefs has survived in the writings of Nammalvar, who taught against advaitan (nondual) positions by describing his relation to God as that of predicate to subject or attribute to substance. As the *gopis* longed for Krishna, so the bhaktist is to experience intense desire for God such as a woman for her husband. The Alvar experience may be described as a passionate spirituality when at its best.

Between the thirteenth and seventeenth centuries, and corresponding to the rise of anti-Moghul sentiments led by Shivaji (d. C.E. 1680), the Marathi people of western India saw the rise of *bhakti* movements. Tukaram (1609–49), a poet who wrote *bhakti* poems, lit a flame of devotion to Krishna and his incarnations which continues to make Maharashtra a center for *bhakti* belief and practice. Vithoba, possibly only a village god originally, is believed to be Krishna reappeared, and yearly throngs of people make pilgrimage to his temple in the western part of the state. Chaitanya (1486–1530) bore a similar role in promoting a frenzy of devotion to Krishna among Bengali-speaking people of eastern India. A classic Sanskrit poem called the *Gita Govinda* describes Krishna's relation to Rhada, his consort. Nimbarka, a Telegu poet from southern India, gained many followers through his hymns in the twelfth century C.E.

Krishna's Distinguishing Marks

When presented as a child Krishna is depicted as a roly-poly and even beautiful boy attempting always to get into the Indian equivalent of the cookie jar. As a youth he plays a flute to mesmerize the *gopis* while his mount, the peacock, stands in the background. Rhada is his consort. Followers of Krishna may adopt the Vaishnavite three vertical marks as their symbol.

Festivals Associated with Krishna

The Janmastami festival, performed in the home or at a temple, celebrates Krishna's birthday. Special sweets are placed around an image of Krishna, who as a child was always one for such things. In one ceremony the author viewed a miniature swing on which the deity was placed for his entertainment. In another setting a toy train chugged around the altar delighting observers as much, presumably, as the deity. A gigantic and famous celebration is held annually in the state of Orissa at Puri for Krishna in his form as Lord Jagannatha. The deity is placed in his car, much like the one described in the Minakshi festival, and is paraded through the city. This attracts thousands of devotees of Vishnu and Krishna from across India.

Rama Bhakti

Rama's story is told in the other Indian epic, the *Ramayana* by Valmiki, dating from about 200 B.C.E. This Sanskrit poem, which may have a historical departure point, tells about a prince from northern India who suffered great peril in his attempts to

Devotees of Lord Krishna celebrate Janmastami—the birthday of the deity. J. Lewis

recover Sita, his wife. She had been abducted by the demon Ravana and taken to the offshore kingdom of Lanka (Sri Lanka). Rama and his brother Lakshman, with the help of Hanuman, the monkey warrior god, pursued. Hanuman and his monkey clan miraculously built a rock bridge across the straits for the army's use. In the fierce battle that followed Ravana and his demons were defeated and Sita was rescued. Her lengthy captivity among the demons raised questions about her marital faithfulness and led to a test of her innocence by fire ordeal. She passed the test. The elements in this story of family solidarity, marital faithfulness, and connubial bliss attract many to worship this divine pair and regard them as models of family happiness. Wherever Hindus traveled in Asia this epic went with them, and in many places the folklore of those countries include it today. Examples include Thailand and Cambodia as well as Indonesia.

Rama Bhakti Texts

Translations of the *Ramayana* into regional languages helped spread the fame of Rama and the family of deities associated with him: Sita, Lakshman, and Hanuman. The *Kamba Ramayana* is the Tamil translation and the Telegu translation is the *Ranganatha Ramayana*. Of all translations that of Tulsi Das into Hindi, called the *Ramacaritmanas (The Mind-Pool of the Deeds of Rama)* and composed about C.E. 1575, is the most famous. It follows the main narrative of Valmiki's original but adds much detail to the life of Rama. It is an intense appeal to readers to give exclusive devotion to Rama as the Supreme Master of the universe and was instrumental in spreading Rama *bhakti* widely in northern India among Hindi-speaking Hindus.

Rama Festivals

Wherever Rama's devotees are found they annually celebrate the Ram Lila festival to reenact the main outline of the *Ramayana*. Virtually every community across northern India ceases all ordinary business and devotes ten days to festivities that often go late into the night. Musicians and actors, some amateurs and others local talents, compete for prizes or recognition of their performances. People come together for relaxation and family reunions. A carnival spirit prevails.

Rama As an Avatar

According to Vaishnavas, Rama is an avatar of Vishnu. Many Hindus who follow these deities do not bother themselves much with these matters. One who worships Krishna may be just as much at home worshiping

Rama, but may or may not connect either to Vishnu. It may be just as one has said: "As intellectual beings seeking reasoned understanding, they turn to thoughtful Bhagavadgita and to the systematic theologies of the Krishna cult. As emotional beings oppressed by the heavy restraints of Hindu social life, they worship . . . Krishna, the carefree divine prankster."[21] The same could be said of Rama.

Shakti Worship

Almost every deity, whether in worship throughout India or confined to local popularity, has a consort. The female deities with which we have already dealt are Lakshmi, Uma or Parvati, and Sita, the wives of Vishnu, Shiva, and Rama, respectively. Shiva is sometimes said to have four wives: Uma, Parvati, Durga, and Kali, each of which has a personal background and iconography. Parvati is the mountain ascetic who attracts Shiva in the Himalayas and with whom he makes passionate love. Uma is known for her more matronly qualities as nourisher and protector. Durga is worshiped apart from Shiva in many places including Maharashtra. She carries a weapon for the killing of Mahisha, the buffalo demon who screams his terror at being defeated by her great power. Her benevolent side is not to be forgotten, however, since she gives prosperity and dispenses food to humankind. Kali is a favorite in Gujarat and especially in Bengal. The famous Kalighat temple in Calcutta, where a goat is sacrificed to her daily, is dedicated to her. This is the only instance of daily animal sacrifice tolerated by government authorities. She may be presented with bloodred tongue extended and bedecked with a necklace of skulls or the decapitated heads of enemies. She drinks blood from a skullcup, indicating her power.

Shakti

The word *shakti* means "power" and when used of these goddesses refers to true power in the world or the power behind the god with which she is associated. Some see *shakti* worship as a fertility cult having its roots in pre-Vedic times among the Indus Valley people and their female figurines. The *Mahabharata* contains a reference to Durga, who accepts offerings of flesh and blood from mountain peoples. However, a modern Bengali interpreter whose family worshiped Kali insists the elements of fertility and militarism have long since been replaced with sincere and joyful devotion for her love and mercy. She combines qualities of awesome fearsomeness and benevolence, and this can be seen in art such as that at Mahabalipuram near Madras, where rock-cut stone reliefs depict highlights of her life.

Shakti Rituals

All the ordinary *bhakti puja* to the deities is accorded to the goddesses. However, their female nature has led to tantric practices. Tantrism has two forms, left-handed and right-handed. Right-handed tantrism involves an exoteric, ascetic, and meditative devotion following yogic disciplines dedicated to *shakti*. The left-handed tantra follows Vamachara (since each Sanskrit word begins with that letter), which is the ritualistic indulgence in the so-called five M's: alcohol, meat, fish, symbolic hand gestures, and sexual intercourse. All except the hand gestures were forbidden by ordinary society. Though motives for following these practices doubtlessly varied, some may have viewed sexual intercourse as an aid to union with the god. Having experienced one kind of absorption of the self, a second kind was easier to attain. Tantrism has not been widely accepted because of its promiscuous and taboo-breaking character.

Vedanta: Hindu Systems of Thought

The word *Vedanta* comes from two words, *veda* (Skt., knowledge) and *anta* (Skt., end), and refers either to that teaching which comes at the end of the Vedic period, namely the *Upanishads*, or that knowledge which is the true aim or final goal of the Vedas. Several competing systems claim to correctly summarize the teaching of the *Upanishads*, which has been called "a fluid search for truth." The abstract and sometimes conflicting strains of thought found in the Vedas made them a fertile field for speculation and system building. We shall look at three of them: Shankara's Advaita Vedanta, Ramanuja's Vishishtadvaita and Madhva's Dvaita.

Shankara's Advaita Vedanta

The influence of Shankara (also Sankara or Samkara, .C.E. 788–820?) is so great that *vedanta* is often, though erroneously, thought to be synonymous with him. He was a Shaivite Brahman from the Malabar country (present-day Kerala state) in south-

western India who founded a monastery at Mysore and possibly in three other places. Perhaps India's most respected intellect, Shankara developed a system that succeeded in synthesizing the diverse and conflicting ideas of the *Upanishads*. He achieved it by reinterpreting some themes and elevating or combining others. Shankara, who wrote commentaries on the *Vedanta Sutra* and nine *Upanishads*, continued the teaching of Gaudapada (C.E. 780). He sought to refute competing religious systems and spared no criticism. Speaking against Buddhists, for example, he said:

> Buddha by propounding the three mutually contradictory systems, teaching respectively the reality of the external world, the reality of ideas only and general nothingness, has himself made it clear either that he was a man given to make incoherent assertions, or else that hatred of all beings induced him to propound doctrines by accepting which they would become thoroughly confused. . . . Buddha's doctrine has to be entirely disregarded by all those who have a regard for their own happiness.[22]

The Nature of Highest Reality

Shankara believed that the *Upanishads* and the *Bhagavad Gita* alone taught the whole truth. These texts had the single purpose of making clear the true nature of highest reality: Brahman. By that word he meant a reality that was unconditioned, eternal, infinite, pure, and unknowable by the ordinary application of reason and mind. It was one and not two; not having duality nor multiplicity. The term *advaita vedanta* (Skt., nondual) is perhaps the best descriptive term that can be used of both the Absolute and Shankara's system. As there were no qualities or characteristics in highest reality, Brahman could be best described only with illustrations or with the use of negatives. This is the same reality in all persons, though appearing by illusion as different individuals. *Atman* is Brahman.

Shankara said that many passages "declare Brahman to possess a double nature, according as it is the object either of knowledge or of ignorance."[23] Brahman, the object of ignorance, is *saguna* (Skt., with qualities) and constitutes an object of devotion. *Nirguna* (Skt., without qualities) is the Absolute without qualities and limiting conditions.

Methods of Knowing the Absolute

He based his ideas of Brahman on *shruti*, the Vedic scriptures, which for him were all equally authoritative and absolutely infallible. He denied that any methods of ordinary knowing such as reason, personal experience, and sense perception could alone lead to truth, since these were subject to error. However, the application of reason to *shruti* was necessary in order to deal with false positions and make *shruti* clear to the understanding.

For Shankara and other Vedantists, the whole body of Vedic scriptures are considered as *shruti*, "that which is heard." This was the truth, final and authoritative, which the *rishis* of the past knew and understood. Shankara uses reason in his system of thought, although it does not take one to ultimate reality since that is beyond reason. It is a state to be experienced, not a truth to be known intellectually. Nevertheless, reason has a value at the lower levels of reality. The unreal is devalued by the application of reason, since such matters are illogical and impossible. For example, the son of a barren woman and the horns of a hare are contrary both to experience and reason. Though it is primarily by more authentic experiences that one moves from the illusory existent to the phenomenally real, reason plays a role there as well. But its role at this level is primarily in understanding *shruti*. By exposition of the *Upanishads*, Shankara concluded that truth was *advaita*. But the highest level of truth is not dependent on reason and is in fact independent of it since the Real is distinctionless. Reason's function, to enable one to avoid the unreal and to know the Real, lies beyond the illusory, but when it has accomplished that, reason must be left behind since there is nothing upon which reason can act in the realm of the Real. Thus reason itself belongs to the realm of illusion since it cannot produce the Real. One may reason "up to" the Real but not "into" it. In the end one either takes *shruti* and Shankara's system by faith or rejects it. Reason cannot prove or disprove it at its highest level since that is self-confirming and self-authenticating.

The Nature of Phenomenal Reality

Compared to Brahman, which alone is real, the world is false and illusory. But the world our senses encounter is not completely illusory; it is just dependent on something else and has a limited reality only in relation to the Real. Shankara thus spoke of degrees of reality; these can be arranged in the following order:

The Real, the Absolute, Brahman (*sat paramarthikha*)

Appearance (*vivarta*)—not Real but not illogical and contradictory; illusory

1. The phenomenal world (*vyavaharika*)—the world of sensory perception. Concepts of a personal deity belong here.

2. The Illusory experience (*pratibhasika*)—dreams fantasies and other illusory experiences.

Unreality (*asat*)—the level of the impossible and contradictory. The illogical.[24]

He denies that the world is void (against Nagarjuna) and that it is a mental construct (against Yogacara). However, though the world participates in reality in some sense, it is not final reality.

The *atman*, or essential self, is identical to Brahman in the experience of *moksha*. But until ignorance is removed the individual self suffers illusory and imaginary pain which disappears when one realizes the identity of Brahman and *atman*.

The Relation Between Brahman and the World

Shankara directly affirms that Brahman is the cause from which the world proceeds. Yet the world is not created since this would imply purposeful acts by an intelligent being, which Brahman is not. Shankara says that "the doctrine of the creation proceeding from an intelligent Being is untenable." [25] The question arises: If the world is not the work of an intelligent creator, how does it arise?

Specifically, how can the multiform world arise out of the undifferentiated One which Shankara believes is the ultimate source? How can purposeful creatures emerge out of purposeless Reality? Shankara cites illustrations such as the following: "As the one luminous sun when entering into relation to many different waters is himself rendered multiform by his limiting adjuncts; so also the one divine unborn Self."[26] Such an answer is couched in a metaphor that seems to answer the question but gives no rational defense, since the rise of the multiform out of the essential unity of Brahman is transrational.

Central to Shankara's answer is *maya*. Brahman possesses the power of *maya* (Skt., occult power to manifest itself). This seems to run contrary to Shankara's contention that Brahman is pure and absolutely* undifferentiated. Critics point out that if *maya* is within Brahman then it is not undifferentiated. If, to safeguard Brahman's distinctionless nature, *maya* lies outside Brahman, then something exists extra-Brahman, and nonduality is compromised. Nonetheless, it is his view that *maya* accounts for the (illusory) existence of the world. Paradoxically, *maya* stands between Brahman and the phenomenal world. Of it Shankara says, "[M]aya is properly called underdeveloped or non-manifested since it cannot be defined either as that which is or that which is not."[27] The world is dependent on Brahman, but the relation between the two is a mystery and can be explained only approximately so far as the topic of cosmic origins is concerned. If one proceeds from the side of the cosmos and moves toward Brahman, some statements can be made. If one attempts explanation starting from the side of Brahman, no statements can be descriptively true. The relation between Brahman and the world is to be believed because "although eternally unchanging and uniform, [the Self] reveals itself in a graduated series of beings, and so appears in forms of various dignity and power."[28]

Liberation

In the understanding of modern thinking, knowledge ordinarily involves making three distinctions: the knower, the known, and the knowledge about the known. But in liberation these distinctions are removed because, according to Shankara, the *atman* or essential self, is not different from Brahman, or the Real. Liberation leads to knowledge but it is a knowledge of a different order; it is an intuitive experience that transcends all distinctions. In a distinctionless knowledge in which the knower and the known fuse, reason is transcended and there is no longer any separation of the principal factors: knower, known, and knowledge. The experience is unitary even as *atman* and Brahman are one.

What are the appropriate and effective means to *moksha*? Study of scriptures may dispel wrong views and point toward the real, but it cannot produce liberation itself. *Sannyasins* who cling to nothing are in an improved situation. However, no means can produce *moksha*. They can only prepare one for the intuitive experience.

Karma and Moksha

Moksha is possible in this life while living. For those who have achieved it there is no *atman* which acts separately. In this state neither good nor evil *karma* can accrue either now or in the future, and hence *samsara* is at an end. However, *karma* that has already begun to bear its fruit cannot be avoided and inexorably has its effects in and on the body. At death the body dissipates and liberation is complete. There is no return.

Ramanuja's Vishishtadvaita

Ramanuja

Some three centuries after Shankara, Ramanuja (d. C.E. 1137) of Madras taught his doctrine of Vishishtadvaita (qualified nondualism). Shankara's interpretation of the *Upanishads* left no room for a personal deity in spite of the fact that the majority of the population, in southern India as elsewhere, were bhaktists worshiping a personal deity. Ramanuja's doctrine was the first to succeed in systematizing a defense of *bhakti* rooted in the same literature used by Shankara and advaitans. His idea was to uphold the legitimacy of devotional worship of a deity while accounting for a world that is not finally or permanently real. His view is called Vishishtadvaita, meaning "qualified nondualism." Van Buitenen summarizes this position as follows: "Unity of the universe's spiritual and non-spiritual substances with and in a God whom they modify as his body."[29]

Brahman and the World

Unlike Shankara, Ramanuja held that Brahman was not entirely without distinctions. Within his nature are the following distinctions: the unconscious material world (*prakrti*), the conscious world of finite *atmans* (individuals), and the source and sustainer of these, which is Brahman, or Ishavara (Lord). There is only one complex reality and all that exists is contained within it. Ramanuja is saying the Real is one but complexly one, not simply one as Shankara held.

An analogy served to illustrate this. Individual persons are a similarly complex unity consisting of body (*deha*) and soul (*atman*). The body is ruled by the soul and its conscious modes of knowing, willing, and feeling. The individual is a microcosm of that one macrocosm: God and his world. Contained within God is all that exists. Things do not exist outside of him but only within him in derived and dependent ways.

Crucial to Ramanuja's thought is the contention that though Brahman in himself is not multiple, there is, nonetheless, complexity encompassed within him. The *Brihadaranyaka Upanishad* (III.vii.3) is cited as proof of this and the *Bhagavad Gita* supplements it. The physical world and individual souls are all within ultimate Reality and have no reality apart from it. In fact, the world and individuals in it constitute the "God-body" of Brahman and serve to manifest him. The universe is the body of Brahman just as Brahman is the soul or *atman* of the world. Moreover, Brahman is personal and not impersonal as in Shankara's view. Specifically, Brahman is the God Vishnu, and followers of him, Vaishnavites, are closest to knowing the final truth. As God is personal, individuals can enter into a saving relationship with him and receive of his grace, which can destroy the harmful effects of *karma*.

Maya for Ramanuja is not the occult force or power by which the world mysteriously arises, as in the case of Shankara, but rather it denotes that which produces various wonderful effects. The Absolute is a *mayin* since he has the power to produce all manner of wonderful things. Thus *maya* is a positive and creative quality of Brahman in contrast to Shankara's view that *maya* cannot be attributed to the Real without destroying its absolute unity.

The following conclusions can be made about Ramanuja's teaching on the self-body relationship (Brahman's relation to the world):

1. There is a true distinction between Brahman and his universe.

2. There is an inseparable dependence of the world on Brahman.

3. Brahman is the causal explanation for the world and souls. The world and souls are alike real and not illusory. Brahman is the material and efficient cause of them both.

4. Brahman is personal and relates personally with souls.

5. The world fulfills the will of Brahman who brought it into existence.

Bhakti and Moksha

Ramanuja held that *moksha* did not consist in becoming one with reality as in Advaita but, rather, in the experience of liberation—the soul and Brahman face each other, each having separate existence. Through meditation and the grace of the deity, one can take on the same attributes as the highest reality. The grace of Brahman enables true meditation and leads the soul to reach its highest potential, that is, to have the same character as the Absolute. The grace of Vishnu removes *avidya* (ignorance), which is the inability of souls to see and understand their dependent relationship with Brahman.

Madhva's Dvaita

Madhva (1199–1278)

Madhva was schooled in Advaita Vedanta but broke from it to take a new direction in opposition to Shankara. He, too, turned to *shruti* and *smrti* for his authority, but extended *smrti* to include the much later puranic literature. His system is sometimes called dualism since he recognizes more than one permanent and real entity: God, souls, and matter. Each is distinct though all are related because the latter two are dependent upon God. It is said Madhva's motivation was to save *bhakti* from the implications of Advaita—if souls are identical to Brahman then surrender to the Lord is, ultimately, not possible.

The One and the Many

The basic problem which Indian thinkers faced was how to explain the relationship between the two catego-ries of the one and the many. A time-honored interpretation of the *Upanishads* had been that the many was absorbed into the one Brahman, though earlier Vedic literature clearly allowed some degree of independent existence to things; a point which Ramanuja incorporated into his thought. Madhva was persuaded of more than one reality not only by his reading of sacred literature but also by the force of direct observation. That things had separate and independent existence from each other and from God was undeniable. Accordingly, he organizes his system around five fundamental distinctions: the Lord is different from a soul; the Lord is different from material particulars; souls are distinct from each other; souls are different from matter; one distinct object is different from another.

God and Reality

The Lord (*paramatman*) is eternal, permanent, self-dependent (*aparatantra*), and totally different from the world, souls, and all other objects. He is an absolutely independent being (*svatantra*) and, in contrast to other Vedantic teaching, does not contain in his being all things (Ramanuja), nor are distinct souls or things an illusion (Shankara). He is not without distinctions but contains an infinite number of perfected differences. Madhva identified Vishnu as the supreme Lord and the only one of whom the Vedas, when correctly interpreted, spoke.

While material things do not arise out of his very nature because all things are distinct, they do, however, arise out of that which he possesses: *prakrti* (matter) and *purusha* (consciousness), both of which are eternal. It would be correct to say that material things as well as souls depend on the Lord but that the Lord is independent of both of them. It would be further correct to say that, while for Shankara there are no ultimate distinctions and for Ramanuja things are distinct in the Lord, things are distinct from the Lord in Madhva's thought.

Souls and Liberation

There are innumerable eternal, distinct souls. The origin of the soul (*jiva*), as an entity separate from God, is mysterious or at least difficult to clearly understand. Yet souls, while suffering in ignorance (*avidya*), contain qualities found in the Lord (*sat, chit, ananda*) that, remain imperfect. While souls are eternally distinct, they are nevertheless dependent on the Lord. Each soul has properties unique to it which distinguish it from another. The self in its natural state is enmeshed with matter and suffers because of the action of *karma* upon it. Two forces may work toward liberation. One is God himself, who is said to determine the destiny of the soul by working in his capacity as creator, sustainer, and destroyer. But each individual has open to it avenues for the awakening to truth. There are eighteen means by which good *karma* is accumulated and right knowledge comes, including:

> study of scripture
> distaste of this world
> attendance upon a *guru*
> performance of rites and ceremonies
> in *puja* for Vishnu
> wearing of proper Vaishnavite symbols
> *bhajans* (devotional hymns)
> worship through proper thoughts and acts

faith in Vishnu while performing all of the above

Yet in the end it is the grace of the deity that saves, and all those who do not reach liberation have one of two destinies. Some will forever course in *samsara*, never escaping the rounds of birth and death. Others will be consigned to eternal torment. An interesting fact is that Dvaita is the only Indian religious system that teaches a destiny of hell for some, from which there is no escape. In liberation souls are alike in perfection but subtly distinct nevertheless, and enjoy uninterrupted communion with God.

New Religions in the Medieval Period

The Sikh Religion

Guru Nanak

The history of the Sikh religion begins with Nanak, who lived in the Punjab region now divided by the Indo-Pakistan border. Nanak's India (1469–1538) was ruled by the Moguls, a Muslim empire centered in Delhi that began in the twelfth century. Nanak and his family were Hindus but, according to Sikh traditions, at an early age he began to refuse Hindu ceremonies such as the *upanayana*. He was attracted by *bhakti* practices and made friends of musicians and poets who spent evenings singing *bhajans* to the deities. Nanak himself composed *bhakti* poetry and with his Muslim friend, Mardana, began attracting a group of followers with common interests. At thirty years of age Nanak had a life-changing experience at river's edge through a vision from God. He told his followers God took him into his presence, gave him a cup of nectar, and commissioned him as follows:

I am with thee. I have given thee happiness, and I shall make happy all who take thy name. Go thou and repeat my Name; cause others to repeat it. Abide unspoiled by the world. Practice charity, perform ablutions, worship and meditate. My name is God, the primal Brahma. Thou art the Holy Guru.[30]

He related this to his followers along with the statement which was to set the tone for the new movement: "There is no Hindu and there is no Mussulman." It was with these words that Nanak set out to establish a religion where Hindus and Muslims could join together in the worship of God. This has sometimes been called a deliberate attempt at syncretism. In this case Nanak intentionally and reflectively sought to unite elements of two religions into a system which would unite both Muslims and Hindus. But what resulted historically was not the joining of the two religions but the establishing of a third, new, and ultimately competing one. What began as an attempt at ecumenism, so to speak, resulted over the years in an entirely new religious tradition (see inset). [31]

Nanak and the Bhakti Movement

For more than fifteen centuries *bhakti* had grown in popular acceptance on the subcontinent, resulting in periods of intense fervor led by charismatic poet-musicians and *gurus* who left their mark on India's religious history. One of those figures was a northern Indian named Kabir (1440–1518). Said to have grown up in Banaras of a low caste and from a Muslim family, he nevertheless rejected all external religious authorities including the Vedas and the Quran in favor of a warm and intense experience with God. In this he might well have been influenced by Sufi or devotional Islam. Kabir, like Nanak, extolled the virtue of praising the name of God in sincere and faithful worship. Through devotional praise and love of God, *samsara* could end and salvation could be achieved. Kabir's influence on Nanak was indirect through his devotional hymns and practices, but nevertheless profound. In the Sikh holy book, the *Granth Sahib*, 74 of his hymns in 423 *slokas* (verses) are found.

Career

Nanak set out, as many *gurus* did, to both seek truth and propound it as he had found it. He went on four journeys across the subcontinent singing his praises of God and explaining his understanding of the True Name, a term by which he addressed the supreme being. He alternately dressed as a Sufi saint and a Hindu bhaktist to appeal to the different religious communities. He returned from his wanderings to settle down in Kartarpur (near Lahore) and establish himself among a group of followers who were to become the nucleus of the Sikh (Skt., disciple) religion. Until his death he continued to accept without distinction both Hindus and Muslims who wished to join with sincere heart in the worship of God. Before passing away he appointed a successor, Angad ("limb"), who would become, as his name implied, a part or extension of the founder himself. He was to become the second of the ten founding *gurus*.

Nanak's Teachings

The goal of Nanak, like that of many
bhaktists, was to be united with God
and enjoy his presence in everlasting
happiness, free from the rounds of
birth and death. The method of
achieving that was devotional experiences of surrender and love through
the grace of God.

God was one and without form and
hence could not be depicted with
statue and image. God is separate
from his creation and this creation is
real, not illusory (*maya*), as taught by
many Hindus. God can be experienced and known, but because he is
beyond all human capacities to understand him, it is a personal and inexpressible union. Nanak used many of
the popular and common names for
God such as Hari and Rama, both
Hindu names. He also used Allah,
Shuda, and even Sahib ("Sir"). But
names to Nanak were merely conven-
tions and he thought it best to use the
nondescript term True Name, which
testifies to Nanak's desire to find a
new linguistic convention or vehicle to
enable humankind to think freshly
about the one true God. God as he
truly is, is absolute, without qualities
and unconditioned. Yet, in his relation to his creation, he is experienced
as person. Nanak combines both personalistic and nondualistic ideas, with
the personalistic somewhat more
prominent.

The Need for Salvation

Salvation is necessary because people
are blinded by willfulness, evil, and
perversity. So long as one fails to
worship God and meditate on him,
one's blinded condition—being unable to see, feel, or experience God—
will continue. One can be roused from
insensitivity by devotional acts such
as meditating on the divine name,
listening to *gurus* explain the truth,
and singing God's praises or listening
to others do the same. This moves one
out of self-centeredness and sensitizes
one for a greater experience. Preoccu-
pation with the world deludes and
blinds. It is not that the material world
is illusory, as in Advaita Vedanta, but
that it detracts and offers false pursuits. Salvation is at the end of a
process whereby, through following
the teachings of the *Granth Sahib* (of
which the *Adi Granth* is the first part)
and the *gurus* of the faith and spiritual
disciplines, one experiences the grace
of God, without which salvation is not
achieved. Sikhs are not explicit about
the experience of saving union with
God. They leave it somewhat unclear
except for affirming the possibility and
even the reality.

The Ten Gurus

The Sikhs accept ten historic *gurus*
who succeeded each other in the
founding period and contributed, at
certain points, new innovations which
together constitute the permanent
marks of the religion. Nine *gurus*
besides Nanak account for a period of
169 years. Nine of these *gurus* and
their ruling dates follow.

Guru Angad (1539–52)

The first to succeed Nanak as leader of the new community, he adopted the Gurmukhi script for sacred writings and introduced the common kitchen (*langar*), later a regular institution attached to all *gurdwaras* (temples), in which disciples could share a communal meal.

Guru Amar Das (1552–74)

He established a center for worship at the side of a well with eighty-four descending steps. This is the first Sikh shrine and is found in Gujarat. His son-in-law was nominated to succeed him and thereafter leadership remained in the Sodhi family.

Guru Ram Das (1574–81)

He established The second and most holy of Sikh shrines under the patronage of the Mogul emperor Akbar (ruled 1556–1605) at Ramdaspur, later called Amritsar ("pool of nectar"), recalling the divine nectar given to Nanak and, in salvation, to all.

Guru Arjun (1581–1606)

Arjun began construction on the shrine at Amritsar called Darbar Sahib by Sikhs or, more popularly because of its gold-leaf covered dome, the Golden Temple. He enlarged the pool to a lake surrounding the temple and constructed four temple doors to illustrate the teaching of Sikh openness to all, regardless of caste or religion. The hymns of Nanak, Arjun, and the previous *gurus* were collected, forming the first stage of the *Granth Sahib* (1604). Under the repressive Mogul emperor Jahangir, builder of the Taj Mahal, Sikhs got their first taste of persecution and began to respond with the militaristic attitudes and practices that have marked them to this day. Arjun was executed for failing to remove passages in Sikh writings which the Muslim ruler deemed offensive. Before he died Arjun instructed his son and successor to "sit fully armed" on the throne and maintain a standing army for protection of the faithful. Sikhs were never to forget these words.

Guru Har Gobind (1606–45)

Sikh men, following Har Gobind's example, adopted the turban that has since been associated with Sikh manhood. He further led them to accept their distinct and separate identity and the inevitable necessity of defending it by force.

Gurus Har Rai (1630–64) and Har K'ishan (1656–64)

Sikhs continued to develop their military strength.

Guru Tegh Bahadur (1666–75)

Continued conflict with the Muslim emperors resulted in Tegh Bahadur's execution, which increased solidarity among Sikhs.

Guru Gobind Singh (1675–1708)

The name Singh (lion) became a common one among Sikhs from this time forward. He instituted a fraternity of warriors called the Khalsa (the pure) who committed themselves to the defense of the truth and the community. Once, to test the sincerity of his warriors, he called for five volunteers to prove their loyalty by dying for the faith. Each entered the tent singly, and shortly after each warrior entered Gobind Singh emerged alone with a bloody sword. The fifth time he emerged he brought with him the brave warriors unharmed; a goat had been slain instead. Through this ordeal the warriors had proven the depth of their commitment. Five new marks of the Sikh man were thereafter required, constituting the so-called five K's: (1) the *kesh*, or long uncut hair on head and face; (2) the *kangha*, or comb; (3) the *kacch*, or shorts worn beneath the trousers signifying preparation for vigorous and unencumbered action; (4) the *kara*, or a steel bracelet; and (5) the *kirpan*, or the sword or dagger without which a Sikh was never to go out in public. Guru Gobind Singh taught his followers from this point to worship only in a Sikh *gurdwara* (temple). Further, as all four of his sons were assassinated in bloody conflicts, he taught that he was the last human *guru*. The *Granth Sahib* would be his successor; they were to follow that alone. He said: "He who wishes to behold the Guru, let him search the Granth."[33]

[The rule of these gurus overlaps sometimes and also there are gaps between rules as well.]

The Granth Sahib

The *Granth* is written in languages and scripts that are old and, in some cases, not understood except by specialists. The initial *Granth*, called the *Adi* (first) *Granth* and collected by Guru Arjan, is thought by some to be the one found today extant at Kartarpur. A small addition of about twenty-seven pages of hymns and *slokas* by Guru Gobind Singh completed the book. It contains

Golden Temple of Sikhs in Amritsar, Punjab. J. Lewis

hymns and devotional material used daily in the worship conducted in the *gurdwaras* across India and around the world, and a copy is an essential element of every temple. Its central ideas include a theistic emphasis with nondualistic overtones, *karma*, and transmigration; the necessity of the grace of God for salvation; the need for and authority of a *guru*; worship through sincere repetition of the True Name; and the need for congregational worship. The *Granth* is centrally positioned under a canopy and on a table covered with embroidered cloth. During services the temple *guru* sings and chants portions from it either from memory or by reading. Sikh worship, unlike Hindu worship, is congregational in that the group listens and participates at certain points. At the conclusion, *prasad* (small snack) may be given to newcomers or guests. This is prepared in the *langar* (kitchen attached to every *gurdwara*), which daily serves one meal to those present, whether they are poor or merely passing through.

Sikhs in Modern Times

Though Sikhs fought to remain independent of British colonial rule, they were not successful. But their extraordinary bravery and loyalty won the respect of the colonializers, whose fairness in turn attracted the Sikhs. A perfect arrangement ensued as Sikhs served the British as crack troops and as the British developed the Punjab, a fertile region like the Gangetic plain, with public works projects. During the period of independence India was partitioned into an independent Muslim state, Pakistan, resulting in the Punjab itself being divided. Hostilities ensued with Hindus and Sikhs of the new state of India joining against Muslims of the new Pakistan.

Worship at the Sikh Gurdwara in Jabalpur, India. J. Lewis

However, Sikhs have grown increasingly dissatisfied with their lack of constitutional recognition as a separate religion. In some sections they are directly or indirectly lumped with Hindus, and some feel they receive unsatisfactory consideration, as a religious minority, for placement in colleges, universities, law schools, medical schools, and civil service positions. Further, they perceive themselves as failing to get the government funds for the improvements that their sizeable tax contributions entitle them to enjoy. The Punjab already has a high standard of public services and utilities compared to much of the rest of India, and their calls for further improvements have gone unheeded. As water resources are always in need of careful management, disputes have arisen in recent years over plans to divert waters. Sikhs believe this jeopardizes their economic way of life. Strong voices in Parliament did not seem to secure the attention desired and hence, in true Sikh tradition, militant and violent measures were advocated and applied in 1983 and 1984. Moderates within the Sikhs did not seem to be able or willing to control the hard-liners, and in June 1984 the Indian central government attacked a minor building within the Golden Temple complex, killing all within and capturing caches of weapons and ammunition. Indira Gandhi, the prime minister, was held to be personally responsible, and as a perceived Hindu she roused old animosities and generated new hatreds. Gandhi was assassinated by two of her own bodyguards, themselves Sikhs, on Wednesday, October 31, 1984. From the Sikh viewpoint, desecration of their temple was a heinous crime for which assassination was merely the just response.

The Parsis

Ethnic and Religious Heritage

The Parsis (Gujarati word for Persians) share a common ethnic and religious background with the Aryans. While some of the Aryans moved eastward toward the Indus Valley, a wave of these same warring nomads earlier swept southward into present-day northwest Iran, where they overcame opponents and established their own way of life. They established worship of powers called *daevas*, which is the same word, *devas*, used by the Indian Aryans for their gods of nature.

Parsis trace their religious heritage, however, to Zoroaster (c. 650 B.C.E.; also, Zarathustra), who was born in Persia and whose teachings mingled with and modified their earlier Aryan beliefs and practices. Ancient *gathas* (hymns) of uncertain dates tell us Zoroaster had a vision in his youth in which one of the *asura* ministering spirits, Vohu Manah (Good Thought), commissioned him as a messenger for Ahura Mazda.

Zoroaster taught that the cosmos was in a titanic struggle between the deity Ahura Mazda, the force of truth and light, and Angra Mainyu, the evil personification of untruth. Under Zoroaster's teaching, *daevas* and *asuras*, spiritual beings which were accepted by his contemporaries, were given a new identity. *Daevas* had been regarded as heavenly deities but now were considered cohorts of the evil Angra Mainyu. *Asuras* were evil but now were seen as divine (Ahura). This inverted the previous understanding of *daevas* and *asuras* that they had held in common with their Aryan cousins.

The world was a battleground between two forces conceived of dualistically because goodness and morality were pitted against evil and immorality. In the beginning two spirits met and made choices of their own free will that was to affect all later times. Spenta Mainyu (good spirit) chose life and truth and Aura Mainyu chose the opposite. Ahura Mazda, father of both spirits, who countenanced their right to make their own choices, was alone

worthy of worship, wholly good and incapable of doing evil. But he is somewhat less than all-powerful and thus does not qualify as an entirely monotheistic deity. His equally powerful counterpart, Angra Mainyu, will some day be defeated through a combination of righteous human choices and divine activity. In the end humankind will be judged, the earth purified, and evil opponents destroyed. Zoroaster condemned sacrifices to the evil *daevas* but incorporated the drinking of *haoma* (Vedic, soma) as a central ritual in the fire temple; all partake of it after it has been offered in the fire to Ahura Mazda.

The Avesta

The Parsi scripture consists of four parts written in languages which only a few specialists can translate and no one can pronounce with any degree of confidence. The *Yasna* is a liturgical collection which contains old hymns (*gathas*). The *Visperad* consists of prayers and ceremonies in honor of the *asuras*. The *Yashts* are hymns of praise and the *Videvdat* contains incantations and spells to deal with evil. "The gathas portrayed the wise Lord as creator of heaven and earth, the source of day and night, the supreme lawgiver of the universe, the center of all nature, the source of the moral order and judge of all humanity."[34]

Indian Parsis

Numbering somewhat less than ninety thousand, the majority of Indian Parsis live in Bombay and Gujarat and are engaged in commerce, finance, and trade. They are known to be generally wealthy, highly educated, civic-minded, and fully at home in Western culture. The most public of Parsi institutions, though not particularly unique architecturally, is the Parsi fire temple which is open only to members. Usually marked by the figure of one or more four-footed creatures with human faces standing at its entrance, the fire temple is so called because in the center is an urn in which burns a sacred fire that is never permitted to die out. The fire, brought originally to the temple from a compound of sixteen purified fire sources, stands as the essence of Ahura Mazda, who is worshiped in prayers and offerings of burned sandalwood. There are no images of the deity nor are there idols of any kind. Attending priests wear masks to avoid contaminating the fire during ceremonies. A declining priesthood is of great concern to many Parsis because the fire is maintained by priests and rituals require their knowledge and services. Many believe that only improved salaries will attract more priests and ameliorate the crisis.

The least public institution of the Parsi community is the *dakhma*, or "tower of silence," in which the deceased of the community are briefly interred. Rising visibly to the height of twenty or more feet on a Malabar hillside in Bombay, but obscured from above by cemetery trees, are towers in which the body is placed to be exposed to the elements and flesh-eating birds. The practice is defended as pure, ecologically superior, humane, and respectful. The earth is not polluted with decaying flesh as in burial. The birds are permitted to satisfy their hunger and fire is not corrupted as happens with cremation, the standard method in

Hindu society. After an hour or two, the bones are stripped clean and placed on the stone floor of the *dakhma* where they can bleach in the sun and dissolve into their constituent elements.

Parsi Fire Temple in Bombay. Entrance to the temple is permitted only for Parsis. J. Lewis

Parsis and Conversion

Some religions hold that unless they energetically press their claims on others to convert, they will eventually decline. Other religious communities welcome converts even if they do not actively solicit or seek them. But conversion according to the Parsi way of thinking, even by marriage, is generally rejected as a threat to the purity of the community, a point that has been upheld by Indian courts.[35] Community attitudes became clear at the 1978 Third World Congress of Zoroastrians held in Bombay under the title "The Zoroastrian Community in a Changing World." Fourteen hundred delegates from around the world heard this statement by an Indian Parsi: "All of you who have come from abroad will put forward dangerous theories in support of conversion and destroy our community." Ironically, this was spoken to a Chicago Parsi who was about to express her own opposition to permitting conversion.[36] As it stands in India today conversion is not only discouraged, it is impossible. Marriage to a Parsi or being born to a couple of mixed marriage guarantees nothing. Children of mixed marriages are members if their fathers are Parsis but not if only their mothers are. The non-Parsi wife of a Parsi can never become one, nor can she even enter the fire temple. This conservative attitude worries the more liberal Parsi element, which fears that delaying of marriage to later years and declining birthrates will further erode community numbers and threaten eventual survival.

Religion in Modern India

The Samaj Movement: Reform and Reaction

India's religious life at the turn of the nineteenth century had been significantly affected by Muslim rule which began after 1236 C.E. and spread over most of India until it peaked under the Mogul emperor Aurangzeb (1658–1707). Thereafter European traders, already present in India, vied to expand spheres of economic and political control: the Portuguese in Goa, the French in Pondicherry and the English East India Company in Bengal and Madras. From 1761 onward until Independence in 1947 the British played the most important and influential role as they gradually consolidated their interests and achieved near-total colonization of the subcontinent.

The English brought challenge and change to Indian social and religious life. Their liberal political, social and scientific outlook forced Muslims, Hindus and others to reconsider their traditional ways. English education and language, provided for and required of all Indians who sought employment with the Company, opened minds to European traditions and views. Through the application of English law, moral standards and social practices of Hindus such as permitting child brides, refusal of remarriage to youthful widows, infanticide, *sati* (obligatory burning of the wife on her husband's cremation fire) and *devadasi* (temple prostitution), were brought under fire.

The arrival in India in 1793 of William Carey, marks the onset of a flood of missionaries who within 50 years had established missions and young churches throughout the provinces. Their critique of Hindu beliefs and practices heightened calls for reform and provoked reaction among Hindu intellectuals. The *samaj* (society) movement was the result and fell into two camps: those seeking to reform Hindu life by accommodating to western ideas and religion and those whose reforms were intended to purify yet defend the Hindu way.

Brahmo Samaj

The Brahmo Samaj (Sanskrit: theistic society) arose under the vision of Ram Mohun Roy (1774–1833). English educated, learned in Persian, Arabic, Sanskrit and his native Bengali language, acquainted with both Greek and Hebrew scriptures, he was India's first modern social critic and advocate of religious reform. While the vast majority of Hindus were polytheists, Roy's brush with Christianity and his study of theistic texts in the Upanishads led him to accept monotheism and oppose idolatry. After flirting with Christian unitarianism, he established the Brahmo Samaj in 1828 to provide a model for the worship of *Brahman*, to rid India of immoral customs not consistent with *shruti*, and to encourage the advancement of women's rights. His movement attracted many but also provoked outrage among many traditional Hindus.

One of the many bright Hindus attracted to the Brahmo Samaj was Keshab Chandra Sen (1838–1884) who joined in 1857. Sen became increasingly fascinated with Christianity and more and more anti-Hindu, rejecting all forms of image worship. A rift led to his departure from the Brahmo Samaj to establish his own movement, The Brahmo Samaj of India. He sought to purify Hindu beliefs but unite the best of them, the theistic ones, with Christian ideas in search of a universal religion of which Christ would be the head. His own movement stalled when he refused to reject the worshipful reverence of his followers and devotees. He goes down in history as one of the earliest modern Indian thinkers to commit himself to Christ, though his religious synthesis did not catch on nor spread far.

Established in 1875 the Arya Samaj (Sanskrit: society of Aryas, or noble ones) expressed the sentiments of many Hindus who while promoting social reforms, defended the teachings of the Vedas and promoted Hindu superiority. Though himself of Brahman caste, the founder of the Arya Samaj, Dayananda Saraswathi (1824–1833), took the revolutionary attitude that the Vedas should be open to all including women and outcastes. The Vedas were regarded as true and inspired in every way. All knowledge could be found in them including the technological and scientific discoveries claimed by Europeans. All India's woes could be corrected by turning "Back to the Vedas" which alone held answers to India's needs. The samaj is also known for *shuddhi*, the practice of aggressively reconverting Hindus who had become either Muslims or Christians.

In his major work *Satyarth Prakash* (Light of Truth) Dayananda Saraswathi devoted one chapter to criticisms of Christianity. He selects certain Old and New Testament passages which he interpreted in a literal way to show their absurdity and concluded that all enlightened Aryas should be careful to escape such superstition and exert themselves to save others from the same. Though his attacks were crude, other younger and more educated Aryas brought forth criticisms which they learned in studies abroad. Durga Prasad attacked the Christian claim of an inerrant scripture by pointing out seeming inconsistencies in the Bible. He also denied that prophecy and miracles were evidences of revealed religion. Thakur Khan-chandra Varma of Lahore used the latest 19th century literary-historical scholarship in Germany and America to refute Christian claims. He argued the scriptures were not only unreliable because of their obvious inconsistencies but went one step beyond saying the Gospel writers were not themselves witnesses of the events and discourses they recorded. He claimed there were no historical proofs for Jesus who was merely a creation of their minds. In this way the Arya Samaj led in a sophisticated and strong counter-attack upon the truth claims of Christianity.

The Arya Samaj today has chapters in every major city and continues its promotion of Hindu superiority and social reform. Recently they have called for prohibition of alcohol and curbs on obscene and pornographic literature. Some Aryas are opposed to the use of English language in the nation and are a force opposing perceived religious advances of non-Hindus.

Ramakrishna Mission

The Hindu revival and renewal movement in India was given great impetus by the life of a Bengali sannasin, Ramakrishna Paramahamsa, and the mission established in his honor. A mystic and yogi in the classical Hindu tradition, Sri Ramakrishna was drawn to meditation and trance in his youth. A priest of the Dakshineswar temple on the bank of the Ganges River near Calcutta, he was intensely devoted to the goddess Kali but is said to have experienced a complete range of bhakti, advaitan, tantric, and even Muslim and Christian spirituality. Ramakrishna was believed by various of his followers to be an *avatar* of Hanuman and Radha, wife of the deity Krishna and had such ecstatic visions some considered him to be mad. His title *Paramahamsa*, "The Supreme Swan," bestowed upon him by his followers, expressed the highest honor a sanyasin could possibly receive.

His disciples, vowing to continue his influence, founded a monastic order whose most famous member was Vivekananda (1863–1902). Trained in English schools, and once a member of the Brahmo Samaj, he was rescued from religious skepticism when he met Ramakrishna and thereafter vowed to advance Hindu spirituality. Vivekananda's fame as a missionary of Hindu beliefs in America is as great or greater than his accomplishments in India. In 1893 he attended the Chicago World's Parliament of Religions and became one of the earliest Hindu spokespersons on American soil. Known to them as Swami Vivekananda, he made his neo-advaitan thought both accessible and acceptable for the first time for many Americans. Bright, engaging, fluent in English and knowledgeable about details of the Judeo-Christian religions, Vivekananda remained in the US after the World Parliament of Religions to establish the Vedanta Society, an organization devoted to the promotion of the teachings of Vedanta and the experiences of his guru Ramakrishna Paramahamsa, to whom he had devoted his life.

The Ramakrishna Mission can be found throughout India and abroad in more than 120 locations and is dedicated to a broad social, religious and educational program under the charter of "the essential unity of all cultures and religions, the potential divinity of man, and service to humanity as a way of reaching the ultimate."[37]

Modern Religious Leaders

It would not be possible to present all of the many important religious leaders in India in the twentieth century but two stand out for their impact both within India and abroad.

Mahatma Gandhi (1869–1948)

Mohandas Karamchand Gandhi was born into a Vaishya caste, Vishnu bhakti family in the northwest coastal city of Probandar, Gujarat. Regarded as the father of the country, his life story is inextricably intertwined with the national struggle for independence. He studied law in England for three years where he came in contact with Christianity and in 1893 moved to South Africa where for twenty-one years he experimented with solutions to racial oppression. In 1914 Gandhi returned to India and rose slowly to become one of the most respected persons in the world for his work as a social activist, political reformer and spiritual guide.

Gandhi became known for his non-violent approach to the conflict with the British from whom Indian nationalists were seeking independence and *swaraj* (self-rule). Steeped in the ancient Jain concept of *ahimsa*, Gandhi counseled his followers and compatriots not to harm their opponents. But ahimsa, to him, meant more than something negative—non-injury to anything in thought, word or deed. Positively, it meant embracing an attitude of love and even the doing of good to the evil doer. *Satyagraha* (holding on to truth) was Gandhi's way of using ahimsa for political ends. He experimented with it in South Africa and applied it successfully against the British by urging Indian nationalists to non-cooperation and civil-disobedience without violence. Gandhi viewed non-cooperation tactics as a way of bringing down an unjust system without destroying people. Gandhi and his followers were well aware of the consequences of defying British laws and spent months and years in jail for their activities.

Gandhi found the ethics of the New Testament to be inspiring and Jesus' Sermon on the Mount stood second only to the Bhagavad Gita for its impact on his non-violent ideals. Gandhi was a seeker as well as a practitioner of truth and on one occasion summarized his outlook in this way. "My religion is based on Truth and Non-violence. Truth is my God and Non-violence is my means to reach Him."[38] Gandhi's affirmation that truth was God meant that for him, God was an abstraction. His life was obsessed with the application of love, truth, ethics, and morality to the times. He recognized that many needed a personalistic conception of God as a foundation for these ideas but he did not and thus he accommodated both personalist and impersonalist ideas in the classic Vedantist tradition. Truth could be known only in the moment but could be had through fasting, self-denial (brahmacarya), meditation and prayer which he regularly practiced. He opposed religious conversion on the grounds that religions were about equal mixes of truth and error and little was to be gained by it.

He opposed untouchability and became the champion of shudras (outcastes) whom he called *Harijans* (Sanskrit: children of God). He believed in karma and reincarnation, and approved cow-protection as a symbol humanity's need to recognize its identity with all that lives. He accepted *varna* or caste not with its modern abuses but as a system whereby the younger generation could follow the hereditary work of the forefathers with no sense of superiority of one caste or vocation over another.

Sarvapalli Radhakrishnan (1888–1975)

Widely regarded as the most brilliant of India's modern intellectuals, Radhakrishnan was diplomat, statesman, orator, author, philosopher and President of India (1962–67). His lifelong desire was to interpret India to the West and defend it from unfair attacks and misunderstandings. His expositions of Indian religious thought have been regarded as among the very best and his academic career took him to posts at major Indian universities as well as Oxford University.

Educated at several Protestant Christian colleges in India he resented that philosophy courses paid no attention to the rich indigenous thinkers of his country. With a full understanding of Hindu texts and a mastery of western religion and philosophy Radhakrishnan set out to show the full equality of Eastern with Western thought, Hindu with Christian thought. *Sanatana Dharma* (Sanskrit: eternal truth) was Radhakrishnan's term for what was central and essential to all religions: the self-realized experience that was common to all great religious leaders. As a true advaitan, he distinguished between intuition and reason and though reason could help one toward self-realization, it had its limits. He distinguished between the historical Jesus, whom he felt could be dispensed with, and the Eternal Christ was no more special than other religions since all imbibe of that true religion found in Hindu texts.

> Christian religion is the continuation and restoration of the ancient religions, of something eternal. The means of salvation is essentially always the same, though its modes may vary in accordance with the different ethnical and cultural environments to which it reveals itself. To be a Christian is not the profession of an outward creed but the living of an inward life.[39]

In response to Albert Schweitzer's view that India's many socio-economic problems were due to its embrace of life-denying Hindu tenets, Radhakrishnan emphasized that the Hindu experience gave an important place to ethical concerns of this world. He justified this by interpreting Shankara's advaitan ideas to teach that the world was real and not maya or illusory, so long as one was in it. The world is not independently real but that is not say it is unreal and meaningless. Radhakrishnan was successful, in the minds of many, in making vedanta relevant to a modern world which increasingly had focused its attention on human and social problems.

Discussion

1. Based upon your studies, what reasons could be given for avoiding the terms *Hinduism* and *Buddhism*?
2. Identify as many religious traditions as you can which have a definite *bhakti* element. What are the similarities and differences? Are there some similarities of form yet differences in substance?

3. Discuss India as a fertile ground for religious life. Is India unique in this?
4. Who are the major religious figures in Indian religious history? Defend your choices.

Notes

[1]H. Kusumaker, "Decoded Harappan Script Alters Indus History," *Indian Express* newspaper, Sept. 14, 1980.

[2]*Indian Express*, Jan. 6, 1980.

[3]Robert F. Weir, gen. ed., *The Religious World* (New York: Macmillan, 1982), 54.

[4]R. De Smet and J. Neuner, eds., *Religious Hinduism*, 3rd revised ed. (Allahabad: St. Paul Society Publications, 1964), 32.

[5]S. Radhakrishnan and C. A. Moore, eds., *A Sourcebook in Indian Philosophy* (Princeton: Princeton Univ. Press, 1957), 23–24.

[6]Arthur Anthony Macdonell, *A Vedic Reader for Students* (Madras: Oxford Univ. Press, 1976), 138.

[7]Franklin Edgerton, *The Beginnings of Indian Philosophy* (London: George Allen & Unwin, 1963), 18.

[8]S. Gambhirananda, *Eight Upanishads*, vol. 1 (Calcutta: Avaita Ashrama, 1977), 61.

[9]De Smet and Neuner, *Religious Hinduism*, 170.

[10]Following the description given in Robert D. Baird and Alfred Bloom, *Indian and Far Eastern Religious Traditions* (New York: Harper & Row, Publishers, 1971), 33–34.

[11]*Majjhima-nikaya*, iii, in *Further Dialogues of the Buddha* , II, translated by Lord Chalmers, Sacred Books of the Buddhists, VI, (London: Oxford University Press, 1927), 296–99; quoted in *A Source Book in Indian Philosophy*, edited by S. Radhakrishnan and C. Moore, (Princeton, New Jersey: Princeton University Press, 1957), 277.

[12]*The Perfection of Wisdom in Eight Thousand Lines & Its Verse Summary*, trans. Edward Conze (Berkeley, Calif.: Four Seasons Foundation, 1973), 188.

[13]Ibid.

[14]*The Three Fold Lotus Sutra*, trans. Bunno Kato et al., with revisions by W. E. Soothill et al. (New York: Weatherhill/Kosei, 1975), 162–63.

[15]Ibid., 89. For an excellent discussion of ethical approaches to the problem of *upaya* read A. L. Herman, *An Introduction to Buddhist Thought* (New York: University Press of America, 1983), 236–247.

[16]Nagarjuna as quoted in "Surendranath Dasgupta," *A History of Indian Philosophy*, Vol 1 (Delhi: Motilal Banarsidass, 1975), 144.

[17]From Nagarjuna's *Sukrllekha* quoted in Surendranath Das Gupta, *A History of Indian Philosophy*, Vol. 1 (Delhi: Motilal Banarsidass, 1975), 144.

[18]Quoted in A. L. Herman, *Introduction to Buddhist Thought* (New York: University Press of America, 1983), 340–41.

[19]Edward Conze, *Buddhist Texts Through The Ages* (New York: Harper & Row, 1954), 213.

[20]Radhakrishnan and Moore, *Sourcebook in Indian Philosophy*, 144.

[21]Niels C. Nielsen, Jr. et al., *Religions of the World* (New York: St. Martin's Press, 1983), 173.

[22]Radhakrishnan and Moore, *Sourcebook in Indian Philosophy*, 535.

[23]Ibid., 513.

[24]After Robert D. Baird and Alfred Bloom, *Indian and Far Eastern Religious Traditions, Religion and Man*, (New York: Harper & Row, 1972), 77–78.

[25]Radhakrishnan and Moore, *Sourcebook in Indian Philosophy*, 533.

[26]Ibid., 536.

[27]Ibid., 516.

[28]Ibid., 513.

[29]Van Buitenen as quoted in Eric J. Lott, *God and the Universe in the Vedantic Theology of Ramanuja* (Madras: Ramanuja Research Society, 1976), 66.

[30]Nielsen, *Religions of the World*, 386.

[31]From the official Sikh book of *Worship and Discipline* (1950) quoted in C. H. Loehlin, *The Sikhs and Their Scriptures*, 3d ed. (Delhi and Lucknow: Lucknow Publishing House, 1974), 42.

[32]Translated from the official book of *Worship and Discipline* in C. H. Loeblin, *The Sikhs and Their Scriptures*, Third Edition (Delhi: I.S.P.C.K., 1974), 42.

[33]Ibid., 390.

[34]Nielsen, *Religions of the World*, 377.

[35]"The Parsi community consists of Parsis who are descended from the original Persian immigrants and who are born of both Zoroastrian parents and who profess Zoroastrian religion, the Iranis from Persia professing the Zoroastrian religion, who come to India either temporarily or permanently, and the children of Parsi fathers by alien mothers who have been duly and properly admitted into the religion." A legal opinion of the Indian courts quoted in Baird, *Indian Religious Traditions*, 96.

[36]Bachi J. Karkaria, "Keeping Alive the Sacred Flame," *The Illustrated Weekly of India*, Jan. 22, 1978, 22.

[37]Taken from "In the Footprints of Vivekananda," in the newspaper, *The Hindu* (Sunday, May 10, 1981): 22.

[38]Quoted in *Religious Hinduism*, 299.

[39]S. Radhakrishnan, *Recovery of Faith* (New Delhi: Orient Paperbacks, 1967), 146.

9 Religion in China

Themes in Chinese Religion

Chinese and Indian civilizations are the two oldest continuous civilizations known to humankind. The earliest Chinese dynasty mentioned in ancient chronicles, but not yet confirmed by archaeology, is the Xia (2205–1760 B.C.E.), which is followed by the Shang (1766–1122 B.C.E.). During Shang and Zhou times (1122–256 B.C.E.) practices and beliefs emerged which are a permanent part of the religions of the Chinese people. Let us turn to these early beliefs and practices, which may be called "themes in Chinese religions."

Yang and Yin

An early myth of creation refers to a cosmic, man Pan Ku, who appeared at a time when the elements were just dividing themselves: the heavier (*yin*) from the lighter (*yang*). From early Zhou times nature was seen to consist of these two. All things were a combination of two contrasting yet complementary energies with one dominant and the other recessive. Not only things, but persons, events, and ideas could be explained by these forces. *Yang* was masculine while *yin* was feminine. From there the contrasts are easy to follow, as *yang* is active, bright, positive, dry, south side of the

The Great Wall of China stands as a symbol of their heroic efforts to shut out the invasion of foreign powers and cultures. Tom White

hill, fire, and warmth while *yin* is passive, dark, negative, moist, north side of the hill, and cool. While contrasting, they are also complementary as is portrayed by the two nesting-teardrops symbol, one dark and the other light, both surrounded by a circle. The heavens, which are dominated by the sun, are predominantly *yang* while the earth is *yin*. This was more than a primitive taxonomy; it was a way to explain the nature of things and constituted a method of determining values. Men are superior to women as heaven is superior to earth. It provided a simple dichotomy by which the complexity of life and experience could be explained. Hence the spirit world, a permanent concern of the Chinese people, consisted of two main categories: the *shen* spirits, which were benevolent or at least benign, and the *kuei*, which were evil, negative, or *yin*. The spiritual aspect of the person, *hun*, was *yang* since it joined the ancestors upon death, while the bodily form was *p'o*, or *yin*, as it went into the ground and, if evil, roamed the world to haunt and bedevil. The *yang-yin* conception served a multitude of purposes in Chinese civilization, including that of artists whose landscape paintings, so world famous, presented their vision in major-minor, dominant-recessive, host-guest motifs.

> *Yin* and *Yang*: opposite and complementary energy forces which served the Chinese in explaining continuity and change in things as well as human experience.

Tian

During the Shang period a supreme ancestor or deity was worshiped called Shang Ti, or Ti. Shang Ti means literally "ruler" and "high," respectively, suggesting the one who rules from on high. He was not well defined though he lived in the heavens and his will could be determined through divination processes which the Shang used regularly. During the Zhou another name occurs which gradually replaces Shang Ti, that of Tian (heaven). While the word could refer simply to the vault above,

or even nature, it also meant a supreme power governing the world in ethical ways. Tian hears all, sees all, and rewards for virtue while punishing evil. Tian was the tutelary ancestor of the Zhou emperor, who was called Tian-zi, "Son of Heaven." The common people did not worship Tian, but the Zhou emperor made sacrifices to Tian on behalf of his people at the winter solstice. In later centuries an altar to Heaven was erected at the imperial capital where offerings of incense, jade, silk, and rice alcohol were made annually until the end of the Qing dynasty in 1911.

One of a pair of gilded lions guarding the entrance of a palace in the Forbidden City, Beijing. This one, positioned on the right was yin *or female while the other was* yang *or male.* J. Lewis

The Spirit World

The Chinese believed the world was inhabited by a myriad of spirits. Some were of greater and some of lesser importance. As Tian was heaven so She chi was "Earth," a power worshiped by the people for its connection with fertility and good crops. In every village a mound of earth was erected where, at the spring equinox, local leaders could make offerings. There is evidence this practice was so important that an altar to Earth was finally erected in Beijing along with the one to Heaven. The Tian-zi would place offerings to the Earth spirit at the summer solstice.

Local spirits were of many kinds and fell into the categories of good or evil. Like deities in the *Rigveda*, they were heavenly, atmospheric, and earthly in their sphere of operation. It was widely believed that spirits haunted dark, difficult, and lonely places. Certain animal forms were associated with both evil and good spirits, respectively. Demons were associated with snakes, tigers, and dogs while good spirits were associated with the phoenix, turtle, and dragon. A folk wisdom emerged on how to cope with evil spirits and how to ensure the presence of good ones. As fire and light were associated with good spirits, any harbingers of the light warded off evil spirits. The rooster, whose crowing signaled the approach of dawn, was depicted in prominent places to assure good luck. At the New Year firecrackers not only scared the evil spirits away with their noise but more importantly gave a brief and brilliant burst of light that dispelled evil spirits. While not all Chinese were always conscious of these ideas, many were and practices developed that have endured until today, perhaps picking up additional associations along the way.

Dao

Dao (also Tao) refers to the way a road or river goes. But as expressed in the text *Dao De Jing* (*The Book of the Virtuous Way*) it also means the way things should go. A single force was thought to govern the relationship of all things to each other. There was a mysterious force, the Dao, which worked for the integration of things harmoniously. This Dao was eternal and worked, if unhindered by people, toward prosperity, happiness, health, and peace. It was to become a topic of much speculation, and with the writing of the *Dao De Jing*, a movement emerged attracting many followers which profoundly influenced Chinese culture in the areas of religion, government, art, and daily life.

Ancestor Worship

As early as Shang times there is evidence of the worship of ancestors. The famous Shang bronze vases were used not only to worship Ti as supreme power but also as the supreme ancestor. Ti granted rain as well as good harvests and was expected to express approval of the emperor's plans. Divination practices emerged to determine the will of the ancestors. Since that time a close association has existed between the Chinese people and their departed ancestors and is expressed through both simple and elaborate rituals occasionally accompanied by divination practices.

Textual reinforcements for this long-established practice are found in the

The Temple of Heaven. Beijing. From the 15th century until 1912, the Emperor, as Son of Heaven, annually conducted religious ceremonies in homage to the Lord of Heaven. J. Lewis

Book of History (Shu Jing), which pictures the ancestors of the Zhou dynasty dwelling "on high" and enjoying a special relationship to the heavenly ruler. In such a position they were able to withhold as well as grant blessing. The implication of these beliefs was not only that one lived on after death but that the dead had extraordinary power to influence the welfare of the living. Furthermore, family solidarity was not ended at the death of a progenitor but was extended into the afterlife. The rule of the elderly in life continued after death with special ceremonies in their honor. Rituals were performed by the ranking male of the family, thus making a special priesthood unnecessary. It has been observed that ancestor worship supported polygamy and concubinage since a male heir was essential to the perpetuation of the family lineage. The family must be continued by any means and at any cost.

The departed dead were considered guardians of family affairs: they were benefactors when pleased but able to punish when displeased. They guarded the morality, good name, virtue, and honor of the family and hence ancestor worship had an important ethical function in Chinese society. It was essential to at least announce important plans or in some cases gain their approval for marriages, purchases of land, or any activity that significantly affected family life.

A portion from *The Book of Poetry (Shi Jing)* preserves the kind of thoughts that well may have been expressed by those making ancestor offerings.

Ah, the glorious ancestors-
endless their blessings,
Boundless their gifts are extended;
To you, too, they needs must reach.
We have brought them clear wine;
They will give victory.
Here, too, is soup well seasoned,
Well prepared, well mixed.
Because we come in silence,
Setting all quarrels aside,
They make safe for us a ripe old age,
We shall reach the withered cheek, we shall
*   go on and on. . . .*
[The ancestors] come, they accept, they send
*   down blessings numberless.*[1]

Literature attributed to Confucius gave specific support for and instruction concerning the proper worship of ancestors. Though he did not express very much support for otherworldly concerns, he repeatedly gave advice on how to reverence the deceased, how long to mourn, and what should be one's inner motive and attitude in it all. This is made clear in passages dealing with *xiao* (filial piety), which is one of the five Confucian principles.

Practices in ancestor worship have

varied greatly both in ancient and modern times among the Chinese people. Ancestor worship was not only expressed to family members but could be extended to certain prominent sages and heroic figures. Ceremonies for deceased family members and others consisted of funeral rites, postfuneral mourning on the death anniversary, and other occasions associated with Buddhist and Daoist traditions. Usually only three generations were revered by the living family members in keeping with Confucian instruction.

Altar to ancestors in a Chinese Malaysian home. J. Lewis

While practices of the past may not perfectly correspond with those known in the present, let us take what we might find in modern Taiwan, Hong Kong, or Malaysia as representative situations. Upon death the corpse is dressed in grave clothes, appropriately called "longevity clothes" in acknowledgment of the Chinese respect for the elderly. In all the ceremonies the eldest son officiates and leads. There may be periods of controlled and formalized weeping during specified times. Friends as well as distant relatives come to join in the affair, which may last from one to three days. The coffin, perhaps prepared long in advance, is positioned in the main room of the home. The ceremony is complex or simple, expensive or inexpensive, or long or short depending on a number of factors, especially whether the deceased is male, a father, rich, and influential. After ceremonies in the home are completed, the coffin will be carried, by cart or motorized vehicle, to the burial ground. A photo of the deceased is usually displayed on the coffin or held by relatives leading the procession. Some Chinese still follow the ancient *li* (prescribed ritual) by wearing coarse mourning clothes of white muslin. The cemetery may be a general one for all persons of the Chinese community or, in some cases, maintained for the dead of a particular clan. Before the final rites at the cemetery, paper miniatures of a house or an automobile may be burned, thus transferring these objects to the afterworld for the relative's use. Finally the coffin is placed in the ground and after final rituals, sometimes led by Buddhist priests, funeral professionals, or a combination of both, earth covers the coffin and the mourners depart.

This may not complete the mourning for, in some cases, special ceremonies will be conducted for one to three years on the death anniversary. After the funeral, the attention shifts from the cemetery to the home or, in special cases, to a separate shrine. Some clans maintain a shrine or temple-alcove for the ancestral tablet on which the name of the deceased is ceremonially inscribed as a memorial. Also, daily and periodic offerings will be made at an ancestral altar positioned in a prominent part of the home. This altar is the family's most precious possession and is made of beautiful woods often with idyllic scenes inlaid with mother-of-pearl. Presents of incense, fruit, chicken or duck, tea or alcohol, flowers, and lighted candles bedeck the altar and are attended to daily with respect by those who speak to the ancestors silently or in lowered voice.

Annually on All Souls' Day special ceremonies mark the return of the ancestors to review family affairs. A place may be set at the eating table. Chinese may be observed presenting food at the ancestral temple accompanied by divination procedures to inquire if the ancestors have been pleased with what was given. A young boy, representing the family, will take two wooden blocks shaped like the halves of a mango seed and drop them on the floor in front of the altar. If they rest in an auspicious way the family will be satisfied that the offering has been received. If not, the family will continue to drop the blocks until they fall properly.

Confucius According to the Analects

Sources

The *Analects* (c. 100 B.C.E.) have been thought by the Chinese to contain the

Terracotta Warriors. Tomb of the 3rd century B.C.E. Chin Emperor. Xian. Larger than life soldiers were buried to ensure a good afterlife in the emperor's tomb city. Max Sawyer

ideas, if not the exact words, of Confucius. It is one of the so-called Four Books of classical Chinese thought, the others being *The Doctrine of the Mean, The Great Learning*, and the *Book of Mencius*. To what degree the *Analects* faithfully record Confucius' teaching is difficult to tell. The book purports to be a collection of the sayings of Confucius and dialogues with his disciples. Said to have been written during or shortly after Confucius' time, the *Analects* were destroyed by the Qin dynasty (221–206 B.C.E.) in one of the infamous book-burning incidents of history. As they opposed Confucian ideas in political matters, the Qin collected all subversive books and put them to the torch. The Han successors are said to have rewritten the classics, but it is not known whether their recreation was entirely faithful. All we can say is that the *Analects* purport to represent Confucius. According to Chinese materials, who was Confucius and why was he so influential?

Life and Times

The dates of Confucius are traditionally given as from 551 to 479 B.C.E. He lived during the Eastern Zhou (771–221 B.C.E.) dynasty, which in its earlier time had consolidated holdings of many petty kingdoms. But the Zhou family had lost its control to a great extent. Though they were still titular heads of government performing annual ceremonies and functions of religion and state, the real power lay among a collection of semi-independent principalities. The *Analects* suggest that these principalities were constantly at war with each other, using ruthless measures to achieve their ends. Historians call the period concluding the Western Zhou the "Warring States" (403–221 B.C.E.) period. Born in humble circumstances in the province of Lu in modern Shandong, Confucius first held a petty position and then became prime minister. After his counsels were ignored he sought a wider audience and set out in 497 B.C.E. to seek support for his program of social and political reform. He returned to Lu without having had great success and died in 479.

Confucius was primarily a teacher or adviser at court. He was a master of the Five Classics, which emerged perhaps in the eighth century, and is said to have himself worked through

them, editing them as he went. His knowledge of these classics—*The Book of History*, *The Book of Poetry*, *The Book of Changes*, *The Book of Rites*, and *The Spring and Autumn Annals* (believed by many to have been written by Confucius himself)—meant he could advise and train on all topics of revered wisdom and knowledge including law, government, moral conduct, duty to ancestors, elders, and the spirits. He offered his services believing that society was in such corrupt and degenerated status that a recommitment to the ideals of the past was the only way to return to the harmony of the past. What was Confucius' program for social, governmental, and personal reform? According to him there were clearly marked principles which, if followed, would enable society to enjoy the peace and happiness of the golden days of the past.

The First Principle: *Li*

Li has several meanings: appropriate behavior, obligatory manners or customs, ceremony, ritual, and propriety. *Li* was not a call for the establishing of rules but for the observing of rules already existing. It could apply to actions of emperors in relation to the spirits or persons in everyday affairs. It is the code which guides all conduct. It is not so much the specifics of a code as it is the obligation to conform to a standard or ideal which is established and accepted. *Li* is acting obligingly and in keeping with socially approved ways. The problem, according to Confucius, was that his contemporaries had forgotten *li* or had chosen to ignore the *li* of the past. This resulted in disharmony and chaos. A portion of the *Analects* on *li* follows:

Duke Ai asked Confucius, "What is this great Li? Why is it that you talk about Li as though it were such an important thing?"

Confucius replied, "Your humble servant is really not worthy to understand Li."

"But you constantly speak about it," said Duke Ai.

Confucius: "What I have learned is this, that of all the things that people live by, Li is the greatest. Without Li, we do not know how to conduct a proper worship of the spirits of the universe; or how to establish the proper status of the king and the ministers, the ruler and the ruled, and the elders and the juniors; or how to establish the moral relationships between the sexes; between parents and children, and between brothers; or how to distinguish the different degrees of relationships in the family. That is why a gentleman holds Li in such high regard."[2]

Li then is a principle that binds details of a code of conduct together and makes it obligatory. It is acting in the appropriate way.

Second Principle: *Ren*

A person who performed *li* was one who embodied *ren*: humaneness, human-heartedness, or virtue. It has the idea of loving others, though this was not extended universally. It certainly applied to family relations and intensified according to ascending rank. One with lesser rank observed *ren* in greater degree when dealing with those of superior rank. The Chinese character for *ren* has two components: "man" and "two," thus indicating the idea of humaneness between two persons. It was not enough to go through the external motions of obligatory behavior (*li*). One had also to feel it in the heart. The *Analects* say, "If a man

is not humane (Ren), what has he to do with ceremonies (Li)?" This word is also sometimes translated "altruism" since it contained the idea of concern for others. This concern was according to rank, and knowing the ranks and the appropriate way one treated persons who were in those ranks was what *li* was all about. Chinese society in classical times was not an egalitarian society but rather highly stratified. Everyone played an assigned role observing appropriate obligations in a fixed society of order. Nevertheless, it was required that one feel one's obligations and thus be humane and virtuous.

Third Principle: *Xiao*

This principle had profound importance for society and government. In all probability it was not new with Confucius, for in many ways his work was to preserve the past and transmit or mediate it to his own generation. *Xiao* is filial piety or filiality. The Chinese ideograph has two components: "old" under which is "son." This indicates that the older is supported by the younger and that the son has the responsibility for this. Each family member is expected to play an assigned role, showing respect and performing duty until death. The place of the father, husband, and eldest son is that of authority. All members of the family know their status and position in relation to these figures. In life there is to be unquestioned obedience and deference. At death, ceremony is to accompany their burial and rituals are performed to honor them in the afterlife. While Confucius seems somewhat indifferent to the spirit world, he supported ancestor worship. "The Master said, 'While the parents are living, serve them with Li; when they die, bury them with Li; sacrifice to them with Li.' "[3]

The family was to be governed by the authority of the ranking male, whether father or eldest son. This authority pattern provided a model for government itself and was extended to the five ranks of human relationships: ruler to subject; senior to junior; father to son; husband to wife; and elder brother to younger brother. Filiality was to be expressed in all these ranks. It was believed that as each performed his or her assigned role in a deferring way, harmony in the home would lead to harmony in society. Similarly, at the top of society, if the emperor would care for the people as a father cared for his children, then prosperity and happiness would result. If not, then he could lose *ming*, or the mandate of heaven permitting him to rule.

Fourth Principle: *Shu*

This is sometimes called the principle of mutuality or reciprocity. Fung Yu-Lan describes it as "conscientiousness to others."[4] It is embodied in this famous saying attributed to Confucius: "Do not do unto others what you would not like done unto you." This has its obvious similarity to the teaching of Jesus, which by contrast is cast in the positive mode: "Do unto others what you would have them do unto you." But it has been praised for its high ethical ideal and civilizing influence across the centuries. The character used for *shu* carries with it the idea of fellow feeling or mutual

consideration. Confucius is quoted as having said:

> There are four things in the moral life of man, not one of which I have been able to carry out in my life. To serve my father as I would expect my son to serve me: that I have not been able to do. To serve my sovereign as I would expect a minister under me to serve me: that I have not been able to do. To act toward my elder brother as I would expect my younger brother to act towards me: that I have not been able to do. To be the first to behave towards friends as I would expect them to behave towards me: that I have not been able to do.[5]

Fifth Principle: *Chung*

This is "loyalty." Loyalty along with reciprocity, filial piety, and humaneness dictate appropriate behavior. Loyalty to those higher in rank was to be unquestioned and constant. When these qualities were combined in a cultured individual—as was Confucius' goal—that individual was called the "Ideal Man" or the Zhun-zi (also Chun-Tzu). He was a man truly fit to rule as opposed to one who ruled merely by hereditary right. Confucius sought to develop the man who through personal exemplification could reverse the moral decline of his day and return to the golden age of the ancients. The Zhun-zi was one who was ideal in every sense of the word: trained in music, poetry, martial arts, personal decorum, and mental prowess. Through him, and those who would follow his lead, Confucius hoped to achieve his religious goal: happiness for society and the individuals in it, now and for the future.

Interpreters and Opponents of Confucius

Meng-zi

Confucius' disciple Meng-zi (often spelled Mencius) lived from 372 to 289 B.C.E. Like Confucius, he tried his hand in some minor government positions, but because his advice to rulers to accept Confucian ideals went unheeded, he withdrew somewhat from society. He believed the Confucian principles could rescue society and became the second-leading Confucian of Chinese history.

While Confucius believed human nature was such that humans would do good if given the proper example, Meng-zi believed in the innate goodness of humanity. Two famous passages are: "The tendency of man's nature to do good is like the tendency of water to flow downward. There are none but have this tendency to good, just as all water flows downward." "If men become evil, that is not the fault of their original endowment."[6] All persons have goodness, feelings of respect and shame, a sense of right and wrong in them as "seeds" or "shoots" which are ready to grow. This is true not just of the wise sages of the past but of all persons, since all possess the nature of a sage.

This inner nature is good but must be developed through education and self-cultivation. Meng-zi looked at the inner goodness of humankind as a seedling needing development or a seed needing to be nourished. The inner nature included feelings of sympathy, modesty, shame, and right and wrong. He proved that compassion or sympathy was natural to humanity by citing what happens when one sees a child about to fall into a well. Without thinking of the fact that the child is not a relative nor that an act to save will bring the praise of his or her fellows, a person naturally acts to save the child. This is a seed virtue natural to humankind. When these innate feelings are cultivated they lead naturally to the full flowering of the Confucian virtues. From feelings of sympathy will emerge *ren*. Out of shame will come *yi* (righteousness). Through cultivation of modesty comes *li* (propriety) and from developing a sense of right and wrong will come *chih* (wisdom).

Meng-zi was not unaware of other tendencies in human beings, but these could be controlled so that evil was avoidable through the cultivation of what was innately good. What plan did Meng-zi have to develop the innate goodness of humankind? Certainly there must be good example and good teaching. The emperor and the nobles must provide a proper example. But direct teaching was of greatest value for character formation. "If men have satisfied their hunger, have clothes to wear, and live at ease but lack good teaching they are close to the birds and the beasts."[7] Teachers aid students to develop their minds, which in turn helps them to know their true nature. "He who has completely developed his mind, knows his nature, He who knows his nature, knows Heaven."[8] Parental guidance and a good environment were needed. Education was essential and hence Meng-zi wed Confucian principles to scholarship, which in time established Confucian ideals as the core curriculum of the civil-service examinations of the Han dynasty and thereafter until the twentieth century. But good teaching must be supplemented by the practice of "self-cultivation." One must engage in the practice of the principles of *shu* and *chung*. These reduce selfishness and lead naturally to other virtues.

Xun-zi

A later contemporary of Meng-zi, Xun-zi (298–238 B.C.E.), took exception to both Confucius and Meng-zi. He rejected the Confucian belief that human nature is innately good. Contrariwise, human nature is essentially bad, though goodness could be learned if properly reinforced and the individual trained. If left to oneself, the seeds of human nature would grow up to be crooked and worthless plants. He said: "The nature of man is evil. . . . Therefore to give rein to man's original nature, to follow man's feelings, inevitably results in strife and rapacity. . . . Crooked wood needs to undergo steaming and bending to conform to the carpenter's rule."[9]

The belief in the evil and selfish nature of humanity had its implications for those who rule. Virtuous example by the emperor* was not enough to produce good results. As human nature was rebellious and disorderly, a rule of conduct had to be enforced to guide people's conduct. While *li*, according to Confucius, meant decorum and propriety, this was reinterpreted by Xun-zi to mean enforced propriety or in simple terms laws, rules, and codes of behavior with appropriate sanctions or punishments. His ideas bore a close resemblance to the School of Law, probably founded by an earlier contemporary, Shang Yan (t. 338 B.C.E.), which became the guiding ideas of the authoritarian and repressive but successful Qin dynasty (221–206 B.C.E.)

Mo-zi

Mo-zi (471–391 B.C.E.) opposed Confucian thought with his view that the ranks of ruler-subject, senior-junior, etc. should be rejected. Mo-zi sought to level society and bring down the elitism he saw advocated by Confucius. Confucius focused his hopes for harmony on leaders and high-ranking persons in society; in their hands lay the possibility of peace, happiness, and social harmony. Mo-zi asserted the doctrine of "universal love," saying that all people should treat all people with care and concern and no special consideration should be given on the basis of rank and position. Confucius placed a value on loyalty and piety to one's family. Mo-zi felt this would never lead to harmony since one's interest was directed too narrowly. All families, all states, all people should have a universal care and concern which transcended the narrow sets of Confucian relationships. Furthermore, he believed this was the will of Heaven, whom he believed was a personal deity who watched over human affairs with great concern. Heaven directly involved himself in human affairs by rewarding good and punishing evil. Mo-zi's writings show a profound interest in the divine-human interrelationship in contrast to Confucius, who was mostly indifferent to things transcendent excepting in the areas of filial piety and respect for ancestors.

The Religion of the Dao De Jing

Lao-zi

Traditionally the *Dao De Jing* has been assigned to Lao-zi, whose dates are disputed butassigned anywhere from 600 to 400 B.C.E. Most scholars are unwilling to positively identify Lao-zi as the author of the book because the very historicity of Lao-zi itself is not established and nowhere is his name given in the book. What follows is a discussion of the religion of the *Dao De Jing* and its ideas.

Without doubt the book reflects ideas about the Dao that are very ancient. They were taken up by many and restated in ways which opposed Confucian ideas. Confucius believed society could return to harmony and stability only as each person understood role and status, kept within his or her assigned rank, and related to others according to the virtuous principles of life: *li, ren, shu, chung,* and *xiao*. Each must play an assigned role in a ranked society held together by authority. This seemed elitist to some, unproductive in the view of others, and pointless to yet others.

For example, Yang-zi of the fourth century B.C.E. felt tranquillity could never be society-wide and advocated an "each man for himself" policy. This uncharacteristic individualism did not set well with Confucians, whom he shocked with the statement that even if he could save the whole world by plucking a single hair from his shank, he wouldn't do it. Lao-zi and others like him took a somewhat similar view

which said that social harmony was indeed a function of individual harmony. Society could find tranquillity but only by individuals getting in step with nature. Efforts to conform individuals to Confucian social norms were both unnatural and unnecessary. The *Dao De Jing* makes the individual the focus and harmony with the Dao the religious goal. The *Analects* made society the focus and happiness through observance of traditional principles the religious goal.

The Dao

The word *Dao* (way, path, road) has many meanings, including the way of the road or the way of the river. The riverbed is the way the river goes. But in the *Dao De Jing* the word refers to the way things are meant to go. Things are meant to go naturally, without interference and restriction. The Dao is mysterious and unquantifiable. Words cannot lead you to it with certainty, and function only to point you toward it. It is wrapped in mystery and is shadowy. But it is nonetheless real. It is that which is behind or within the power or energy of the world. It is that singular reality which stands behind all that is and when understood and incorporated into life leads to harmony. It is obvious that the Dao is not known through direct inquiry or formal analysis but is sensed or, better put, apprehended intuitively. The opening chapter of the *Dao De Jing* states:

> The Tao that can be told of is not the eternal Tao;
> The name that can be named is not the eternal name.
> The Nameless is the origin of Heaven and Earth;

The Named is the mother of all things.[10]

The Confucians were concerned broadly about harmony between heaven and earth and practically about order in human society. The *Dao De Jing* held that heaven and earth attain complete harmony by letting the Dao take its course. The task of rulers was to attune themselves to the Dao, to get in step with the Dao, to conform to the Dao. The problem, implied in the *Dao De Jing*, is that rulers have made their own plans as to how to achieve harmony without concern for what was natural and noninterfering. Out of this penchant for rules and principles spring the ills of society. The current of the Dao flows in one way while rulers, including the Confucians, swim against it.

The Dao may be thought of as the natural way things are intended to go: harmoniously, effortlessly, without striving or self-assertion. Action consistent with the Dao is natural or effortless. Individuals and societies that do not understand the Dao work against it and never succeed; they ruin themselves through strivings and rules which are not in step with nature. But in the end the Dao has its way. One may swim against the current rather than with it and in the process drown! Governments, sages, and societies may fly in the face of the Dao and achieve some temporary success, but in the end their efforts will fail.

An inexorable law determines that things will always return to the natural way, the way they were intended to be. This eventual return to nature is called the principle of the "reversal of

the Dao." When operating against the Dao a point is reached where it is exhausted. It is certain you must reverse and return to the point from which you started. The bow may be stretched only to a point, then it returns. The sword may be sharpened, but if you go too far it becomes dull, just as it was before you began. For those following the Dao it was inevitable that Confucian conformist principles would come to an end and things would return to the way things were intended to go. "Returning is the motion of the Dao."[11]

The Sage and the Dao

Those followers of the *Dao De Jing* and similar Daoist writings viewed their main contribution to society to consist in personally modeling the lifestyle that was best suited to meet the chaos of the times. They acted spontaneously, naturally, and without affectation. To be in touch with the Dao meant positively that one acted in quietude, sought to act without self-assertion and work, yet without striving. The *Dao De Jing* placed the emphasis on an enlightened quietude: "Attain complete vacuity. Maintain steadfast quietude."[12] This did not mean passivity nor mere "do-nothingism" but activity which would not interfere in the smooth and natural course of things. It meant to observe *Wu-wei*.

Wu-wei

Wu-wei is sometimes defined as quietism, nonaggressive or nonmeddling acts. It had the idea of noninterference. It was not passivism nor donothingism. It did not mean to stand by and let the world pass you by, though this is the way some recluses and ascetics took it. Indeed, there was a strong "stay at home" and "live in nature" attitude. But at its heart it meant acting, yet so as to avoid wrongly acting. It came close to do-nothingism but with this important difference. One could and should act, but always in conformity with nature or the Dao. "Do nothing and everything is done" meant that one's acts were so in harmony with the Dao that one did no interfering, disruptive, contrary-to-the-Dao acts. No acts at all were right acts if they were in harmony with the Dao. Acts were right and proper if they were in step with the Dao. The Dao was not inactive; it acted. So the sage got in step with the Dao by acting but with noninterference.

The Dao and Politics

One might wonder how such a position could be seriously advocated as a viable principle for the body politic. How could a ruler rule if *wu-wei* was a first-order principle? It is obvious that Daoist thought is close to laissez-faire. That government rules best which rules least. "Get government out of daily affairs" might be the Daoist watchword. "If kings and princes could but hold fast to this principle, all things would work out their own reformation."[13] The Daoists believed that rules, prescribed ways of behaving (Confucian *li*), laws, and restrictions inhibited the flow of the Dao. "The greater the number of laws and enactments, the more thieves and robbers there will be."[14] The *Dao De Jing* gives us a picture of the ideal community living in harmony with the Dao.

Take a small country with a small population. It might well be that there were machines which saved labor ten times or a hundred times, and yet the people would not use them. . . . They would not emigrate to distant countries. Although there might be carriages and boats, no one would ride in them. Although there might be weapons of war, no one would issue them.[15]

According to the Dao there is no room for measures of aggression and war though there may be some room for self-defense. There is even a better way.

Therefore, if a great kingdom humbles itself before a small kingdom, it shall make that small kingdom its prize. And if a small kingdom humbles itself before a great kingdom, it shall win over that great kingdom. Thus the one humbles itself in order to attain, the other attains because it is humble. If the great kingdom has no further desire than to bring men together to nourish them, the small kingdom will have no further desire than to enter the service of the other. But in order that both may have their desire, the great one must learn humility.[16]

The Dao and Personal Longevity

The concern to live in harmony with nature led to the belief that there were ways to prolong life and prevent the processes of decay from setting in. Personal immortality was believed to be a distinct possibility, and various methods were explored toward this end including alchemy, breathing exercises, restricted diet, and potions of eternal youthfulness. These concerns are sometimes called "religious Daoism" to distinguish them from the concerns of "philosophical Daoism" as described above. But to the extent that any concern is a dominating one in one's life, it is a religious concern. The *Dao De Jing* gives advice to those interested in longevity and eternal life. For example, it says that those who understand the Dao become immune to the attack of wild animals and armed men. It states: "He who attains the Dao is everlasting." Another influential Daoist book along this line is *Zhuang-zi* (also *Chuang Tze*), which is attributed to the person of that name. It tells the story of a person who, though of great age, had the complexion of a child. Upon inquiry it was revealed the secret was in knowing the Dao. This secret was not gained by study but through the instruction of a sage who could transcend the mundane world and the whole of material existence. He could even transcend the past and present and had entered the state where death was no more. Such stories sparked great interest and the nobility openly sought the elixir of life during the Han dynasty. The common people were not unaffected by this, and in time Daoist shrines and temples emerged which incorporated divination, meditation, rituals, and ceremonies designed to enhance life, avoid danger, secure a long life, and guarantee a better future in the beyond. It took many forms from spiritism and spirit possession to divination, fortune-telling, and herbal potents. Such practices are found widely among the Chinese today in free Chinese communities of Asia and elsewhere. Thompson offers this comment concerning the place of Daoist priests and practitioners among Chinese today: "The main functions of the Taoist are exorcism and the protection of the well-being and security of the mortal world against the attacks of Kuei, and performance of rituals on behalf of clients and community."[17]

Chinese Followers of the Buddha

It is not known precisely when Buddhist traditions were introduced to China, but it is widely believed Buddhist missionaries came as early as the first century C.E. Early on it was considered an occult sect and even a Daoist variation. At certain points early Buddhist beliefs and practices were similar enough to Daoist ideas that it was speculated that Lao-zi must have been the Buddha's teacher. It was not until the third and fourth centuries C.E. when Buddhist *sutras* had adequate Chinese translations, that the scriptural ideals of Indian Buddhist schools were understood. Thus the *Tipitaka* and Mahayana texts became available to the Chinese in their own language, though the Mahayana texts had greater appeal.

The Chinese understanding of Buddhist texts varied considerably at certain points and led throughout history to the rise of new ideas and distinctive Chinese movements. For example, while the *Tipitaka* taught that the *atman* was nonpermanent the Chinese, at least during the later Han period, frequently failed to accept the radicalness of such doctrine. Through Mahayana influence it was broadly believed among some Chinese Buddhists that the soul was indestructible. In holding to this they were close to traditional views of the Chinese that a person, upon death, became a spirit with knowledge and feeling which could harm or help. Even Confucians believed spirits survived death as seen in the practice of "the recall of the departed spirits" where relatives would call out for the dead to return to the body.

But Buddhist notions sometimes conflicted with popular thought as well. The suppression of desires and the attempt to limit attachment was not found in either Daoist or Confucian thought and served to create suspicion and doubt about the new religion.

A fact which influenced the interpretation of Buddhist ideas among the Chinese was that early translations of Indian Sanskrit texts were often inadequate and even misleading. Complex ideas of the original texts were sometimes garbled or misinterpreted by the Chinese terms used to convey them. It is believed that Daoists were among the earliest Chinese to be interested in translation efforts and they preferred to use their vocabulary. This inevitably led to a less than accurate rendering. When more accurate translations were completed in the fourth and fifth centuries C.E., ideas had already gained acceptance which were impossible to completely correct.

The Buddhist School of Chan

Though its ideas were introduced long before, Chan gained an influential and even dominating position among intellectual Buddhists in China from the tenth century onward. Also called *dhyana* (Skt., meditation; of which the Chinese and Japanese is *chan* and *zen*, respectively) it traces itself back to Bodhidharma (C.E. 470–543), who is called the first patriarch of the Chinese school. Little credible evidence exists about Bodhidharma, but he is said to have come from a Kshatriya or Brahman family in southern India. He was sent as a missionary to China by his teacher Prajnatara and after three years travel arrived in Guangzhou (Canton) around C.E. 500. His chief disciple was Hui-k'o, who learned meditation and studied the *Lankavatara Sutra* under Bodhidharma. He died in Lo-yang. He was said to have been a bad linguist whose Chinese was poor and wrote nothing scholars can attribute to him. It should be noted however, that many manuscripts discovered at Tunhuang in northern China in the early twentieth century are ascribed to him but were probably written by later Chan monks.

Early Chan

The *Tipitaka* scriptures contain much instruction on meditation (*dhyana*). Some of these were translated by Chinese scholars as early as about C.E. 150, two of which are entitled: *The Sutra Spoken by the Buddha on Keeping Thought in the Manner of Great Anapana*, and *The Sutra on Perception in the Law of Practice of Meditation*.[18] A second major wave of translations came with Kumarajiva's efforts from C.E. 402 to 412.

Chan as a School

Early on, until about the fourth century in China, those interested in Buddhist thought were not much concerned with the contradictory nature of the flood of texts coming out of India. For one thing, the translations from Sanskrit were known to be imperfect, and the fine points of distinction in the original Sanskrit were often

incorrectly or inadequately made in translation. Some Chinese Buddhists concluded that the distinctions, whatever their merit, were not really so important. Whatever the distinctions of language, it was the experience toward which the language pointed that counted. Tao-sheng (C.E. 360–434) said: "The function of a symbol is to illustrate an idea, when one gets the idea, one may forget the symbol; and the purpose of a language is to explain the meaning, when one gets the meaning, the language may cease to function."[19] This he illustrated by saying that the purpose of the fish trap was to trap fish, and when the fish was in hand one could lay aside the trap. This seemed to characterize Chan attitudes toward texts and formal scholarship. Others seriously pursued the different positions of the various texts, but the history of Chan was to prefer to view this as an unnecessary and superficial matter. For Chan, it was better to have the revolutionary spirit of "getting at the essentials."

About the eighth century in China a number of schools flourished along with Chan, including Pure Land, Tian-Tai, Dharmalaksha, and The Three-Shastras. Each of these schools, having no exact parallel in India, nevertheless derived its teaching from specific Indian Buddhist texts. Chan, too, can look to certain Indian texts in translation but depended more on writings and recorded teachings of the Chinese Chan masters whose general view was to sift texts to get at the experience. This meant that textual study, recitation, memorization, elaboration, and commentary took a decided second place. Put another way, the learning of books was only instrumental to getting at the experience. Knowledge was not an end but only a means to an end.

Hui-neng and Chan

Though Bodhidharma and Tao-sheng were earlier figures in Chan development, it was really Hui-neng, the so-called Sixth Patriarch, who articulated a position that set Chan apart from all other views. He and his successors held to the following: (1) There existed from the beginning a special tradition passed from master to disciple containing the teaching of the Buddha and not found in any scripture. (2) There is no need to depend on books or writings to get to the heart of this teaching. (3) The focus was to be upon personal experience. (4) To become a Buddha one needed only to see, truly see, one's own nature as it really was.

The most fundamental truth of all,

taught Hui-neng, is that the true nature of all things, including the self, is emptiness. That is, things have no nature of their own, so whenever one must talk about things such as the mind or the Buddha (both of which were hotly debated) the most that could be said about them was "not-mind" and "not-Buddha." This application of the *Tipitaka* said nothing has existence in itself. Hence, for Hui-neng, the truth about mind was that it was nonmind and the truth about the Buddha was it was non-Buddha. Hui-neng once made this point when he offered a corrected version to the following poem:

The body is like unto the Bodhi-tree,
And the mind to a mirror bright;
Carefully we cleanse them hour by hour
Lest dust should fall upon them.

To this Hui-neng responded:

Originally there was no Bodhi-tree,
Nor was there any mirror;
Since originally there was nothing,
Whereon can the dust fall?[20]

The experience of enlightenment was when one came to a personal and existential experience of this. This could, generally, only be achieved by contact with one who had the experience. But the methods of instruction varied. Some felt that meditation was an aid and meditational techniques were used especially by the so-called northern school. But the southern school of Hui-neng, in an attempt to lead seekers to the truth that reality was inexpressible, would either respond to ignorant questions with silence or with an enigmatic response.

The *koan* (J.; C., *kung-an*), or enigmatic statement, has become one of the more well-known features of Chan. It is used both to facilitate and lead to enlightenment as well as to express its achievement. The Chan masters sought to create in their disciples a mental state whereby seekers came to the end of themselves and had exhausted their mental powers. It was believed that only when one gave up scholastic thought and logic was one properly prepared for the experience. One had to give up logic because logic stood in the way of the experience. The *koan* helped to exhaust the mind and at the right moment the intuitive insight into the true nature of self and things occurred.

An example of a *koan* is the following. "A student wanted clarification on a point of common debate and asked: 'What kind of man is he who is not linked to all things?' Ma-tsu answered: 'Wait until in one gulp you can drink up all the water in the West River, then I will tell you.'" As it was impossible to gulp all the water of the West River, so it was impossible to answer the question under debate, as it was unanswerable in the terms given. Only he who had transcended belief in "all things" could then be linked to them.

Chan accepted as true the rounds of birth and death, *karma*, and many of the assumptions of the *Tipitaka*. However, in seeking the experience of enlightenment there was no need to withdraw from the world. It was possible to achieve it in this life, in this worldly setting and without withdrawal from the world. Chan was, then, a counterestablishment movement seen by some as a threat to their more traditional ways of seeking enlightenment.

The Tian-Tai School
Mahayana Texts

Indian Buddhists were prolific in producing texts which purported to be authentic teachings of the Buddha. These took differing positions on the nature of the Buddha, the existence of the Buddha-nature, the nature of things, the character of the experience of liberation, and a whole host of other questions. They made fine but important distinctions that were not easy to understand in Sanskrit, let alone when translated into Chinese. Some of the earliest texts to be translated were the *Astasahasrika Prajnaparamita* (*Perfection of Wisdom in Eight Thousand Lines*) and *Vajracchedika* (*Diamond Sutra*). These took the position, generally, that the nature of every discrete entity (*dhatu*) was without any discriminating marks and expressed as "emptiness" or the "void."

Developed along other lines was the *Sukavativyuha sutra*, which pictured a transcendent Buddha whose merits were so great he ruled a cosmic sphere known as the Western Paradise. The Tian-Tai school, named after the mountain in Zhejiang province to which its founding monk retired to establish his monastery, sought a way to embrace the perspectives of all Buddhist texts and incorporate them into a comprehensive system.

Founding Monk

A major concern of Zhi-yi (also Chih-i) was to find a way of reconciling all the many texts which by his time (C.E.

538–97) had collected in the hands of Buddhist monks. In an attempt to accept them all with their diverse and logically contradicting positions, he came to hold that the Buddha taught all the ideas of these texts, but during the years of his earthly ministry he wisely suited his teaching to the level of maturity of the disciples. The Buddha used *upaya* (Skt., skill-in-means), which meant he gave instruction only at the disciple's level of understanding. When the lesson was mastered the Buddha would go on to higher truths. Further, he believed the Buddha's teachings were progressively more complex and complete; texts taught in the Buddha's early career were preliminary and basic. These were followed by texts with the highest truth. Zhi-yi arranged the Buddha's teachings in five stages, which was his way of accommodating all the Buddhist texts at hand and reconciling their differences.

Five Stages of Gotama's Teachings

According to Zhi-yi the Buddha presented his teachings to his disciples in five stages. (1) During the earliest period, lasting for 21 days, the Buddha taught the Hua Yan doctrine which was too difficult for his followers to understand. Realizing that its abstract doctrine of the interchangeability of all entities was beyond beginners, he determined to present a truth which they could more easily comprehend. (2) The second stage, lasting for twelve years, was spent in presenting the truth of the *Tipitaka*. Such doctrine was simpler than the first stage and constituted an example of the Buddha's *upaya*—skill in presenting truth suited to the capacity of the hearer. (3) For eight years after-

wards, the Buddha took his followers one step further into what may be

Buddhist monk holding Hua Yan Sutra. Datong, People's Republic of China. J. Lewis

called the elementary Mahayana sutras. (4) For the next 22 years the Buddha taught advanced wisdom such as that found in the *Astasahasrika Prajnaparamita Sutra*. The truth proposed there teaches that all constituent elements are empty (*shunya*) of own being (*svabhava*). Such truth had the practical advantage of leaving no place for the suffering world to cling. (5) In the final period of eight years, the Buddha was able to return to and even transcend the higher truth he had sought to teach in the very beginning. Incorporated into the *Saddharmapundarika Sutra* (*Lotus Sutra*), the doctrine presents the Buddha as a cosmic principle found in every person and object. This meant there existed the possibility that all things in the chain of being could attain Buddhahood. The Buddha is pictured surrounded by a host of attendants including *arhants*, deities, and *bodhisattvas*. Listening to him are three levels of seekers after the truth. Some are seeking enlightenment in hopes of becoming *arhants*. Others, called *pratyekabuddhas* are near enlightenment but are seeking it for personal and selfish reasons. But the ideal beings of the text are compassionate *bodhisattvas* who are postponing *nirvana* until they can rescue a host of others who need their help.

The Pure Land School

The Pure Land

This school called Jing-Tu (C., pure land; also Ching-Tu) is based on the *Sukhavativyuha Sutra*. Tan-luan (C.E. 476–542) taught that there were several paths one might pursue toward *nirvana*. But since society was in a state of moral and spiritual decay more difficult disciplines were impossible for the masses. There was a way, however, the way of faith and devotion. If one were to even once say, in faith, "I take my stand in Amitabha Buddha," it was sufficient to save. This was the "easy path." Its simplicity and popularity made it the leading school among the lay Buddhists of China until the Communist Revolution.

The Pure Land was a paradise existing in cosmic worlds to which one would go at death. It was from here that *nirvana* was guaranteed, though its pleasant surroundings and good life tended to obscure the need for further pursuit of final liberation.

The Goal and the Means

The religious goal among the Pure Land Buddhists varied as some were not fooled by the good life of the Pure Land. They viewed this heavenly paradise as only one step toward final release from *samsara*. But for the majority of Chinese Buddhists, reaching the Pure Land was quite good enough. Its heavenlike atmosphere was a satisfactory final goal and nothing beyond this was of great concern.

The means to attain the Pure Land was faith in the Buddha and devotional acts which expressed one's faith. One text indicates that if one has the means to do so, support of the temple through grants and gifts would be good, but if one is poor, even building a small temple playfully in the sand while meditating in faith would be meritorious. Practicing the recitation of the Buddha's name (*nian-fo*) was assisted by ritual prayer beads used much like the rosary in the Roman Catholic tradition. Acts of worship and devotion in the home were incorporated with ancestor worship, the two existing side by side.

Followers of the Buddha in Tibet

History

Using trade routes through northwestern India, Buddhist missionaries established communities of belief at several places between India and the

centers of Tibetan culture. However, it was not until the seventh century C.E. that Buddhist institutions gained courtly endorsement. Srong Tsan Gam Po's two wives from China and Nepal wished to practice their Buddhist beliefs, so the prince sent emissaries to invite Buddhist teachers. This was the beginning of Buddhist impact on national life. The Tibetan people were slow to accept the foreign religion but gradually adopted it under the tutelage of Bengali monk Padma-Sambhava and his associate, Shantarakshita. Padma-Sambhava followed Vajrayana or tantric practices which combined basic concepts of the *Tipitaka* with yogic meditation, sexual symbolism, and spiritism. This unique blend of Buddhist theory and practice characterizes Tibetan Buddhist believers to this day.

Buddhist beliefs were combined with indigenous Tibetan Lamaism. The word *lama* (Tib., superior one) is the equivalent to the Sanskrit word *guru* and means supreme teacher. The *lama* was a spiritual master who engaged in shamanistic practices and taught a mysterious knowledge transmitted secretly. This combination of existing Tibetan religion and Buddhist beliefs went through many changes and periods of reform.

The Buddha

Unlike the idea of the *Tipitaka* which pictures Gotama as a human being, Tibetan Buddhists accepted a view of the Buddha found in later *prajna* (wisdom) and *bhakti* (devotion) texts where the historical Buddha is regarded as only one of many cosmic Buddhas inhabiting unfathomable time and deep-space worlds. These Buddhas had their own special names, families, genealogies, and spiritual realms with mythologies which described their wives, attendants, exploits, and characteristics. Closely associated with the Buddhas were the *bodhisattvas* (enlightenment beings) who had gained great spiritual power by postponing *nirvana* because they did not want to enter enlightenment without helping others attain it too.

They were regarded as the essence of mercy and goodness for such selfless attitudes and hence were worthy of worship. While the Buddhas were cosmic and removed, the *bodhisattvas* seemed nearer and more approachable.

The Religious Goal

Many of the teachings of the *Tipitaka* are assumed in Tibetan Buddhist religion. The three marks of existence still hold, but combined with them is a devotion to the many Buddhas, *bodhisattvas* and spiritual beings. Accompanying this was a need to ward off, if possible, evil spiritual beings who were believed to populate the world and hinder spiritual progress.

Each Buddha had his female sexual counterpart. Amitabha's consort was Pandara, with whom he lived in the cosmic West. Akshobhya lived with Mamaki in the East; Tatnasambhava with Locana in the South; and Amoghasiddhi with Arya-tara in the North. Arya-tara, sometimes called simply Tara, was a popular figure whose nature could be fierce but was generally benevolent. At the center of the four cardinal points was Vairocana with his wife Vajradhatvisvari. These pairs cohabited and their descendants generated heaven and earth. This is one of many stories of cosmic origins found in Tibetan literature. One offspring of Amitabha was Avalokita, who brought the earthly figure Gotama into being.

The relationship between these couples is explicitly sexual, but the sexual element can also be seen as symbolic of the goal of the unitary experience.

On the one hand, there was a stream of thought which said that craving and passion could be overcome by repeated sexual indulgence. The idea was to rise above duality and passion by exhausting oneself in the experience of sex. On the other hand, *prajna* Buddhist texts spoke of the experience of the "void" or the "empty" characterized by nonduality. Sexual union had the benefit of giving one a real, though momentary, taste of the unitary nature of things by blissful oblivion in coitus. Tibetan Buddhist iconography has explicit sexual scenes which may, in part, be understood in view of the religious goal: overcoming desire and passion by exhausting it on the way toward the nondualistic experience.

To aid in the pursuit of *nirvana* and to secure protection from evil forces one could attach oneself to any of these Buddhas or divine beings. Aids to mystical union with the deities could be *mantras*, fasting, prayer, meditation, and devotional acts. Certain ceremonial instruments were made of human skulls and bones, thus reinforcing in nonverbal ways the message of human transience. Practical external aids included prayer beads, the famous hand-held prayer wheels (the prayer was repeated with every revolution of the wheel), and temple prayer cylinders. Priests could also perform protective rites and positive ceremonies to enhance one's progress.

The Dalai Lama

In their early history Tibetan Buddhists believed spiritual knowledge was passed to worthy recipients in a master-disciple relationship. Followers of particular *lamas* developed schools which vied for followers and courtly favor. A full account of Tibetan Buddhist developments would chronicle these schools' struggle to dominate the religious and political scene. In time, Tibetans of all schools accepted that when the ruling lama died, his successor was reincarnated as an infant. Using divination practices a child was identified as the reincarnated *lama* and taken to the monastery and given the respect and education proper to him. The current Dalai Lama is identified by the faithful as a "living Buddha" and, consistent with past Tibetan practice, is regarded as both temporal and spiritual leader of Tibetans who fled their homeland in the wake of the Communist Chinese occupation of Tibet in 1951.

Religion in China Since the Communist Revolution

The Status of Religion Before the Communist Revolution

The constitution of the new Republic established in 1911 guaranteed freedom of religion. The ruling party, the Guomindang (also, Kuomintang), or Nationalist party, saw no conflict in affirming the classical Confucian virtues as the ethical and moral basis of their government. These were loyalty, filial piety, benevolence, human-heartedness, fidelity, harmony, and peace. Later, when Jiang Jieshi (also, Chiang Kai-shek; 1887–1975) established the New Life movement (1934), four Confucian ideas were again central: *li* (propriety), *yi* (uprightness), *lien* (integrity), and *ch'ih* (self-respect). The attempt to use these principles to

effect social reform did not succeed in as much as political unity, economic health, and national peace evaded all efforts. China in the early twentieth century was torn by fratricidal strife and later, Japanese aggression. The rise of the Communists under the leadership of Mao Zedong (1893–1976) brought an end to the Republican phase of modern China and instituted a totalitarian state in which religion had no place.

The Communist Theory of Religion

A general theory about religion has guided Chinese Communists in their policies and practices toward religion. This theory follows classical Marxist ideas which hold that religion arose first in primitive societies in response to their fear of the unknown in nature. When primitives encountered natural phenomena that frightened or awed them, they mistakenly identified nature's rhythms, spectacles, and powerful events as deriving from the spiritual world. Being unscientific in their reasonings, they could not know that nature was subject to impersonal laws and forces that had nothing to do with spirits and gods. Nevertheless, they believed in them and religion was born.

As society moved toward more settled and civilized forms, classes developed and these classes began to struggle for position and power. Upper classes found the widespread belief in supernatural forces a convenient tool to control and subjugate the less powerful. Thus began the long and mutually beneficial relationship between religion and the ruling class.

The religious hope of the workers could be used to the advantage of

> Since we cannot free ourselves from various hardships brought on by serious natural and man-made disasters within a short period of time; since class struggle continues to exist within certain limits; and given the complex international environment, the long term influence of religion among a part of the people in a socialist society cannot be avoided. Religion will eventually disappear from human history. But it will disappear naturally, only through long term development of socialism and communism, when all objective requirements are met.
>
> —From "The Party's Central Committee Directive of March 1982"[21]

their oppressors by directing attention toward transcendent matters— heaven and eternal concerns. Miserable conditions of life and labor were momentarily forgotten when workers were absorbed in pursuit of God and the world to come. Religion and religious institutions demanded of believers patience in a pilgrimage that inevitably involved suffering and disappointment. The emphasis on spiritual values thus left little time for material concerns which were presented as less important, less honorable, and less pleasing to God.

According to Marxists, the clergy benefit as much as the ruling class from such an ideology. In communist understanding religious leaders are parasites on society, for they receive the fruits of the workers' efforts without contributing to the creation of wealth. They do not enter into production; they only, so to speak, take

the collection. Furthermore, Roman Catholic and Protestant churches and their missions permitted themselves to be used by imperialist opponents of communism to carry out their attacks from within the countries.

With the rise of Marxist understanding of life, politics, and economics, religion came to be seen for what it was, an enemy of the people. The overthrow of the bourgeoisie meant that religion would no longer have upper-class support since communism would satisfy the material needs of society.

Religion, like all social institutions, is governed by a dialectic. It has its own laws of origin, growth, and extinction. Because it is subject to these laws, ideally there would be no need to legislate it out of existence. Progress in socialism should be naturally accompanied by the demise of religion. In the Chinese Communist view, religion would gradually disappear with the elimination of the bourgeoisie. In theory this is the way it would work, but the history of communist treatment of religion shows that state measures were brought against it to hurry the process along.

Religion Under Mao

With the takeover of China in 1949 by the Communists, organized religion began to experience the application of the theory of religion mentioned above. Though at first moderation prevailed, in time religion was dealt a crushing though not fatal blow. All properties and lands in the hands of religious associations were appropriated through the land reform move-

Monument of the Heroes of the Communist Revolution, Tian Anmen Square, Beijing. J. Lewis

ment. Though no consistent and systematic practice was followed, it was clear from the beginning that religion was not to enjoy constitutional protections found in many other countries in the world.

The government's policies have changed and moderated somewhat since the death of Mao but are still rooted in ideological considerations found in classical Marxist thought. Based on these antireligious ideas, even Confucian ideals were denounced because they were regarded as instruments of feudal oppression of the masses. Daoists were held in contempt for beliefs that were superstitious. Persons who persisted in religious beliefs and duties were, at minimum, ostracized, and those who were uncooperative with the new system were often severely punished by imprisonment or even death. The full

story of the suffering of religious persons in the Mao era is not well known even to this day. We await the emergence of a more open Chinese society for this story to be told.

Religion Prior to the Cultural Revolution (1966–76)

Absolute repression of religion did not seem to be a major concern of the Communists in the earliest years of the revolution. It might be said that there was limited toleration, and this is reflected in the statement on religious freedom found in the first constitution. Article Eighteen states: all citizens "enjoy freedom of religious belief." A summary of the provisions includes the following. First, people who believe in a religion have freedom. Second, people who do not believe in a religion have freedom. This freedom includes the right to be against religion and those who are religious. Third, people have freedom to change religious belief. Fourth, no religious service may be held outside so-called religious buildings. To do otherwise is to infringe upon the rights of those who are against religion. Religious activities must be confined to authorized buildings such as temples, churches, synagogues, and mosques. Fifth, an individual may hold no more than one religion. In 1950 the Bureau of Religious Affairs was established to supervise religion and implement socialist policies. The bureau's major function was to neutralize those groups and individuals who might seek to use religion as a pretext for resisting communist policies for social change. This could best be implemented by forcing all religions to come under state-sponsored

(The following appeared June 1986 in the English language newspaper "China Daily" produced by Xinhua, the official news bureau of the People's Republic of China.)

Religious Belief Affirmed—Bishop Ding Re-Elected

Bishop Ding Guangxun, 71, has been re-elected President of the Christian Council of China and Chairman of the Three-Self (self-administration, self-support and self-propagation) Patriotic Movement Committee of the Protestant Churches of China.

The election took place at the fourth National Christian Conference of China which closed in Beijing on Saturday.

With a 40-year church career, Ding began to hold the leading posts in two national Christian organizations of China in 1980. He is also a member of the Standing Committee of the national People's Congress. A graduate of the Central Theological Seminary of the Chinese Anglican Church, Ding was ordained pastor in 1942. From 1946 to 1951, he studied in the New York Union Theological Seminary, serving as secretary of the Student Christian Movement of Canada and as secretary of the World Student Christian Federation in Geneva.

After returning to China in 1951, he was appointed President of the Nanking Union Theological Seminary and was consecrated bishop in 1955. He was elected Vice-Chairman of the Three-Self Patriotic Committee Movement of the Protestant Churches of China in 1961.

The conference also issued a message to Chinese Christians everywhere, urging them to make a concerted effort to maintain the Protestant churches of China and to contribute to modernization and world peace.

During the one-week conference, 280 participants revised the constitutiuons of the two organizations.

Christianity in China has succeeded in running its church independently, Xi Zhongxun, member of the Political Bureau of the Communist Party of China Central Committee, said in Beijing on Friday. Xi told the Christian conference that the Three-Self Patriotic Committee and the Christian Council of China have made outstanding contributions in helping the government implement the policy of freedom of religious belief, in training younger clergymen, in uniting Christians to take part in socialist modernization, and in safeguarding a world peace.

Xi said the past 30 years' practice has shown that the principles of self-administrating, self-supporting and self-propagating of Chinese Protestant churches is completely right.

In a related matter, another central government official said freedom of religious belief is a long lasting and fundamental policy of the Chinese Communist Party and a democratic right the Chinese people enjoy.

nationwide associations which, to some extent, resulted in effective surveillance and control of all religious groups. Accordingly, the Protestant Three-Self Patriotic movement was established in 1951. Similar Buddhist, Daoist, and Catholic associations were approved shortly thereafter.

In 1949 there were estimated to be 750,000 Protestant Christians spread through 30 denominations with a Chinese clergy assisted by 8,000 missionaries. Roman Catholic strength was estimated at 3.2 million served by 5,000 priests, of whom 2,090 were expatriates. The midfifties, prior to Mao's 1958 Great Leap Forward, were years of considerable church activity, but pressures began to build under

the massive collectivization programs instituted in that year. Thereafter most Sunday schools were closed and the forced unification of all recognized Christian bodies under the leadership of the Three-Self Patriotic movement began. This was followed by a ten-year period leading to the complete dissolution of separate denominational organizations.

As an example of state measures applied in 1958, the following is a partial list of things pastors in Shanghai were required to agree to:

1. Guarantee that eighty-five percent of their congregation would participate in every social program.

2. Learn six patriotic songs.

3. Send back all rural people who had come to the city to seek employment to work the farm.

4. Observe the "five don'ts": don't

Moen Tang Church service, Shanghai, People's Republic of China. The Christian population of China has increased many fold in spite of years of religious suppression. J. Lewis

break laws, preach reactionary sermons, use healing to attract converts, invite unauthorized evangelists, or participate in house-church activities.

5. Accept the "five musts": cooperate with the government religious policy, expose unauthorized evangelists, be economical, discipline the body, and participate personally in every socialist campaign.[22]

After 1958 local church buildings were gradually closed and congregations were forced to unite for survival. Many congregations ceased to meet publicly resulting in loss of both property and autonomy. In 1958 the sixty-five Protestant churches in Beijing were reduced to four and the two hundred in Shanghai were combined into twenty-three.[23] Denominations lost separate identities as they were forced to accept common leaders, rituals, and liturgies. The Roman Catholic Church broke with the Vatican in 1958 when it consecrated twenty Chinese bishops without the approval of Rome. This painful decision gave some proof to the Communists that the Catholic Church was in charge of its own affairs and was not controlled by a foreign body.

With the onset of the Cultural Revolution in 1966 Christians and Roman Catholics suffered a complete and total ban on public meetings and a corresponding suppression of religion at every observable level.[24] The few churches that had been permitted to remain open before the Cultural Revolution were now closed and their buildings turned into factories, libraries, warehouses, and other purposes to advance the socialist program of the government. Church furniture, hymnals, Bibles, and property were destroyed or appropriated by Red Guards. Clergy were laicized and any meetings of any kind were held under fear of the most severe consequences if discovered. All churches in China, Christian or Catholic, were closed except one in Beijing reserved for the use of foreign legations.[25]

With the death of Mao in 1976 came the end of the Cultural Revolution and ten years of national horror. By 1978 a slight improvement in official attitudes toward religion resulted in opening a few churches and cathedrals as showcase proof to the world that China deserved to be reconsidered as a member of the civilized world. With the coming to power of Deng Xiaoping in 1981, religious communities began to experience some further relief from state pressures. It is reported that Deng said: "If the people work hard the government doesn't care which religion they practice."[26] A new constitution adopted in 1982 made official the more tolerant view: "[N]o state organ, public organiza-

tion, or individual may compel citizens to believe in or not to believe in, any religion; nor may they discriminate against citizens who believe in or do not believe in any religion."[27]

Christians who have visited the People's Republic in the mid- and late-1980s have been encouraged and a bit surprised at the resilience and vitality of Chinese Christians. While no one knows the size of the Christian community today, claims by Chinese leaders clearly indicate a remarkable resurgence in numbers and evangelistic zeal. The head of the Chinese Christian Church, Bishop Ding Guangxun, reports a conservative estimate would be four million, but informed world Christian leaders are likely to accept a figure more like ten million if one counts those attending both the registered and the home-based unregistered churches.[28] The Reverend Peter Tsai of Hangzhou has stated that in Zhejiang Province lying to the south of Shanghai there are more Christians in 1987 than there were in all of China in 1949.[29]

Buddhist Fortunes

What happened to the followers of the Buddha in China after the Communist takeover? As background it is important to recognize that Buddhist institutions and monasteries were in poor shape in the period from 1900 to 1940. As Chinese intellectuals learned more of Western political and philosophical ideas, they disdained popular beliefs and practices of Buddhists. The monks were not respected since they were poorly trained and performed the various rituals often merely for monetary gain.

The Communists moved cautiously and even preferentially with Chinese Muslims but ruthlessly with Buddhists. By February 1950 numerous changes began to affect Buddhists. Monks were accused of being parasites on society since they took from the fruits of production but contributed nothing to the creation of wealth. Throughout China a massive disestablishment of Buddhist monasteries and nunneries took place. In Shanghai five hundred of the two thousand monks serving three hundred temples were summarily removed from office and sent back to their rural homes to farm. The younger monks were retrained to work at factories, farms, and national enterprises. As with Christian churches, temples were appropriated and turned into print shops, warehouses, and small factories.

The earliest days brought the most severe reversals. Some reports by Buddhists from within China state that the early days of the revolution were most destructive for the Buddhists. Whereas before the revolution there were one hundred thirty thousand Buddhist temples throughout China, only 100 remained open by 1955. In major cities that had scores of major temples, such as in Guangzhou, Hangkow, Nanjing, and Shanghai, only one remained in each city as a showcase for propaganda purposes. Many culturally valuable Buddhist scriptures were burned. By 1963 fewer than 2,500 monks and nuns were alive in all of China. All lands belonging to Buddhist organizations had long since been nationalized according to the Land Reform Bill of 1950.

In 1953 the Chinese Buddhist Association had been effectively politicized, as can be seen in their three objectives published in 1953: (1) Unite the Buddhists of China so as to participate under the leadership of the People's Government in the movement to love the fatherland and defend the peace. (2) Help the People's Government to thoroughly carry out the policy of freedom of religious belief. (3) Cooperate with Buddhists of other countries in order to develop the excellent traditions of Buddhists.[30] The Chinese Buddhist Association went on record as condemning superstition, heterodox beliefs, the burning of paper money, and sacrifices to deities and the ancestors. To engage in such practices was "to cheat the masses" through an expenditure of money and time which could be better put to production. The association committed itself to protecting the people from "bad people," i.e., monks who sought to undermine the association's goals and refused to cooperate with the Peoples Government. Heads of monasteries had to pledge not to provide food and lodging to traveling monks. This was to break the back of the centuries-old practice of support for monks who were dependent on the general population for basic necessities. The new rule was enforced to discourage "vagrancy" on the part of those who did nothing for productivity.

Tibetan Buddhists

The presence of a minority of Tibetans in China prior to the revolution gave the Communists putative cause to invade Tibet in 1950. Tibet's claim of independence and autonomy was supported vigorously by India. An appeal to the United Nations was to no avail as the Peoples Government was committed to the idea that Tibet was a part of China. In May 1951 a delegation of Tibetans went to Beijing for consultations. An "agreement" was reached stating that Tibetans were only a Chinese minority and not a separate people, race, or nation. In 1952 Mao said freedom of religion would be upheld, but in the following two years the revolution proceeded with vicious suppression and land confiscations. In 1956 further repressive measures followed, including executions, not for religious but for "counterrevolutionary" statements.

Throughout this transitional period the Dalai Lama remained in his seat of government, but in March 1959, when he was summoned to appear before authorities in Beijing, he secretly escaped over the high mountains of the southern Himalayas to India, where he set up his kingdom in exile. Upon reaching the free world the Dalai Lama told how the Communist Chinese sought changes that were radical and unacceptable. More than one thousand monasteries were destroyed up to 1958, and in 1959 a full-scale program of religious extermination was underway. The Communist officials went so far as to insult the Buddha himself by calling him a "reactionary." Zhou Enlai stated that ninety percent of the Tibetan monks had been secularized.

Maoism

It has frequently been observed that the rise of Mao led to the introduction of a "religion" which forcibly replaced, or attempted to replace, all other religion. If religion means "that which is of supreme importance to individuals and groups," then it is certainly true that a new religion characterized much of China under Mao. The Communist leaders and intellectuals had embraced Marx, though they sought to apply the principles in a distinctively Chinese way. A process of thought reform or virtual conversion of national beliefs was undertaken at every level of society. Every vestige of counterrevolutionary religious belief was to be rooted out through a variety of techniques. Foremost in the Communist approach to brainwashing was the employment of a new vocabulary which turned the minds of the people to Communist values and goals. Mao's demise has removed this powerful symbol of new China and the hysteria that seemed to pervade the nation during his lifetime. Maoism is dead and it remains to be seen who, if anyone ever again, will capture the unreflective devotion and obedience of the Chinese people as he did.

Discussion

1. Identify "themes" in Chinese religion. Which seem to be most enduring in the Chinese experience? Give examples.
2. In what sense are the principles of Confucius found in the *Analects* "religious" ideas?
3. Give a description of Dao according to the *Dao De Jing*. What practical implications were there for the Chinese who followed its ideas?

4. What distinctives identify the Chan, Tian-Tai and Pure Land Buddhist schools?
5. What is the Chinese Communist theory of religion? How does that theory seem to be working out in China today?

Notes

[1]Laurence Thompson, *Chinese Religion: An Introduction* (Belmont, Calif.: Dickenson, 1978), 45.

[2]David S. Noss and John B. Noss, *Man's Religions* (New York: Macmillan, 1980), 271.

[3]Thompson, *Chinese Religion*, 40.

[4]Fung Yu-Lan, *A Short History of Chinese Philosophy* (New York: Free Press, 1966), 43.

[5]Noss and Noss, *Man's Religions*, 273.

[6]Ibid., 285.

[7]Meng-zi, 3a, p. 4; quoted in Fung Yu-Lan, *A Short History of Chinese Philosophy*, 73.

[8]Meng-zi, 7a, p. 1; Ibid., 76.

[9]Noss and Noss, *Man's Religions*, 287.

[10]*The Way of Lao Tzu* (1958:97).

[11]Noss and Noss, *Man's Religions*, 248.

[12]*The Way of Lao Tzu*, 128.

[13]Noss, *Man's Religions*, 251.

[14]Ibid.

[15]Ibid.

[16]Ibid., 252.

[17]Thompson, *Chinese Religion*, 107.

[18]Wang Pachow, *Chinese Buddhism: Aspects of Interaction and Reinterpretation* (Washington: Univ. Press of America, 1980), 5.

[19]Ibid., 26.

[20]Fung Yu-Lan, *A Short History of Chinese Philosophy*, 256.

[21]P. Quoted in Richard P. Bohr, "State and Religion in the People's Republic of China Today: The Christian Experience," paper presented to the Fifteenth Sino-American Conference on Mainland China, June 1986, Taipai, Formosa, 10.

[22]Richard C. Bush, Jr., *Religion in Communist China* (New York: Abingdon, 1970), 229.

[23]Raymond Pong and Carlo Caldarola, "China: Religion in a Revolutionary Society," in *Religions and Societies: Asia and the Middle East* (New York: Mouton, 1982), 562.

[24]The words *Christian* and *Roman Catholic* are used by the Chinese themselves in distinguishing these two bodies.

[25]Pong and Caldarola, *Religions and Societies*, 564.

[26]Bohr, "State and Religion," 9.

[27]Ibid., 13. For the entire article see *Beijing Review* 26, no. 52 (December 27, 1982), 10–29.

[28]"Growth of Protestant Church in China," *Beijing Review*, 30, no. 52 (December 28, 1987), 18.

[29]Interview with J. Lewis, June 25, 1987.

[30]Bush, *Religion in Communist China*, 305.

10 Religion in Japan

Earliest Mythology

Many of the earliest religious beliefs and practices of the Japanese are imbedded in mythical materials which Japanese scholars collected in the eighth century C.E. These legends and stories have been accepted as indisputable facts by the Japanese throughout most of their history even into the twentieth century. The *Kojiki* (*Records of Ancient Matters*) and *Nihongi* (*Chronicles of Japan*) deal with the deities and heavenly figures who created the world, the Japanese islands, and the Japanese people. Cosmogonic methods of the *kami* (gods) include interdeity sexual union, bisection of *kami*, and the use of blood. One myth indicates the *kami* stirred the ocean with a spear and the islands appeared.

The earliest ancestors were called Izanagi (male principle) and Izanami (female principle), who after stirring the ocean to create the Japanese islands, stepped down upon them and began to procreate the Japanese race. Both the land and the people have thus been thought of as having come from a divine source. One progeny was Amaterasu (Sun Goddess), another was Susano-o (Storm God) whose many activities have a bearing on later practices, including ritual pollution which subsequently became a central concern in the religious life of the Japanese.

The Japanese claimed descent from these cavorting earth-heaven deities through Jimmu, a fifth-generation descendant of Amaterasu. Jimmu dates from 660 B.C.E. according to Shinto calculations, and this marks the beginning of the line of human emperors whose rule continued unbroken until the midtwentieth century and ended with Hiro Hito. The mythology tells of sacred items belonging to both the *kami* and the divine emperors, including a mirror, jewels, and a sword. A shrine at Ise, located two hundred miles southwest of Tokyo, is reported to contain these items and remains a center of pilgrimage and Shinto worship today.

Shinto

The word *Shinto* comes from two Chinese loan words, *shen* and *dao*. The word *dao* means "way" and *shen* refers to "good spirit" beings. The Japanese equivalent of *shen* is *kami*, but as Japan was strongly influenced by Chinese language, religion, and culture in its formative period beginning in the seventh century C.E., *shen* was preferred in order to distinguish the indigenous religion, Shinto, from imported ones. The Japanese term would be *Kami-no-michi*, or "the way of the Kami." Shinto, then, is the beliefs and practices of the Japanese about the *kami*.

Kami

Since the *kami* Amaterasu is the divine ancestor of Jimmu, the earliest human being, it is easy to see the close and unbroken connection between divine and human beings. Ordinary mortals may be thought of as *kami*, though they typically are not. According to Japanese thought, all things are *kami* though some are more potent and influential than others. The word connotes that which is high, lifted up and therefore unusual, powerful, and special. *Kami* comes close to the South Sea island-world idea of *mana*, or "power." The important *kami* figure prominently in the legends, but also include emperors, ancestors, national heros, and special scholars as well as spirits known to inhabit shrines, mountains, seas, rivers, and impressive natural settings. But even this does not exhaust the idea of *kami*. It cannot be limited or pinned down, for *kami* are without number. Though Hindus claim 330 million deities for a starting figure, Japanese might speak of 8 million. The point is that *kami* are innumerable and universally found in their experience.

Ancestral *Kami*

It may be helpful to indicate some categories of *kami* recognized by the Japanese. The Japanese recognize the presence and influence of ancestral *kami* such as Amaterasu and her descendants in the imperial lineage. Until he was dethroned by the defeat of the Japanese in World War II, the emperor was considered a divine and living *kami* to be revered, worshiped, and obeyed. But as the Japanese were socially organized around clans (uji) from earliest times, shrines throughout the nation have been erected to and maintained for the clan ancestors who in some sense are believed to dwell there. Festivals, so much a part of the annual calendar, celebrate their presence and power.

Nature *Kami* and *Kami* of Skill

All aspects of life are populated with *kami*, but as natural surroundings impinge so dramatically on the lives of the Japanese people, nature *kami* are prominent in Japanese life. *Kami* include, therefore, natural powers and objects and are associated with mountains such as Fuji, oceans and seas surrounding the islands, rivers and fields, animals and herbs. There is a rice *kami* and even a complex of *kami* which receive special attention at planting and harvest of rice. There are also *kami* governing relationships, those guaranteeing good luck, and others which ensure fertility. There are *kami* of trades, businesses, and skills such as fishing and shipbuilding. A proper relationship with these *kami* signifies potential for skill and hope for protection and success.

Kami of Revered Heroes

Shrines are found throughout the country dedicated to the souls of departed heroes whose lives, exploits, status, or extraordinary deaths warrant special attention. These include nobility, commoners, scholars, and some semimalevolent characters whose shrines are maintained in regions across the nation.

Yasukuni Shrine, Tokyo. Controversy surrounds this Shinto Shrine. Constitutional separation of religion and state cause many to question official visits by the Prime Minister and his cabinet ministers to pray for war dead enshrined here. Ken Milhous

Shinto: From Classical to Modern Times

Shinto and the State

Prior to the sixth century C.E. Chinese culture and religion periodically influenced the court and leading clans, but from C.E. 645 onward Chinese contribution was profound. Confucian and Buddhist thought was patronized by the court and intermixed with native Shinto ideas. During the Ritsuryo state period (645–1185), Shinto integrated certain Chinese ideas, particularly Buddhist and Daoist, but maintained an identity of its own. While separate Buddhist and Confucian rituals and festivals were extremely popular with the nobility, Shinto was not forgotten nor displaced. There is much to suggest it was even favored by some emperors. Buddhist festivals were performed at temples or shrines but Shinto celebrations were held within the court. For the most part the imperial court gave financial support to what it regarded

as the best in Buddhist and Confucian traditions.

Prince Shotoku (574–622) incorporated these with native beliefs. Buddhist ideas were concerned with the afterlife, Confucian ethics promoted family solidarity and loyalty to the state, and Shinto beliefs enabled control of nature and helped in meeting the crises of daily life. The several religions were seen as complementary and not conflicting or exclusive. This gentle accommodation was not always to remain the prevailing view, but it was very common in the past, and even today it is widespread among many Japanese.

Classical Shinto

Until the twelfth century Shinto had no formal organization with ordained priests, controlling officials, and formally controlled practices. Its priests, shrines, and rituals were perpetuated nonformally, loosely, and naturally since they had been established in prehistory and were simply a regular part of Japanese life. There was nothing comparable to a formal organization until medieval times when it was considered expedient by the state to promote Shinto over against other religions considered as having become too powerful.

Shinto Shrines and Ritual

There is a theory that earliest Japanese beliefs located the *kami* in a particular area or associated them with natural objects such as trees or mountains. Only later were buildings erected on these precincts. The earliest shrines, built prior to Chinese architectural influences, consisted of platforms on poles above ground covered with thatch. The Ise shrine to Amaterasu is built like this. The typical shrines today consist of various parts. The shrine precincts, which may be small or large, are surrounded by walls or a fence and entered through a *torii* (sacred gate). Situated in the center of the courtyard is a *haiden* (worship hall), which may be entered by the public, and provides a sheltered place for priestly activity and individual prayer. Separate from the *haiden* is the *honden* (*kami* shrine) which may have two parts. One part may be open to the public and contain strips of cloth associated with prayer. But the other part is the most sacred of all as it is the home of the *kami* and the item or items the *kami* inhabits, usually a mirror though possibly also a sword or jewels. This sacred shrine, holding these objects, is opened at certain times, but only when the shrine precincts are closed to the public. It is opened to radiate, as it were, its powers, but is too sacred for human contact. Naturally, these items must be attended to from time to time by the local priests.

Today, shrines are most likely to be visited by the Japanese on festival occasions, at the New Year, or during special events in individual or family life such as a wedding or crisis. Before entering the *haiden* water purification is necessary; water is always available in every shrine for this purpose. The mouth and hands are first washed, after which the person stands before the *haiden*, often ringing a bell to gain the attention of the *kami*. The hands are then clapped and silent prayer is offered to the *kami*. Priests are available for help and their assistance may be called on in advance, usually for special purification rituals. The majority of worshipers can carry on themselves without priestly assistance. Some worshipers also attach paper slips containing prayers to trees in the precincts before leaving.

Purification is very important to the worshiper and finds its origin in the earliest Shinto religious texts. In the mythical past the *kami* could become ritually polluted and some worshipers had to go through various ceremonies to be purified. Pollution is caused by a variety of things such as contact with the dead and sexual activity, but is not necessarily based on moral or ethical considerations. To be pure it is not necessary to be morally pure. It is not particularly important to shrine visitants to understand why they must go through ritual purification. It is the expected ritual and that is good enough. Before going through the acts leading to water purification, they are impure and only after this are they suited to come into the presence of the *kami*. As the *kami*'s activity is primarily to bestow protection and good for-

Main Shrine, Izumo. One of two most important shrines, it is believed that each Fall all Shinto Kami leave their respective shrines to go to Izumo for "vacation." The main buildings at Izumo are a National Treasure because they are the oldest Shinto structures in Japan. The resident Kami, Okuninushi, is the god of marriage. Ken Milhous

tune, one needs to be appropriately prepared to take advantage of this.

Shinto Priestly Activity

While priests in some religions are called upon to offer explanations to the faithful concerning the religious texts and received traditions as well as perform ceremonies, Shinto priests are nearly wholly limited to ritual performances. They assist the believers in establishing and maintaining contact with the *kami* through regular and special ceremonies. Priests do not preach sermons nor comment on the meaning of texts. They are ritual intermediaries who know the right things to do and say and provide guidance for those who do not.

Some priests are professional religious functionaries with full-time paid posi-

tions, having been trained on the job or at one of the few training institutions established in modern times. They may, however, hold full-time employment at other professions and serve part time as priests with little or no training other than that gained assisting others. Since most shrines are small and lacking in large attendance, and since priests may marry, the majority of priests are simple practitioners who supplement their income with occasional service at the shrine.

The vestments of priests may be very colorful and elaborate or rather simple and drab. Some women serve as priests, which corresponds well with ancient documents that connect women as intermediaries, or shamanists, between the human and the divine world. Shamanism is not typi-

Shinto ceremony to purify the gounds before starting a new building project. J. Lewis

Shinto Prists in full costume. J. Lewis

cal of Shinto, but priests who serve as spirit mediums are not unknown, either.

Shinto Festivals

Most shrines of significance hold festivals at the New Year and at other times which are appropriate to the history of the resident *kami*. At festival time the visitants may offer food to the *kami*; priests chant special *norito* (formal prayers); dances are performed in the streets; and the *kami* symbols may be paraded through the community. The procession through the streets is accompanied by a carnival or festive attitude as the *kami*-box, containing treasures symbolic of the *kami*, is carried by designated worshipers through throngs of onlookers. Whether the *kami* is stationary in the *honden* or paraded through the streets, it has power both to provide and to protect. One might discover the details of this by asking members of the Shinto community, "What does this *kami* provide or protect?" In farming communities the *kami* may guarantee good harvest while in fishing villages the *kami* may protect the fishing fleet when out to sea.

Two young women commune with the Kami at one of Japan's 80,000 Shinto shrines. Tom White

Shinto shrines across Japan prior to World War II numbered about 110,000. But since that time the number has declined to around 80,000. The busiest time for most shrines is at the New Year when a series of five ceremonies are conducted. The first three days of the New Year are national holidays, and as people are off work, many throng to the nearest or most famous shrine available. Other festivals include the Seven Herb festival, which marks the ancient custom of eating a dish of rice flavored with herbs to mark the people's resump-

tion of ordinary activities. Festivals in March, May, July, and September are popular but not universally observed in all shrines.

Shinto Worship in the Home

Much closer to the lives of the people are rites and practices in the home centering around the *kami-dana* (god shelf). Nearly all non-Christian homes have a simple or more ornate shelf with memorial tablets, upon which are inscribed the names of ancestors and local or special *kami*. The *kami* Amaterasu and the goddess of rice (Inari) are signified by symbols such as a mirror, strips of paper, or other ritual items. Small cups of tea and offerings of rice and incense are given daily, accompanied by prayers and gestures of worship. In moments of great personal or family need, special ceremonies may be performed with gifts of cloth and food. Some evidence of respect for the Buddha may be visible as well, though many have a separate shelf for this called the *butsu-dana* (Buddha shelf); they accommo-date the worship of the Buddha with similar offerings. The two are seen as compatible and overlapping centers of worship in the home with no thought of competition or conflict.

Shinto-Buddhist Interpenetration

From the seventh century C.E. onward Buddhist texts, institutions, and schools proliferated, sometimes with court approval and endorsement and sometimes suffering reversals and persecution. Being identified with Chinese culture, Buddhist practices had the advantage of association with haute culture, even though they suffered the disadvantage of emanating from a foreign religion. During the Nara period (710–84), named after the city to which the capital was moved, Buddhist religion was endorsed and financed by Emperor Shomu. During his time the Todaiji temple was built to enshrine a large statue of the Buddha. Furthermore, he ordered Buddhist temples to be constructed in every province of the land, along with a monastery and nunnery. While Buddhist practices were sanctioned by the court, the Buddha and the divine figures associated with him were considered by many as Shinto deities or *kami*. For example, the Buddha displayed at Todaiji was the Maha Vairocana (J., Dainichi), or Locana, the Sun Buddha, a specific Buddhist figure with its own mythological history. But many Japanese associated Vairocana with Amaterasu, the sun goddess referred to in the ancient Shinto legends. In summary, though Buddhist traditions gained acceptance in the court among the aristocracy during the Nara and subsequent periods, the practices of Shinto went on as before. Buddhist and Shinto practices sometimes were combined, although separate identities were often recognized by the people. The intermixing of the two traditions sometimes championed the one, sometimes the other.[1]

In the medieval times of the Heian and Kamakura periods (1192–1336), Shinto actively borrowed from Buddhist, Confucian, and Daoist practices, thus becoming a synthesis of Japanese indigenous beliefs and Chinese imports. This took place continuously thereafter from the twelfth to the sixteenth centuries. Under the belief that *kami* had their Buddhist counterparts and vice versa, Buddhist deities were erected in Shinto shrines and worshiped alongside the *kami*. This was possible under the Buddhist theory of *Honji-suijaku*, which taught that the Japanese *kami* were merely the "manifest traces" (*suijaku*) of the original substances of Buddhas and *bodhisattvas*. In short, the *kami* were none other than expressions of the Buddha-nature and hence legitimate objects of Buddhist worship. Some

Buddhist schools in Japan worked out systematically the problems associated with the intermixing of these two powerful religious traditions. One was called Shingon and the other, Tendai (C., Tian-Tai).

The Giant Buddha of Kamakura. This bronze Buddha, initially housed in a wooden temple, was cast in 1252 C.E. but has been in the open since 1494 when the temple was swept away in a tidal wave. Ken Milhous

Written prayers are tied on a stand at a shrine frequented by both Shinto and Buddhist followers. J. Lewis

Some thinkers, however, were not content to see Shinto, a national and

335

native religion, so intertwined with foreign religions. Two who made protests and championed Shinto over all others were Kitabatake Chikafusa (1273–1354) and a later defender, Motoori Norinaga (1730–1801). Chikafusa defended the belief that the emperor was descended from ancient *kami*, and Norinaga sought to restore Shinto to its pristine purity by study of the earliest literature prior to "contamination" by Chinese religious thought.

Shinto's improved fortunes in the modern period begin with the so-called Meiji Restoration (1867), which returned ruling authority that had long been in the hands of military rulers to the imperial family. Emperor Meiji took over formal rule in January 1868 and immediately attacked Buddhists because of their association with things foreign. Buddhist images and priests, so long intertwined with Shinto, were purged. In 1872 a state edict made it a criminal offense to teach that *kami* were Buddhist manifestations. It was a time of great persecution for Buddhist followers and especially priests, who were so accustomed to special favors. Buddhist priests were demoted to laymen and forbidden to conduct their ceremonies. While Buddhist practices were disallowed Shinto was elevated as the national religion. Technically it was called "State Shinto" and declared to be a matter of national patriotism and hence not religious at all. Worship of the emperor and the mythical *kami* were nonetheless required in schools as a sign of support for the Japanese nation. Only defeat in World War II brought the dismissal of Shinto as a state religion and made possible religious freedom for groups which had earlier been suppressed.

Japanese Buddhist Traditions

Beginnings

The known period of introduction of Buddhist traditions to Japan begins in 538 C.E. when the ruler of Korea, then a colony of China, sent to Japan a Buddhist statue, religious texts, and some priests. From this time forward the Japanese aristocracy was fascinated with things Buddhist. This earliest experience with Buddhist traditions came at the time Japan was learning and modifying the Chinese writing script for use with its own language. The Buddhist priests were skilled calligraphers as well as able expounders of the texts. The texts were often difficult for the Japanese to understand, which fact seemed to add to their fascination. Further, the Buddhist priests had special knowledge of medicine to cope with disease and pregnancy, and their rituals were full of pageantry and ceremony. Buddhist priests could officiate at funerals that were forbidden to Shinto priests because contact with death was polluting. Also, many of the priests were schooled in statecraft and had valuable skills in administration and bureaucracy management, thus further influencing the Japanese court. Thus Buddhist traditions won their way among the Japanese by contributing in ways that were religious, political, and practical.

It was under Prince Shotoku's leadership (C.E. 573–621) that Buddhist traditions were incorporated into state practice and documents. Shotoku saw

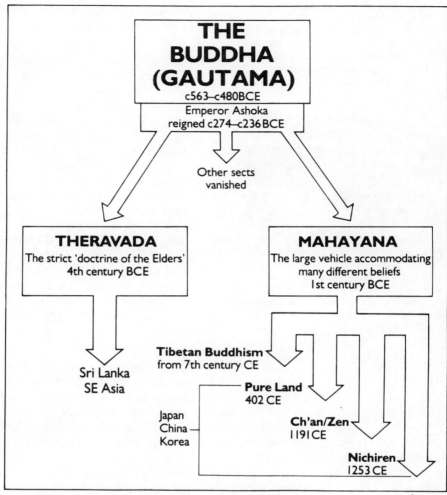

THE
BUDDHA
(GAUTAMA)
c563–c480BCE

Emperor Ashoka
reigned c274–c236 BCE

Other sects
vanished

THERAVADA
The strict 'doctrine of the Elders'
4th century BCE

MAHAYANA
The large vehicle accommodating
many different beliefs
1st century BCE

Sri Lanka
SE Asia

Tibetan Buddhism
from 7th century CE

Pure Land
402 CE

Japan
China
Korea

Ch'an/Zen
1191 CE

Nichiren
1253 CE

© DIAGRAM

The main streams of Buddhist traditions. Religions on File

in them values for society and in the famous seventeen articles of his "constitution" he included both Buddhist and Confucian ideas. Furthermore, he showed his personal interest and devotion by writing several commentaries on difficult Buddhist texts. Later, Emperor Shomu's efforts (reigned C.E. 724–49) to increase the number and importance of Buddhist institutions encouraged the founding of six formal schools of Buddhists during the Nara period (C.E. 710-84). One of them, the Kegon school, had its center at the Todaiji temple in Nara which is still surviving today. Scholars have concluded that Buddhist strength at this time was primarily in the court and among the nobility more than among the masses of people. Earhart concludes the following about Buddhist traditions in the eighth century.

We might say that Buddhism already was considered a state religion of Japan, and later, with increasing popularity, became a national religion of Japan. Buddhism tended to dominate the whole religious scene, but actually paralleled Shinto rather than superseded it.[2]

Main hall of Todaiji Temple in Nara. Originally built in 1180 C.E. and rebuilt in 1709, it houses the Great Buddha of Nara and is considered to be one of the largest wooden buildings in the world. Ken Milhous

Tendai

The Chinese school of Tian-Tai was brought to Japan under the name Tendai and first introduced by the monk Saicho (762–822), whose name means "the master who brought the message." He, like many Japanese monks of the time, traveled to China in search of a better understanding of truth. Typical of Buddhist priests of his day, he was also a sincere believer in the *kami*, and before he left Japan he appealed in prayer at *kami* shrines for their help and protection as he set out on the long and dangerous trip. In China he spent most of his time at the monastery on Tian-tai mountain, after which the school gets its name. He became convinced this school taught the *dharma* (truth) in its fullness and

returned to spread its doctrine and erect an ordination altar in his native land based on the Chinese model.

Chinese Tian-Tai believed that the historical Buddha taught different texts throughout five stages of his earthly career. Based on the maturity of his hearers, he suited his instruction to their abilities (*upaya*). When Saicho returned he established a monastery on Mount Hiei near the city of Kyoto. Here Buddhist scriptures were studied, chanted, memorized, and commented upon. The *Lotus Sutra* was given special attention as it was thought to be the culmination and zenith of the Buddha's thought. This text had special significance to Saicho since it reportedly was a favorite of Prince Shotoku, who had written a commentary on it some two centuries earlier.

Saicho accepted the Tian-Tai doctrine of the superiority of the *Lotus Sutra* but gave it an interpretation different from and opposed to the Chinese ones. In fact, he held that the Chinese view was false since it restricted liberation to only a few. He believed the essential teaching of the text was that all could experience liberation because the nature of all beings was fundamentally the same. He also tied the fortunes of Tendai, the true religion, to that of the nation and regarded the monastery as a guarantor of national safety. He claimed it was the center for the protection of the Land of Great Japan. He also regarded the training which Japanese monks received in China to be woefully inadequate and instituted in Japan a twelve-year study curriculum, during which time students were not allowed to leave the mountain monastery. The magnitude of Saicho's influence in Japan can be appreciated by the fact that at one time there were thirty thousand monks training in temples and study halls numbering in the thousands and scattered across the mountainside.

Saicho is credited, therefore, with casting Tendai in a unique Japanese mold. He is also known for having introduced into Tendai two other innovative elements: faith in Amida and many Chan practices. Equally important for later developments is that he and his followers taught that the *kami* were manifestations of the one Buddha-reality. This is something similar to the Hindu *avatara* (descent) concept. The Buddha had priority, however, since *kami* were considered dependent manifestations. Such ideas provided the grounds for Buddhist and Shinto practices to exist side by side for most of Japan's religious history.

Nichiren

In the thirteenth century a young Tendai monk named Nichiren (1222–82) believed that the centuries since the founding of Tendai had brought in unnecessary formalism, complexity, and scholasticism which obscured the essentially simple message of the *Lotus Sutra*. The original teaching of Tendai accepted all Buddhist texts as authoritative teachings of the Buddha. Nichiren rejected this in favor of the view that the *Lotus Sutra* alone was the sole and entire truth. After having an enlightenment experience wherein Nichiren is said to have seen the identity of Buddha Maha-Vairocana and the Buddha-reality of the *Lotus Sutra*, he

set out to proclaim that all teachings but his own were false and harmful. He upheld the *Lotus Sutra* as the only hope for returning to the pure teaching of the Buddha. In addition to founding a monastery and gathering a community about him, he took to the streets, preaching wherever he could gain a hearing. He preached against moral degeneracy and explained that the darkness of the age was the result of departing from the pure teachings of the *Lotus*. A special evidence of moral corruption, in his view, was the popularity of Amidaism (Pure Land School; Jodo), wherein people expected to find the good life in Amida's Pure Land. He also regarded the emphasis on faith in Amida as undercutting human effort and striving. Since Jodo had such widespread popular support, his views offended many government officials and twice he was exiled. He did not endear himself with other Buddhist leaders either, since he demanded that national leaders require belief exclusively in his teachings and banish all others. Like a Jeremiah who preached to a corrupted Israel, he predicted that unless the nation turn from its error, embrace his teachings, and worship the *Lotus Sutra* it would suffer severe national consequences. For making such a threat he suffered his second exile only to be recalled when an attempted shipborne Mongol invasion across the Japan Sea was narrowly averted. The armada of ships was destroyed by high winds which contemporaries gratefully called *kamikazi* (divine wind).

According to Nichiren, the worship of the *Lotus Sutra* was necessary for liberation, along with the following essentials. The Trikaya doctrine,

Amida Buddha. This giant—sized wood sculpture, 9'2" x 7' x 4'10", was lacquered and richly gilded when used in Jodo worship. Muromachi period (1392-1568). The Nelson—Atkins Museum of Art. Kansas City, MO.

which held there were three Buddhabodies (historical in Sakyamuni, universal in all things, and the bliss-body which periodically appears in various forms), was expressed by Nichiren in *mandala* (magic-diagram) form. By the veneration of the *mandala* one could experience the universality of the Buddha-nature referred to in the Trikaya doctrine. A second means to liberation was the repetition of the *daimoku*, a phrase exalting the *Lotus Sutra*. While Jodo encouraged devotion to Amida as Buddha of the Western Paradise, Nichiren presented worship of the *Lotus Sutra* itself as the only enabling means toward liberation.

Jodo: Honen's Pure Land School

Japanese monks learned Jodo from China, as they did almost all things Buddhist. The belief that Amida Buddha would save sentient beings and bring them into a pure land from which *nirvana* was a certainty appealed to the masses. At first this belief was incorporated by Tendai as an inferior but useful method. The preferred means to escaping *samsara* was meditation on the *Lotus Sutra* and other pious activities such as memorizing and chanting the text.

Butsudana: *altar used for worship in Japanese Buddhist home.* J. Lewis

Honen

Honen (1133–1212) was trained in Tendai practices on Mount Hiei, but at the age of forty-two he came to believe that the proper way for liberation in the present age was recitation of the name of Amida Buddha in faith. Basic to this was the understanding of the three periods of the *dharma*. According to Pure Land texts, each Buddha-age could be divided into three periods: the success of the *dharma*, the decline of the *dharma*, and the low point of the *dharma*. Honen and others believed their times corresponded to the last, in which the moral and spiritual nature of humanity was so enslaved to crav-

ing, lust, and self-indulgence that the spiritual achievements of earlier times were beyond grasp. In these times the practice of *nembutsu*, uttering or thinking the phrase "*namu-amida-butsu*," was sufficient. This meant literally "name of Buddha," but when uttered with pious intention it meant "I put my faith in Amida Buddha." Other acts were meritorious, such as meditating on texts, giving offerings, and supporting temples and monasteries. But recitation of the Buddha's name was best of all.

Pure Land Scriptures

One of the most important of the texts was *Muryojukyo* (*The Teaching of Infinite Life*), which is Japanese for the Chinese title translated from the Sanskrit. In it is recorded the forty-eight vows taken by the Buddha Hozo, who when a *bodhisattva* (one who postpones enlightenment voluntarily though fully ready for it) decided to create a perfect land for sentient beings. He went to all the existing Buddha-worlds, noting their perfections, and vowed to incorporate them all into his own. He is known by the name Amitayus, or the Buddha of Infinite Life. His twelfth vow is as follows: "If, after my obtaining Buddhahood, my light should be limited and not be able at least to illumine hundreds of thousands of kotis [an astronomical number] of Buddha countries, may I not attain the highest enlightenment." He was entirely successful in achieving his vows and thus created a pure land where all who would recite or even think piously on his name could go.

A second text is *Amidakyo*, which is very short but indicates that the Pure

Land, though a place of bliss, is not one of physical pleasure and material benefits. It is a land in which the moral climate is so superior and the teaching of the *dharma* is so pure that one can go on to enlightenment easily.

Shinran's Jodo Shinshu

Shinran's Problem

Shinran (1173–1263) was a Tendai monk who feared he had somehow missed the true path. Accordingly, he left off following Tendai and from 1201 to 1207 followed Honen, saying, "I . . . Shinran . . . in the year 1201 abandoned the different practices and took refuge in the Original View." But in time Shinran also broke with Honen over a point of great importance to him. According to Honen, since it was impossible, due to moral decay (*mappo*), to observe the classical disciplines that formerly led to enlightenment, the practice of *nembutsu* was alone effective and meritorious. But Shinran believed that man was so corrupted and enslaved to self and lust that not only were the disciplines of classical times impossible, but even *nembutsu* had become corrupted. People did not say *nembutsu* out of pure faith, but out of selfish motives. Their selfish desire to gain the Pure Land rendered these recitations nonmeritorious. Shinran concluded that Honen's system rested not on the merits and grace of Amitayus but purely on the self-effort of individuals. Further, it did not reckon with the absolute corruptness of human nature which in Shinran's view was not capable of any meritorious deeds whatsoever.

Shinran's Solution

Shinran did not deny the validity of *nembutsu*, but he insisted that the attitude in reciting it must be one of faith. Faith meant utter reliance and total trust without any ulterior motives. This kind of faith was impossible unless it was graciously given to the person by the Buddha. It was a gift of grace and not something one could produce unassisted. What is necessary to have faith? One must have a sincere or selfless mind, trust, and a desire for rebirth in the Pure Land. But these things come only from without; they are a matter of "other power,"not "self power." They are a gift. How does one know one has true faith? How can one be sure? True faith is the absence of doubt. How does one know doubt is gone? It is gone when one does not continue to strive. If one continues to be anxious about the future life then doubt remains, faith is absent, and salvation is not real. Confidence is, therefore, a sign of true faith. When one is at rest about these matters then faith, which comes from Buddha, is real. According to Honen one could have certainty of *nirvana* only after being reborn in the Pure Land. But Shinran taught that true faith, being a gift, brought certainty in this life. According to Honen, only at the moment of death would one know for sure. According to Shinran, one could be fully confident during one's life that *nirvana* was attained. But this was totally by Buddha's grace.

Zen

Zen (the Japanese equivalent of the Chinese Chan), although it had been in existence for centuries, rose to prominence during the Kamakura period (1185–1333), at a time when Nichiren and Jodo had gained popularity. Japan saw the rise of not one but two schools of Zen. Under the name of Rinzai (Japanese for the Chinese school Lin-chi) sudden enlightenment was promoted through the efforts the monk Eisei (1141–1215). Eisei's student, Dogen (1200–1253), later broke with his master to found a competing movement called Soto Zen.

Rinzai

The Southern School of Chinese Chan, led by Hui-neng, argued that the experience of *satori* could not be gained in stages but rather came suddenly through a variety of devices to exhaust the mind. Rinzai followed the school that said meditation was necessary to gain enlightenment. This involved seated meditation presided over by a Zen master in a controlled situation such as a Zen monastery. Still, meditation was only instrumental to the experience of *satori*. Rinzai preferred to add the *koan* and other exercises to facilitate *satori*.

The experience Rinzai and other Zen schools sought was described in various ways. It was described as achieving the Buddha-nature, Buddha-reality, Buddha-principle, "nothingness," or the "void." Nagarjuna, the Buddhist scholar of India, taught that all entities were empty of permanent reality and hence there was really nothing to grasp or cling to. This view of the "emptiness" of all things was to be taken up by Chinese and Zen thinkers as a way of describing not only the nature of things generally but the very nature of the ultimate reli-gious experience. The "void" meant that the experience was of such a nature that nothing could be said about it without falsifying its intrinsic emptiness. It transcended the very categories of thought itself and was the nondual experience wherein all things were nondifferent.

Zen masters established centers of meditation where one could be spared distractions to concentrate on the rigorous goal of *satori*. In the meditation centers the masters taught the proper position for the body, since one had to get comfortable or the body itself was a distraction. Meditation's goal was to progressively cut oneself off from distractions so as to think on a single object or idea. The next step was to cease thinking about even that one object, since only if one broke out of thought and reason itself could *satori* happen. Meditation could lead to ecstasy or trance, but this was not *satori*. Zen masters said there must be a general mental upheaval and an awakening which would lead to seeing old things from a fresh and new perspective.[3]

Religion in Japan in Modern Times

Discussion about religion in modern Japanese society is troubled by the same ambiguity that seems to surface wherever the term is used. Are the Japanese still "religious" as they were in the past, or have they been "secularized" like their contemporaries, the industrialized technocrats of America? Robert N. Bellah in an essay comparing society and religion in the United States and Japan makes this observation: "Clearly, in both societies religion is still a force, though exactly what that means requires close attention."[4] How much of a force religion is in this or any society can only be determined by reference to what is meant by "religion."

In this text we have chosen to use the word *religion* to refer to that discernible pattern in the lives of individuals or groups which is the expression of what they hold to be more important than anything else in life. As we discuss the so-called new religions we will see how the values held supremely high by some new movements have to do with world peace as much as personal inner peace, and with group ideals as much or more than individual satisfaction.

Soka Gakkai

The Soka Gakkai (J., value-creation society) movement is an example of one of Japan's new religions. A summary of goals stated by Soka Gakkai is as follows:

> Soka Gakkai is an organization that puts into practice the doctrine of the dignity of human life as expounded in the Buddhism of Nichiren Daishonin (Japanese: "Nichiren the Great Holy One"). It also promotes various social movements. In particular, with regard to the problem of world peace, it has spoken out publicly many times and has taken concrete actions in the cause of peace. Peace, indeed, is a theme that cannot be separated from our religious belief that human life is of supreme value in and of itself and cannot be sacrificed as a "means" to any "end."[5]

Soka Gakkai also offers the hope that individuals can change and improve their lives. Emphasizing the need to change oneself, the process is called "changing poison into medicine" through following the tenets of Soka Gakkai. Yet individuals cannot be entirely happy so long as society follows principles that affect the masses negatively. Every member of Soka Gakkai therefore has a responsibility to work for Japan's improvement by advancing the teaching of the movement. By the same token the truth must be spread to other societies, which gives Soka Gakkai an international mission.

History of Soka Gakkai

Soka Gakkai is a Buddhist lay movement begun in 1930 by Makiguchi Tsunesabure (1871–1944) to support and advance the religion of Nichiren Shoshu. One of eighteen Nichiren groups in Japan today, Nichiren Shoshu ("The true religion of Nichiren") claims to be the authentic successor to Nichiren (1222–82). Thus Soka Gakkai is not a new religion in one sense because it accepts doctrines of a seven-hundred-year-old Buddhist school. But it is new in the sense that it uniquely combines those beliefs with new goals for individual happiness and social change related to issues created by the nuclear age.

Soka Gakkai considers itself to be the only accurate transmitter of Nichiren's doctrines and the sole proponent of "true Buddhism" and even "true religion." To be a member of Soka Gakkai one must also be a member of Nichiren Shoshu. For all practical purposes they may be considered as one since in Japan they are known as Soka Gakkai and internationally as Nichiren Shoshu.

By 1957 it claimed the support of seven thousand households, many of whom were gained through the technique of *shakubuku*, a Buddhist term meaning literally to break (*shaku*) and subdue (*buku*), and refers to aggressive tactics used in gaining converts. This practice subjects inquirers to endure persistent repetition of its doctrines in the context of group pressure. Members of Soka Gakkai defend their conversion tactics, believing they were sometimes necessary to get obstinate persons to accept the absolute truth. Since 1960 these tactics have moderated as the group gained greater acceptance in society.

By appealing to the large urban salaried class in the post–World War II period, it entered political candidates in the 1955 elections and won fifty-three seats in metropolitan and prefectural assemblies on a platform pledging to "purify politics," work for "fair elections," and seek to unite individual happiness with social prosperity. It claims ten million to sixteen million members in Japan and about one million overseas, including many in the United States, Great Britain, and West Germany. It supports publishing houses, a national daily newspaper (circulation 4.5 million), nationwide meeting halls, schools and universities, and Komeito, Japan's third-largest political party.

Makiguchi and His Theory of Value

Makiguchi, the founder, was an educator in an elementary school in Tokyo who developed an educational theory called "value creation." This led him to establish a society by that name (Soka Gakkai) which sought to combine the teachings of Nichiren Shoshu

and Makiguchi's own thought centering on the ideas of value, benefit, beauty, and goodness. He opposed certain state Shinto religious requirements during World War II and was charged with disloyalty and subsequently imprisoned along with twenty other leaders in 1943. His fledgling society was outlawed by the imperial government and he died in prison during the war.

According to Makiguchi, truth and value are two distinct and separate realms. Values are created whereas truth exists independent of human support. Truth is identified or discovered, but value is created as people first identify truth and then go on to see the connection between a truth and themselves, between a fact and themselves. This connection is the value placed on the relation to truth. One does not create truth—it exists independently—but one does relate truth to one's self, others, and, more broadly, even to one's own culture. The relating of truth to individuals is the arena of value.

A fact exists independent of one's feeling about it and truth is not necessarily connected to goodness, nor is nontruth connected to evil. "Sometimes the true is evil to man; sometimes the false is good. For example, a man hears the rumor of an earthquake and fire. If the rumor is substantiated it is not good to him, but evil. If the rumor is proven to be false, it is good."[6]

Values do not entail any truths intrinsically. There is no such thing as "true value" or "false value." Value is not identical with truth and hence philosophical pragmatists who equate the two by teaching that what is beneficial (value) is necessarily true are wrong. Something may be beneficial but such a decision depends on the creation of value and not identifying truth with value.

One might well ask how all this theory connects with the practice of Soka Gakkai. First, it is believed that the truth given in and through the teaching of Nichiren is objective, fixed, and absolute, like all other truth. Soka Gakkai's exclusivism is rooted in Makiguchi's belief that truth stands alone and is immovable. Since religious truth is an aspect of general truth, Nichiren's doctrines are absolute and final.

Second, much of life is subject to our ordering according to the three values of beauty, benefit/gain, and the good. These three values can be experienced individually and as a society and world. "An individual can arrange his environment in such a way as to create what is good, beautiful and beneficial."[7] The ultimate goal of Soka Gakkai is to create happiness through satisfying the spiritual, material, and altruistic desires of humankind corresponding respectively to beauty, benefit, and the good. Soka Gakkai is therefore a this-world, life-affirming movement having little or no place for ascetic, world-withdrawing, or self-denying themes. Its goal is to achieve happiness for all persons through creating a world permeated with beauty, benefit, and goodness.

Soka Gakkai: Individual Happiness and Religious Claims

Its ambitious societal aims notwithstanding, a chief aim of Soka Gakkai is to assist individuals in finding happiness. This can only come by finding the one true religion. The following steps of Soka Gakkai lead one to the truth. First, one must acknowledge that the chief end of humanity is to find happiness and peace. Thus Soka Gakkai espouses a noncontroversial goal that most individuals find easy to accept. Second, one should agree that it is usually the function of religion to achieve this state. Third, one must resolve the conflicting truth claims of the religions, since each makes exclusive claims and promises. How can an individual decide which is correct? According to Soka Gakkai each religion must be judged according to a threefold test.

The threefold proofs (*shansho*) of the true religion are: the literal, the theoretical, and the actual. The literal proof (*monsho*) means that when compared to the *Lotus Sutra*, all other texts, Buddhist or not, lack the teaching it contains. Though numerous Buddhist *sutras* are taught by the Buddha, Soka Gakkai believes the historical Buddha intentionally delayed teaching the highest truth until the end of his career, at which time he taught the *Lotus*. The current president of Soka Gakkai, Ikeda Daisaku, said: "I can state positively, taking many scriptures as literal proof, that the Buddhism of Nichiren Shoshu is the highest religion."[8] This exclusivist conviction can be found in the teachings of Nichiren himself, who proposed a series of comparisons between religions and *sutras*. Working from the general to the particular, he preferred Buddhist religion to non-Buddhist, Mahayana to Hinayana doctrine, the *Lotus* as the highest of all *sutras*, the last half of the *Lotus* to the first half, and the "hidden" meaning to the literal. The *Lotus* alone was effective in the degenerate spiritual climate of the latter days (*mappo*).

In the apologetics of Soka Gakkai only Nichiren Shoshu passes the theoretical proof (*risho*) because it alone has the doctrine of cause and effect and is therefore consistent with both science and reason. Unlike other religions which are inconsistent and irrational, Soka Gakkai is scientific and plausible. Finally, only their followers possess actual proof (*gensho*), for they alone, by their own testimony, are happy and moving forward. President Ikeda says, "Proof is better than argument. It is easy to merely mouth good opinions, but what is essential is whether the actual proof of faith is acquired and whether the followers have become happier or not, whether their diseases are cured, or they have realized the eternity of life, or if they have gained spiritual enlightenment, peace and a happy state of life—these are the actual proofs."[9]

Once one elects to test the claims of Soka Gakkai, the following practices, called the "three great secret laws," are essential. First, one must recite the *daimoku* daily and frequently. This verbal act mysteriously encapsulates in a single sentence the whole of the teaching of Buddhist *sutras*, the *Lotus*, Nichiren, and the Buddha. It consists of four words: *Namu-Myoho-Renge-Kyo*: "Adoration to the Lotus of the Wonderful Law." While such is the literal meaning, the deeper reference is to Ultimate Law, which is the essential reality permeating all phenomena in the universe. When the

daimoku is thus repeated it has both positive and negative benefits. Negatively, it alters *karma* by canceling the effects of previous unwholesome deeds. Positively, it operates by the principle of cause and effect to confer a universal range of benefits including happiness, health, and prosperity. Chanting *daimoku* could be called salvation by repeated invocation. However, rather than being considered a means to salvation, Soka Gakkai teaches that the act is one with and inseparable from the benefits it dispenses.

Faith in the *daimoku*, Nichiren, or the teaching of Soka Gakkai is not a prerequisite to successful recitation. This contrasts with the teaching of one of Soka Gakkai's religious competitors, Risho Koseikai, which holds that repeating the *daimoku* serves only to affirm preexisting faith in the *Lotus*. Frequent repetition is of no great value.

But in Soka Gakkai one needs no faith to undertake chanting *daimoku* since faith results from practice. It works and this is why people have faith in it. Some, like the American entertainer Tina Turner, testify that the act of recitation empowers and transforms by linking one with the Ultimate Law or principle of the universe–the Buddha himself. She is quoted as saying: "I joined NSA [Nichiren Shoshu of America] ten years ago. The first time I ever chanted daimoku was four years before my divorce. At that time, my father and the rest of my relatives were baptists. I didn't understand anything about Buddhism, so I used to chant daimoku five times and say

'Amen'. But once I began chanting good things kept happening to me."[10]

> "I joined NSA ten years ago. The first time I ever chanted daimoku was four years before my divorce. At that time, my father and the rest of my relatives were baptists. I didn't understand anything about Buddhism, so I used to chant daimoku five times and say 'Amen'. But once I began chanting good things kept happening to me."
>
> —American Rock star Tina Turner

A second requirement is to worship, respect, and adore the Gohonzon. This *mandala* tablet, displayed prominently in the Nichiren Shoshu temple at the foot of Mount Fuji, has in its center the *daimoku* which is believed to have been inscribed by Nichiren himself in C.E. 1279. Just as the *daimoku* is the spoken phrase of incomparable universal power, so the Gohonzon is the visible object of unlimited and unmatched importance. While recitation of the *daimoku* is most efficacious when done before the original Gohonzon, one can purchase a miniature to enshrine in one's home for the same purpose. Recitation before the *mandala* brings into convergence the two most powerful forces in the world resulting in promised benefits to the individual. Tina Turner testifies to the effects of doing Gongyo (chanting *daimoku* plus selected *Lotus* passages) before the Gohonzon: "It took me ten years to get to where I am today. Before I could achieve success, I had to purify my own life. That purified life is my source of power. Through my Buddhist practice, I gained the ability to judge people correctly, so I could find a good manager. . . . If I hadn't been practicing [Gongyo] to the Gohonzon,

I probably would have gone to five, six, seven or even eight managers, one after the other and experienced nothing but a succession of hardships."[11]

The third of the essential spiritual laws is to support and defend the head temple where the Gohonzon is enshrined at the foot of Mount Fiji. Nichiren is believed to have predicted and ordered the erection of the Taiseki-iji temple as the center from which the faith would spread throughout Japan and the whole world.

Seicho No Ie

Founder

Taniguchi Masaharu (b. 1893), founder of Seicho No Ie, was at first a follower of Omoto-kyo, a shamanistic new religion of the 1920s. This movement was one of many responding to the felt needs of the mass of Japan's working class. Taniguchi broke with Omoto after reading "New Thought" spiritualist materials that said matter was not real—only the good and the true were real. His ideas are contained in the forty-volume scriptures, *Seimei No Jisso (The Truth or Reality of Life)*, made up of selected articles from the journal *Seicho No Ie*.

The first issue of *Seicho No Ie* was published in 1930 and marked the beginning of the movement which brings together ideas from a variety of religious traditions. From traditional Japanese thought Taniguchi affirmed the existence of *kami* from whom the Japanese descended. Western ideas from the Bible, Christian Science, and spiritualism were influential, especially *Law of Mind in Action* by Fenwicke L. Holmes. In the period prior to 1945 the movement patriotically supported Japan's imperialist policies. World War II moderated its supremacist attitudes but in the 1980s there has been evidence that the movement has revived its support for Japanese supremacy by calling for restoration of the influence of the imperial family.[12] In the late 1970s it had 3.1 million followers, which was the third largest of the new religions after Soka Gakkai (16.5 million) and Risho Koseikai (4.7 million).[13]

Nature of Reality

While some kind of nondualism is doubtless a correct description of Seicho No Ie's view of ultimate reality, most written material stops short of drawing out the full implications of such teaching. Rather, believers are taught to affirm the qualities of goodness and truth by accepting a positive message such as "The World of Reality is filled with goodness."[14] In public meetings the congregation may be led in continuous chanting of the words *Jisso Enman Kanzen*, "reality is absolutely perfect."

Discussions about reality, either in public services or in literature, use popular theistic language such as "God" even though such language has personalistic, and hence dualistic, connotations. But such language is an accommodation to the ignorance of humankind, since reality is beyond our grasp of it. Reality is mind and this is the opposite of matter. Matter, including all that takes place in the material world such as sickness and hate-filled relations between persons, is ultimately false and nonexistent.

"There is no such thing as material appearance. Don't be tricked by things that are not. Know that things that are not are not! Only spiritual reality exists. You are reality. You are Buddha. You are Christ. You are infinite. You are inexhaustible."[15]

The nonmaterial world of purity unfolds into the concrete as a projection of the mind, but the concrete is not the real. Exactly how the material world derives from the realm of pure mind is vague and reminds one of the classical Hindu concept of *maya*, or illusion. The material world is illusory or at least lacks any final reality. These details are not entirely self-consistent since the movement has little interest in focusing on the theoretical. It is the practical results that are sought.

The Religious Goal

The goal which Seicho No Ie promotes is, positively, to accept the truth that there is only God and good in the world. Negatively, the goal is to reject the erroneous idea that evil exists. Steps are presented to assist one to live in this truth as it touches one's life practically. The truth about the world is that it, like God with which it is identical, consists only of love and goodness with no evil admixture. As there is no evil in God, so there is no sickness or disease if one brings one's mind to accept that only goodness and purity exist. This has a curative effect on many, especially those who face a broad range of emotional, psychosocial, and psychophysical problems.

The similarity of this to Christian Science is evident since both deny the existence of evil. Taniguchi's writings bear this out.

There is nothing real in the true sense of the word but God, and those that have come of Him. Sins are not perfect, so they are not of reality. Diseases are imperfect, so they are not real. Death is imperfect, so it could never be of reality. Do not take the things to be real that have not been created by God. Never dream of things in your bad dreams which have no existence in reality nor be afraid of things unreal. Sins, diseases, and death are not what God has created; they have ever assumed the garb of reality. I have come to unmask them to show that sins, diseases and death have no existence in reality.[16]

Evil and Ethics

If evil is illusory in some sense, then on what basis is one to make moral choices? If evil, error, and wrong do not exist, what reason is there to be ethically concerned? An ethical problem based on a Christian teaching is used to illustrate how Seicho deals with this problem. The issue can be put this way. The Bible tells us to love our enemies. But how can one deal with one's "enemies" if, in fact, there is no enemy? The answer of Seicho is that one must begin with first principles: there is no enemy. But, if one believes (wrongly) that enemies exist, it is impossible, humanly speaking, to be reconciled. If enemies do exist at least in the mind, then the hope of reconciliation is not possible. But since there are no enemies, if one accepts Seicho's doctrine one can then be reconciled to those formerly considered enemies. "Only when you realize that you have no enemy will you be able to love anyone without trying to do so purposely."[17]

The voluntary death of Jesus for sins, as viewed by Christians, is reinter-preted along similar lines. Though there is no such thing as sin, there is the mistaken notion that there is. Christ died not to take away sins that truly exist, but to put away such an erroneous notion. "Christ had himself crucified as atonement for humanity's sin in order to exterminate humanity's sin-consciousness."[18] Recognition of a real physical death of Christ, so inconsistent with Seicho's doctrine of none-vil, does not seem to create any tension in their explanation.

Religious Means

The means by which one attains the goal of returning to the original state of purity and goodness include the following:

The *shinsokan* (practice of divine mind) is "prayerful meditation in concentrating the mind." The ultimate purpose is to aid an individual in realizing that the individual, God, goodness, and perfection are one. This practice, which Taniguchi is said to have learned from Omoto-kyo, is believed to have extraordinary power to assist individuals in accepting the truth about reality. But the meditative technique seems intended to influence the unconscious mind as much as the conscious. Since it is the mind that creates sickness, it is through the correcting of the mind that a cure comes.

Public services usually include *shinsokan* undertaken in a kneeling or sitting position with clasped hands held over the nose, elbows hanging straight down, and eyes closed. The leader chants some verses and punctuates them at one point with a shrill cry which, though it is anything but meditative, acts as a verbal signal that something significant has occurred. The period of meditation may end in silent contemplation until hands are clapped twice to signify that the exercise is over.

The focus of meditation can be the *bodhisattva* Kannon (Indian: Avalokitesvara) or the Buddha. *Shinsokan* is not the attempt to still the mind as in Patanjali's Yoga or to empty the mind as in Zen, but to fill it with the positive realization that love and goodness is all that exists.

The end product is the affirmation of the mind that only goodness, perfection, and life exist. One might be tempted to compare it to the modern Western doctrine of "positive thinking," but such a description would fail to acknowledge the underlying metaphysical foundation behind *shinsokan*.

Nempa

While *shinsokan* is effective for the individual who practices it, *nempa* refers to that power, generated by meditating persons, which influences the lives of others. Sometimes described as a kind of spiritual wave, the power of *nempa* can affect others from a distance or impact even the souls of the deceased. "The thought waves are far more delicate than those of the radio; distance will not be a hindrance to receiving them. We have an example of a patient in Manchuria who could neither walk nor sit with his legs folded. He was healed instantly by practicing meditation at the same time that we were praying for the benediction of all the members of Seicho-No-Ie."[19]

Healing of Sickness and Disease

The appeal of Seicho to many Japanese is the promise concerning and testimony about physical healing. In fact, it has been described as "a religion of healing" due to this strong emphasis. Disease simply cannot exist given the truth about a world consisting only of goodness, light, and life. Taniguchi used psychoanalytical explanations to show how sickness could arise from false thinking. "You think something can hurt you. This false idea arouses anger and fear which creates a negative mental wave. And according to the Law of Affinity your negative mental wave will call forth evil mental waves broadcast from the miserable and unhappy people prevailing in the universe. The objectivication of these evil mental waves is so-called disease and misfortune."[20] Such explanations have convinced many Japanese that Siecho No Ie is a significant religious movement in modern Japan.

Discussion

1. Describe *kami*, their diversity, and the ancient mythical supports for them.
2. Discuss shrine Shinto worship.
3. Characterize as best you can the functions of a Shinto priest.
4. What were the fortunes of Shinto after the Meiji Restoration?
5. Compare Honen's and Shinran's views on the Pure Land and how to get there.

6. To what extent is Soka Gakkai dependent on Nichiren's doctrines and to what extent is it a "new religion"?
7. What, in your opinion, might be the appeal of Seicho No Ie to the Japanese people?

Notes

[1]A more complete discussion of this may be found in Niels C. Nielsen, Jr. et al., *Religions of the World* (New York: St. Martin's Press, 1983), 338–42.

[2]H.Byron Earhart, *Japanese Religion: Unity and Diversity* (Belmont, California: Dickenson Publishing Company, 1969), 25–6.

[3]David S. Noss and John B. Noss, *Man's Religions* (New York: Macmillan, 1984), 154.

[4]Robert N. Bellah, "Religion and the Technological Revolution in Japan and the United States," a lecture at Arizona State University, February 19, 1987.

[5]*Soka Gakkai News*, 11, no. 207 (May 1986), 2.

[6]Noah S. Brannen, *Soka Gakkai: Japan's Militant Buddhists* (Richmond: John Knox, 1968), 134.

[7]*Abingdon Encyclopedia of World Religions*, 698.

[8]*The Nichiren Shoshu Soka Gakkai* (Tokyo: The Seikyo Press, 1966), 145.

[9]Ibid., 146–47.

[10]*Soka Gakkai News* 11, no. 206 (April 1986), 2.

[11]Ibid., 3.

[12]*Insight* 4, no. 29 (July 18, 1988), 8–9.

[13]H. Byron Earhart, *Japanese Religion in the Modern Century* (Tokyo: Univ. of Tokyo Press, 1980), 170–71.

[14]Harry Thomsen, *The New Religions of Japan* (Rutland, Vt.: C. E. Tuttle, 1963), 157.

[15]Taniguchi, *Seimei no Jisso*, as quoted in Clark B. Offner and Henry van Straelen, *Modern Japanese Religions* (Leiden: Brill, 1963), 73.

[16]Quoted in Thomsen, *New Religions of Japan*, 159.

[17]Taniguchi, *Seimei No Jisso*, as quoted in Thomsen, *New Religions of Japan*, 163.

[18]Ibid.

[19]From August, 1953, *Seicho No Ie* as quoted in Thomsen, *New Religions of Japan*, 157.

[20]Taniguchi, as quoted in Thomsen, *New Religions of Japan*, 164–65.

Part Five

Contemporary Theologies of Religion

The Pluralism of John Hick

John Hick is a British-born philosopher-theologian who taught at Birmingham University and since 1982 has occupied the Danforth Chair in the Philosophy of Religion at the Claremont Graduate School in California. He is one of the foremost spokespersons of pluralism, a position he took in his 1973 book *God and the Universe of Faiths* and has refined in numerous books and articles since.[1] Other pluralists of one kind or another in this century include Ernst Troeltsch in his later writings, William Hocking, Paul Knitter, and Wilfred Cantwell Smith.

Hick uses the categories of exclusivism, inclusivism, and pluralism in his writings as ways by which Christians see their truth claims in relation to other religions. In so doing he has helped to popularize these categories and, hence, these are the ones which will be followed in this section.

By exclusivism he refers to the view, held almost universally among Christians until this century, that Christ is the only savior and outside him there is no salvation. Hendrik Kraemer's 1938 publication, *The Christian Message in a Non-Christian World* was a major defense of this position. Inclusivists, by contrast, hold that though Christ is God's only way for salvation, sincere followers of the other religions un-knowingly participate in the grace of God in the forms of their own religion. If they cannot hear the Gospel through no fault of their own, they are still saved. This view emerged in the twentieth century among both Protestants and Catholics as a reaction to exclusivism. Its most powerful spokesman is the Catholic theologian Karl Rahner, who coined the phrase "anonymous Christians" to describe followers of other religions who are nonetheless saved.

Hick's position is pluralism which, in contrast to exclusivism and inclusivism, is the belief that the world religions are true and equally effective in reaching liberation, freedom, or salvation. His view can be summarized in a verse from the *Bhagavad Gita* which he cites as being a remarkable revelation. "Howsoever man may approach me, even so do I accept them; for, on all sides, whatever path they may choose is mine."[2]

Hick believes that "Christianity is not the one and only way of salvation, but one among several."[3] He is uneasy with a view of Christianity which sees itself as absolute, unique, final, normative or exclusively true in contrast to other religions. He proposes that world religions such as Judaism, Islam, Buddhism and Hinduism have the same general goal which is moving from self-centeredness to "Reality-centeredness." He arrives at this position not so much by a descriptive analysis of the beliefs of the respective religious communities as by material that is couched in philosophical, theological, historical and phenomenological concerns. These concerns lead to two main points. First, Christianity's claim to either an exclusive or inclusive salvation must be given up and, second, pluralism is correct since all religions save.

Hick's Objections to Exclusivism and Inclusivism

Exclusivism

Biblical and Theological Problems

Hick cannot accept claims about the absoluteness and finality of Christ and the Christian faith. Though himself a member of the Christian religion, Hick is ready to give up the usual marks of Christian uniqueness: claims that the Godhead is triune, Christ is divine and salvation from sin is by the atoning death of a Savior. He recognizes that the linchpin of Christian claims to uniqueness is the Incarnation. Belief in the uniqueness of Jesus as God incarnate and its concomitant, the absoluteness of Christianity, is doubtless an ancient belief of the church that, in his view, must be given up on the grounds of both biblical scholarship and a revised and more appropriate theological interpretation.

Recognizing that New Testament criticism is prone to change its consensus from generation to generation, nevertheless he says scholarly belief that Jesus claimed to be the Son of God "is

no longer generally held."[4] Quoting Wolfhart Pannenberg he agrees that John's gospel is not historically dependable as a source of Jesus' teaching and says that the Christological sayings of John were the creations of the church at the end of the first century. Furthermore, the term "Son of God" cannot be taken literally but only mythically and certainly not factually. The "real meaning" of the Incarnation is not that God fathered Jesus in a literal way with the Holy Spirit acting as male parent. Rather, he is the Son of God in the sense that he is "the saving point of contact" with God. There is something absolute about him which we discover when we experience the presence of God through obedience to Christ. He serves functionally as our point of contact just as other religions have their own point of contact with God. One can affirm salvation in Christ in this way without denying salvation through others who have a similar function.

Selected theologians are called on to supplement his argument against orthodox claims that Christ was uniquely divine and human. Hick examines the attempts of several more adventurous contemporary theologians to explain the meaning of the Incarnation. He looks at the works of Presbyterian Donald Baillie, Anglican Geoffrey Lampe and Roman Catholic Karl Rahner. Each of the three explain the Incarnation differently but have this in common: they suggest that what was true with respect to the interpenetration of the human and divine in Christ's person is merely the perfected form of what can be operative in ordinary persons though, no doubt, to a lesser degree.

Rahner's Christological reflections are the most conservative of the three because, though they come close to overturning the orthodox Chalcedonian formula, in the end he returns to it. The creed made it clear that Christ was both human and divine in a way that was "substantially" different from any other commingling of the divine and human; Christ was human and divine in an absolutely unique way not shared by other humans. But Rahner's statements indicate the possibility that Christ's incarnation can be understood as his possessing in completeness what obedient persons might experience as well. *Incarnation* is a term that can apply to both Christ and his followers since it signifies the operation in the human soul of the grace of God which effects a self-transcending love for others. But Rahner, bound as he is to the Chalcedonian tradition, ultimately turns away from accepting that the Incarnation is a sharable experience. He falls short of affirming that Christ and his disciples in some way occupy only slightly different points on a common continuum.[5]

Baillie is much more bold. In search of an explanation suitable for modern understanding and echoing ideas found in Irenaeus, Augustine, and Origen, he takes as his starting point Paul's words in 1 Corinthians 15:10: "It was not I, but the grace of God which is with me"(RSV). This unlocks for him the paradox of both the Incarnation and the relation between sovereign grace and human freedom. Paul's choices were driven by divinely sover-

eign initiative and yet were freely his own. He experienced both the divine and the human in that most sacred of all arenas, volition. Yet he gives God the glory for whatever element in his choices that were good. The human and the divine commingle with the divine, which achieves its purposes through the human agency. In a more profound and mysterious way the Incarnation was like that but to a perfected degree. The paradox of the grace of God in Christ's incarnation is that though he was human the divine was so perfectly and completely at work that Paul could say, "It was not I but God." In Christ this union was absolute though in others, like Paul, it is present to a lesser degree. Lampe's reflections on the Incarnation take an entirely different approach, but his conclusions are similar to Baillie's. All three seem to either affirm or come close to affirming that the activity of God in the Incarnation is not so unique; all humans may share in it to some degree.

The implications of these ideas about the Incarnation for Hick's theology of religion are momentous and may be summarized as follows. First, these modern explanations of the Incarnation, some of which link up with ancient ideas, show that what Christ was in full, humanity can become in part while in ordinary terrestrial experience. Therefore, Christ was not unique in the sense of having no like nor equal in essential nature; Christ is not absolute. Second, without an absolutist Christ there seems to be no absolutist religion. Hick puts it this way:

> [I]f one says, with the older Christian formulations, that the divine

357

substance was present on earth once and once only, namely in Jesus Christ, it follows as a corollary that the Christian religion, and no other, was founded by God in person; and it certainly seems in turn to follow from this that God must want all human beings to accept Christianity as the religion which God has created for them. . . . But if, with Baillie, we see in the life of Christ a supreme instance of that fusion of divine grace and creaturely freedom that occurs in all authentic human response and obedience to God, then the situation changes.[6]

Ethnocentric, Historical, Moral, and Phenomenological Issues

Once the biblical and theological grounds for Christ's nonuniqueness are shown, Hick believes the explanations for exclusivist claims for Christianity reduce to ethnocentric, historical, moral, and phenomenological ones.

Christians have engaged in a kind of religious ethnocentrism, a self-serving pride which, along with the above dogmatic considerations, have played a major part in their exclusivist claims. This ethnic or "tribal" pride, though regrettable, is inevitable since it is natural for religious groups to believe themselves superior to others. The danger is, however, that such exclusivism has in some cases led to "policies of persecution, coercion, repression, conquest, and exploitation."[7] Critics of Hick have pointed out that just because it is "natural" for religious groups to be self-serving, that does not mean this is the main reason nor the true reason for their truth claims.

The history of Christianity is a history of just such imperialism. Citing "historical facts," Hick refers to Christianity's record of social, economic and political evils due to partnership with nineteenth- and twentieth-century Western colonial powers. This record makes it morally impossible to claim an absolutist faith. Rather than leading colonies to a better world, the Christian faith was guilty not only of partnership in exploitation and oppression but of poisoning inter-religious relations with arrogant claims to superiority. Hick assumes that claims to absoluteness, if justifiable, should be accompanied by a righteous performance by those who hold it but such has not been the case. Rather, fallen human nature, which Hick credits as the source of all such breakdowns of performance, leads to exploitation of the weak, acts of violent aggression, and intolerance. Christianity is not the only religion with such a track record, of course. But it is a damaging fact against exclusivist-type Christianity. Hick takes James Michener's novel *Hawaii* as a dependable source of information about the typical paternalism and prejudice of missionaries everywhere at that time.

Claims to exclusivity in more recent centuries were made without benefit of knowing much about other religions. This situation was significantly altered by the events of the nineteenth century wherein colonialists of Christian Europe gained extensive firsthand contact with Hindus, Buddhists, Muslims, and others. The progressive increase of knowledge about the non-Christian religions since that time has made it intellectually impossible for Christians to claim exclusivism. The study of non-Christian texts and religions has corrected mistaken stereotypes of these religions and taught Christians the depth of the spiritual riches in the very religions to which they had, in ignorance, compared themselves so favorably.

The failure of Christianity to convert the world to its position is a practical argument against exclusivism. Past expectations that Christianity would take over the world due to its absoluteness are not supported by current statistics. Though the number of Christians is increasing worldwide, the percentage of Christians relative to world population is dropping. This fact militates against the idea that Christianity is succeeding due to its superior status.

Further evidence against the absoluteness of Christianity comes from a phenomenological comparison between Christianity and the other religions. By phenomenological he refers to what meets the eye and the ear; those features of the religions which present themselves to an observer by participation or observation. Citing prayers of Jewish, Muslim, Sikh, and Hindu *bhakti* believers, he holds that while the forms of the religions may be different, and while the names for God may differ (examples are Adonai, Allah, Param Atma, and Rama), there cannot be different gods but the names must refer to the same God. Hick says only three possibilities exist to explain these different gods. All may have separate existence; only one may exist (the true God as espoused by one of the religions); or all may exist but not in the sense of each having separate, ontological existence. (In one context, Hick fails to recognize another option: none of these may exist.) The true view is that each name stands for one and the same God. God is one though there are "different, overlapping concepts or mental images of him."[8] Hick bases this conclusion on his belief that the conflicting phenomenological claims can only be reconciled in one way: by accepting that each entity essentially refers to the same reality.

Lastly, Hick believes that the history of religion, governed by an evolution from simple and low to higher and better, militates against any exclusivist claim. The history of religions demonstrates that earliest religions were succeeded by the "higher religions" which share much in common. At first "natural religions" worshiped spirits, nature gods, and bloodthirsty deities. This was followed by what Karl Jaspers called the axial period during which the "higher religions" emerged out of Greece, Palestine, India, and China from 800 B.C.E. on and included figures such as the Hebrew prophets, Zoroaster, Confucius, the Buddha, upanishadic writers, Socrates, and Plato. Jesus and Muhammad continued in that tradition. All the religions or ideologies formed at this time were somewhat isolated from each other and Hick accepts *a priori* that it is "a natural and indeed an inevitable hypothesis" that God revealed his presence to a number of sensitive persons. Due to the isolated linguistic, social, and cultural contexts in which each revelation was given, each form of the divine revelation was different. Nonetheless, Hick is certain the message is the same to all.

Problems with Inclusivism

The above factors have contributed to a significant shift away from exclusivist theology in the modern period. Nowhere is this seen more dramatically than in the theology of the Roman Catholic Church, which has drastically revised its view of the relation between the church and the non-Christian religions. The classic exclusivist view of the Roman Catholic Church, *extra ecclesiam nulla salus*— "outside the Roman Catholic Church there is no salvation"—has been radically modified. Documents issued after Vatican II (1963–65), together with the papal statement *"Redemptor Hominis"* (1979), demonstrate how the Catholic Church has exchanged its earlier exclusivism for the belief that non-Christians receive the grace of God and are united with Christ in a manner which, though mysterious and known only to God, truly saves. The newer view, as held in some form by both Hans Küng or Karl Rahner, is called "anonymous Christianity." Its fundamental mark is that though the truth of other religions is not adequate in itself for salvation, nevertheless world religions—Hindu, Muslim, Buddhist—can be a means of saving grace. Protestants have developed similar views of inclusivism. In both camps, inclusivism says that persons in other religions are saved, but the basis of salvation is on Christian grounds and not on the grounds of the non-Christian religion. It is the Gospel that saves, Christ who is the Savior, and the God of Jesus who is at work in other religions. Many of the arguments Hick brings against exclusivism are also directed against the inclusivists' Christology and their belief in a normative Gospel.

Hick and Pluralism

Hick believes the earlier "intolerant exclusivism" of the church, subsequently replaced by "benevolent inclusivism," must now yield to pluralism. This will take Christian theology further in the direction it is "naturally heading." The effect of Hick's view is sweeping. Gone are the direct or indirect claims of absolute truth in either their exclusivist or inclusivist forms. As Hick says, "the whole terrain of Christian truth is bound to look different."

Hick's argument for pluralism has been successfully popularized by his use of an analogy based on the Ptolemaic and Copernican theories of astronomy. It will be remembered that Ptolemaic astronomers mistakenly regarded the earth as the center of the universe and explained the orbits of other heavenly bodies as anomalous epicycles not conforming to their theory. It was not until Copernicus proved that all bodies in the earth's universe rotate around the sun that the earlier view was abandoned. What the geocentric view of the universe was to the heliocentric view, exclusivists/inclusivists are to the pluralist position. The new and correct view is that it is God around which things center and not Christ or Christianity. Christianity, so long thought to be the truth-center of the universe, is itself only one of many religious spheres which pivot around the central point of God himself. Any other view is, theologically speaking, Ptolemaic. In summary, this powerful analogy teaches the following:

1. God (better the Real, the Ultimate, the noumenal) is the center of the religious world.

2. Any view that makes Christ or Christianity the center and test of religious truth is erroneous.

3. The world religions are, in fact, theocentric. They have their center in the one Reality which is common to them all.

4. The truth of these religions is judged not by their distance from Christ but from God.

5. Christianity is only one of the many religions and the test of its truth is no different than the test of truth for the others: Does it manifest the noumenal and is it effective in morally changing lives?

More recently Hick has preferred the term noumenal to the term God. "Noumenal" has the advantage over the English term "God" in that it can serve as a referent for either personal or impersonal conceptions of the real. According to Hick the religious experience of the noumenal is inevitably understood in cultural forms and ideas that to some extent express the noumenal but to some extent distort it as well. It is essential to his theory of religious pluralism that all phenomenal expressions of the real in the world religions have as their true and only referent a noumenon which can be simultaneously understood as either *personae* (Yahweh, Allah, Amida Buddha, Vishnu, Shiva) or *impersonae*

(non-personal Brahman, Tao, Shunyata or emptiness). The Jewish, Christian, Muslim and Jodo Buddhists have apprehended the noumenal in theistic terms while Hindu advaitans, Taoists, and Zen Buddhists apprehend the same reality in non-personal ways. The logic of Hick's view of the relationship between the noumenal and its phenomenal manifestations has stimulated considerable debate among scholars.

Some may want to ask how Hick's theory of pluralism can serve as a unifying theory of religion if the noumenal can be properly taken as both personal and impersonal.[9] How can both be descriptive of it? If it is a personalist noumenon then his theology of religion has its general appeal to those who likewise affirm that the Real is personal. This would include most Christians, Muslims, Hindu bhaktists, Jews and others whose systems are basically theistic. But such a conception leaves out a vast number of religious believers who either do not believe in a personal deity or whose traditional theology does not so believe. Examples would be Tipitaka Buddhists, Vedantic Hindus of advaitan persuasion and Zen Buddhists. If Hick affirms the one conception, it seems he must exclude the other and thus what becomes of his central affirmation that there is a God who is at the center of the *universe* of faiths? If he affirms that the personal and impersonal are both expressions of the Real, which he clearly does, there is question about the coherence of his concept of the noumenal.

Pluralism is Hick's term for the way the religions are related to truth: the major religions share equally in the truth of salvation. But it is essential to understand what Hick means by "salvation" here. By this he means "the transformation of human existence from self-centeredness to God- or Reality-centeredness."[10] Though he does not identify it as such, by offering this as the universal definition of salvation for all religion, Hick is proposing his own theological interpretation of the religious goals of the major religions. He makes no attempt to describe the religious goals of the world religions, in part or in whole, in a way that shows how his and theirs are congruent. That is, his definition of salvation does not arise out of, nor is it shown to be demanded by, the historical religions. It is his meaning for salvation which he imputes to them and assumes is true about them.

Since the world religions have, in his view, a common understanding of salvation, he proceeds to offer support for his position of pluralism. "Historical evidence" and "observable facts" are called upon to demonstrate that all these religions are equally true, no one religion has a monopoly on the truth and all are transformative in nature.[11] Two general evidences of transformation in the religions are brought forward: individual and social. The saints of all the religions are the first evidence and the social transformations effected by the religions constitute the second. Mahatma Gandhi of India is a prime example of a "saint" who personally embodied self-giving love and inspired it in others. Each of the great religions has persons who, like Gandhi, have given themselves to God in similar ways. However, he recognizes that such a claim

cannot be proved since "we do not at present command the conceptual precision . . . for objective comparative judgments."[12] In other contexts we have seen that Hick cited "historical facts" as discrediting claims to exclusivism. However, he recognizes that empirical facts are a questionable support for pluralism due to a "very partial and unsystematic body of historical knowledge."[13] It appears that Hick is in the position of saying that history can disprove the absoluteness of Christianity (its moral performance in nineteenth- and twentieth-century imperialist colonialism was lacking) but cannot prove the truth of pluralism. It would seem that historical facts cannot be used as a major support for either position.

Analysis of Hick's Ideas

Some critique has been implied in the description above but let us now turn more directly to a brief analysis of Hick's pluralism under the following topics: incarnation and the centrality of Christ, Hick's Copernican revolution in theology, the relationship of the noumenal to the phenomenal, and connection between religious morality and the claims of truth.

The Incarnation and the Centrality of Christ

Hick is correct in choosing the Incarnation as the most significant issue for the Christian claim to absoluteness. For if it is true that God himself came in human form in the person of Jesus Christ of Nazareth and proclaimed a message for humanity to hear and heed, then claims to absoluteness stand. We have seen that Hick seems to accept the witness of only one side of this Christological controversy.

Coward refers to the work of New Testament scholar James Dunn as representative of investigations not in substantial disagreement with the traditional understanding of the nature of Christ.[14] Dunn is of the opinion that much modern scholarship agrees that, while biblical passages relating to Christ's person may not explicitly affirm preexistent divine sonship, neither do they deny it. Some passages accommodate that conception rather well even though others may not be easily identified with it. The effect is that modern critical scholarship is not nearly so negative about the nature of Christ as the material Hick draws on for his conclusions.

Has Hick been able to successfully replace Christ at the center of his theology with a nondescript noumenon? D'Costa has shown that Hick has consistently stated in writings in 1978 and 1981 that the Christian only knows God's love experientially through Jesus Christ. This is in some considerable tension with his other statements that Christ is not God. But has Hick, at least for himself, been able to sever his view of God from Christ? D'Costa doesn't think so. He examines Hick's complex view of the incarnation and concludes that even though Hick rejects a unique incarnational disclosure so as to avoid the implication that Christ alone saves (exclusivism), he cannot avoid concluding that Christ in some sense is the one through whom Christians experience the love and grace of God. Hick seems to be in the position of

rejecting an exclusive Christ but affirming a normative one. Thus his theocentrism is compromised, Christ becomes to some extent essential, and Hick's position remains, to some extent, Christocentric.[15]

A Copernican Revolution in Theology?

Hick's earlier formulations of his theory of pluralism seemed to place a great deal of weight on the analogy of the Copernican revolution. By citing Copernicus's undeniable finding that the earth and the planets revolve around the sun rather than all planets revolving around the earth, he has seized on an excellent analogy for his position. He believes that the center of truth is God and not a human Jesus, just as the center of the solar system is the sun and not the earth. The religions, including Christianity, are like planets which reflect the light of the central source.

However, it must be remembered that this is only an analogy and cannot tell us anything whatsoever about the correctness of his theology of religions. Hick, or perhaps his readers, may be easily caught up in the rhetoric and momentarily forget that illustrations only illustrate. But in at least one place, noted above, he comes close to making it serve an *evidential* end. In his essay "Whatever Path Men Choose Is Mine" he speaks of Copernicus's scientific discovery. "Copernicus *realized* that it is the sun, and not the earth, that is at the centre, and that all the heavenly bodies including our own earth, revolve around it. And we have to realize that the universe of faiths centres upon *God* and not upon

Christianity or upon any other religion."[16] A reminder seems in order here. What it means to "realize" something scientifically and what it means to "realize" something theologically involves radically different methods of evidence. But the language seems to blur this fundamental distinction and functions to give his theological conclusions the strength of a crucial scientific discovery.

An exclusivist might reverse the Ptolemaic-Copernican analogy to illustrate the cogency of his argument. It might go something like this. As theory making does not change reality, so throughout religious history humankind and the various religions have advanced their theories and been engaged in a search for the truth. All the religious thinkers of history have been, so to speak, theoreticians of divine astronomy. They have been the Ptolemaic seers. Some have not been able to see beyond their own planet to conjecture about their relation to others. Others have peered outwardly into the universe of truth inaccurately but not entirely mistakenly. The sun has been there all along, but the inaccuracies or inadequacies of their instruments have meant they have not understood exactly how that sphere related to their own existence. Some religions have mistakenly claimed all other religious spheres revolved around their own. Such conclusions did not change the reality. All along God in Christ has been the epicenter of their universe. In the coming of Jesus Christ God has made it clear that his truth is in the Son of God. He is the pivot of all truth and all human religions, societies, and cultures must take their bearings from him.

The Noumenal and the Phenomenal: A Troubled Relationship

Harold Netland has raised questions about Hick's views of the relationship between the Real *an sich* (as it is) and the Real as it is experienced and conceptualized as diverse *personae*, "images," or "manifestations" of the religions.[17] Though it is true that theologians of many religious traditions have made a distinction between the infinite Real and conditioned human experiences of it, all have had to deal with problems concerning continuity and discontinuity between the two. Hick seems to affirm both continuity and discontinuity.[18]

If there is continuity and if the diverse *personae* (Yahweh, Allah, Nirguna Brahman, Amida Buddha, Shunyata, Vishnu) are all manifestations of the one Real as Hick says, why is there such diversity and contradiction amongst them? Not only do each of these function differently within their religious systems but there are fundamental differences in their natures since some are non-personal (Nirguna Brahman, Shunyata) and others are personal (Yahweh, Allah, Amida Buddha and Vishnu). Can the Real be a single divine reality, as Hick claims, if accurate expressions of it are mutually exclusive? Perhaps reality is not singular (noumenon) but plural (noumena) in which case polytheism would be closer to the truth than either theism or monism. Netland's comment seems helpful here.

Now here it is not just a question of whether the Eternal One can be *experienced* as personal and non-personal, it is a question of whether its ontological status is such that can correctly be described as both personal and non-personal. For it *may* be possible for the divine reality to be experienced as personal and non-personal without necessarily being both. (Perhaps the Eternal One is able to present itself in certain situations as a non-personal ground of being.) But since the respective traditions are making significant ontological claims it seems that the divine reality must actually be both personal and non-personal if these claims are to be taken seriously.[19]

On the other hand, if there is discontinuity, and Hick seems to affirm there is, then how do we know the *personae* are representative of it? The problem for Hick is that if the Real *an sich* is unknowable, then on what grounds can one be sure the religious conceptions are distortions proper to the Real. In other words, if there is the discontinuity which Hick claims, how then can criteria arise to make judgments between conceptions that are proper to the Real and those that are false, imaginary or delusory?

Hick seems to be saying the *personae* are both accurate expressions and also distortions of the Real. If the *personae* are accurate expressions and there is some degree of continuity, then Professor Hick must elaborate the ontological and epistemic nature of that continuity in such a way as to provide greater coherence to his theory. If there is discontinuity, then the knowledge of the ultimate referent behind religious conceptions and Hick's theory of religious pluralism are both in some jeopardy. Altogether, these issues raise significant questions about the adequacy of Hick's theory of pluralism to give a unified account for the

diverse conceptions of the Real found in the world religions.

Religious Morality and the Claims of Truth

While not his main argument against the exclusivist position, Hick argues that Christianity cannot be the true and only religion due to its rather poor performance ethically and morally. It must surely be admitted that Christian colonialists were sometimes abusive and arrogant. Native clergy and foreign missionaries no doubt both took advantage of their connections with colonial rulers to gain followers by intimidation and ignoble means. Further, the peoples and cultures they sought to convert were indeed sometimes dealt with in insensitive and unjust ways. Newbigin acknowledges all this when he speaks of the "acute bad conscience of western man" in modern times, many of whom were confessing Christians.[20] The immoral and inhumane performance of some Christians for their part in genocide, slave running and cultural imperialism has been a source of historical embarrassment and humiliation. What should be said in response to this?

First of all, there is no doubt the church in many places has repented, is still repenting and must continue to carry the memory of its guilt. It has sinned and is in need of the forgiveness and grace of God just like other sinners. It might be noted, however, that not all the wrong attributed to Christians was in fact committed by Christians. Specifically, it was not only Christians that were involved in slave trading. Muslim Arabs were as much or more involved in this as the Christian west and Newbigin wonders aloud about the signs of repentance for that among the modern Muslim states. Jesus himself warned in the parable of the wheat and the tares in Mt. 13:19–30 that the false would mix with the true. This is not to excuse the wrong or shift the blame but to realistically identify the larger group of wrong-doers.

But can the history of flawed Christendom in one era discredit the claims of the Gospel in that era or another? Is the truthfulness of a religion dependent on the moral performance of its followers? Hendrik Kraemer was probably right to argue that the Biblical faith and the social and ecclesiastical expressions of it must be kept separate. Not that this separation can ever be total but still it is not for Christendom that exclusive claims are made; the claim is for the truth that judges both it and all other religio-ecclesiastical entities. Thinking Christians maintain that Jesus Christ, as the Way, the Truth and the Life, came temporarily *into* history not that His kingdom has yet come enduringly in history. Thus while Hick's statement sounds a warning to Christians about their oft inadequate moral performance, it does not discredit the exclusivist position.

Discussion

1. What do you think are Hick's strongest supports for pluralism?
2. How does Hick view Christ and how important is Christology to his pluralist position? Similarly, how important is it to the exclusivist position?
3. What use does Hick make of Copernicus' heliocentric discovery in presenting his pluralist position?
4. What implications follow for pluralists and exclusivists if, as Hick claims, God and not Christ is the true center of all religions?

Notes

[1]A recent revision of his theory of religious pluralism is *An Interpretation of Religion* (New Haven, Conn.: Yale University Press, 1989).

[2]John Hick, "'Whatever Path Men Choose Is Mine,'" in *Christianity and Other Religions: Selected Readings*, ed. John Hick and Brian Hebblethwaite (Philadelphia: Fortress, 1980), 190. A more extensive definition of pluralism is as follows: ". . .the view that the great world faiths embody different perceptions and conceptions of, and correspondingly different responses to, the real or the ultimate from within the major variant cultural ways of being human; and that within each of them the transformation of human existence from self-centeredness to Reality-centeredness is manifestly taking place—and taking place, so far as human observation can tell, to much the same extent. Thus the great religious traditions are to be regarded as alternative soteriological spaces within which, or ways along which, men and women can find salvation/liberation/fulfillment." John Hick, "Religious Pluralism and Absolute Claim," in *Religious Pluralism*, ed. Leroy S. Rouner, Boston University Studies in Philosophy and Religion, vol. 5 (Notre Dame, Ind.: Univ. of Notre Dame Press, 1984), 194.

[3]John Hick, "The Non-Absoluteness of Christianity," in *The Myth of Christian Uniqueness: Toward a Pluralistic Theology of Religions*, Faith Meets Faith Series, ed. John Hick and Paul F. Knitter (Maryknoll, N.Y.: Orbis, 1987), 33. See also John Hick, "'Whatever

Path Men Choose is Mine,' " in *Christianity and Other Religions: Selected Readings*, eds., John Hick and Brian Hebblethwaite (Philadelphia: Fortress Press, 1980); and John Hick "Religious Pluralism and Absolute Claim," in *Religious Pluralism*, Boston University Studies in Philosophy and Religion, ed. by Leroy S. Rouner, 5 (Notre Dame, Ind.: The University of Notre Dame Press, 1984).

[4]Hick, "'Whatever Path,' " 184.

[5]Hick, "Religious Pluralism," 204–205.

[6]Ibid., 209–210.

[7]Ibid., 197.

[8]Hick, "'Whatever Path,' " 178.

[9]Harold Coward, *Pluralism: Challenge to World Religions* (Maryknoll, N.Y.: Orbis, 1985), 30.

[10]Hick, "The Non-Absoluteness of Christianity," 23.

[11]Ibid.

[12]Ibid., 24.

[13]Ibid.

[14]Coward, *Pluralism*, 29–30.

[15]Gavin D'Costa, *Theology and Religious Pluralism: The Challenge of Other Religions* (New York: Basil Blackwell, 1986), 30ff. But see Hick's response on this to D'Costa in "Straightening the Record: Some Response to Critics," *Modern Theology*, Vol 6, no. 2 (January 1990): 188–191.

[16]Hick, "'Whatever Path,' " 182; first two italics mine.

[17]Harold Netland, "Professor Hick on Religious Pluralism," *Religious Studies*, Vol. 22 (June 1986): 258–61.

[18]John Hick, *God Has Many Names* (Philadelphia: Westminster Press, 1982), 59, 83.

[19]Harold Netland, "Professor Hick on Religious Pluralism," 259.

[20]Lesslie Newbigin, *The Finality of Christ* (Richmond: John Knox, 1969), 11.

12 The Inclusivism of Karl Rahner

Inclusivism is that position which "affirms the salvific presence of God in non-Christian religions while still maintaining that Christ is the definitive and authoritative revelation of God."[1]

This position is not exclusively a Roman Catholic phenomenon, but its most able spokesperson was the Roman Catholic theologian, Karl Rahner. Rahner was born in Germany in 1904 and after becoming a Jesuit priest, he distinguished himself as one of the church's most influential theologians in the years before and after the Second Vatican Council (1962–65). He wrote extensively and his works were collated into twenty volumes under the title *Theological Reflections*. To the extent that he paid attention to non-Christian religions at all, he was more interested in general facts about their traditions than he was in the details of their belief systems. In this sense he was much like other Western theologians such as Karl Barth, Hans Küng, or Carl F. H. Henry.

One very practical theological issue dominates Rahner's theology of religions. What about all the people, both before and after Christ, who have had no opportunity to hear of the grace of the one true God? Even the biblical Israelites knew nothing of the historical Jesus, and what is to be said about

their eternal destiny? The majority of humankind up to and perhaps including the present generation has not had opportunity to hear an intelligent presentation of the Gospel of grace. Rahner regards it as "senseless" and cruel to hold that all people outside of Christ are so evil and rebellious that "the offer of grace ought not be made" to them somehow.[2] It is "impossible to think" that the personal guilt of man is so great that it would render ineffective the grace of God. "[W]e have no really conclusive reason for thinking so pessimistically of men."[3]

Compounding the situation is the steady loss of Christian influence in areas once strongly held by the church. Rahner was aware of the decline of Catholic Christianity in Europe and the world in modern times. "It is almost two thousand years since the Church received her commission to preach the message of Christ to all nations unto the ends of the earth. In principle we have reached those ends. . . . Yet what position does the message of Christ occupy in it? In the ancient cultures of Asia it has never been able to gain a foothold, and in the West where it became one of the historical roots it is still steadily losing in importance and influence."[4]

An additional problem is that due to

the general failure of Christianity, religious pluralism persists and expands, invading lands where Christianity was the established religion. Further, newer ideologies such as Marxism and other ungodly worldviews rise with the force of religion to capture hearts and minds formerly solidly under the influence of Christian thought. The exodus, in the heartland of Western Christendom, of former Christians to these religions and ideologies constitutes for many Christians a "vexation" and a "scandal."

Thus, in view of the halting spread of Christianity, its demise in its own strongholds, and the rise of competing religions, the question must be asked: Is Christianity's success at an end and its claim to uniqueness and absoluteness to be given up? Rahner's answer is in the negative. He comes forth with a program for understanding the success of Christianity as a complex reality having two basic forms: explicit and anonymous.

"Explicit Christianity" exists on the historical and descriptive level. In this sense Christianity has its historically tangible and socioecclesiastical manifestation in the church founded on Jesus, the apostles, the Scriptures, the sacraments, and the teachings and traditions of the church. It refers to individuals who have entered the faith by conscious acceptance of the teachings and sacraments. Those who belong have been baptized and have formally entered the church. This "Christianity" has not been, for all people at all times, the way of salvation, but is the objective and socially visible manifestation of God's salva-tion which is available to all humankind and comes to them at a moment in their own personal history.

"Anonymous" or implicit Christianity is different from explicit Christianity. This term, which he first used in 1960, is at the heart of the theology which has become a central part of late-twentieth-century Catholic orthodoxy. Without ever having heard the name of Jesus, people from all religions, whether polytheists, atheists, or pantheists, can experience the grace of God in Christ and thus become anonymous Christians enjoying saving faith. This saving faith comes only through a Christ they do not know, yet can be enjoyed even when the person is not conscious of any of the realities that make him or her a Christian. Rahner believes that the anonymous Christian, being nonofficial and possessing a low degree of membership in the church, must still move toward a more explicit faith when given an opportunity, and that the church should continue its missionary mandate. However, even if the details of the Gospel should fail to be presented, the individual would still have saving faith.

Several questions arise concerning Rahner's theology of religions. First, what are Rahner's presuppositions or axioms? Second, what is the nature of the objective action which brings about universal salvation? This has to do with Rahner's Christology. Third, under what circumstances is this salvation appropriated by people in the non-Christian religions? This deals with his anthropology. Fourth, what is to be done about the non-Christian religious beliefs of those he accredits as anonymous Christians?

Rahner's Theological Axioms

Two axioms lie at the heart of Rahner's theology of religions and he constantly returns to them.[5] The first is that salvation is in Christ and Christ alone. This axiom drives Rahner to attempt to construct a theology of religions based on the central doctrines of the Catholic faith in its most modern expressions. The second is that God wills all the world to be saved. Rahner's theology is an attempt to bring these two axioms to bear upon each other and universally upon humankind in its various religious traditions. Outside of Christ there is no salvation, yet the possibility of salvation must, on unambiguous Christian grounds, extend to all humanity.

Rahner takes it as a given of both Catholic theology and Scripture that God wills all the world to be saved and has set in motion the necessary means to accomplish that end. "God desires the salvation of everyone. . . . It is a salvation really intended for all those millions upon millions of people who lived perhaps a million years before Christ—and also for those who have lived after Christ—in nations, cultures and epochs of a very wide range which were still completely shut off from the viewpoint of those living in the light of the New Testament."[6]

He examines several historic models of redemption in search of one which will accommodate his Christocentric universalism. It goes without saying that he rejects the view of an earlier Catholic theology of mission, one still held by many evangelical Protestants, that those who do not explicitly receive Christ are lost and bound for perdition. In Rahner's view this mistakenly places salvation on an individualistic basis wherein each person must consciously hear of God's grace and respond to it. The fact that the whole world *cannot* and does not have access to salvation in this way, together with a second fact that the whole world *must* have access, means that another way of understanding redemption must be discovered.

Other models of universal redemption are also flawed. One model has been belief in a saving natural revelation derived through observations and interactions with nature similar to what is suggested in Paul's statements in Romans 1:19–20. This Rahner rejects since it leads only to a "purely metaphysical knowledge of God" which is not a saving knowledge, for it leaves out the human, social and historical experience essential for salvation.

Rahner also rejects any explanation which would ground salvation in doctrines outside of Christ, such as the explanations of pluralists who bypass Christ and generalize "salvation" in such a way that all religious goals are made to couple with Christian salvation.

Rahner appeals to John 3:8, Acts 10:47, and especially 1 Timothy 2:4, which Rahner returns to frequently since it speaks of God "who wants all men to be saved."[7] Boutin recognizes, however, that the passages Rahner cites do not, themselves, teach his anonymous Christian conclusions. He indicates that a critic of Rahner "was apparently right when he stated, in 1973, that there is no accurate study of the question of salvation of so-called non-Christians according to Scripture."[8]

Rahner's Christology: The Objective Action That Makes Possible the Salvation of Non-Christians

There is a full recognition of the historical Jesus in the theology of Rahner. What is unclear is whether the historical Jesus is definitive for Rahner's Christology.

Rahner's Christology addresses anew the question which medieval theologians debated: Why did God become human? Anselm's *Cur Deus Homo*, a classic response to this difficult issue, articulated a position which Rahner specifically rejects. Anselm held that the death of Christ was required because God was angry at sinful humankind and needed to be placated. The Cross satisfied God's demand for justice and resulted in the forgiving and saving grace of God toward sinners. In contrast, Rahner holds that the death of Christ was not required because of some lack or need in God, not even the need for him to receive judicial satisfaction required by the sinful offenses of humankind. Furthermore, it wasn't Christ's incarnation, death, resurrection, and ascension that effected God's will to be gracious, rather it was God's voluntary and preexisting grace right from the start that brought about the incarnation and death of Christ. "God is not transformed from a God of anger and justice into a God of mercy and love by the cross; rather God brings the event of the cross to pass since he is possessed from the beginning of gratuitous mercy and, despite the world's sin, shares himself with the world, so overcoming its sin."[9]

The significance of the Incarnation is thus brought forward into humankind's history and makes its contribution in connection with fallen human nature and universal redemption, not subsequently in time. But the incarnation and cross have universal significance on other grounds as well since both are "signs." Signs can be of two kinds: those that signify something beyond themselves and those that embody the reality signified. The cross is the latter. It has causal significance as a unique sign whereby the grace of God becomes universally operative in the world. "The cross has primary sacramental causality for the salvation of all men."[10] In sum, though the cross is a particular historical event, treated as a sign, it has universally saving effects.

Rahner's Anthropology: The *Theiosis* of Human Nature

The universal effects of the incarnation, cross and resurrection, treated as sacramental signs affect the ontology or being-ness of human nature. Thus Rahner sees the universal meaning of the cross as manifest in history but located primarily in creation so far as the majority of humanity is concerned; the very nature of mankind is graciously affected. This is an assertion of Rahner which he reasons on theological, philosophical, linguistic and psychological grounds.[11]

The ontological impact of the Incarnation on human nature is referred to as the "supernatural existential." While Rahner never deals with this idea systematically in any one place, it is used throughout his writings and may be defined as the grace-given existential capacity or modality in human nature to freely accept the self-communication of God through proper response-decisions. In short, humankind has a transcendental essence which can lead to its salvation without ever having heard of Christ.[12]

The keys to this thought are revelation, grace, and human nature and how these ideas relate. In the supernatural existential Rahner seeks to preserve salvation as grace-given while making it possible for all humans, even those in non-Christian religions, to freely choose it since the potential is given in their very nature.

The nature of the human being has two important characteristics: self-consciousness and God-consciousness. By "God-consciousness" Rahner means that humankind is not closed in upon itself but is open to a "mysterious Infinity." Thus the human being is both "self-aware" and "Transcendent-aware." Both are steady, not intermittent, states of experience. But just as one does not conceptualize self-awareness, so one does not typically objectify in analytical thought the givenness of the Transcendent. The Transcendent in human nature is present as "Question," which is implicit and incoherent. This is the "way of being" that characterizes the human being.

Revelation is an accepted fact for Rahner, first in the traditional sense of God entering history in Old Testament events, and in the God-man Jesus Christ. But revelation also occurs in the supernatural existential, a revelation which is internal and personal existing in two modes. First, as we have seen, God is truly present to human beings as Question but, secondly, for some he is manifest as "Answer" as well. This revelation within, whether as vague Question or more specific Answer, is the result of the operation of the grace of God. Rahner says that the very fact of the human being's openness to mystery is the evidence of the reality of revelation and grace.

God experienced as revelatory Answer is the experience of a truly transcendental, supernatural, and saving revelation. But when God reveals his mysterious presence supernaturally yet objectively in history, it is the same mystery that addresses every human being either as unconscious Question or more sharply as objective Answer. This mystery is the triune God: Father, Son, and Holy Spirit.

In Rahner's view there is a continuum between the transcendental supernatural, whether experienced as Question or Answer, and the objective historical form of revelation. All is revelation to some degree; all is an experience of grace. There is no difference in kind, only in degree of saving grace. The objectified form of revelation in history is no more revelation, even though more specific, than revelation as Answer in the human experience. The revelation as Answer is no less saving to those who respond than revelation in history is to believing persons. "The expressly Christian revelation becomes the explicit statement of the revelation of grace which man always experiences implicitly in the depths of his being."[13]

Revelation of God as Question and Answer occurs in the religions because it occurs in religious persons. Religion is the result of a combination of sinful hearts and corrupted natural reason. It is also the result of the steady-state openness of religious persons to the Mystery given graciously by God to all humans. While persons in the non-Christian religions have an experience of God, the highest manifestation historically of the Transcendent God is experienced in explicit Christianity.

Rahner's complex understanding of human nature seems to indicate that sinful humanity is not, by virtue of the operation of human nature alone, able to experience God. He wishes to say that the experience of God is not natural but is due to the operation of the grace of God as a mode of human nature. How does God's grace come to humankind and when does it come?

The answer is connected to Jesus and the Cross but resides in human nature. As we have seen, the Cross is the result of God's grace. God decides to save and humankind is ontologically affected by this intention, since God's sovereign end for humanity cannot fail to have its effect. Human beings must have the innate ability to receive a self-communication from God, that is, a transcendental revelation outside historic or explicit Chris-

tianity. This intention of God to save becomes a constitutional modality in the operation of human beings wherein or whereby individuals are able to freely accept or reject the self-communication of God. The supernatural existential is the potential to experience God as Question while yet freely choose God as Answer.

Jesus is present in the supernatural existential. How? Rahner affirms that God as Question includes a reference to the incarnate Christ. In Rahner's essay on "The Universality of Salvation" he makes it clear that the unthematic quest of humankind is a Christological quest and that "this Christological search is in fact directed to Jesus, for it is Jesus who in reality is its proper goal."[14]

How does the person untouched by explicit Christianity become an anonymous Christian? Here we take up the question of how the universal salvation available in Christ is appropriated by those in the non-Christian religions. Individuals do so by their response to the grace of God in them in the supernatural existential. Rahner speaks of the individual experiencing the self-communication of God when he or she "really accepts *himself completely*. . . . Prior to the explicitness of official ecclesiastical faith this acceptance can be present in an implicit form whereby a person undertakes and lives the duty of each day in the quiet sincerity of patience, in devotion to his material duties and the demands made upon him by the persons under his care."[15]

Put in practical terms one becomes an anonymous Christian enjoying God's saving grace in Christ when one loves one's neighbor as referred to in Matthew 25. The capacity to love another is grace-given and hence an experience of God and Christ. "Love does not find its full realisation out of its own resources but from the radical unity it has with the love of God in Jesus Christ. It implies a unity of the love of God and the love of neighbour, in which the love of neighbour is the love of God and so has an absolute quality, even if this lacks thematic expression."[16] The salvation of non-Christians presupposes only that they "are of good will, even when this good will has absolutely nothing to do with Jesus Christ."[17]

Rahner's Theology of Religion and the History of Religion

Rahner's goal is to construct a theology which, though it does not depend on history of religion, at least does not totally ignore it, either. The following are questions of some importance: What status do non-Christian religions have relative to the Christian faith and how is the answer to this question decided? How do the two disciplines of theology and history of religions relate in the "inclusivism" of Karl Rahner? Let us take up these questions one by one.

First, what is the status of non-Christian religions? Until Christianity is "really present" among a people, their pagan religions are more than "natural theology" combined with error. They contain elements of the authentic grace of God which saves. Hence, pagan religions become as "lawful" as

Christianity itself, though to some lesser degree. They are given positive value generally, though when considered separately the degree varies.

A non-Christian religion is a "lawful" religion in the following sense. First, until its followers have a Christian witness it is a means by which non-Christians gain a "right relationship to God." Second, the religion is included in God's plan of salvation since its followers are under God's grace.[18] To deny this is "certainly absolutely wrong."[19] This is supported by reference to the old covenant with the Jews. The religion of Israel was, like pagan religions, a "lawful religion" marked by a mixing of truth and error, divine laws and human corruptions. It lacked the institution of the Catholic Church, by which, Rahner is convinced, some permanent "norm of differentiation" was finally and infallibly erected for the judging of religion. Old Testament religion was a unity of truth mixed with error which was "willed by God" providentially for the salvation of Jews. It had only the status of "lawful religion" since neither written scriptures nor the institution of the prophets provided concrete standards for Israel by which corruption, error, and moral wrong could be judged.

How does Rahner arrive at the position of "lawful religions"? His conclusions are not based on any descriptive examination of the religious truth claims of others. The history of religions does not play any role in this. This is purely a theological conclusion. Rahner has not felt it necessary to examine the truth claims of the non-Christian religions in formulating his view of the theology of religions. As a theologian he comes to the religions with *a priori* assumptions, which is a different approach from the historian of religions who believes that one must inquire about religious claims first and only then formulate conclusions and make distinctions between the religious traditions.[20]

Another reason non-Christian religions are "legitimate" is because it is through them, as social and historical entities, that salvation is mediated. Through the religions as historical entities one may become an anonymous Christian.

The historical and objective claims of the religions are not really considered and do not seem to count for much. This is no doubt due to the fact that Rahner's theology of religion cannot be reconciled with the doctrinal description of a religion on any rational basis. That is, to claim that a religious person belonging to the Buddhist faith is an anonymous Christian is bound to conflict sharply with the self-understanding of that person.

Rahner has a defense for this and an explanation. His defense is that talk about anonymous Christians had never been intended for discussions with non-Christians. Hence misunderstandings might easily arise. Second, he explains that it is not unusual for someone other than the individual to have a better understanding than the person himself or herself does of realities impacting that person. In this he appeals to Kant and depth psychology. It really does not matter what the person believes since the grace of God functions *ex opera operato*: independent

of the consciousness of the Buddhist or Hindu.

Analysis

Rahner's Theological Axioms

The point of departure for Rahner, as for many other inclusivists, and the main point of criticism by both pluralists and exclusivists, has to do with two central axioms. The first is that there is salvation only in Christ. A pluralist like John Hick would disagree, while Lesslie Newbigin would be in substantial agreement. Some exclusivists might see a problem in whether we should say there is salvation only in Christ, or only in the faith response to the revealed word of God. The former seems far too narrow, whereas the latter is most consistent with the New Testament. That is, Abraham was saved, as Paul says, in faith response to God's word (Romans 4). God spoke to Moses and the prophets with revealed instructions which, when accompanied by the response of faith, saved Israel. When the revelatory activity of God came to its fullness in the person and work of Christ, the faith response had him as its object of faith. And we are given to know that this time it is a final word and a final act beyond which God does not go. Rahner makes a good point about the finality of Christ when he says, "God's promise of himself as our salvation has become in Jesus a historical event in a unique and irreversible way."[21]

But it is the second axiom of Rahner (God wills to save the whole world) which many exclusivists find problematic. Rahner repeatedly returns to scriptural passages which support his idea of universal salvation. His primary text is 1 Timothy 2:4, which speaks of a universal saving will of God, a God who "desires all men to be saved." It could be observed that there seems to be no equal attention paid to the rest of the verse, "and come to the knowledge of the truth." Paul and the other writing apostles were certainly conscious of the religious pluralism of their day which ranged from polytheism and atheism to pantheism and ideologies of nature. In view of the missionary mandate of Jesus and the energetic preaching of the Gospel of truth by the early church, it seems to be a misreading of the New Testament to maintain that Paul envisioned salvation for those who have not "come to the knowledge of the truth." Exclusivists find it difficult to avoid the conclusion that there is a body of truth apart from which there can be no salvation.

Nevertheless, as in the case of Newbigin, there are exclusivists who believe there may be a loophole in Scripture for those who have never heard a clear presentation of the Gospel. Braaten cites relevant passages such as 1 Corinthians 15:22 and 28, Colossians 1:19–20, Ephesians 1:9–10, Philippians 2:10–11, and 1 John 2:2. He is in substantial agreement with Newbigin about the grounds of salvation for sinners. "There are stern warnings in the New Testament threatening eternal perdition. There are reservations; there are qualifications of universal hope. . . . New Testament universalism, however, is always a predicate of the uniqueness of Jesus Christ, not a metaphysical attribute of the world in process . . . or of a saving potential inherent in the world religions or of an existential possibility universally available to every person in a moment of decision."[22]

Hans Küng reportedly objected to Rahner's use of the term *anonymous* to describe any kind of Christian experience. His concern was how the individual could be saved by or through Christ if he or she knew nothing about the historic person of Christ and his teaching and divine work. His point is that since Christ is a name, Christianity cannot be anonymous. Kres quotes Ernst Jungel as offering a similar thought. "In its very essence Christianity is not only not anonymous, it is downright anti-anonymous. The Christian faith not only wants to be recognized by the name of him to whom it owes its existence and continued sustenance, it also wants to be recognized by his name and charged with it."[23]

Rahner and the Heart of the Christian Faith: Christology

Most Christian thinkers recognize that how one interprets the person and work of Christ is crucial for Christian theology. Rahner's Christology seems to come close to a variety of the *Logos Spermatikos* doctrine comparable to that of the church father Justin. Justin's idea of the Logos was that Christ, similar to Greek philosophical understanding of Principle/Mind/Thought (*logos*), is the divine power in all things giving the world its meaning and structure and accounting for change and continuity. Greek philosophers came close to reasoning out the truth of God due to the innate presence of Christ in the core of human experience. All humankind experienced a divinizing force from creation.

Though Rahner's understanding of the Logos differs from Justin's, his ideas are not different in some important ways. Like Justin, Rahner sees the Logos operative universally since the beginning of creation. There are intimations of this in John 1. What is unique is that Rahner's Logos is the dynamic of the saving will of God in the "supernatural existential." The Logos is incarnated in Jesus Christ who experiences the Cross-Resurrection, which is necessary since salvation must have its historical grounding. But the operation of the Logos, connected formally to the Cross and history, is transhistorical. Further, universal salvation provided through the Logos-Christ seems to have theological priority.

The operation of the Logos as the universal saving will of God is primary, "first cause," and "efficacious," while the Cross is reduced to the "final cause."[24] The center of salvation seems to have moved away from the Cross and history and into the abstract and the ideal. The Logos saves universally outside of time through the ontology of humankind, while the Cross saves particularistically within time and history. According to Rahner, the activity of the Logos accomplishes the universal self-communication of God to the world in and through one's own personal existence and choices.

For Rahner it seems that the historic Christ and his historic Cross are not definitive of who Christ is and what he does. The historic Cross alone according to Bible writers, deals with the human problem—sin. But sin is not humankind's basic problem according to Rahner: not having a transcendent nature is. The primary significance of Christ is not as historic Savior from sin but as cosmic Savior of humankind from not being. Jesus becomes, as Kres has said, "an ontological savior."[25] There is a shift away from the concrete historical Jesus to a kind of cosmic Christ.

In Rahner's view Christ's prehistory is saving; for the New Testament it is Christ's acts in history that are saving. What is really essential for salvation? Is it the redeeming work on the historic Cross or the ontological work of Christ? For Rahner, it is the latter that can save all and the former that saves some.

Rahner and World Religions: Implications for Dialogue

From the perspective of the other religions, to be considered an "anonymous Christian" and one's religion an "anonymous Christianity" seems patronizing and unacceptable. This is very apparent in the story Rahner tells of meeting the Zen philosopher Nishitani.

Nishitani, the well known Japanese philosopher, the head of the Kyoto school, who is familiar with the notion of the anonymous Christian once asked me: What would you say to my treating you as an anonymous Zen Buddhist? I replied: certainly you may and should do so from your own point of view; I feel myself honoured by such an interpretation, even if I am obliged to regard you as being in error or if I assume that, correctly understood, to be a genuine Zen Buddhist is identical with being a genuine Christian, in the sense directly and properly intended by such statements. Of course in terms of objective social awareness it is indeed clear that the Buddhist is not a Christian and the Christian is not a Buddhist. Nishitani replied: Then on this point we are entirely at one.[26]

This anecdote indicates the gulf existing between Rahner's theology of religions and a more objective history of religion. For on the theological level Rahner indicates that in his understanding, "in the sense directly and properly intended,. . . to be a genuine Zen Buddhist is identical with being a genuine Christian." On the other hand, when the two religions are examined historically, that is in terms of "objective social awareness," Rahner readily admits that "the Buddhist is not a Christian and the Christian is not a Buddhist."

What connection does he see then between history of religion and theology of religion? There is some mutual contribution. The conclusions of the historian of religions may assist the theologian's work by pointing out religious beliefs and practices which have obvious similarities to the Christian faith. This seems to be what Rahner means when he refers to the possibility of a historian "discovering" Christ in the religions.[27] Examples would be savior figures in the various religions by which Rahner probably means, for example, the Hindu Bhagavan or the Buddhist *bodhisattva*. But Rahner does not seek any substantial contribution from history of religion, since on that level a unitary theory of religions is not achievable. Indeed it must be denied. As the Zen master

said, "the Buddhist is not a Christian and the Christian is not a Buddhist."

If history of religion provides some slight service to theology, can theology also provide a service to history of religions? Rahner hints that it might. He seems to say that after the theologian has assumed that Christ is present in the religions and has made "provisional hints" in that direction, the historian might then "direct and sharpen his search and his inquiry for a task which the dogmatic theologian cannot assume."[28] The idea seems to be that the theologian might provide an agenda for investigation, namely that salvation is present in the religions, which the historian might investigate to see if there are historical evidences. The widespread belief in world saviors among Hindus and Buddhists is cited as an example.

But taken as a whole, history of religion and theology of religion do not seem to mix well in Rahner. When religious beliefs and testimony explicitly exclude Christ, Rahner finds Christ there. His transcendent theology, which takes precedence over historical statements and facts, takes priority. The Logos of God operating in the essence of humankind reveals the Triune God: Father, Son, and Holy Spirit, thus making salvation by faith possible. Where the historian does not find Christ, it does not mean he is not there. It perhaps only means the historian's method cannot perceive him.

Since the doctrines and teachings of the world religions seem only incidental to Rahner's inclusivism, there seem to be significant implications for interreligious understanding and dialogue.[29] For one thing, to claim that Christ is in the religions with no examination of the traditions themselves seems to treat the religions superficially. From the standpoint of non-Christians Rahner achieves a certain kind of unity of religions by denying what is final and precious to them, their distinctive truth claims and doctrines. He claims to understand non-Christian religions better than do the persons in the religions themselves. This does not seem to promote interreligious understanding.

In religious dialogue inclusivists find the objective differences between the religions something of a problem. But exclusivists who say that the historic Christ is the only Savior have a stake in the descriptive approach, since this sharpens the diversity between religious traditions. The exclusivist invites non-Christians to interpret their own religion, and expects that right for his or her own in return. But Rahner's inclusivism seems to leave no room for debate between truth-claimers because at bottom the non-Christian is an implicit Christian or an anonymous Christian, though he or she does not know it.

Can there be rational interreligious dialogue if one follows the inclusivist path of Karl Rahner? It does not seem that there can be. How can it be rationally maintained that a religion that denies God's existence (as in the case of many Theravada Buddhists today) nonetheless believes in him, and that one which rejects Christ's physical death (most Muslims) nonetheless accepts him?

One might reasonably expect a greater place for history of religion in Rahner's inclusivism since he seems to place an emphasis on the importance of historical religion in anonymous Christianity. The non-Christian religions as historical phenomena have saving significance for the non-Christian since salvation must be mediated through some social or historical institution.[30] However, Rahner's place for the historical has not to do with objective, descriptive, and hence, historical understandings. It is not the religions as they are historically experienced that is important but merely history as a formal category. This in spite of the claim that "it is through the content of historical experience that man becomes conscious of his own transcendental nature."[31]

One wonders what "the content of historical experience" means for Rahner. One might think that discussion about "history" would at least involve the descriptive task of the historian, if not also the testimony of religious persons. But such does not seem to be Rahner's understanding. Whatever the word *content* here means, it clearly does not take seriously the conscious beliefs and practices of a particular religion. We are left with the conclusion that the historical nature of religion which is important to Rahner is merely the abstract recognition that religion operates in the social and historical realms. It does not have to do with specific beliefs and practices which are a vital part of the history of a religious community. The role religions play in salvation is a formal one, one that is logical and abstract, and not an operative one on the level of religious persons and their self-understanding.

It stretches credulity to accept Rahner's theological interpretation of the religions. In his view if a person is personally self-sacrificing, even if it be for the Devil, he or she is experiencing the grace of God nonetheless. In the context of discussing persecution and the enemies of the church, Rahner confirms this. Those "who oppose her are merely those who have not yet recognized what they nevertheless really already are (or can be) even when, on the surface of existence, they are in opposition."[32]

Discussion

1. Rahner is concerned with the problem created by the fact that the majority of humanity, both before and after Christ, have not had the opportunity to hear of the grace of God in Christ. What are the main points in Rahner's solution? What is your solution?

2. There are two axioms basic to Rahner's theology of religions. What are they and how central are they to the New Testament message as you understand it? Do you support or take exception to Rahner's choices and the use he makes of them?

3. Rahner is of the opinion that Christ's death is of both historical and transhistorical significance. What do you think?

4. Debate the notion that "anonymous Christian" is a Biblical notion.

5. Compare Rahner's Christology to Hick's. How does yours compare to each?

Notes

[1]Gavin D'Costa, *Theology and Religious Pluralism: The Challenge of Other Religions* (New York: Basil Blackwell, 1986), 81.

[2]Karl Rahner, "Christianity and the Non-Christian Religions," in *Christianity and Other Religions: Selected Readings*, ed. John Hick and Brian Hebblethwaite (Philadelphia: Fortress, 1980), 63.

[3]Ibid., 64.

[4]Karl Rahner, *Theological Investigations: Concerning Vatican Council II*, trans. Karl Rahner and Boniface Kruger, Vol. 6 (Baltimore: Helicon, 1969), 390 (hereafter cited as *TI*).

[5]Rahner, "Christianity and the Non-Christian Religions," 56ff; *TI*, 6:391; 16:218; 17:40.

[6]Rahner, "Christianity," 63.

[7]Other Scriptures include Matt. 8:1–13; 1 Cor. 5:9–13, 15; Acts 17:23; 1 Tim. 4:10; Phil. 4:8; and Rom. 2:15.

[8]Maurice Boutin, "Anonymous Christianity: A Paradigm for Interreligious Encounter?" *Journal of Ecumenical Studies* 20, no. 4 (Fall 1983), 609.

[9]Rahner, *TI*, 16:207.

[10]Ibid., 16:212–20.

[11]Kern R. Trembath, "Our Knowledge of God," *Evangelical Quarterly* 87:4 (1987), 329.

[12]Karl Rahner, *Foundations of Christian Faith: An Introduction to the Idea of Christianity*, trans. William V. Dych (New York: Seabury, 1978), 312.

[13]Rahner, *TI*, 6:394.

[14]Rahner, *TI*, 16:222.

[15]Rahner, *TI*, 6:394; italics Rahner's.

[16]Rahner, *TI*, 16:223.

[17]Rahner, *Foundations of Christian Faith*, 312–13.

[18]Rahner, "Christianity and the Non-Christian Religions," 66–67.

[19]Ibid., 69.

[20]Rahner, *TI*, 17:39–40; where Rahner distinguishes theology from history of religions by saying the former takes the *a priori* approach and the latter the *a posteriori*.

[21]D'Costa, *Theology and Religious Pluralism*, 96.

[22]Carl E. Braaten, "Who Do We Say That He Is? On the Uniqueness and Universality of Jesus Christ," *Occasional Bulletin of Missionary Research* (January 1980), 5.

[23]R. Kres, *A Rahner Handbook* (Atlanta: John Knox, 1982), 57, 59.

[24]Rahner, *TI*, 16:204, 211; 17:44, 46.

[25]Kres, *A Rahner Handbook*, 44.

[26]Rahner, *TI*, 16:219.

[27]Rahner, *TI*, 17:39–40.

[28]Rahner, *Foundations of Christian Faith*, 312.

[29]Relevant readings here are Rahner, "Christianity and the Non-Christian Religions"; and Rahner, *Foundations of Christian Faith*, 311–21.

[30]Rahner, *Foundations of Christian Faith*, 314.

[31]Rahner, *TI*, 17:48.

[32]Rahner, "Christianity and the Non-Christian Religions," 78–79.

13 The Exclusivism of Lesslie Newbigin

The position called exclusivism has many variations and many spokespersons. Among the most notable in this century are Samuel Zwemer, Hendrik Kraemer, W. A. Visser't Hooft, and Lesslie Newbigin.[1] We will take Newbigin as our representative for this position.

Lesslie Newbigin served as the Anglican missionary bishop of the Church of South India where he came into living contact with the rich diversity of Indian religious traditions. His years of contact and acquaintance with non-Christian religions makes him a respectable spokesperson for exclusivism. An early work during those days, *The Household of God*, gained him international recognition as a churchman sensitive to the problems of the younger church competing in a context of the overwhelming numerical superiority of the non-Christian religions.[2] He has served as associate general secretary of the World Council of Churches and professor of mission at Selly Oaks Colleges in Birmingham, England.

Newbigin accepts the term *exclusivism* to describe his thought, even though he differs with other exclusivists on the topics of the nature of Scripture, the presence of truth in the non-Christian religions, and the possibility of non-Christians being ultimately saved. Though certainly not a professed "evangelical," he regards his theology as being in continuity with much of traditional Christian thought throughout the centuries. Further, he sees himself as a defender of this orthodoxy against what he calls the newer "orthodoxies" of pluralism and inclusivism, theologies which have, in his view, collapsed into skepticism and irrationalism.

The Starting Point

Newbigin holds that Jesus Christ is the only one whom the true God and personal Creator sent into the world for the redemption of individuals and the world. Adopting language popularized by Robert Speer in his monograph *The Finality of Jesus Christ*, Newbigin accepts that Christ is final in that he provides the only meaning for human experience, the only hope for human community and the true goal of human history. Jesus will, through the church and the Holy Spirit, bring all history to a grand climax which glorifies the one true God. Finality with respect to Christ means he is the unique and only Savior essential to salvation. Finality with respect to the world religions means there is no salvation in them.

He finds the New Testament documents and the resultant church tradition about Jesus to be convincing and objective supports to the uniqueness of Jesus, the key to which is New Testament material concerning the Resurrection. A personal experience of commitment to Christ brings assurance of the uniqueness of Christ, though such subjective experience cannot alone be persuasive to the critical minds of nonbelievers. When all is said and done it is only the future which can fully and finally prove claims about the uniqueness of Christ to an unbelieving world.

Newbigin testified to his belief about the finality of Jesus Christ for humankind in *The Finality of Christ* (1969), and has explicitly embraced exclusivism in *The Gospel in a Pluralist Society* (1989). In the former work he begins by considering three posssible starting points for a discussion about the theology of religions.[3] One can approach the relationship between religions as a religious outsider (those who are not religious nor members of any religious affiliation), as one who is agnostic to religion (Durkheim and Freud could be examples), or as one from within the religions. Newbigin identifies himself as one who begins from within and believes that as an insider it is essential to make explicit his faith commitment from the very outset. In doing this he is reminiscent of Hendrik Kraemer. Like Kraemer, Newbigin does not accept the possibility of an unprejudiced, totally objective, and impartial treatment of religion. In his view, to lay claim to achieving that, as some did who were in the *Religionswissenschaft* school, requires the suspension of the researcher's complete personality. Since that is impossible and since there can be no total objec-

tivity, the best one can do is to acknowledge one's presuppositions, try to state correctly the views of others, and even enter into the experiences of others in limited ways.

More precisely, the starting point for Newbigin is in accepting the historic affirmation of nearly all Christians throughout the centuries. The presupposition of "all valid and coherent Christian thinking is that God has acted to reveal and effect his purpose for the world in the manner made known in the Bible."[4] Newbigin thus begins with a trustworthy Bible which faithfully records historic events which have decisively changed the world and which change individuals who accept the offer of grace brought to its climax in the resurrected Jesus. The words of Scripture are instrumental to conveying the truth of these events and point the reader to a God who acts in history to save the world.

Newbigin defends the use of the Bible as a beginning point on the following grounds. First, to begin in this way is not different, in principle, from all others who, in pursuing systematic thought, build their explanations on *a priori* assumptions. All alternative positions must of necessity begin from some unargued departure point, too. If one wishes to ground one's view of truth on the Buddha rather than Christ, on the Quran or *Das Kapital* rather than on the Bible, on belief in a purposeless rather than purposeful cosmos, then one must begin with some givens that provide a place to stand and a point from which to move ahead. All points of departure, he would argue, have in common that they cannot be proven by appeal to some higher or more ultimate authority. Newbigin's argument is that at least his assumptions are out in the open, unlike some whose starting points are unconsciously assumed and uncritically examined.

Second, the Bible's story has coherence and rationality. If there is a God who exists and he is personal and capable of showing his will and purpose to humankind, it is not unreasonable that he should do precisely what the Bible describes—come in the flesh for the redemption of the world. Those who fault the Bible's story as "unreasonable" hold that opinion because they are captives to that which is "reasonable" as determined by the currently reigning "plausibility structure" of Western world culture. The notion of "plausibility structure," drawn from American sociologist Peter Berger, is that within every society there exists an accepted pattern of beliefs and practices which determines which of the welter of beliefs and practices are to be sanctioned as true and proper. The current plausibility structure in the Western world, based on notions inherited from the Enlightenment and sustained by many professionals in the social sciences and scientific community, rejects the idea that history can witness to an absolute and is explainable by a divine will and purpose. Tragically, in Newbigin's opinion, the reigning plausibility structure of the American and European world has replaced the biblical one for the average person and has negatively impacted many Christians and most contemporary theologians. Newbigin withholds no criticism of pluralists like John Hick, Paul Knitter, and Wilfred Cantwell Smith whose theologies, in his view, have degenerated into anthropology and who have given up the search for a unifying truth by lapsing into skepticism and irrationalism.

Newbigin is critical of pseudosources of truth including reason, religious experience, and tradition (authoritative interpretations of Scripture by a believing community) which depart from the biblical story of a unique Jesus. He does not say reason is of no value, for, in fact, he believes it is essential to understanding truth and plays an important role in confirming it. But reason and revelation are not coequal sources of truth. That reason is flawed which, on the grounds of naturalism and antisupernaturalism (the central assumptions of today's plausibility structure), rejects the idea of a God who shows himself, speaks, and saves in Jesus Christ.

Those who claim that truth can be known not from the Bible but from rational reflection on human experiences (including religious experiences) are doomed to failure. It is not that nothing can be learned about God and truth by the rational analysis of human experiences, but that no criteria for such truth can be discovered by such an approach. Newbigin does not hesitate to speak of revelation as that which provides such criteria. Though the Bible is not an inerrant Scripture, its story is about the revelation of God to Israel and the world, attested to by prophets and apostles and transmitted to successive generations by the believing community of the church. The essential trustworthiness of the Bible is important to Newbigin.

Third, Newbigin believes that the Bible provides practical hope for avoiding global fratricide since its message alone provides the true solution to human problems and destiny. The Bible "is the light by which things are seen as they really are, and without which they are not truly seen." [5] Against all who would offer their own personal values as the answer to unite the world, whether they be those of the philosophers or the pluralist theologians, the Bible is not the assertion of one set of values in the midst of others from which humankind can pick and choose as though in a supermarket shopping for the best bargain in values. Rather, the Gospel of Jesus is the only hope that the world can avoid disastrous conflicts based on greed, hatred, self-interest, and conflicting tyrannies.

With the message of the Bible as a starting point, Newbigin's exclusivism seems to hinge on four correlated elements: history, personal experience, the believing community of the church, and the future.

Finality and History

History is important to Newbigin's exclusivism in two ways. First, historical investigation serves to corroborate the Bible's story. Second, history is essential to the exclusivist's claim to the universal applicability of the Gospel.

The New Testament is history and not just "religious history." The apostolic writers were not merely attempting to advance their religious movement or encourage a particular religious experience with indifference to the facts.

Jesus was a real person in the coordinates of time and space who lived, died, and was resurrected. Historical arguments convince Newbigin of these things. He is especially convinced about the Resurrection. "The tomb is empty. Jesus is declared to be the Son of God with power. This is a fact of history in the only sense in which we can speak of a fact of history, namely a judgment of the evidence."[6] The events recorded in the Gospels are factual.

But Newbigin agrees with many historians that history inevitably involves interpretation. Like all historical facts, New Testament facts are interpreted facts. What does this mean and how does this affect the reliability of the New Testament?

Historians inevitably present facts wrapped in interpretation. "Historical facts" are not the recording of events, acts, and occurrences independent of the interests of the observer. Rather, "facts" are the statements historians make based on the multitude of details they select, integrate, and interpret.[7] For Newbigin, history never consists merely in recounting "facts." The historian selects the raw material used for the history according to some interest and tells the story according to some perspective. Interpretation is unavoidable. As applied to the Gospel writers the "facts" reported in the New Testament are, like the "facts" of ordinary history, accompanied by an interpretation.

This being true, can the Gospels be trusted, since they inevitably blend fact with interpretation?[8] On one hand they can, since the authors of the New

Testament were not giving reports based merely on what they felt. Theirs was no sentimental, self-serving, religious myth spinning based on purely personal, inner, and spiritual ideas. Personal faith is not necessarily subjective faith cut loose from objective reality.

But while the New Testament is historically trustworthy, its story cannot be confirmed with finality until all humanity experiences the outcome which the story confidently predicts. The Gospels claim that the historical Jesus will be the world Savior who at the end of human history will save and judge the world. But it is only in the future that the claim of the believer about the reliability of the Gospel story can be proven to the unbelieving world.

Second, history is essential to Newbigin's exclusivist claim that the Gospel has universal applicability. The events the Gospels record have significance beyond that local place (Palestine) and that historical moment of two thousand years ago. Those events have local and universal, as well as past, present, and future, significance. The New Testament story is presented with "universal intention," which is language Newbigin has borrowed from Michael Polanyi.[9] That is, the New Testament writers' intention in telling the Jesus story was to indicate that its implications extended beyond the immediate audience/time/setting and were significant for all people for all time.

Newbigin recognizes that existentialists and Hindus find problems with his emphasis on the historicity of

Jesus. For the existentialists the pastness of Jesus fails to guarantee anything about their future. For Hindus history does not enhance the significance of Jesus; rather, it diminishes it. Let us look at each of these positions and Newbigin's response.

Newbigin recognizes that his claim about the importance of the historicity of Jesus is problematic for modern existentialists. For them meaning is found in the present interior experience of the individual human person regardless of historical matters. Existentialist New Testament scholars recognize significance in the historical moment but see no meaning beyond that. Newbigin characterizes such a position in this way: "The only thing which is real is the present, and the 'finality' of the Gospel message can only mean that it is ultimate for me personally at this moment, not that it gives assurance about what will be at the end of the time series."[10] But the interpretation of the facts by Bible writers is true for me personally precisely because, Newbigin believes, God will bring to pass the predicted outcome. Christ will be King of all the world and I am part of that world.

Newbigin defends the truth of a revealed absolute within history against the misunderstandings of Hindus. They have a problem with identifying absolute truth with historical events or personages. Truth that is inextricably tied to the accidents and particulars of history loses its universal validity. How can the universal be restricted to the particular? If the teachings of Jesus and the truths about God and the world are true, are they not true regardless of whether or not there truly existed a person, Jesus of Nazareth, who uttered words and accomplished deeds? To insist that absolute truth is personified in Jesus Christ and is revealed at the historical coordinates of time and place is to localize and thus limit.

But the New Testament writers saw the issue of universal truth quite differently. They deliberately avoided historically decontextualizing the Jesus story and went to great lengths to demonstrate that the events they recorded were given not only an accurate historical setting but were placed in the matrix of a broader history, or "secular" history as Newbigin calls it. It is the "secular meaning of Christ" that is important. This can be seen most clearly in the gospel of Luke, where the author takes pains to place the Christ-event in the framework of secular history: Roman Emperor Caesar Augustus, Governor Quirinius of Syria, and Pontius Pilate who was governor of Judea. The importance of this is that the authors of the Gospels did not see the life and times of Jesus as significant just for local and individual believers but for the whole of human and even cosmic history. The finality of Jesus means that he affects the outcome of secular history or world history as well as each individual's history.

If Gospel writers had presented an ahistorical Jesus, this would reduce salvation to an abstraction which individuals could either appropriate or ignore as they chose. But the presentation of the Gospels has to do with a universal yet concrete Savior whom individuals could not escape even if they wished and must deal with ultimately even if they would prefer not to.

Finality and Personal Faith

The uniqueness and finality of Jesus is based not exclusively on history but also on the grounds of personal faith. Newbigin accepts the point made by Pascal that upon hearing the claims of Jesus everyone must respond, everyone must make a choice; everyone, in effect, wagers. If one chooses to believe the Gospel and Jesus Christ does not turn out, in the end, to be the World Savior, one has lost nothing. But if one chooses not to believe and it turns out Jesus is the universal and unique Savior, everything is lost.

Newbigin raises the question whether such an argument can be convincing to a person of another faith. His answer appears to be to some significant extent no. While the member of another faith can follow his argument, it may seem inadequate. He says, "It is a personal commitment to a faith which cannot be demonstrated on grounds established from the point of view of another commitment."[11] It is only when one becomes convinced, as he is, that Scriptures tell a true story and when that story grips one to the point of surrender that conviction can follow. Conviction about Jesus as the universal and unique World Savior can only come when, like the apostle Paul, one can say, "Necessity is laid upon me. Woe to me if I do not preach the gospel! For if I do this of my own will, I have a reward; but if not of my own will, I am entrusted with a commission" (1 Cor. 9:16–17 RSV).

But personal faith is not merely a subjective experience to be dismissed because it is too internal and private to merit universal attention and acceptance. Newbigin sees a close analogy between the personal faith of a Christian and the trust a science student has of the doctrines of science. The student who is told authoritatively that the three angles of a triangle make 180 degrees must believe the teacher until such time as the individual "sees" for himself or herself that it is true. When that insight is achieved, then the student in retrospect finds it impossible to understand how he or she could have been so unseeing, so unconvinced. Faith thereby is rewarded by understanding.

There is, in the case of both science and the biblical faith, an important place for authority as the necessary precondition for personal understanding. Without these authoritative truth claims most individuals would probably not come to understanding by the process of trial and error. But when understanding occurs, it is not an absolutely unique and private experience but one that has been shared by others previously and has been attested to by the authoritative body of scientific (or religious) doctrines and by those who have also experienced the truth of these doctrines.

The experience of one who understands Christian truth is, as Newbigin says, held with "universal intent." Personal faith about Christ is not a subjective or private faith any more than the experience of knowing geometry is totally subjective. It is embraced in the context of a community of people who have had the same experience and who can stand alongside to confirm and corroborate one's belief experience as authentic. The faith of the Christian in Jesus Christ is one that is undertaken with "universal intent." It is a faith that begins with certain basic truths and proceeds by acting on those truths. When one "sees" or experiences God's grace, one is open to guidance and correction by those who understand the realities of God and the Bible's story about Jesus, and who have themselves embraced the truth of Jesus' Lordship.

Finality and the Future

The apostolic witness about Jesus is true, but trusting its truthfulness is a commitment of faith analogous to a reader of history trusting the judgments of a historian. If it is true, time will show it to be true and in the meantime we act in faith. "The claim that Jesus is final is the claim that at the end of the story this judgment will be seen to be the true judgment, the true interpretation of history."[12]

There is no way of proving to unbelievers in advance of the end, the truth of the interpretation given by New Testament writers which culminates in a prediction concerning the end of the age. The future cannot be known with certainty from the vantage of the present. Newbigin likens one's faith acceptance of the Gospel announcement to that of one who accepts the interpretations of secular historians who do megahistory or, in Newbigin's terms, universal history. Both are taking risks since, strictly speaking, both go beyond what is expressly required by the bare facts. Newbigin believes that the Christian theologian's faith in the "end" proposed by the Gospel writers is no different than the "end" accepted by historians who do universal history by seeing all the parts of history working toward a particular conclusion. The finality of Jesus Christ is not only that Christ is the fulfillment of the purposes of God but also that he is the clue to the meaning of history.

Finality and Its Competitors

Finality and Pluralists

The acceptance of secularism and pluralism by recent Christian thinkers has contributed significantly to a rejection of exclusivist notions. By secularism, Newbigin refers to the modern belief that truth and fact are knowable in technology and science but that no similar confidence is possible about God and salvation. Religious pluralism is defined by Newbigin as the belief that "the differences between the religions are not a matter of truth and falsehood, but of different perceptions of the one truth; to so speak of religious beliefs as true or false is inadmissible."[13]

The issue is whether there is reason to believe absolute truth about God is knowable. The biblical plausibility structure has been cashiered by pluralists and in its place a secularized and skeptical structure has been substituted. Newbigin says: "In a pluralist society such as ours, any confident statement of ultimate belief, any claim to announce the truth about God and his purpose for the world, is liable to be dismissed as ignorant, arrogant, dogmatic. We have no reason to be frightened of this accusation. It itself rests on assumptions which are open to radical criticisms, but which are not criticized because they are part of the reigning plausibility structure."[14]

Newbigin recognizes that the pluralist position is motivated, in part, by a commendable concern for finding some unifying principle which can bring about global friendship and address the critical conflicts that face the world. The exclusivist claim that Christ is God's offer to humanity to accomplish world community, justice, and unity is rejected as divisive and arrogant. As seen by the pluralists, it exacerbates rather than ameliorates. In Newbigin's view this concern to promote human unity is a legitimate and urgent problem to be solved.

But the pluralist counterproposal seeks to establish unity on faulty and inadequate grounds. First, it must be recognized that pluralism is itself a brand of exclusivism. While excluding Christ as the central truth through which humanity can experience harmony and fellowship, it proposes a variety of organizing principles, each of which is of an exclusive nature. The absolutist language expresses, in fact, only the personal desires or values of the proponents. In this sense pluralists propose a secularized ethical pragmatism. This can be seen in several of the pluralist essays in *The Myth of Christian Uniqueness*. For example, Gordon Kaufman of Harvard substitutes salvation in Jesus with his own exclusivist view that only "modern historical consciousness" can furnish the basis of human unity.

In this same volume pluralists who have given up the belief in a biblical plausibility structure offer proposals which land in skepticism and irrationalism. Wilfred Cantwell Smith's claim that all religious experiences are of the gracious Transcendent One has the effect of reducing this Transcendent to a purely formal category with no qualties that are known or can be known. According to Newbigin, Smith's position ends in "total subjectivity" and leaves the Transcendent unknowable. The essay of Tom Drive proposes a unifying conception for humanity around a God who has different and rationally conflicting natures whereby to some he shows himself as one and to others he shows himself as many gods. Newbigin concludes that the twin poles of theological skepticism and epistemological irrationalism have had disastrous consequences for the conclusions of these theologians. "Physicists, faced with the problem of reconciling relativity with quantum theory, do not fall back on the supposition that reality has different natures, acts in different ways, is fundamentally incoherent. They continue with unwearied energy to seek a unified theory which will hold the whole of physics together. The religious pluralism represented in *The Myth* is evidence of cultural collapse."[15]

The pluralist position, speaking of the movement as a whole, must be seen for what it is. Ostensibly it is a claim to know based on what is "reasonable" but in fact the position often reduces to unfounded dogmatisms. The pluralist asserts: "The whole truth about God cannot be disclosed in Jesus Christ." But Newbigin responds: "What is your source of knowledge that this is so? How do you know so much about the unknowable?"

The pluralists call for an open mind on truth but violate that very principle with the dogmatic assertion that truth must be larger and more complex than the one found in the biblical story. In short, their dogma is that they have discovered a larger truth; namely, there is no absolute truth. This self-refuting assertion becomes the newest and most arrogant of dogmatisms.

John Hick's position is an example of this. He seeks to illustrate his pluralist claim that truth is one and that people just see it differently by telling the story about the king of Banaras who brought an elephant before five blind persons. Each describes the elephant differently depending on which part of the elephant the person comes in contact with: head, ears, tail, side, leg. Hick tells the story in order to teach that believers of the great religions should accept that none of them have any more than part of the truth. Each of the blind is right but only partially right; each is wrong in some respects but not entirely. In the story the king alone knows the whole truth.

Newbigin's criticism is that the story illustrates the exact opposite of what Hick intends. The story is told to warn against arrogant truth-claimers. But the story backfires on the pluralist since it is the storyteller who is the most arrogant of all by claiming that he alone has the full truth.

Hick is also famous for his claim that the pluralist position accomplishes the religious equivalent of a Copernican revolution. Newbigin's response is as follows.

Professor John Hick has proposed a "Copernican revolution" in theology which would solve the problem of interreligious understanding by means of a shift from the dogma that Christianity is at the centre to the realization that it is God who is at the centre and that all the religions of mankind, including our own, serve and revolve round him. Clearly there is a logical fallacy in comparing this proposal to the shift from a Ptolemaic to a Copernican view of the solar system. The sun, the planets, and the earth are all objects capable of investigation by the same methods of observation; they are equally objects of sense-perception. God and the religions are not objects in the same class. If the analogy of the Copernican revolution is to be applied to the relation of Christianity and the other religions without logical fallacy, then like must be compared with like. God is not accessible to observation in the same sense in which the world religions are, and we have no frame of reference within which we can compare God as he really is with God as conceived in the world religions. The two realities which are accessible and comparable are God as I conceive him and God as the world religions conceive him. What claims to be a model for the unity of religions turns out in fact to be the claim that one theologian's conception of God is the reality which is the central essence of all religions. . . . This is the trap into which every program for the unity of the religions is bound to fall.[16]

Newbigin's conclusion is that Hick and the pluralists have a universe not centered in Christ, not centered in God, and not centered even in salvation. It is a universe that is centered in the self; the self-generated ideas of the pluralists who prefer their own ideas to that of the revelation given in Christ attested to by the Bible.

It is Newbigin's belief that every attempt, including the pluralist one, to reduce the truth claims of the religions into some kind of unity is impossible. Every proposal is the superimposition of a theological position and not the demonstration of real unity. And it will not do to say that one's proposal for unity works for most. If it is not universally useful, that is, applying to all the religions, then it does not universalize and we are left with particular claims, albeit a somewhat reduced number of them. Hick's essence of all religion relativizes these religions and they are made to serve his truth claim. They do not affirm it themselves.

Finality and Inclusivists

Newbigin finds himself in both agreement and disagreement with inclusivists. He disagrees with inclusivists like Rahner who think non-Christians can be saved in their own religion if they have no Gospel witness. Non-Christian religions can not be vehicles of salvation. In sum, Newbigin holds that Christ alone saves for all time and all peoples but that salvation may come to non-Christians in ways not known to us excluding, of course, non-Christian religions.

He is, however, in agreement with inclusivists like Rahner in that he refuses to limit salvation only to those in the Christian church. There may indeed be salvation for some who never learn about Christ, but we should not presume upon that. Rather, we should pursue the path which the New Testament offers for the salvation of humankind.

Finality and Other Exclusivists

Newbigin parts company with other exclusivists on at least two counts. First, he differs with some over the nature of Scripture, and second, he parts company with those who say conclusively that all who either do not know of Christ or do not accept him are forever lost.

Scripture

While there can be no doubt that Newbigin has a high view of Scripture and affirms that in some sense it is revelation, he denies that it is an inerrant Scripture. There are two reasons for this. For one thing, in his view, fundamentalist-type exclusivists have shown a penchant for insisting that the Gospel consists in an affirmation of Bible propositions as true. He parts company with those "who seek to identify God's revelation as a series of objectively true propositions, propositions which are simply to be accepted by those who wish to be Christians."[17] In doing this they miss the point that God came into the world to save sinners, not merely to give them some neurological and objectively true accuracies. Such a position has too much in common with eighteenth-century apologists who viewed the Bible as metaphysical truths independent of the cultural and historical setting. The truth of the Bible he believes is not a "set of timeless propositions: it is a story."[18] But it is an unfinished story and one that is not yet entirely clear.

Second, the Bible has undeniable errors in numbers and secular matters and to claim otherwise is to be ignorant. There are "contradictions between parts of the Bible and things we certainly know as the results of the work of science," and there are "obvious inconsistencies" within the Bible itself on factual matters.[19]

Conservative evangelicals would be justified in concluding that Newbigin holds to a partial infallibility of Scripture. That is, where Scripture words speak about the story of redemption they are accurate and trustworthy. Though the truth of the revelation can never be fully understood and grasped, the words of Scripture are true witnesses to the event and to the interpretation Bible writers give to them. Further, Scripture acts to sustain, nurture, and test the individual's subjective experience with God. Without this objective test there may be no criteria for discriminating invalid or even demonic claims to divine revelation.

But rational reflection on propositions as abstract truth, whether it be of creeds, dogmas, or doctrines, is not the whole of truth or even the most important part of truth. Truth considered in this way is necessarily limited, flawed, and incomplete. What the Bible teaches is that truth is a gift of grace to be received by faith, and this is bound up in the person, redemptive work, and cosmic goals of Jesus Christ.

But if Newbigin denies plenary inspiration, he nonetheless seems to have affirmed in his most recent writings a closer connection between revelation and Scripture. Some of his earlier comments about revelation—that it is invariably personal and cannot be otherwise—seem to have been tempered. In *The Finality of Christ* (1969) he said: "Revelation happens when God actually communicates himself to men, and that communication happens only if there is a response."[20] But this position seems to lead into a trap he later wishes to avoid. Wilfred Cantwell Smith's insistence that revelation can only be "to the person and in the present" is not unlike Newbigin's earlier position.[21] Such a view makes it impossible to affirm that in Jesus Christ the absolute has been made manifest timelessly in history. Since, according to this view, it is agreed that no person can grasp the fullness of the absolute, the absolute cannot be identified with Jesus Christ.

Newbigin seems to have sharpened and broadened his understanding of revelation to encompass not just revelation to persons but revelation in and through written words found in Scripture. Following the scholarship of James Barr, Newbigin accepts that revelation is not just of events in the past and present but inevitably of words. How else could past events be communicated except through words?

Taken as a whole, Newbigin's view of Scripture is at least complex if not in some ways contradictory. In *The Gospel in a Pluralist Society* he speaks of Scripture as revelation and denies reason and tradition as coequal sources. Reason must be used to understand the givens of one's life, but it cannot, on its own, give us any clues to meaning about life and human history. Scripture alone has let us into

God's secret and this way of talking is to talk "the language of revelation."[22] "The Bible . . . is that secret by those who have been chosen to be entrusted with it as bearers of it, agents of it, witnesses of it."[23]

He celebrates Vatican II's rejection of tradition as equal to Scripture; the former is "not a separate source of revelation from Scripture."[24] He hopes Anglicans will follow the lead of Catholics by repudiating reason as well as tradition as independent sources so that the only criterion for truth would be Scripture. His high view of Scripture as revelation is reflected in the statement that "the Bible speaks of things which are not simply products of human culture but are words and deeds of God, creator and sustainer of all that is."[25] He rejects any false division between revelation as event and revelation as word since "we have access to the knowledge of these events only through the words which embodied the understanding of those who witnessed them."[26] For Newbigin therefore, revelation is both in the events of the Old and New Testaments and in the words of Scripture.

The Fate of Those Outside Christ

Newbigin hesitates to say that those who have never known about Christ or are outside of Christ are doomed to hell. Two reasons are offered. The first one seems to be that no human is authorized to make such a statement since this involves judging a matter which must be left to God himself.

But he also calls on Scripture to support his view that some may be saved who have never known about him. He hesitates because he sees Jesus and Paul teaching that the ones who think they are saved should beware while those who appear to be lost may be accepted. The unsuspecting in Jesus' parable in Matthew 25 are surprised when they are received into the glories of paradise. On the other hand, an element of fearful uncertainty about his eternal destiny grips the apostle Paul when he says, "lest I, myself, should be a castaway." In the final analysis Newbigin says salvation outside of Christ may be possible, but he does not say it does, in fact, happen.

Finality: World Religions and Dialogue

Newbigin is concerned about dialogue. In his view it is best always in conversations with persons of other religions to be clear, honest, and frank about one's commitment to Jesus Christ: one should openly confess that Jesus is his or her authority. In dialogue with others one should take the position primarily of truth witnessing, not merely truth seeking. A pluralist like Hick sees this as unproductive since it leads, in his view, to only two ends: conversion or alienation. Two things can be said in response to this. First, conversion or alienation are not the only alternatives since a third position is clearly possible: understanding and respect. In religious dialogue one does not have to either convert or be angry. Rather, when the truth claims of the given religions are more clearly understood, tensions can be reduced rather than raised. It is misunderstanding that leads to tension. Understanding, while not always leading to acceptance and often leading to rejection, at least does not, in principle, among persons of good will, lead to conflict. Hick's call for exchanging truth claiming for truth seeking does not, in principle, offer any more hope for reduced tension.

Newbigin holds that it is mistaken to think, as Hick does, that those who claim to know truth are not seeking truth. For the person committed to Jesus Christ it is true that the search for truth is not entirely open-ended, but neither is that search ever complete. There is no omniscience among Christians; there is the recognition that the infinite cannot be fully grasped by the finite. And there is little doubt that by examining the beliefs, scriptures, and experiences of others one comes to a more full appreciation of the truth; truth that is both outside Christian Scriptures (though consistent with it) and within Christian Scriptures.

Discussion

1. What is meant by a "plausibility structure" and how, according to Newbigin, does this influence the current discussion on the finality of Christ?
2. Newbigin's exclusivism hinges on three elements: history, personal experience and the future. How convincing are these separately? Taken together?
3. What does Newbigin mean by the "secular meaning of Christ?"

4. What do you understand Newbigin to mean when he says that only the future can prove the truth of the finality of Christ?
5. Would you agree with Newbigin that in inter-religious dialogue one can take the position of "truth-witnessing" while at the same time be a "truth seeker?" Is there a conflict between these two?

Notes

[1]Other somewhat less well known exclusivists include Carl E. Braaten ("Who Do We Say That He Is? On the Uniqueness and Universality of Jesus Christ," in *Occasional Bulletin of Missionary Research* [January 1980], 2–8) and Stephen T. Davis ("Evangelicals and the Religions of the World," in *Theological Students Fellowship* 5 [September/October 1981], 8–11, where he defines and defends exclusivism against the criticism of John Hick and Wilfred Cantwell Smith); and Harold A. Netland, "Exclusivism, Tolerance, and Truth," *Missiology: An International Review*, Vol. XV, No. 2 (April 1987): 77–95.

[2]Leslie Newbigin, *The Household of God: Lectures on the Nature of the Church* (New York: Friendship Press, 1954).

[3]Lesslie Newbigin, *The Finality of Christ* (Richmond: John Knox, 1969), 15; Lesslie Newbigin, *The Gospel in a Pluralist Society* (Grand Rapids: Eerdmans, 1989), 8.

[4]Newbigin, *Gospel in a Pluralist Society*, 8.

[5]Ibid., 6.

[6]Newbigin, *Finality of Christ*, 85.

[7]Ibid., 70.

[8]Ibid., 76.

[9]Newbigin, *Gospel in a Pluralist Society*, 92.

[10]Newbigin, *Finality of Christ*, 51.

[11]Lesslie Newbigin, *The Open Secret: Sketches for a Missionary Theology* (Grand Rapids: Eerdmans, 1978), 17.

[12]Newbigin, *Finality of Christ*, 85–86.

[13]Newbigin, *Gospel in a Pluralist Society*, 4.

[14]Ibid., 10.

[15]Ibid., 161.

[16]Newbigin, *Open Secret*, 184–85.

[17]Newbigin, *Gospel in a Pluralist Society*, 24.

[18]Ibid., 12.

[19]Ibid., 97.

[20]Newbigin, *Finality of Christ*, 75.

[21]Newbigin, *Gospel in a Pluralist Society*, 163.

[22]Ibid., 91.

[23]Ibid., 92.

[24]Ibid., 53.

[25]Ibid., 192.

[26]Ibid., 76.

14 Toward An Evangelical Theology of Religions

All evangelicals are exclusivists of some kind or other but not all exclusivists are evangelicals. Lesslie Newbigin and Carl E. Braaten are both exclusivists but each are critics of evangelicals who hold that salvation comes only to those who have a personal knowledge of Christ.[1] However, in other ways the evangelical position is quite compatible with that of most exclusivists. Where does an evangelical theology of religions begin and what does it look like? It begins with a revealed and inspired scripture. While evangelicals are not entirely of one mind on how to understand inerrancy, all have a high view of scripture as revealed, inspired and infallible. This approach to scripture is regarded as basic to all doctrinal issues since it is scripture, both what it says and what it does not say, that is determinative and not philosophy or speculative theology. The evangelical sees scripture as final in every theological discussion and that includes the relationship between the Christian faith and other faiths.

It is possible to *oppose* the position of pluralists and inclusivists by showing how, for example, pluralists land in skepticism and have abandoned the pursuit of truth. This is Newbigin's criticism of Hick and both Netland Newbigin would agree that any approach to a unifying theory of religion

which skirts the issue of reconciling the conflicting truth-claims of the religions fails to deal with one of the most important, as well as the most perplexing, issues. But evangelicals view scripture as essential to the *construction* of their exclusivistic theology of religions. Other sources of authority such as church creeds, historical traditions, and human reason are secondary and supportive but without a revealed Bible evangelicals doubt that anyone can be confident about a theology of religions.

For example, the Lausanne Covenant of 1975, which expresses the theological agreement of a large number of influential evangelical thinkers from around the world, unapologetically derives its conclusions from scripture. Basic to their confidence in the authority of scripture is the belief that revelation has occurred and is found in the words of scripture as well as God's acts in history. Revelation is propositional and is not merely historical acts nor personal experience.

The Lausanne document serves to provide a basic outline for the evangelical theology of religions. It states:

> We affirm that there is only one Savior and only one Gospel, although there is a wide diversity of evangelistic approaches. We recognize that all men have some knowl-

edge of God through his general revelation in nature. But we deny that this can save, for men suppress the truth by their unrighteousness. We also reject as derogatory to Christ and the Gospel every kind of syncretism and dialogue which implies that Christ speaks equally through all religions and ideologies. Jesus Christ, being himself the only God-man, who gave himself as the only ransom for sinners, is the only mediator between God and man. there is no other name by which we must be saved. All men are perishing because of sin, but God loves all men, not wishing that any should perish but that all should repent. Yet those who reject Christ repudiate the joy of salvation and condemn themselves to eternal separation from God. To proclaim Jesus as "the Savior of the world" is not to affirm that all men are either automatically or ultimately saved, still less to affirm that all religions offer salvation in Christ. Rather it is to proclaim God's love for a world of sinners and to invite all men to respond to him as Savior and Lord in the wholehearted personal commitment of repentance and faith. Jesus Christ has been exalted above every other name; we long for the day when every knee shall bow to him and every tongue confess him Lord.[2]

The above statement provides skeletal answers, which we wish to flesh out below, to the following questions:

1. Has God revealed himself in non-Christian religions?

2. Is the truth found in the religions salvific?

3. How is Christ unique and universal?

4. What is the fate of those outside of Christ?

5. What is the responsibility of the Christian to those in other religions?

1. Has God revealed himself in non-Christian religions?

General revelation, described in part in Romans 1 and Psalm 19, affirms that there exists a bona fide knowledge about God in the human heart. This results from observation of the natural world but it is supplemented by the conscience which is constitutional in human nature (Romans 2:14–15). It is only a short step from this to the affirmation that some knowledge of God can be found in the religions of the world since these are the result of human strivings and understandings.

Some evangelicals still hold to a position, now largely given up, that the religions, root and fruit, are evil and Satanic. But this is both unfaithful to scripture and disconfirmed by close contact with many non-Christians. Most evangelicals these days, who have had any contact with informed and sincere followers of the world religions recognize there is some knowledge of God. Religions can be satanic as systems if, as Pinnock says, they claim ultimacy for themselves.[3]

Phil Parshall's contact with Muslims in Metro-Manila and Bangladesh and Don Richardson's life among the tribals of Irian Jaya have convinced them that God has made himself known among the peoples of the world. Reading the prayers and devotional literature of Hindu bhaktists and the Sikh *Japji* shows without doubt some experience with God and truth.

But the other side of this affirmation is the realization that this knowledge is severely limited and incomplete as well as mixed with error and falsehood. The Muslim's theology has much in common with Judeo-Christian thought: monotheism, God as creator and judge, revelation of truth through the prophets, and divine judgment and heavenly bliss. But Muslims (Sufis less so) emphasize right belief and do little with personal experience. They claim to know the will of God but are most cautious about claiming to *know* God personally. Jesus is, next to Muhammad, perhaps the most important prophet, but the Quran's respect for him is so great that it cannot believe he suffered death at all. Thus, Muslims end up with a doctrine of a God that many do not personally experience, a forgiveness they cannot be assured of and a Christ who cannot save. Moreover, they do claim ultimacy with all its implications.

Hindu *bhakti* literature, for all its sublime grasp of the Transcendent, moves easily between *nirguna* Brahman and *saguna* Brahman, between an impersonal deity and one who is intensely personal. When the bhaktist speaks of God in personalist terms the Christian senses commonality. When the nondualistic elements arise, the Christian is left questioning if there is as much commonality as once thought.

The Bible-believing evangelical is often left with the conclusions of the Apostle Paul in Athens as recorded in Acts 17. Many followers of the world religions worship God, but the God they worship is largely unknown to them. The result is that the Christian is obliged to kindly but confidently inform and correct where the religions are either incomplete or erroneous in their beliefs.

2. Is the truth found in the religions salvific?

The answer to this question pivots on what we mean by "truth" and, more importantly, what is meant by "salvation." The Bible is sufficiently clear that salvation has certain characteristics: it is *from* sin and death, *by* personal faith, *in* Jesus Christ and *to* life everlasting with the triune God (Acts 4:12, John 14:6). Basic to the Christian view of salvation is who the Savior is; related to this is whether one needs a personal knowledge of the Savior to be saved. Rahner's answer is that such personal knowledge of the historic Christ is unnecessary for those in the world religions who have had no opportunity to know the Christian message since he is known and experienced in their ethical decision-making. For Rahner salvation is *by* Christ but not directly *in* Christ. Hick's pluralism argues that salvation is neither *by* Christ nor *in* Christ but equally in all the world religions.

But evangelicals, like other Christian exclusivists, affirm that since salvation is both *by* and *in* Christ, those religions that exclude him, intentionally or otherwise, cannot be salvific even when their texts and teaching hold general truths which Christians both accept and laud.

The evangelical consensus on this issue is twofold. First, the truth which is found in the religions is mixed with non-truth, in part because the human condition is to both know and distort truth. Romans 1 tells us that humanity "suppresses" truth resulting in condemnation. Second, God has sent Jesus to the world as Savior of the world and there is no salvation outside of him. Though he rejects it as true, Hick acknowledges that if Jesus Christ is the God-man, the Incarnate One sent to the world as the Savior, then the Christian message alone is salvation. (Of course Hick denies this is the case.)

Carl Braaten's defense of Jesus as the incarnate God turns on his examination of the titles of Jesus such as Lord, Savior, Christ, Son of God, Logos. He says:

> Both God and Jesus are spoken of as Savior. Both God and Jesus are spoken of as Lord. Jesus is the Savior because he will save his people from their sins. Jesus is the Lord because God has raised and exalted him above all others. Jesus is the subject of names that are above all other names because they are the name of God. They speak eloquently of the uniqueness of Jesus.[4]

The key to the question under consideration here has not to do with truth alone but with salvation. If salvation is in Christ and by Christ, and it is, then no truth is saving which fails to recognize this, since it is, at best, incomplete.

3. How is Christ both unique and universal?

Christ is unique in a way other than what we mean when we say that each person is unique. It is true that each person is unique as to fingerprint ,

DNA code, personality, personal history and vision about life. But Christ is unique not in degree but in kind. His uniqueness is so absolute that, as God-man, there never was and never will be another like him. He is unique as to his purpose and accomplishments as well: he is the Savior of the world.

His universal significance is more difficult to articulate but one thing is sure, his universal meaning and his uniqueness are mutually supportive. He is unique because he is the one and only Savior; he can be world Savior because, and only because, he is Lord, Christ, and Son of God. He alone stands in relation to all (universal Savior) because he alone stands supreme over all (unique Savior).

Braaten and other exclusivists are one with evangelicals in holding that salvation is only *by* Christ and *in* Christ. But they differ from many evangelicals in declaring that salvation is not only *for* the whole world (salvation in principle) but shall be successfully extended *over* much of humanity (salvation in fact) through some unspecified provision whereby "God is at work behind the backs of the plurality of world religions" since "they also *somehow* speak of Christ."[5] Braaten believes in some kind of universal salvation; most evangelicals believe only in a universal Savior.

The Lausanne statement recognizes this distinction when it says: "To proclaim Jesus as 'the Savior of the world' is not to affirm that all men are either automatically or ultimately saved." The meaning of Jesus as universal Savior is that his salvation is unrestricted in offer since there are no racial or cultural conditions. But it is restricted in its application since it is effective only for those who have faith. The scriptures that teach the necessity of personal faith are numerous including the following: Acts 2:38 "Repent and be baptized, every one of you, in the name of Jesus Christ for the forgiveness of your sins. And you will receive the gift of the Holy Spirit."; 1 Timothy 1:15–16 "Christ Jesus came into the world to save sinners— of whom I am the worst. But for that very reason I was shown mercy so that in me, the worst of sinners, Christ Jesus might display his unlimited patience as an example for those who would believe on him and receive eternal life." John 3:36 "Whoever believes in the Son has eternal life, but whoever rejects the Son will not see life, for God's wrath remains on him."; Acts 17:30–31 "In the past God overlooked such ignorance, but now he commands all people everywhere to repent. For he has set a day when he will judge the world with justice by the man he has appointed. He has given proof of this to all men by raising him from the dead."; Romans 3:22 "This righteousness from God comes through faith in Jesus Christ to all who believe."

The evangelical position, however, must wrestle with and be faithful to other scriptures as well which Braaten calls the "universalist thrust" in Pauline theology:[6] 1 Corinthians 15:22 "For as in Adam all die, so in Christ all will be made alive;" Colossians 1:19–20 "For God was pleased to have all his fullness dwell in him, and through him to reconcile to himself all things, whether things on earth or things in heaven, by making peace through his blood, shed on the cross;" Ephesians 1:9–10 "And he made known to us the mystery of his will according to his good pleasure, which he purposed in Christ, to be put into effect when the times will have reached their fulfillment—to bring all things in heaven and on earth together under one head, even Christ;" Philippians 2:10–11 "That at the name of Jesus every knee should bow, in heaven and on earth and under the earth, and every tongue confess that Jesus Christ is Lord, to the glory of God the Father."

Both Braaten and Rahner place great emphasis on 1 Timothy 2:4 as a key text. "God our Savior . . . wants all men to be saved . . . ." Rahner selects this to uphold his inclusivism : many shall be saved through "legal" religions of the world when there is no other way. Braaten also turns to this text to uphold his form of Biblical universalism: more will be saved than just those who confess Christ personally in a pre-mortem state.

What is often left unquoted is the rest of the verse and that which follows. After affirming that God wills all humankind to be saved it continues, "and . . . come to the knowledge of the truth. For there is one God and one Mediator between God and men, the man Christ Jesus . . . ." This passage seems to support the following thoughts consistent with the rest of the New Testament.

First, to "come to the knowledge of the truth" is a deliberate and conscious step on the part of the sinner. God wills all mankind to be saved but this is through the method of pre-mortem, intentional faith in Christ.[7] There have been reports of conversions to Christ preceded by extraordinary angelic or supernatural phenomena. Through a shaman's trance in 1950, Hmong tribals in Xieng Khuoang province of northern Laos learned enough details about the coming of a new religion to recognize the missionaries when they arrived. But there is no unambiguous example or teaching in the New Testament that salvation will come to anyone without a pre-mortem, conscious, and deliberate response of faith.

Secondly, the meaning and purpose of Jesus' pre-ascension instructions and the early church's self-understanding of those instructions coincide. They understood themselves to be the instruments by which humanity could come to faith. Indeed, Paul directly acknowledges his responsibility in this very passage when he says "for this purpose I was appointed a herald and an apostle . . . and a teacher of the true faith to the Gentiles." 1 Timothy 2:7.

If "intentional pre-mortem salvation" is our best understanding of scripture, what about those who either reject the truth or, through no fault of their own, can make no choice due to lack of opportunity?

4. What is the fate of those outside of Christ?

An increasing number of evangelicals have been struggling with the awesomeness of the implications of two deeply held truths: Christ is the only Savior and only those who consciously put their trust in him can be saved. The implications are twofold. First, since only a small number of humanity past, present and future will have opportunity to embrace Christ intentionally, only an even smaller number will actually do so. Secondly, the vast majority, those who do not personally confess Christ, are eternally lost. What does the evangelical say to the person from another religion who asks: "I am considering Christ for myself, but what of my ancestors who had no opportunity to hear? What will happen to them?"

The Christian church has had more than one response to this question. A qualified *universalism* of some sort, though only one option, is very popular at the moment. A majority of exclusivists take this position and an increasing number of evangelicals seem to be warming to it in one of its many variations.[8] A second option is annihilation or *conditional immortality* which teaches that eternal life for the sinner beyond the grave has two conditions: "God must give it and man must receive it."[9] The fate of those who either refuse to accept the Gospel or have no opportunity to do so cease to exist upon the occasion of their death. Grounds summarizes conditional immortality in this way, "Their end is an ended existence. Thus their doom while not conscious is eternal, their punishment forever irreversible and unchanging."[10] A third option is a reflective *agnosticism* such as that seemingly held, at present, by John R.W. Stott, who says: "I cherish the hope that the majority of the human race will be saved" though he does not specify how it might be accomplished.[11]

A fourth response may be called, borrowing Hendrik Kraemer's term, *Biblical realism*. This position calls for those who accept the authority of scripture to acknowledge that all humankind is headed for one of two destinies. Hell and heaven are both taught by Jesus and the Apostles and to soften the realities of either may have implications for the other. Downplaying hell or widening the "narrow road," as some do, seems to be called for by emotional as much as exegetical concerns.

For example, Braaten says evangelicals generally "restrict salvation in the end to those who actually hear the gospel and put their faith in Christ. Under this restriction the rift that has been opened up in the world through sin will widen to an eternal chasm, splitting the one world of God's creation into two unreconcilable halves, only God's half will be much smaller than the devil's, in fact, only a remnant of the whole. There is not much for the angels to sing about if the evangelicals get what they expect—a heaven sparsely filled with only card-carrying Christians."[12]

But many evangelicals are willing to accept the burden of an unpopular truth if it is, in their judgment, biblically sound. The truth about hell and eternal separation is not addressed only to those who are outside the Gospel, it is addressed to those who are apparently insiders too. No more sobering words are found in scripture than those found in Matthew 7:21–23 and 25:31–46. Jesus says to those least expecting it: "Depart from me, you who are cursed, into the eternal fire prepared for the devil and his angels."

(Mt. 25:41) Nevertheless, the judgment of God is according to both mercy and fairness. To his listeners Jesus says that it would be more tolerable for those from ancient Sodom and Gomorrah than those in the contemporary seaside cities of Bethsaida and Korazin. Paul confirms that the wrath of God will fall upon mankind in just and fair ways. He quotes the Old Testament in Romans 2:6 saying: "God 'will give to each person according to what he has done.'" Contrasting the believer (or pre-Christian faithful Jew) and the evil doer Paul says: "To those who by persistence in doing good seek glory, honor and immortality, he will give eternal life. But for those who are self-seeking and who reject the truth and follow evil, there will be wrath and anger."

Rather than adopt qualified universalism, conditional immortality, or reflective agnosticism the traditional evangelical opts for a recognition of the realities of heaven and hell knowing that the just judge of the world will do justly. "Scripture leaves no doubt that in the world to come sin's punishment shall be real and searching. We know that it will entail banishment from God and further we know that infinite love and perfect justice shall measure the cup each must drink. But beyond this we know absolutely nothing."[12] The church must be faithful to its mandate and leave the outcome to God.

5. What is the responsibility of the Christian to those in other religions? The Call for Enlightened and Caring Evangelicals

Mark Thomsen has rightly observed that the key issue facing world Christians is "whether and how to confess Jesus Christ within religious pluralism."[14] Many evangelicals remain convinced that scripture and history support the uniqueness of Jesus and for them the question is not whether to confess Jesus Christ as Lord of the earth, it is only "how" to do this. The raging debate about the theology and sociology of religious pluralism is sensitizing evangelicals about the "how" of confessing Jesus Christ. There is more sensitivity to the faith of others than ever before. This means the claims of Christ will still be proclaimed but in less strident and arrogant ways. Confidence will be accompanied by gentleness; persuasion will be preferred to bombast.

How can enlightened evangelicals present the uniqueness of Christ in better ways? First, it is necessary to become better informed about the truth claims of other religions. Knowing the religions of others does what we claimed it would do at the beginning of this book. It removes ignorance, sharpens distinctives, and provides bridges of communication. It puts a real face on the religious person we wish to win to Christ. Most of all, it will press on us all the more that what Christ offers is what they lack. Second, there is no substitute for loving people. All the right knowledge and all the correct doctrine will not substitute for caring and loving. The need today is form minds that are keen and hearts that are loving.

Discussion

1. Discuss the meaning of the statement: "All evangelicals are exclusivists of some kind or another but not all exclusivists are evangelicals."
2. How do your views on the topic of the theology of religions compare or contrast with that found in this chapter?
3. How do you answer the question: "What is the fate of those outside of a knowledge of Jesus Christ as Savior?"

Notes

[1]Carl E. Braaten, "Who Do We Say That He Is? On the Uniqueness and Universality of Jesus Christ," *Occasional Bulletin of Missionary Research* 4, no. 1 (January 1980): 5.

[2]Taken from John Stott, *The Lausanne Covenant: An Exposition and Commentary* (Wheaton, Ill.: Lausanne Committee for World Evangelization, 1975), 9.

[3]Clark H. Pinnock, "Toward An Evangelical Theology of Religions," *Journal of the Evangelical Theological Society* 33, no. 3 (September 1990): 364.

[4]Braaten, "Who Do We Say That He Is?", 3.

[5]Ibid., 7. Emphasis mine.

[6]Ibid., 5.

[7]1 Peter 3:19 and 4:6 are often cited as Biblical hints which challenge this.

[8]Pinnock, 'Toward An Evangelical Theology of Religions," 367.

[9]The view of David Dean as quoted in Vernon Grounds, "The Final State of the Wicked," *Journal of the Evangelical Theological Society* 24, No. 3 (September 1981): 214.

[10]Ibid., 215.

[11]D. Edwards and J. Stott, *Essentials: A Liberal-Evangelical Dialogue*, (London: Hodder and Stoughton, 1988), 327.

[12]Braaten, 'Who Do We Say That He Is?', 5.

[13]Robert Anderson as quoted by Vernon Grounds, 'The Final State of the Wicked," 219.

[14]Mark Thomsen, "Confessing Jesus Christ within the World of Religious Pluralism," *International Bulletin of Missionary Research* 14, no. 3 (July 1990): 115.

Bibliography

General

Anderson, Norman, ed. *The World's Religions*. 4th ed. London: InterVarsity Press, 1975.
Bowker, John. *The Problems of Suffering in Religions of the World*. London: Cambridge Univ. Press, 1970.
Comstock, Richard, gen. ed. *Religion and Man: An Introduction*. New York: Harper & Row, 1971.
de Bary, Wm. Theodore, gen. ed. *Sources of Indian Tradition*. Vol. 2. New York: Columbia Univ. Press, 1958.
Eerdmans' Handbook to the World's Religions. Grand Rapids: Eerdmans, 1982.
Ellwood, Robert, Jr. *Many Peoples, Many Faiths*. 2d ed. Englewood Cliffs, N. J. : Prentice-Hall, 1982.
Moore, George Foot. *History of Religions*. 2 vols. New York: T. & T. Clark, 1913–19.
Nida, Eugene A. *Customs and Cultures: Anthropology for Christian Missions*. New York: Harper & Row, 1954.
Nielsen, Niels C., Jr. et al. *Religions of the World*. New York: St. Martin's Press, 1983.
Noss, David S., and John B. Noss. *Man's Religions*. 7th ed. New York: Macmillan, 1980.
Smith, Wilfred Cantwell. "Comparative Religion: Whither and Why?" In *The History of Religions: Essays in Methodology*, edited by Mircea Eliade and Joseph M. Kitagawa. Chicago: Univ. of Chicago Press, 1959.
————. *The Faith of Other Men*. New York: Mentor Books, 1961.
————. *The Meaning and End of Religion*. New York: Mentor Books, 1964.
————. *Toward A World Theology: Faith and the Comparative History of Religion*. Philadelphia: Westminister, 1981.
van der Leeuw, G. *Religion in Essence and Manifestation*. Torchbook Series. New York: Harper & Row, 1963.
Weir, Robert F., gen. ed. *The Religious World: Communities of Faith*. New York: Macmillan, 1982.

Ancient Religions

The Ancient Egyptian Book of the Dead. Translated by Raymond O. Faulkner. Edited by Carol Andrews. Revised edition. New York: Macmillan, 1985.
Ferguson, John. *Greek and Roman Religion: A Source Book*. Park Ridge, N.J.: Noyes, 1980.
Finegan, Jack. *Myth and Mystery: An Introduction to the Pagan Religions of the Biblical World*. Grand Rapids: Baker Book House, 1989.
Guthrie, William K. *The Greeks and Their Gods*. Boston: Beacon Press, 1950.
Jacobsen, Thorkild. *The Treasures of Darkness: A History of Mesopotamian Religion*. New Haven: Yale University Press, 1976.
Kerenyi, Karoly. *The Religion of the Greeks and Romans*. Westport, CT: Greenwood Press, 1973. Reprint of the 1962 edition.
Mendelsohn, Isaac, trans. *Religions of the Ancient Near East: Sumero-Akkadian Ugaritic Epics*. New York: Liberal Arts Press, 1955.
Morenz, Siegfried. *Egyptian Religion*. Translated by Ann E. Keep. Ithaca, NY: Cornell University Press, 1973.

Rice, David G. and John E. Stambaugh, eds. *Sources for the Study of Greek Religion*. Missoula, Mont.: Scholars Press, 1979.

Seltzer, Robert M., ed. *Religions of Antiquity: Religion, History, and Culture: Selections from the Encyclopedia of Religion*. New York: Macmillan, 1989.

Buddhist Traditions

Bapat, P. V., gen. ed. *2500 Years of Buddhism*. New Delhi: Publications Division; Ministry of Information and Broadcasting of the Government of India, 1956.

Chang, Garma C. C. *The Buddhist Teaching of Totality: The Philosophy of Hua Yen Buddhism*. University Park, Pa.: Pennsylvania State Univ. Press, 1971.

Conze, Edward, ed. *Buddhist Texts Through The Ages*. Harper Torchbooks. New York: Harper & Row, 1954.

————., trans. *The Perfection of Wisdom in Eight Thousand Lines & Its Verse Summary*. Berkeley, Calif.: Four Seasons Foundation, 1973.

Herman, A. L. *An Introduction to Buddhist Thought*. New York: University Press of America, 1983.

Palihawadana, Mahinda. "Is There a Theravada Buddhist Idea of Grace?" In *Christian Faith in a Religiously Plural World*, edited by Donald G. Dawe and John B. Carma. Maryknoll, N.Y.: Orbis, 1978.

Suzuki, D. T. *On Indian Mahayana Buddhism*. Harper Torchbooks. New York: Harper & Row, 1968.

Welch, Holmes. *Buddhism Under Mao*. Cambridge, Mass.: Harvard Univ. Press, 1972.

Christianity

Ahlstrom, Sydney E., ed. *Theology in America: The Major Protestant Voices from Puritanism to Neo-Orthodoxy*. Indianapolis: Bobbs-Merrill, 1967.

Baldwin, Marshall. *The Mediaeval Church*. Ithaca, NY: Cornell University Press, 1953.

Bettenson, Henry, ed. *Documents of the Christian Church*. Second edition. New York: Oxford University Press, 1963.

Bokenkotter, Thomas. *A Concise History of the Catholic Church*. New York: Doubleday, 1990.

Constantelos, Demetrios J. *Understanding the Greek Orthodox Church: Its Faith, History, and Practice*. New York: Seabury Press, 1982.

Frend, W. H. C. *The Early Church*. Philadelphia: Fortress, 1982.

Gonzalez, Justo L. *The Story of Christianity*. Two volumes. San Francisco: Harper and Row, 1985.

Hudson, Winthrop S. *Religion in America: An Historical Account of the Development of American Religious Life*. Fourth edition. New York: Macmillan, 1987.

Leith, John H., ed. *Creeds of the Churches: A Reader in Christian Doctrine from the Bible to the Present*. Third edition. Atlanta: John Knox, 1982.

Marsden, George M. *Understanding Evangelicalism and Fundamentalism*. Grand Rapids: Eerdmans, 1991.

Meyendorff, John. *The Orthodox Church: Its Past and Its Role in the World Today*. Third revised edition. Translated by John Chapin. Crestwood, NY: St. Vladimir's Seminary Press, 1981.

Spitz, Lewis. *The Protestant Reformation, 1517–1559*. New York: Harper and Row, 1985.

Christianity and the Religions

Bavinck, J. H. *The Church Between the Temple and the Mosque*. Grand Rapids: Eerdmans, 1966.

Brooke, Robert Taliaferro. *Lord of the Air*. London: Lion, 1976.

Castro, Emilio. "Mission in a Pluralistic Age." In *International Review of Missions* 75, no. 299 (July 1986).

Conn, Harvie. *Eternal Word and Changing Worlds.* Grand Rapids: Zondervan, 1984.

Drummond, Richard. *Gautama the Buddha.* Grand Rapids: Eerdmans, 1974.

Geffre, Claude, and Mariasusai Dhavamony, eds. *Buddhism and Christianity.* New York: Seabury Press, 1979.

King, Winston L. *Buddhism and Christianity: Some Bridges of Understanding.* Philadelphia: Westminister, 1982.

Kraemer, Hendrik. *The Christian Message in a Non-Christian World.* Grand Rapids: Eerdmans, 1963.

Maharaj, Rabindranath R., and Hunt, Dave. *Escape into the Light.* Salem, Ore.: Harvest House, 1984.

Manglewadi, V. *The World of Gurus.* New Delhi: Vikas, 1977.

Matrisciana, Caryl. *God's New Age.* Salem, Ore.: Harvest House, 1985.

Newbigin, Lesslie. *The Finality of Christ.* Richmond: John Knox, 1969.

Nida, Eugene A. *Customs and Cultures: Anthropology for Christian Missions.* New York: Harper & Row, 1954.

Pobee, John S. *Toward an African Theology.* Nashville: Abingdon, 1979.

Rousseau, Richard W., ed. *Christianity and the Religions of the East: Models for a Dynamic Relationship.* Vol. 2. Scranton, Pa.: Ridge Row, 1982.

Samuel, Vinay, and Chris Sugden, eds. *Sharing Jesus in the Two Thirds World.* Grand Rapids: Eerdmans, 1983.

Siegmund, Georg. *Buddhism and Christianty: A Preface to Dialogue.* Tuscaloosa: Univ. of Alabama Press, 1968.

Utuk, Efiong S. "From Wheaton to Lausanne: The Road to Modification of Contemporary Evangelical Mission Theology." *Missiology* 14, no. 2 (April 1986).

Islam

Ahmad, Imitiaz. *Ritual and Religion Among Muslims in India.* New Delhi: Manohar, 1981.

Esposito, John L. *Voices of Resurgent Islam.* New York: Oxford Univ. Press, 1983.

Fry, C. George, and James R. King. *Islam: A Survey of the Muslim Faith.* Grand Rapids: Baker, 1980.

Haddad, Yvonne Yazbeck. *Contemporary Islam and the Challenge of History.* Albany: State Univ. of New York Press, 1982.

_____. *The Islamic Impact.* Syracuse, N.Y.: Syracuse Univ. Press, 1984.

_____. *Islamic Values in the United States: A Comparative Study.* New York: Oxford Univ. Press, 1987.

_____. "Muslims in America: A Select Bibliography." *Muslim World* 76, no. 2 (April 1986): 93–122.

_____. "Muslim Revivalist Thought in the Arab World: An Overview." *Muslim World* 76, nos. 3–4 (July-October 1986): 143–67.

Kateregga, Badru, and David W. Shenk. *Islam and Christianity.* Grand Rapids: Eerdmans, 1980.

Lewis, Bernard. *Arabs in History.* London: Hutchinson's Univ. Library, 1950.

Pickthall, Mohammed Marmaduke. *The Meaning of the Glorious Koran.* New York: Mentor Books, 1953.

Smith, Wilfred Cantwell. *Islam in Modern History.* Princeton, N.J.: Princeton Univ. Press, 1957.

Titus, Murray T. *Islam in India and Pakistan.* Rev. ed. Madras, India: Christian Literature Society, 1959.

Trimingham, J. Spencer. *The Sufi Orders in Islam.* London: Oxford Univ. Press, 1971.

Watt, W. Montgomery. *What is Islam?* 2d ed. London: Longeman Group, 1979.

Judaism

Dawidowicz, Lucy S. *The War Against the Jews, 1933–1945*. 10th anniversary edition. Ardmore, PA: Seth Press; New York: distributed by Free Press, 1986.

Encyclopedia Judaica. 16 volumes. Jerusalem: Keter Publishing House, 1972.

Glazer, Nathan. *American Judaism*. Second revised edition. Chicago: University of Chicago Press, 1988.

The Jewish Experience in America: A Historical Bibliography. Santa Barbara, Calif.: ABC-Clio, Inc., 1983.

Neusner, Jacob. *The Oral Torah: The Sacred Books of Judaism: An Introduction*. San Francisco: Harper and Row, 1986.

Sachar, Howard M. *A History of Israel: From the Rise of Zionism to Our Time*. New York: Alfred A. Knopf, 1976. Volume two: *From the Aftermath of the Yom Kippur War*. New York: Oxford University Press, 1987.

Scholem, Gershom. *Kabbalah*. New York: Quadrangle/New York Times Book Company, 1974.

Seltzer, Robert M. *Jewish People, Jewish Thought: The Jewish Experience in History*. New York: Macmillan, 1980.

Strassfeld, Michael. *The Jewish Holidays: A Guide and Commentary*. New York: Harper and Row, 1985.

Tannenbaum, Marc, Marvin Wilson and A. J. Rudin, eds. *Evangelicals and Jews in an Age of Pluralism*. Grand Rapids: Baker Book House, 1984.

Wiesel, Elie. *Souls on Fire: Portraits and Legends of Hasidic Leaders*. Translated by Marian Wiesel. New York: Random House, 1972.

Method in the Study of Religion

Baird, Robert D. *Category Formation and the History of Religions*. The Hague: Moulton, 1971.

_____. *Methodological Issues in the Study of Religion*. Chico, Calif.: New Horizons Press, 1975.

Lott, Eric J. *Vision and Interpretation: The Interaction of Theology and the Study of Religion*. The Hague: Mouton de Gruyter, 1988.

Merton, Robert K. *Social Theory and Social Structure*. New York: Free Press, 1957.

Penner, Hans H. "Creating A Brahman: A Structural Approach To Religion." In *Methodological Issues in Religious Studies*. Chico, Calif.: New Horizons Press, 1975.

Religion in China

Bohr, Richard P. "State and Religion in the People's Republic of China Today: The Christian Experience." Paper presented to the Fifteenth Sino-American Conference on Mainland China, June 8-14, 1986, Taipei, Formosa.

Bush, Richard C. *Religion in Communist China*. New York: Abingdon, 1970.

Fung Yu-Lan. *A Short History of Philosophy*. New York: Free Press, 1948.

Pachow, W. *Chinese Buddhism: Aspects of Interaction and Reinterpretation*. Washington: University Press of America, 1980.

Thompson, Laurence. *Chinese Religion: An Introduction*. Belmont, Calif.: Dickenson, 1969.

Religion in India

Chaudhuri, Nirad C. *Hinduism: A Religion to Live By*. New Delhi: B.I. Publications, 1979.

De Smet, R., and J. Neuner, eds. *Religious Hinduism*. 3d ed. Allahabad: St. Paul Society Publications, 1965.

Edgerton, Franklin. *The Beginnings of Indian Philosophy*. London: George Allen & Unwin, 1963.

Gambhirananda, S. *Eight Upanishads*. Calcutta: Advaita Ashrama, 1977.

Loehlin, C. H. *The Sikhs and Their Scriptures*. 3d ed. Delhi and Lucknow: Lucknow, 1974.

Lott, Eric J. *God and the Universe in the Vedantic Theology of Ramanuja*. Madras: Ramanuja Research Society, 1976.

Macdonell, Arthur A. *A Vedic Reader for Students*. Madras: Oxford Univ. Press, 1976.

Radhakrishnan, S., and C. Moore, eds. *A Sourcebook in Indian Philosophy*. Princeton, N.J.: Princeton Univ. Press, 1957.

Singh, Gursaran. *Guru Nanak's Japji: The Morning Prayer of the Sikhs*. Delhi: Atma Ram & Sons, 1972.

Tiliander, Bror. *Christian and Hindu Terminology*. Uppsala: Almqvist & Wiksell, 1974.

Welbon, G. R. "Person, Text, Tradition: India's Acarya." In *History of Religions* 25, no. 4 (May 1986): 368–77.

Religion in Japan

Earhart, Byron. *Japanese Religion: Unity and Diversity*. Belmont, Calif.: Dickenson, 1969.

McFarland, H. Neill. *The Rush Hour of the Gods*. New York, Evanston, and London: Harper & Row, Publishers, 1967.

Offner, Clark B., and Henry van Straelen. *Modern Japanese Religions*. Leiden: Brill, 1963.

Thomsen, Harry. *The New Religions of Japan*. Rutland, Vt.: C. E. Tuttle, 1963.

Religions of Select Societies

Archer, Wm. George. *The Hill of Flutes: Life, Love and Poetry in Tribal India*. London: Geo. Allen and Unwin, 1974.

Berglund, A. I. *Zulu Thought Patterns and Symbolism*. Cape Town: Philip, 1976.

Bodding, P. O., ed. *Santal Folktales*. 3 vols. Oslo: H. Aschehaug, 1925.

Durkheim, Emile. *The Elementary Forms of the Religious Life*. New York: Free Press, 1965.

Dutta-Majumdar, Nabendu. *The Santal: A Study in Culture-Change*. Memoir No. 2, 1955. Delhi: Government Press of India, 1956.

Gill, Sam D. *Beyond the Primitive: The Religions of Nonliterate Peoples*. Englewood-Cliffs, N.J.: Prentice-Hall, 1982.

Hultkranz, Ake. *Belief and Worship in Native North America*. Syracuse, N.Y.: Syracuse Univ. Press, 1981.

———. *The Religions of the American Indians*. Berkeley, Calif.' Univ. of California Press, 1979.

Idowu, E. B. *African Traditional Religion: A Definition*. London: SCM Press, 1973.

King, Noel Q. *African Cosmos: An Introduction to Religion in Africa*. Belmont, Calif.: Wadsworth, 1986.

———. *Religions of Africa*. New York: Harper & Row, 1970.

Lawson, E. Thomas. *Religions of Africa: Traditions in Transformation*. San Francisco: Harper & Row, 1984.

Lee, S. G. "Spirit Possession Among the Zulu." In *Spirit Mediumship and Society in Africa*, edited by J. Beattie and J. Middleton. New York: Africana Pub. Corp., 1969.

Malinowski, Bronislaw. *Magic, Science and Religion*. New York: Doubleday Anchor, 1954.

Man, E. G. *Sonthalia and the Sonthals*. Delhi: Mittal, 1983.

Mbiti, John. *African Religions and Philosophy*. New York: Anchor Books, 1970.

Mukherjea, Charulal. *The Santals*. Calcutta: A. Mukherjee & Co. Press, n.d.

Nida, Eugene A., and William A. Smalley. *Introducing Animism*. New York: Friendship Press, 1959.

Nordyke, Quentin. *Animistic Aymaras and Church Growth*. Newberg, Ore.: Barclay Press, 1972.

Parrinder, Geoffrey. *Religion in Africa*. London: Penguin Books, 1969.

Presler, Henry H. *Primitive Religions in India*. Madras: Christian Literature Society Press, 1971.

Ranger, T. O., and I. Kimambo, eds. *The Historical Study of African Religion*. Berkeley, Calif.: Univ. of California Press, 1970.

Ray, Benjamin. *African Religions*. Englewood Cliffs, N.J.: Prentice-Hall, 1976.

Ray, Ujjwalk, Das Amal K., and Basu Sunil K. *To Be With Santals*. Special Series No. 28. Delhi: Indian Gout. Press, Bulletin of the Cultural Research Institute, 1982.

Troisi, J. *Tribal Religion*. New Delhi: South Asia Books, 1979.

Zahn, Dominique. *The Religion, Spirituality and Thought of Traditional Africa*. Chicago: Univ. of Chicago Press, 1979.

Theology of Religions

Boutin, Maurice. "Anonymous Christianity: A Paradigm for Interreligious Encounter?" *Journal of Ecumenical Studies* 20, no. 4 (Fall 1983): 602–29.

Braaten, Carl E. "Preaching Christ in an Age of Religious Pluralism." *Word and World* 9, no. 3 (Summer 1989): 244–50.

————. "Who Do We Say That He Is? On the Uniqueness and Universality of Jesus Christ." Ventnor, N.J.: *Occasional Bulletin of Missionary Research* (January 1980): 2–8.

Davis, Stephen T. "Evangelicals and the Religions of the World." *Theological Students Fellowship* 5 (September/October 1981): 8–11.

D'Costa, Gavin. *Theology and Religious Pluralism: The Challenge of Other Religions*. New York: Basil Blackwell, 1986.

Hick, John. *God and the Universe of Faiths*. New York: St. Martin's Press, 1973. Also paperback, London: Collins/Fount, 1977.

————. *God Has Many Names*. Philadelphia: Westminister, 1982.

————. "The Non-Absoluteness of Christianity." In *The Myth of Christian Uniqueness: Toward a Pluralistic Theology of Religions*. Faith Meets Faith Series, edited by John Hick and Paul F. Knitter. Maryknoll, N.Y.: Orbis, 1987.

————. "Religious Pluralism and Absolute Claim." In *Religious Pluralism*, Boston University Studies in Philosophy and Religion, edited by Leroy S. Rouner, vol. 5. Notre Dame, Ind.: Univ. of Notre Dame Press, 1984.

————. *Second Christianity*.

————. "'Whatever Path Men Choose is Mine.'" In *Christianity and Other Religions: Selected Readings*, edited by John Hick and Brian Hebblethwaite. Philadelphia: Fortress, 1980.

Kres, R. *A Rahner Handbook*. Atlanta: John Knox, 1982.

Küng, Hans. *On Being a Christian*. London: Collins, 1977.

Maddox, Randy L. "Karl Rahner's Supernatural Existential: A Wesleyan Parallel?" *Wesleyan Theological Journal* 5 (1987): 3–14.

Moltmann, Jurgen. *The Church in the Power of the Holy Spirit*. London: SCM Press, 1975.

Newbigin, Lesslie. *The Finality of Christ*. Richmond: John Knox, 1969.

————. *The Gospel in a Pluralist Society*. Grand Rapids: Eerdmans, 1989.

————. *The Light Has Come*. Grand Rapids: Eerdmans, 1982.

————. *The Open Secret: Sketches for a Missionary Theology*. Grand Rapids: Eerdmans, 1978.

Piet, John. "Where in the World is God?" *Reformed Review* 27, no. 3 (1974): 131–47.

Rahner, Karl. "Christianity and the Non-Christian Religions." In *Christianity and Other Religions: Selected Readings*, edited by John Hick and Brian Hebblethwaite. Philadelphia: Fortress, 1980.

————. "Jesus Christ in Non-Christian Religions." In *Foundations of Christian Faith: An Introduction to the Idea of Christianity*. Translated by William V. Dych. New York: Seabury Press, 1978.

_____. *Theological Investigations.* Vol. 6 "Anonymous Christians." In *Concerning Vatican Council II.* Translated by Karl Rahner and Boniface Kruger. Baltimore: Helicon Press, 1969. Vol. 12 *Confrontation.* Translated by David Bourke. New York: Seabury Press, 1974. Vol. 16 *Experience of the Spirit: Source of Theology.* Translated by David Moreland. New York: Seabury Press, 1979. Vol. 17 "Jesus Christ in the Non-Christian Religions." In *Jesus, Man and the Church.* Translated by Margaret Kohl. New York: Crossroad, 1981.

van Rooy, J. A. "Christ and the Religions: The Issues at Stake." *Missionalia* 13, no. 1 (April 1985): 3–13.

Schreiter, Robert J. "The Anonymous Christian and Christology'" *Missiology: An International Review* 6, no. 1 (January 1978): 29–52.

Trembath, Kern R. "Our Knowledge of God According to Karl Rahner." *Evangelical Quarterly* 87, no. 4 (1987): 329–41.

Yandell, Keith E. "On the Alleged Unity of All Religions." *Christian Scholar's Review* 6, nos. 2 & 3 (1976): 140–55.

Toward an Evangelical Theology of Religions

Chapman, Colin. "The Riddle of Religions." *Christianity Today* 34, no. 8 (May 14, 1990): 16–22.

Covell, Ralph R. "The Christian Gospel and World Religions: How Much Have American Evangelicals Changed?" *International Bulletin of Missionary Research* 15, no. 1 (January 1991): 12-17.

Davis, Stephen T. "Evangelicals and the Religions of the World." *Theological Students Bulletin* 5, no. 5 (September-October 1981): 8–11.

Edwards, D. and Stott, John. *Essentials: A Liberal-Evangelical Dialogue.* London: Hodder and Stoughton, 1988.

Grounds, Vernon C. "The Final State of the Wicked." *Journal of the Evangelical Theological Society* 24, no. 3 (September 1981): 211–220.

Netland, Harold. "The Challenge of Religious Pluralism." *Theological Students Fellowship* 10, no. 5 (September-October 1986): 20–25.

_____. "Exclusivism, Tolerance, and Truth." *Missiology: An International Review* 15, no. 2 (April 1987): 77–95.

_____. "Religious Pluralism and Truth." *Trinity Journal* 6 (new series), no. 2 (Spring 1985): 74–87.

Parshall, Phil. *The Cross and the Crescent.* Wheaton, Il: Tyndale House Publishers, Inc., 1989.

Pinnock, Clark H. "Toward An Evangelical Theology of Religions." *Journal of the Evangelical Theological Society* 33, no. 3 (September 1990): 359–368.

Richardson, Don. *Eternity in Their Hearts.* Ventura, Calif.: Regal Books, 1981.

Sanders, John. "Is Belief In Christ Necessary For Salvation?" *Evangelical Quarterly.* Vol. LX, no. 3 (July 1988): 241–259.

_____. "The Perennial Debate." *Christianity Today* 34, no. 8 (May 14, 1990): 20–21.

Scott, Waldron. "'No Other Name'—An Evangelical Conviction." *Christ's Lordship and Religious Pluralism.* Anderson, Gerald H. and Stransky, Thomas F. (S.P.), eds. Maryknoll, New York: Orbis Books, 1981.

Stott, John. *The Lausanne Covenant—An Exposition and Commentary.* Lausanne Occasional Papers, no. 3. Wheaton, Il: Lausanne Committee for World Evangelization, 1975.

Thomsen, Mark. "Confessing Jesus Christ Within the World of Religious Pluralism." *International Bulletin of Missionary Research* 14, no. 3 (July 1990): 115–118.

Index

Religious Traditions of the World was typeset by the Photocomposition Department of Zondervan Publishing House, Grand Rapids, Michigan on a Mergenthaler Linotron 202/N. Compositor is Susan Koppenol Editor for Academie Books is Leonard G. Goss

The text was set in 10 point Palatino, a face designed by Herman Zapf in Germany in 1948. He used this face often in designing his exquisite *manuale Typographicum* (1954). The italic of this face was originally called medici italic. Palatino is admired for its penlike, calligraphic strokes, and is popular for bookwork. This book was printed on 50-pound S. D. Warren Sebago paper by R.R. Donnelley, Harrisonburg, Virginia.